100
NEW ZEALAND CRAFT ARTISTS

100
NEW ZEALAND CRAFT ARTISTS

HELEN SCHAMROTH

GODWIT

For Melina, Natalia and Nikki, with love

Author's acknowledgements
My heartfelt thanks go to Jane Connor of Godwit Publishing, who offered me the opportunity to write this book and supported me through the process. I thank her and Sarah Bowden for their patience and considerable assistance. It was a pleasure to work with Haru Sameshima, who took many of the beautiful photographs, and Jane Parkin, who edited the book. The preliminary research for this book was undertaken as a dissertation for a Bachelor of Spatial Design degree at AIT, and my thanks go to members of staff who encouraged me. I especially appreciate the cooperation, support and friendship of the craft artists represented. My search for 100 practitioners opened considerably more than 100 doors, and I have been greatly enriched by the many conversations I had with those who make, teach, curate, write about and sell craft arts. I particularly acknowledge Carole Shepheard, Louis le Vaillant, Warwick Freeman, Moyra Elliott and Howard Williams. The person I thank most is Michael Smythe, who has lived with this project for nearly two years. His unflagging support, encouragement and rigorous criticism were invaluable.

Illustration credits
The author and publisher gratefully acknowledge the co-operation of all living artists and the family of the deceased artist, in granting permission to reproduce works and providing material for reproduction. Photographers are as follows: Michael Smythe, 33; Ian Hobbs, 62; Phil Fogle, 87; Norman Heke, 133, 153, 175; Howard Williams, 169; Kelly Thompson, 183, Haru Sameshima 15, 17, 23, 29, 35, 39 41, 45, 57, 59, 61, 63, 65, 71, 73, 75, 81, 83, 89, 91, 95, 99, 101, 103, 105, 107, 111, 113, 117, 119, 123, 129, 131, 139, 141, 145, 149, 151, 157, 161, 165, 167, 173, 177, 179, 181, 187, 189, 191, 193, 195, 197, 199, 201, 209. All other photographs were supplied by the artists.

A GODWIT BOOK
First published 1998 by
Random House New Zealand
18 Poland Road, Glenfield, Auckland, New Zealand

First published 1998

© 1998 text, Helen Schamroth; illustrations, individual artist or artist's estate

The moral rights of the author have been asserted

ISBN 1 86962 030 5 (hardback)
      1 86962 036 4 (paperback)

Front cover illustration: 'Flotsam', 1998, by Garry Nash, collection of the artist, photograph by Haru Sameshima
Typesetting and production: Kate Greenaway
Printed in Hong Kong

CONTENTS

vii	Preface	42	Heather Kilgour
ix	Introduction	43	Rangi Kiu
		44	Maureen Lander
1	Brian Adam	45	Phillip Luxton
2	Brendan Adams	46	Toi Te Rito Maihi
3	Peter Alger	47	Linley Main
4	Raewyn Atkinson	48	Owen Mapp
5	Ruth Baird	49	Paul Mason
6	Penelope Barnhill	50	Elizabeth McClure
7	Tony Bond	51	Royce McGlashen
8	Kobi Bosshard	52	Mike McGregor
9	Christine Boswijk	53	Peter McKay
10	Barry Brickell	54	Matt McLean
11	Freda Brierley	55	Hamish McWhannell
12	Alan Brown	56	Ross Mitchell-Anyon
13	Emma Camden	57	Gael Montgomerie
14	Len Castle	58	Gaeleen Morley
15	Madeleine Child and Philip Jarvis	59	Garry Nash
16	Peter Collis	60	Manos Nathan
17	Jim Cooper	61	Chester Nealie
18	Paerau Corneal	62	Michael O'Brien
19	John Crawford	63	John Parker
20	Deborah Crowe	64	Richard Parker
21	Ann Culy	65	Diana Parkes
22	Andrea Daly	66	Tania Patterson
23	Peter Deckers	67	Suzy Pennington
24	John Edgar	68	Alan Preston
25	Moyra Elliott	69	Louise Purvis
26	Penny Ericson	70	Baye Pewhairangi Riddell
27	Warwick Freeman	71	Darryl Robertson
28	Steve Fullmer	72	Ann Robinson
29	Eléna Gee	73	Caroline Robinson
30	Matarena George	74	Willa Rogers
31	Jude Graveson	75	Rick Rudd
32	Rose Griffin	76	Emily Siddell
33	Jens Hansen	77	Yvonne Sloan
34	Niki Hastings-McFall	78	Robyn Stewart
35	Gavin Hitchings	79	Margaret Stove
36	Ola and Marie Höglund	80	Wallace Sutherland
37	Susan Holmes	81	Wi Taepa
38	Megan Huffadine	82	Juliet Taylor
39	Humphrey Ikin	83	Diggeress Rangituatahi Te Kanawa
40	Lynn Kelly	84	Christine Thacker
41	Hilary Kerrod	85	Kelly Thompson

86	David Trubridge	**97**	Merilyn Wiseman
87	Andrew Van Der Putten	**98**	Peter Woods
88	Jeannie Van Der Putten	**99**	Gloria Young
89	Ann Verdcourt	**100**	Marc Zuckerman
90	Peter Viesnik		
91	Gwen Wanigasekera		
92	Chris Weaver	**ccxii**	Glossary of Maori Terms
93	Kate Wells	**ccxii**	Glossary of Craft Terms
94	Areta Wilkinson	**ccxviii**	Other Practitioners mentioned in the Text
95	Carin Wilson		
96	Christina Hurihia Wirihana	**ccxx**	Bibliography

PREFACE

When I was invited to write about 100 New Zealand craft artists, the task of researching the topic seemed overwhelming. There had been no book covering a range of crafts since *Craft New Zealand—The Art of the Craftsman* by Doreen Blumhardt and Brian Brake, published in 1981. There had been no Crafts Council since 1992 nor a crafts magazine since 1993. My research had me exploring work in many fields, including the margins surrounding craft—interfacing on one side with fine art and on the other with design. I saw some very fine work that was neither fine art nor design, and some that could be classified as both. This defined the scope of my subject.

Nonetheless, there were some nagging questions. On the one hand there seemed to be few reasons for separating craft art from fine art and design in the 1990s. Old demarcations evident in previous decades appeared to have broken down. Furthermore, practitioners were choosing to define themselves in a multiplicity of ways that included craft artist, designer, sculptor and mixed-media artist as much as by medium, such as ceramist, glass blower, blacksmith and weaver. The most compelling reason for allowing craft art to merge with fine art and design was to acknowledge the seamlessness of these practices within Maori and Pacific Island cultures.

On the other hand, there was a very real need for a book that covered a category of creative production that was missing out on being documented. Since the magazine *Craft New Zealand* ceased publication discourse about crafts practice has been infrequent and spasmodic, and there has been no real forum for debate. During this period craft design courses, initiated more than a decade ago within the polytechnic system, have progressively changed to visual arts or 3D design courses. Craft art as an independent entity is struggling to remain visible.

This might not have mattered if the visual arts umbrella comfortably accommodated craft practitioners. The reality, however, is that only a few have received recognition as artists or designers. The recording of a significant aspect of New Zealand's culture has been incomplete and the sector has run the risk of becoming invisible, absent from collections, major exhibitions and critical discourse.

The term 'craft' has a certain ambiguity. For many it evokes the craft of roadside stalls rather than work at the leading edge of craft practice. This seems at odds with the way we consider painting, which is far more likely to be associated with Rembrandt, Picasso, Georgia O'Keefe or Colin McCahon than with Sunday painters. Many practitioners, however, believe that 'craft' is still an honorable term, and I agree with them. Besides, we found it impossible to find a suitable alternative name for the sector. The term 'craft art' seems to encompass the diversity of practice I wanted to cover, and it focuses on the essential qualities of the genre that I had identified. 'Craft art' it remains.

Two books by Warwick Brown preceded this one—*100 New Zealand Paintings by 100 New Zealand Artists* and *Another 100 New Zealand Artists*. The second of these, which included sculptors, printmakers and photographers, provided a further reason for this book. Many practitioners who create significant works were not included in Brown's books. Brown included what he defined as 'fine art' and excluded what he considered to be 'craft art' because of the medium or because the work had developed within the Crafts Movement. The exceptions were practitioners Bronwynne Cornish,

Gordon Crook, Mark Lander and Kazu Nakagawa, whose work I could have included in this book. In order to avoid duplication I have not done so.

To select 100 practitioners I used personal networks, guilds, societies, art and design schools, galleries and museums to expand and update the information I held. In the process I heard some wonderful stories and saw many outstanding works. The search has been exhilarating, humbling and exhausting, and my travels have taken me from Northland to Southland, from the east coast to west coast. The riches have included the vibrant changing landscape that has inspired so many practitioners, new insights into the lives and work of some of the most talented, innovative people of this country, and their warm hospitality.

Each practitioner is represented by a page of text and a single image. For a number of craft artists this seems minimal, given the diversity and complexity of their work. It does, however, provide a springboard for further research. The practitioners are listed alphabetically to remove any hierarchy, and some connections may not be readily apparent. There are, however, cross-references within the book and to Warwick Brown's two books to assist those who wish to make some links. Additional artists mentioned in the text are listed on page ccxiv with brief notes; glossaries of Maori words and art and craft terms used in the text are on pages ccxii–ccxiii. These, along with a bibliography that was of assistance to me, are provided to aid further research.

This book is not a definitive history, nor does it document the work of all the significant pioneers. It is based on the criteria I established during my research, as discussed in the introduction, and is a personal snapshot of the late 1990s that offers a representative sampling of a broad range of recent work by practitioners active in their craft during this decade. Included is a handful of pioneers, a few emerging practitioners and a generous proportion of mid-career practitioners who work in clay, fibre, glass, stone, metal and wood. I have interviewed all of them, and they each had an opportunity to review the draft material. What has emerged is a rich mix of stories and images. All these practitioners make work that fits within the broad parameters I established and, most importantly, that in some way touched and impressed me.

Helen Schamroth
Auckland
1998

INTRODUCTION

As we come to the end of the twentieth century it is appropriate to reassess the objects in our lives and their significance, and to acknowledge that our material culture is much more than the 'essential' equipment and ephemera of contemporary life. I come in daily contact with a number of small crafted objects which mingle with the clutter of domesticity—I instinctively fondle them before repositioning them, and my life is enriched.

Crafted objects offer more than usefulness and visual gratifaction—they fulfil the human need for tactile experiences. These works embody human enterprise and satisfy the desire to make objects that someone will value—a tangible expression of materials and process. We can look at a work and sense the pleasure of the maker: clay squeezed through fingers, fragrant harakeke stripped for its fine inner threads of muka, fine wood shavings falling from a turned vessel, silver jewellery being polished to a gleaming finish, and glowing molten glass gathered on the end of a blowpipe.

In 1859 John Ruskin wrote: 'Fine art is that in which the hand, the head, and the heart of man go together.' (*The Two Paths*, 1859, Lecture 2.) Today the description is apt for craft art. The human desire to make things by hand, the intellectual exploration of ideas, and the passion for expression and contribution come together in craft practice. Many craft artists talk of 'thinking through their hands', their familiarity with materials and process leading intuitively to forms imbued with personal philosophies.

A number of craft practitioners make reference to craft history in their work and philosophies. Craft guilds date back to the eleventh century in Europe, but it was during the European Renaissance in the fifteenth century that craft and fine art were intellectually separated. Painters and sculptors achieved success in terms of status and money—a situation that continues to this day. They removed themselves from the restraints of guild systems and allied themselves to the more intellectual pursuits of literature and the liberal arts. The Arts and Crafts Movement of the later nineteenth century, led by William Morris, was inspired by Ruskin's writings. Ruskin saw craft as a way of counteracting the dehumanising aspects of industrialisation.

In the early twentieth century the Modern Movement in Europe encompassed the socialist aspects of the Arts and Crafts Movement, although there was a strong desire to link craft with industry. Walter Gropius in his Bauhaus Proclamation identified craft as a way of re-energising art and design. Modernism was characterised by a rejection of decoration and an emphasis on simple forms and functionalism. It remains a significant strand of contemporary craft practice. Some craft artists are revisiting modernism; others never left it. The more contemporary art movements like expressionism also appear in recent craft art, often as sculptural works.

A crafts movement developed in a number of Western countries including New Zealand in the 1960s and '70s. Its values contrasted with pop art and accelerating mass consumerism. The movement was integral to the emerging 'alternative' rural lifestyle—a reference to the earlier Arts and Crafts Movement in its ideals and opposition to mainstream values. A number of craft pioneers developed significant work during this period and continue to work in this way. Latterly a few practitioners have engaged with post-modernist notions of deconstruction and reference to other movements and disciplines. Parallels can be drawn between the work of these craft artists and fine artists.

Diversity and plurality are the hallmarks of contemporary craft art. Even the notion of functionalism, traditionally a core characteristic of craft practice, has expanded. By including physical, social, emotional, cultural, spiritual, narrative and iconographic functions we gain new insights into the concept. The broad definition also finds common ground with the visual arts of Maori and Pacific Islanders.

The unique cultural factors of New Zealand offer a particular challenge. The work of many Maori and Pacific Island practitioners, like that of a number of other indigenous people, has achieved fine arts status but has never completely left its craft roots. In the languages of Maori and Pacific Islanders there are no separate words for craft, art and design, which are experienced as integral to life. Nonetheless, there is an acceptance by a number of Maori and Pacific Island practitioners that their contemporary work in ceramics, fibre, jewellery, sculpture and furniture can be seen as part of the genre of craft art.

Thematically, craft art has few limitations. There are explorations of decoration, function, the human figure, animal life and the environment juxtaposed with commentary on social, political, historical, ecological and gender issues. References to human emotions, psyche and behaviour, spiritual, cultural and narrative expressions, myth, metaphor and material culture all feature, as do the histories of craft, art and architecture.

Some work develops incrementally and remains strongly rooted in craft traditions. Processes and forms are learnt from family, mentors and teachers. Pieces might take the form of exquisitely fine muka cloaks with pre-European traditions, or organic ceramics firmly grounded in the Hamada-Leach tradition which was so influential in this country. They might be formal geometric patchwork quilts with European and North American antecedents; elegant jewellery with Bauhaus formality; or seductive, Italian-inspired glass goblets.

Innovation plays a major part in contemporary craft art. Instances of ingenious methods and pragmatic solutions to practical problems show that the pioneering spirit has not been lost. The relative isolation of some practitioners contributes to innovative processes and imagery. Stories include the devising of glass-casting techniques by learning about bronze casting, the ingenious modifications of equipment for the solo glass blower, ceramists emulating ancient wood-carving processes with ballpoint pens or hosing off layers of colour from clay works. For many, personal expression is a response to a unique cultural mix and environment.

Just as there are multiple strands of craft practice, there are a number of ways in which practitioners develop proficiency. Many older practitioners developed an interest in craft and were self taught with the aid of overseas books, travel and research, and sharing knowledge with each other; some were introduced to the genre at teacher training colleges; others found craft through fine arts, design or architecture training. They adopted, adapted and ingeniously innovated. Virtuosity is often a feature of their work, not as an objective but as a product of considerable enthusiasm and practice.

Tertiary craft education commenced in the mid-1980s and many pioneer craft artists with well-honed skills turned to teaching in the polytechnic system to supplement their incomes. Most of these courses have since evolved into Visual Arts and 3D Design degree programmes requiring tertiary education of the educators. Some craft artists returned to teaching in less formal situations, while a number undertook further education. There are now more tertiary-qualified craft practitioners than ever before.

One of the outcomes of craft design education is 'urban craft'. Many graduates align themselves with design, and there is considerable energy in this sector. They frequently identify as 'designer-makers'—a term used freely in Australia—and some produce accessories for trendy lifestyles: jewellery, glass objects and furniture that often integrates elements of fashion. A number share studios as an extension of their collegial experiences.

The relationship between craft art and design is more developed in Australia than New Zealand and few local craft practitioners work directly with industry. However, a number of craft design graduates from tertiary institutions are seeking a level of credibility, status and income that matches that of their designer peers. They do this by the way they define and market themselves and their products, recognising that craft arts are identified by the background of the maker, where the work has been exhibited and sold, and who has written about it in which publication. Like more senior practitioners they make one-off pieces, series of related works or short production runs. Their perception is that it may be easier to be aligned with design than with architecture in an environment where architectural commissions are infrequent. Those who might have worked on architectural commissions in the 1980s or even the early '90s are being forced to re-evaluate how to continue in their chosen media.

Much fine work is still being created in the provinces as a continuation of the rurally based 'alternative lifestyle' of the 1960s. A number of co-operative retails outlets established in the 1970s and '80s no longer exist, but some persevere. Several established practitioners have retail outlets attached to their studios, and these become tourist attractions. Suburban craft remains predominantly recreational—historically the seedbed for professional practice, especially in the fibre arts.

In pulling together the many strands of crafts practice I have erred on the side of widening the scope rather than limiting it. My selection embraces work that moves into the spaces between craft art and the neighbouring genres of fine art and design—it is my belief that some of the most interesting work is being produced in those areas. Much has been made of the 'art/craft' debate over the past two decades, and however much one would like to see endless discussion laid to rest, it continues to affect a few practitioners, curators, writers, educators, collectors and administrators.

The language of craft art has altered over time, as has the point of entry into the genre, but there are constants: the need to make by hand, and the desire for tactile expressions of our environments, our ideas and our cultures. I remain optimistic about the future of the genre. However difficult the social and economic environment, there are always people who are driven to make objects that enhance our lives. Contemporary craft art is an integral part of the material culture that touches us in many ways. We might wear a favourite piece of jewellery, sit on a carefully crafted piece of furniture, pour from a lovingly formed teapot or jug, enjoy the ritual associated with a christening gown, or open a hand-forged gate; maybe we live with a piece of sculptural clay or stone, or see it in a gallery or museum; the cover of a handmade book might invite us to turn the pages; we might wrap ourselves in a cloak, a quilt or a piece of wearable art. In each instance a relationship between maker and audience is established.

Craft art offers us many perspectives. Some works have immediate appeal; others invite contemplation and further understanding. My pleasure is in sharing with readers the broad spectrum, from innovative and provocative works to those in the continuum of tradition. This book is a window to an under-valued but rich expression of our culture.

1

BRIAN ADAM

Born Greymouth 1949.
School of Design, Wellington Polytechnic 1968–71.
Lives in Waitakere.

Brian Adam makes eyewear, jewellery for the face as objects of utility and frivolity. It is work that evokes the 1700s, a time when jewellers combined pure silver, gold and copper ingredients to produce alloys with particular working properties. The ingots were then rolled into solid sheets and fabricated into frames for spectacles.

However, Adam is not stuck in the past, and since 1996 he has combined a historical attitude with computer technology. It makes sense to him to use a two-dimensional CAD program for producing accurate symmetrical designs and making size variations for clients. The process is not necessarily faster; it is just better to fine-tune the design on computer rather than on graph paper and the metal, and he can easily keep a record of the changes.

He started making spectacle frames in 1981, both as a response to a group jewellery exhibition *Paua Dreams* at Fingers Gallery, Auckland, and because he himself wanted to wear something less conventional than was commonly available. He wanted less of a contraption, something more expressive of the wearer. Alone in his endeavours in New Zealand, he sought dialogue elsewhere. He found makers in the USA also interested in making jewellery that functioned for the eyes and fitted with the wearer's facial expression. Historical research revealed that the eighteenth century was a time when eyeglasses were heavily embellished as a fashion item and an attention-seeking badge of rank. Eyeglasses and, by association, their wearers were historically considered to portray success and scholarship, though paradoxically were also seen as a sign of pitiful weakness.

The resultant eyewear has at times been fairly whacky—humorous pieces made mainly for exhibitions, a lively antidote to the frames Adam made for prescription lenses. He was interested in changing people's attitudes to what is often regarded as a burden by creating conceptual, funny, absurd, even ugly frames. By juxtaposing different materials in a lighthearted way, he introduced an element of surprise, sometimes making frames that conjured up imaginary wearers. Several functioned as sculptural works.

One cannot live on spectacle frames alone in New Zealand, so Adam produces earrings and rings, with the same approach to materials. His fascination for melting metals, discovering alloys and developing new ways with materials is put to use in all his jewellery. The most recent works he calls *Metros*, which relate to city detritus. Tin cans as an expression of kiwiana are not new materials for artists, but he puts his personal stamp on these works which make reference to Kiwi Nugget, Golden Syrup and Lipton's Tea. He values urban found objects as others might value natural found ones.

Like many working as craft artists, Adam has taught jewellery part time for a number of years, and now shares his craft in private workshops. He has been the recipient of a number of Arts Council/Creative New Zealand grants, has exhibited in the USA and Australia, and is represented in a number of private collections.

Ferns and Looking Glass
Silver
60 x 150 mm each
Collection of the artist

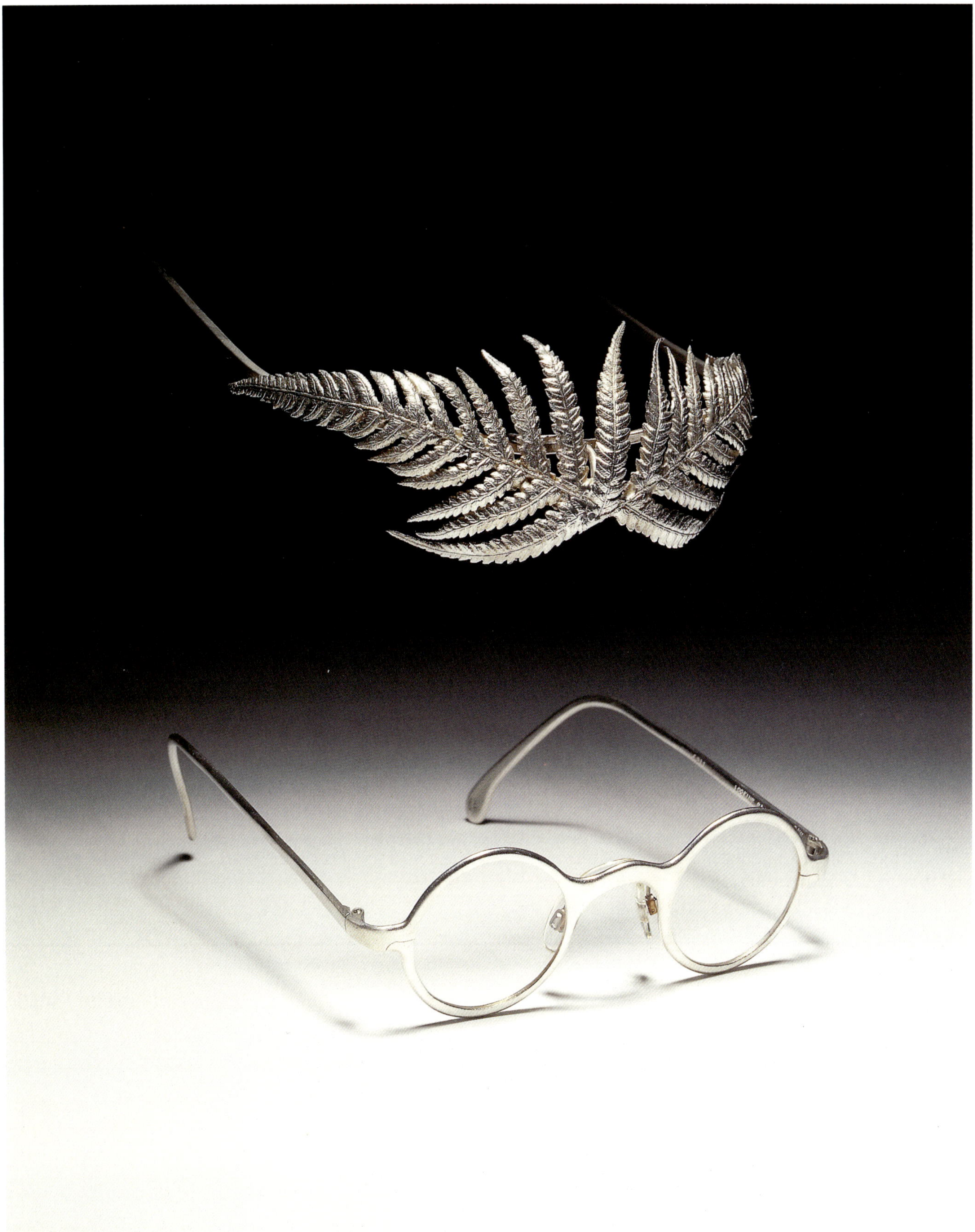

2

BRENDAN ADAMS

Born Auckland 1961.
DFA, Otago Polytechnic 1985.
Lives in Auckland.

There is a slightly mischievous quality to a lot of Brendan Adams' work, a great deal of which is domestic ware with exuberant colour, unexpected forms and lively detail. Some of his clay teapots have strange-looking spouts and handles which could have stepped out of a children's story book. In others the spout is the teapot, maybe in the form of a cone with a hole in the end. His teapots and clocks have a life beyond their expected function, and are amusing, self-parodying and playful—almost self-indulgent. Sometimes it is surprising that the pieces are indeed physically functional.

Clay hasn't always been Adams' primary interest. At art school he majored in painting, but clay became a means to an artistic end, just as slip casting became his means of self-expression, complemented by an ongoing interest in drawing and working with other materials like metals. However, the more he used clay, the more respect he gained for the tradition and the more he grew to appreciate it as a medium.

Adams is inspired by Italian painters and sculptors of the 1950s. Locally he acknowledges the support received through his association with ceramic artists like Christine Thacker (84) and Matt McLean (54). Slip casting is a favoured process, never as a substitute for other processes, but for its own special qualities, and he uses the cast components in a variety of combinations to make intricate objects. These objects become vehicles for the bright colours and subtle textures of his playful decoration.

In another genre of work Adams takes further risks, and his installations and sculptural work bring together ideas which had their genesis at art school. He has won a number of awards, has been represented in several Fletcher Challenge Ceramics Award exhibitions, has tutored in ceramics, and in 1997 was Artist in Residence at Unitec. The residency allowed him time to explore paper clay as a medium, and this resulted in a new direction in his sculptural work. Thematically his sculptures, which are random rather than sequential, have ranged from figures in landscapes to commentaries on urban landscapes. The figures have a cartoon quality, and Adams enjoys applying a kinetic quality to seemingly static objects.

The intention extends beyond the playful. *Factory*, created in 1997, demonstrates a play of lines, a rigid space frame enclosing the work and a fluid, organic, almost sinister cloud floating above a factory building. The physical constraints of combining the materials do not detract from the formal composition, which manages to retain a certain looseness. The work is a product of extensive drawing, revealing a graphic quality that is enhanced by the work being partially three-dimensional, so the cloud is able to cast literal as well as metaphoric shadows over the landscape. *Factory* illustrates a substance to Adams' ceramic art not generally associated with his more populist work. It is one of his most mature sculptural works.

**Factory
Earthenware and steel
760 x 530 mm
Collection of the
James Wallace
Charitable Arts Trust**

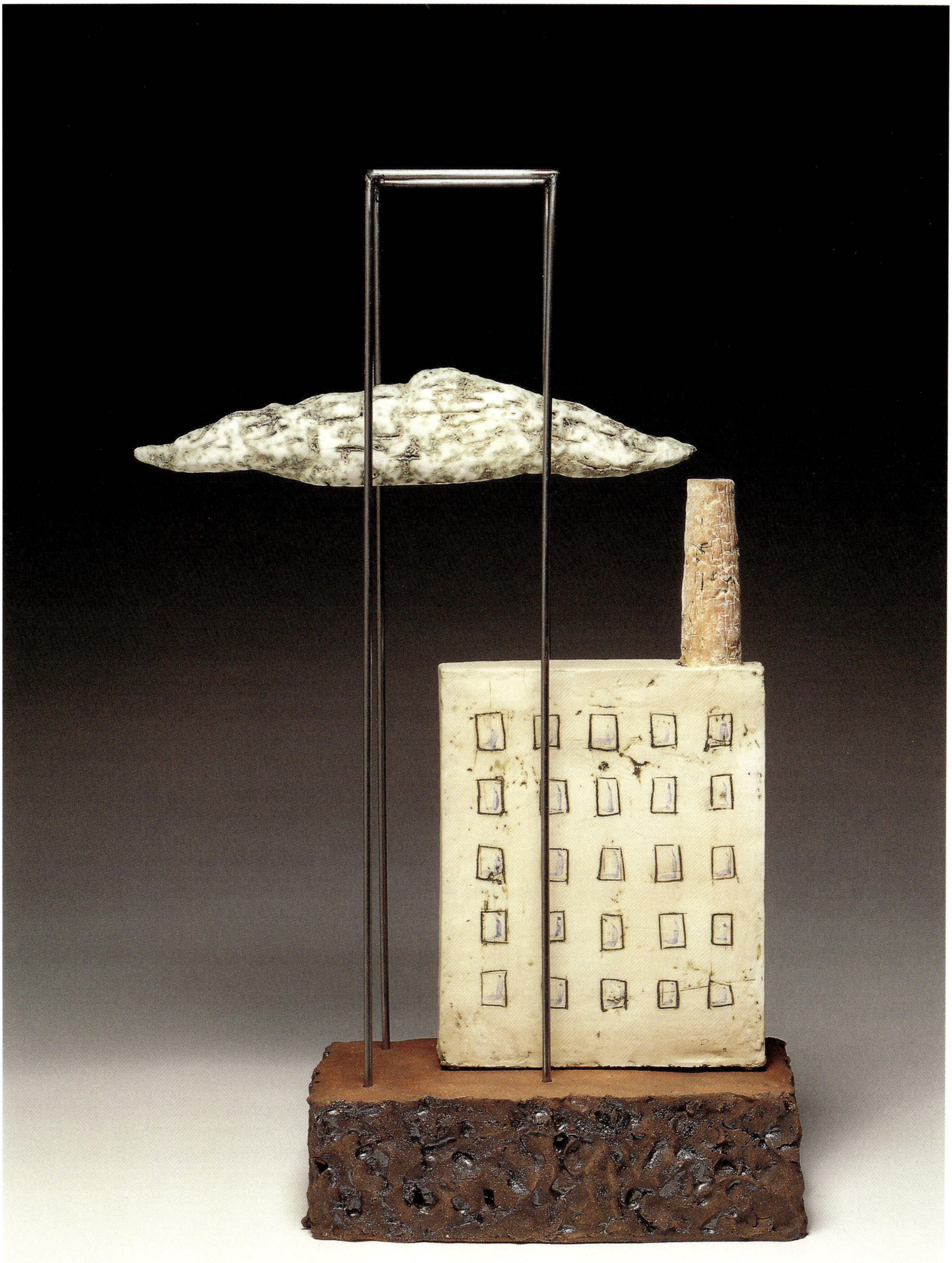

3

PETER ALGER

Born New Brunswick, Canada 1952.
Emigrated to New Zealand 1959.
Apprenticed to Warren Tippet, Coromandel 1968.
Lives in Waiotira, Northland.

Fish are potent images for Peter Alger, who is known best for his practised handling of clay vessels. As a child he used to go fishing with his father at Mercury Island, and he fondly recalls the time when snapper were plentiful. The experience never left him, and trying to capture fish has become the stuff of dreams as well as a means of financial survival in recent years. Those dreams, interlaced with readings from Carl Jung, inform Alger's creative work. He acknowledges that the fish in the sea can't be recreated, but he works from the premise that fish are the spiritual contents of an ancestral home. His intention is to create a symbol, to imbue it with energy that comes from a real affection for his subject matter.

His sculpted fish are demanding, labour-intensive works, and he makes them infrequently. However, he finds the process an energising one. The pieces are thrown on a wheel like a bottle; he squashes the body, then inflates it to form the fish, stands the work on its head and extrudes the neck of the bottle into a tail. Making the porcelain teeth, then closing the mouth becomes a symbolic action: something about art work being food that you don't put in your mouth. Alger sees this as a different statement from his fish on a plate with which viewers are more likely to identify—a fish on a plate is less a trophy than a symbol of the food one eats.

Much of Alger's work has an enduring earthy, rustic quality with rich textures. His dinner sets, teapots and mugs are made as personal items with individual personalities rather than as production ware. He makes strong, sophisticated, yet understated forms which develop their personalities as a direct response to the reaction between clay and fire. His process plays with the way clay shrinks on firing. Sometimes raw clay is applied to already fired and glazed areas; different shrinkages occur and the resultant crevices can fill with glaze. Alger's surfaces are about construction and deconstruction in a fundamental way, and he creates images that evoke the cracking of ice in the Antarctic and the forces of nature at work.

The teapot is a favourite form of expression, a crossover between domestic and sculptural genres. For Alger teapots that don't pour well are always a disappointment, so his are designed to be totally functional, symbolic of the tea-drinking ritual while never losing sight of their literal purpose. Large-scale works, including generous bowl forms, have also appealed to him, and for some years he also made planters. Ironically, when a changing economic environment and inexpensive imported planters forced him to re-assess his output, it was liberating for him, and freed him from market forces.

An apprenticeship with Warren Tippet was the formative clay experience for Alger. He has gone on to win many awards, has been represented in a number of Fletcher Challenge Ceramics Award exhibitions, and has exhibited in Japan and the USA. Self-effacing, and the most rigorous critic of his work, he tutors in clay, and brings to all his work a strongly developed philosophy and an eloquent personal imprint.

**When the Boat Comes In
Stoneware 1300°C
700 x 400 mm
Collection of Whangarei Art Museum**

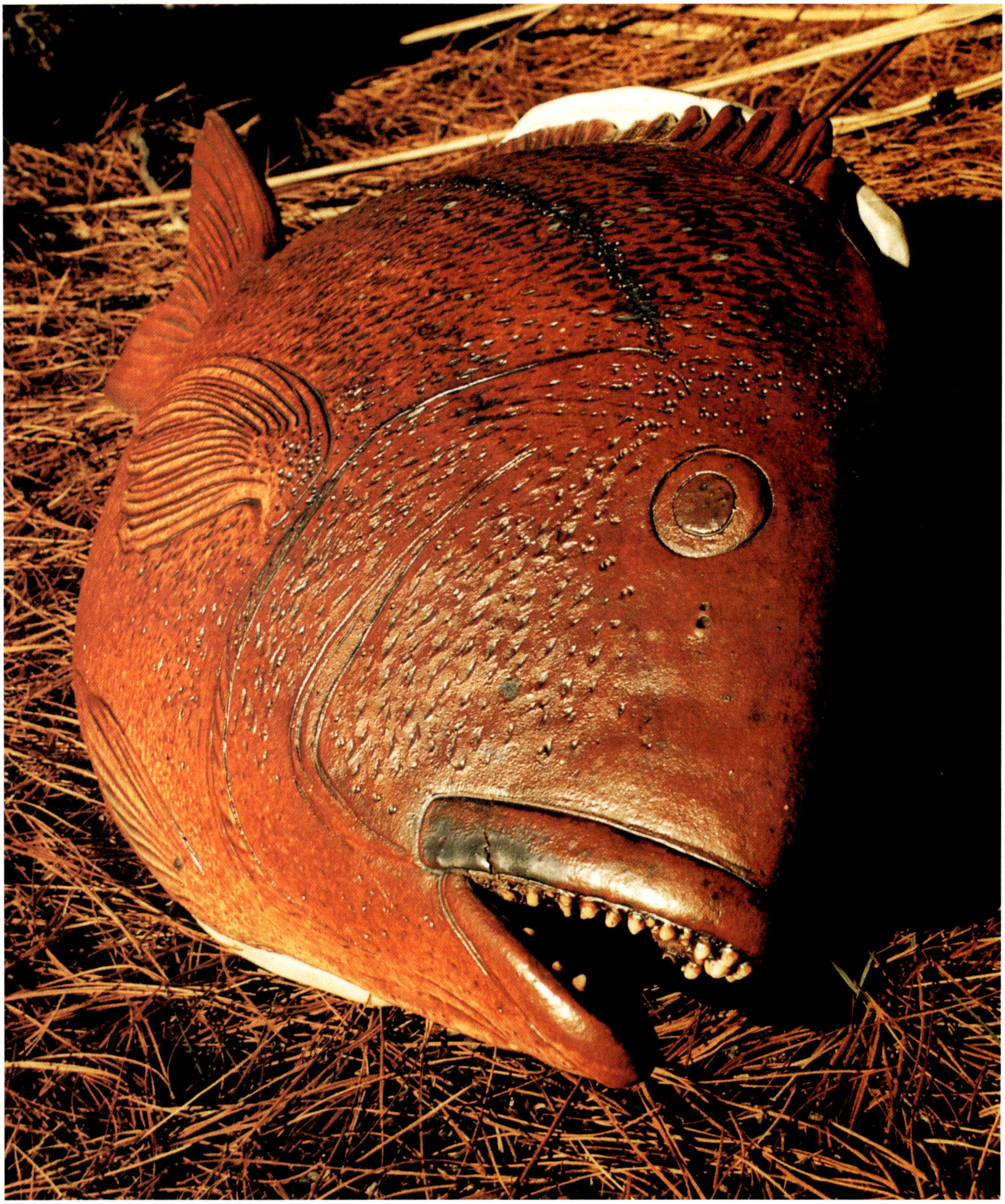

4

RAEWYN ATKINSON

Born Napier 1955.
Dip Early Childhood Education, Palmerston North Teachers College 1975;
completing BA (Art History), Victoria University Wellington 1998.
Lives in Wellington.

A distinctive style, eloquently evocative of her environment, characterises Raewyn Atkinson's ceramics. She has captured the essence of the bush, sea and hills in her work in a celebratory way, identifying motifs that signify New Zealand.

The nikau has provided inspiration for a number of her textured handbuilt works in recent years. In earlier stoneware tableware she used images of the nikau as decoration. More recently she took the nikau as the basis for her forms, her process changing from throwing on the wheel to handbuilding. She developed an evocative palette of textures to accompany the forms. First came the partially glazed goblets: gorgeous green cups on tall stems, adorned with red berry-like globules at their necks. The chevron markings on the cups with their torn edges were undeniably the fronds of the nikau palm, and the loose clayness of the work was an endearing characteristic.

The goblets were re-interpreted as totems exhibited as clusters—human-scale pieces, very upright, vulnerable in their slenderness, yet proudly tall, straight and breathtakingly beautiful. Partially inspired by the Pukumani burial poles of the Australian Aborigines, the works were created as markers of life, a celebration. The scale required some technical expertise, an ability to create sections which could be assembled into a cohesive whole that appeared as seamless and effortless as the uncontrived goblets.

Atkinson takes whatever is within view and allows it to emerge through clay in her hands. Heart forms developed, emulating the shapes of heart nikau and kina. A snorkelling holiday in the Coromandel had triggered her interest in kina. Before long Atkinson was crossing and combining the forms, letting the surface textures speak of their influences, the forms referencing and abstracting their origins. The tops of the kina evolved into hill forms that evoked the hills of Colin McCahon's (Vol.1, 50) paintings. They became an emotional, direct response to her environment that indicates how New Zealand is identified by land forms.

Her recent work focuses on the vessels which were originally the bases of the kina. The vessels, which can be seen as boats as well as domestic containers, are aged-looking forms which suggest decomposition, referring to the dead rather than to the living. A journey to the South Island had raised Atkinson's awareness of whaling, an activity about which she had always felt negative. Her research revealed different perspectives on whaling history and she realised that the experience of early whaling stations had little bearing on contemporary views of the industry. The whale became a symbol, stimulated by museum images seen in Picton, and she created her own narrative about whales on the surfaces of her vessels. Her images evoke early cave drawings with their minimal sgraffito marks and subtle areas of colour. She documents her personal response to the whales rather than intellectualising what they mean to other people— her depiction is less social commentary than an expression of how she herself was moved by their history.

The integrity of her work is unquestionable. Her works are featured in a number of significant collections and have won awards, including a Merit Award at the prestigious Fletcher Challenge Ceramics Award in 1997. Atkinson held and a residency at Shigaraki, Japan, in 1998.

Green Totems
Clay/glaze
1750 x 190 x 190 mm
Collection of
Natural Habitats Ltd

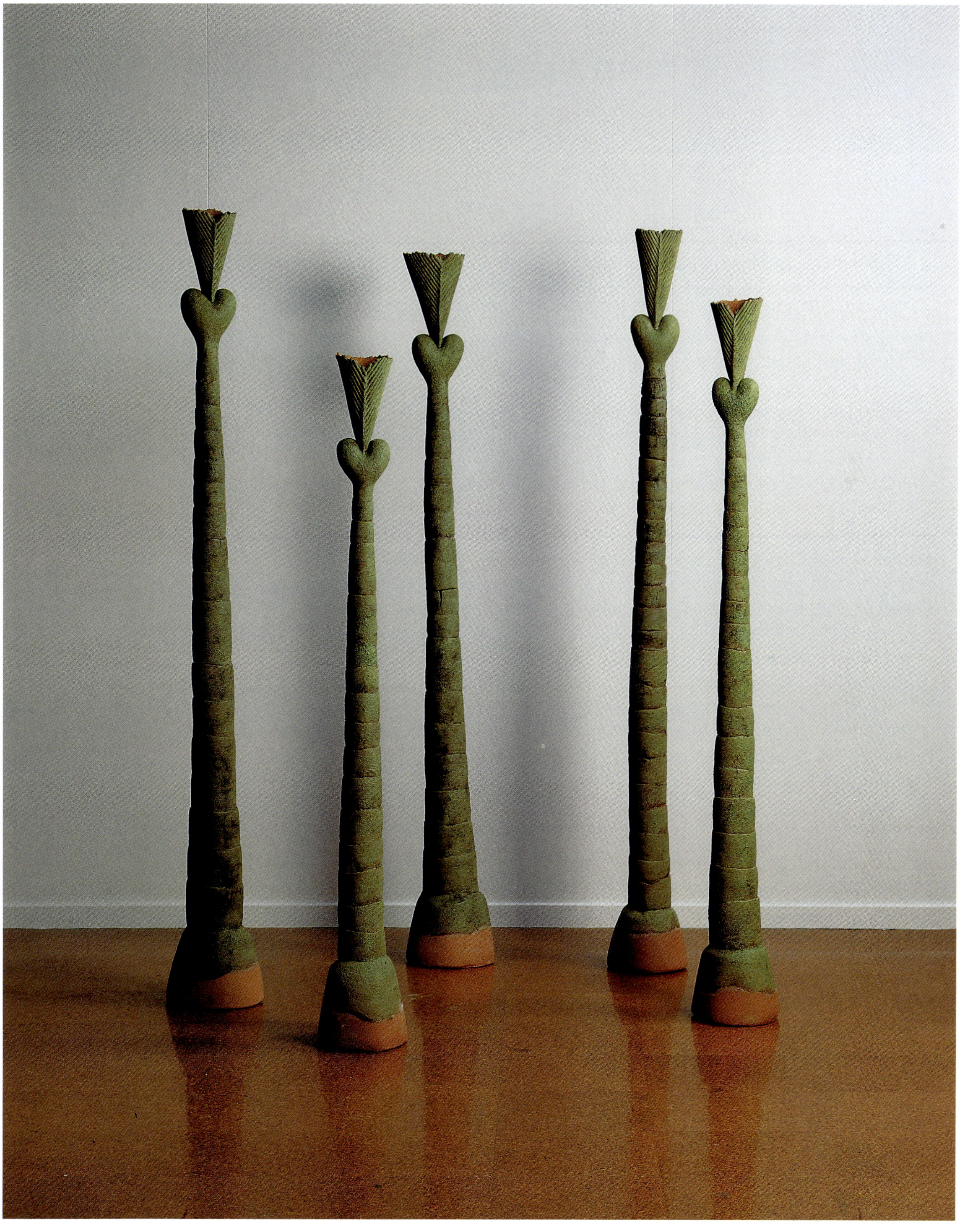

5

RUTH BAIRD

Born Norfolk Island 1941.
MA Classics, University of Auckland 1964.
Began making jewellery in London 1969.
Lives in Titirangi, Waitakere City.

Domestic fibre traditions, in the form of crochet, knitting, weaving or twining, are often part of Ruth Baird's delicate jewellery. Most are processes she learnt as a child, and they appeal to her as an expression of female activity. They also fit with her preference for using her hands rather than working with machinery, and provide quiet, contemplative work while sitting in her home studio that overlooks her garden. Strong links between making jewellery and domestic life have thus been established, philosophically and in reality.

Baird was a foundation member of the Fingers collective in 1974. She describes the group at that time as 'amateurs playing it by ear', learning from public feedback and each other. It took time for each of them to develop a clear philosophy, but it was an optimistic period for craft, and contemporary jewellery was a welcome new phenomenon in Auckland.

The changes in Baird's imagery have often been incremental. She had studied the classics and spent time overseas visiting museums in the 1960s. Jewellery from the time of Tutankhamun, and the sinuousness of art nouveau as expressed in Lalique jewellery, were early sources of inspiration, and that leaning to European culture remains a constant. In 1985 she knitted silver wire necklaces that were like collars, perhaps a reference to the Egyptian collars she had seen in her travels, perhaps also a reference to homemade knitted clothing.

Nonetheless, she has looked to her immediate environment for imagery—the sea, the bush and her garden. Her shapes and textures are generally derived from nature, like the recurring image of the butterfly, and leaves. They frequently develop into a series of similar works, perhaps with slight variations of colour, rather than as an edition of identical pieces.

Crocheting has come and gone in Baird's work, and for a while she was weaving wire, but found the process produced very rigid results. She discovered working with a single hook and a length of fine wire to be more flexible, and the results readily became three-dimensional forms. Titanium has been a favourite material since 1986; it meets Baird's need to work with colour. In the past she incorporated colour through the inclusion of small stones and, later, by using paua. Now she oxidises the surface of titanium by heating it with a torch, and produces a range of glorious soft glowing greens, golds and pinks not generally associated with titanium. She varies the processes to produce different intensities of colour, and has developed a concise vocabulary of techniques to express her ideas effectively. She might let twined skeletal leaves of fine silver wire dance in front of a softly hued pair of leaf earrings; or she might play with the colours and fine textures on simply articulated brooches. Her necklaces are a distinctive trademark—tubes of crocheted silver or anodised titanium wire support a series of leaves, the graphic shapes of which are taken directly from her garden.

Baird has exhibited nationally, in the USA and Australia. Her quietly resolved work is known for its wearability and sense of joy.

Pohutukawa necklace
Silver and titanium
150 x 150 mm
Collection of the artist

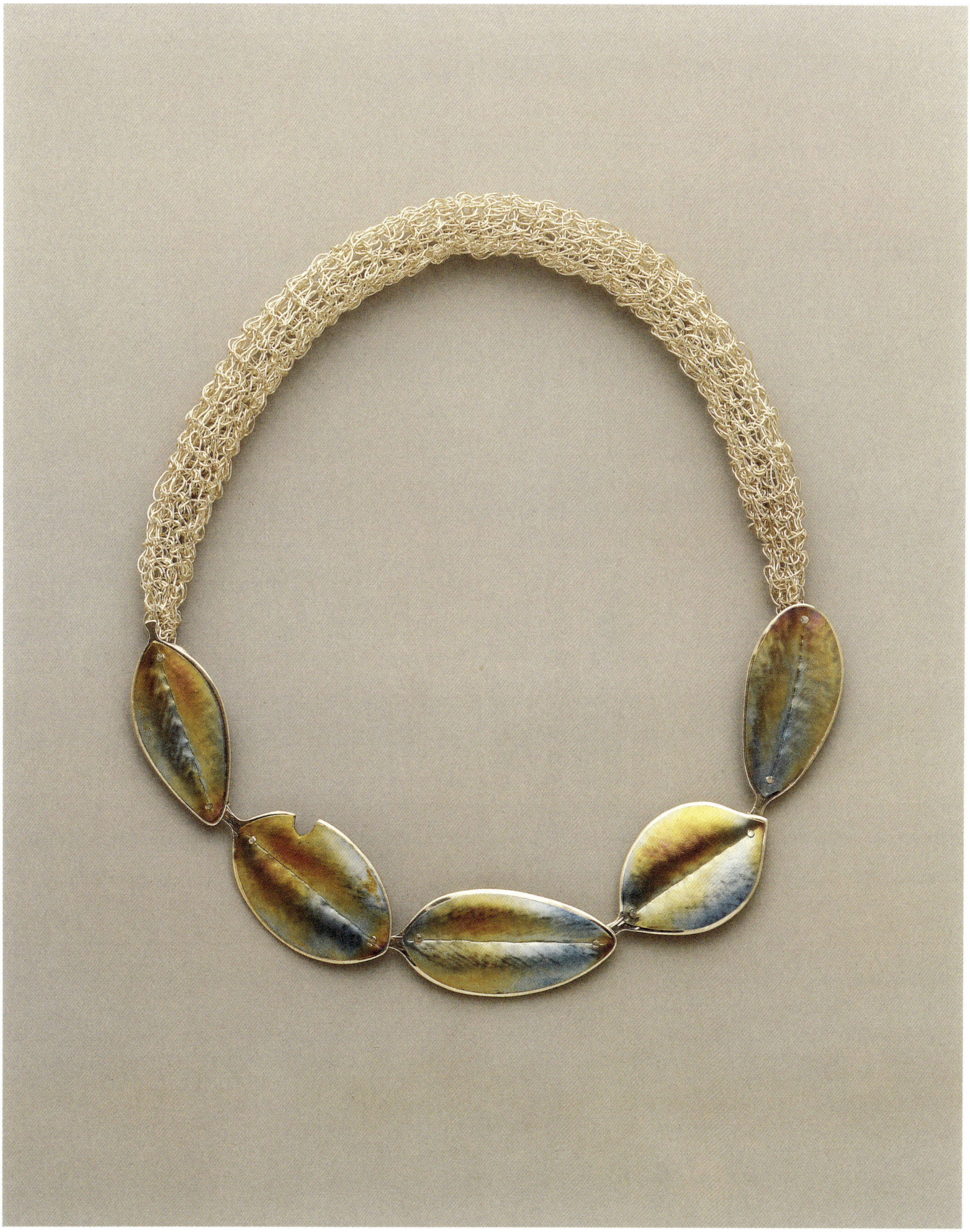

6

PENELOPE BARNHILL

Born Auckland 1969.
Certificate Craft Design, Christchurch Polytechnic 1990;
Dip Visual Communications Art and Craft Design, Christchurch Polytechnic 1991.
Lives in Auckland.

Roses, expressing preciousness, mortality and fragility of spirit, feature in Penelope Barnhill's jewellery. The theme of the rosary, derived from the Latin *rosarium*, which also means 'rose garden', was her starting point. Roses became a personal symbol that expressed sentiment and change, sometimes appearing as petals or caged rosebuds—encased but not trapped. As they dried and shrivelled, the owner could become involved in the work by replacing them. Barnhill is not alone in her use of roses. Parallels can be drawn with the poignant jewellery and small sculptures of the late Joan Atkinson, and Carole Shepheard (Vol. 2, 78) has also used roses and thorns as symbols of love and pain.

When Barnhill was a student close family members died, and a number of works in which roses had special meaning were made as memorials, a way of processing her bereavement. However, during this period she concentrated on printmaking and sculpture more than jewellery. When she graduated she went to the USA, then in 1991 returned to Auckland, where she worked with jeweller Warwick Freeman (27). In 1993 she moved to Christchurch where she had spent her childhood. That year she received a QEII Arts Council grant and held her first solo exhibition, *Fragile Hearts*, which featured hearts and roses, at Lynx Gallery.

Barnhill works in a number of media. Her jewellery is mainly of silver, and she enjoys working with fine gold for its colour and softness. Greywacke pebbles, leaves, copper—quenched to achieve a range of beautiful colours—and concrete all play a part. When she includes lush, green components they break down against the body, and dry and change in nature. She anticipates this distortion and seeks unknown developments.

Her works have developed using her life and her changing emotions as primary resources. She draws on themes of sexuality, ritual and rites of passage in one-off pieces that change, grow and develop within a series. She fabricates with wire and sheet metal, enjoying forging and manipulating. Her forms vary according to her mood, becoming free and whimsical when she is excited. In more controlled periods she tends to use solid, graphic shapes, contrasting open with solid, closed forms, and using recurring symbols that include hearts, crosses, spikes, cages and roses. The heart depends on context for meaning and is an expression of happiness, contemplation or hurt; the cross becomes a symbol of pain, protection or protest. *Whispered Memories*, from a 1998 exhibition at the Salamander Gallery, Christchurch, packages up the sentiment of ten years following her bereavement, and creates a token of love.

Experimental work encompasses working with paper, plant matter and fibre. Time working in the garden, cooking and exercising nourishes the process. She draws to resolve works before making them, but a fully resolved drawing is a completed journey which needs no further work. She aims for mystery, spontaneity and freshness.

In addition to jewellery Barnhill makes sculptures and mosaic works. Many of the former are personal works, a sorting-house for ideas and emotions. Her mosaics are made from tiles which she handpaints, then breaks, re-assembling the fragments as mirror frames, fireplaces, blackboards, benches and door frames. This original young artist has exhibited throughout New Zealand, and in Australia, Germany and USA.

**Precious Memories—
Series Honesty Crown
Silver, fine gold,
rose buds
1200 x 170 mm
Private collection**

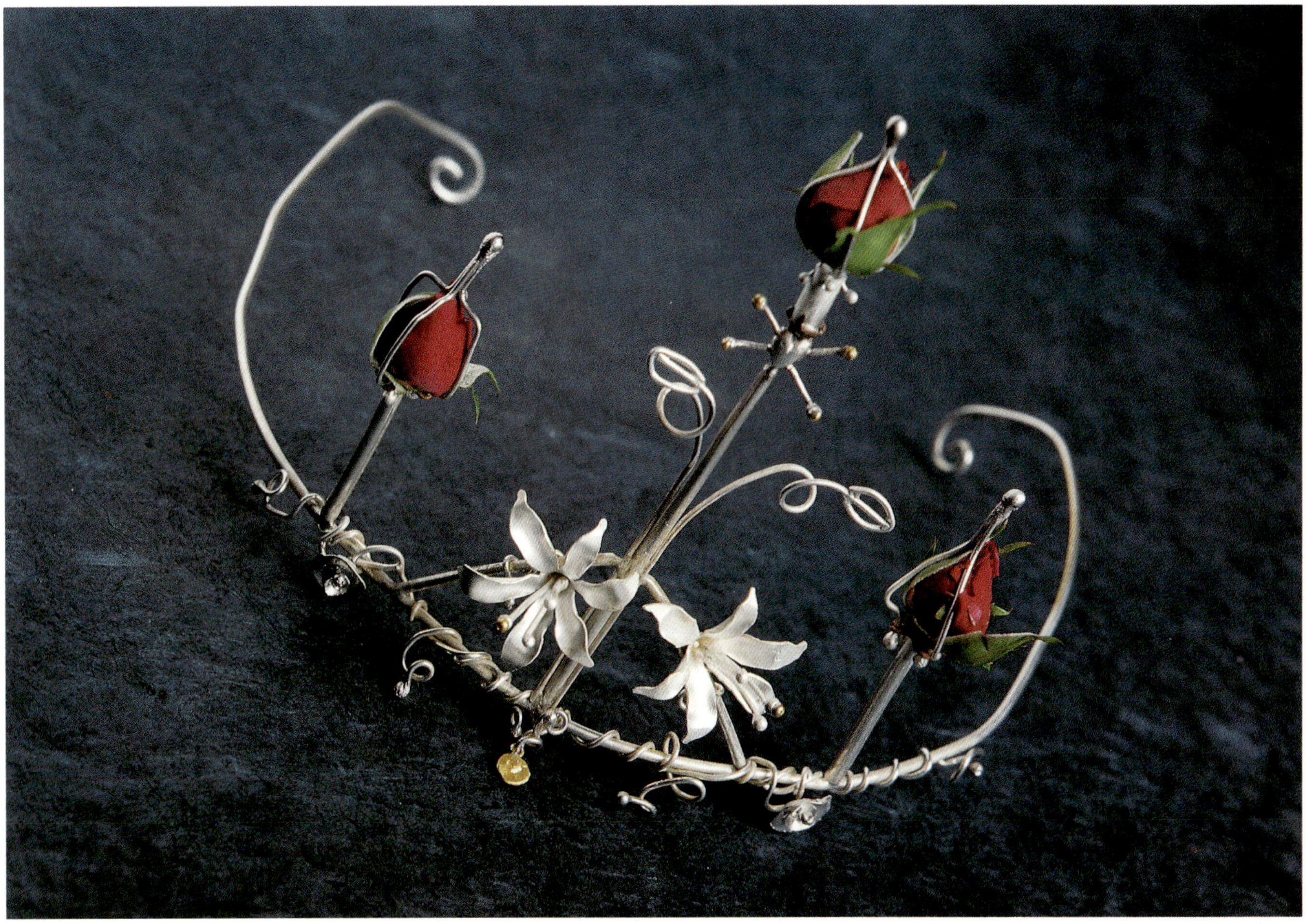

7

TONY BOND

Born Christchurch 1958.
Certificate in Visual Communication, Christchurch Polytechnic 1984;
Certificate in Fine and Applied Arts (Ceramics and Printmaking),
Wanganui Regional Community Polytechnic 1991.
Lives in Corsair Bay.

Tony Bond started working with clay at Wanganui Regional Community Polytechnic in 1991 as a sculptor rather than a potter. Before this he had worked as a graphic designer for six years, and he continues to produce etchings. Printmaking, stone carving and bronze casting became part of his repertoire, yet the unique qualities of working with clay appealed most, as a way of recording ideas, like a diary. He made frequent clay 'jottings' which would later reveal themselves, and drew a lot—not actual pieces, but doodles or visual clues.

The intriguing imagery on his vessels was never designed to sit on the surface. He has aimed more for integration of narrative and vessel, a marriage of two-dimensional concerns with three-dimensional form. Many works are small, intimate vessels designed to be hand-held. Bond likes them to be handled and the viewer to be led around the work to discover the imagery. They are surprisingly heavy pieces made of solid clay that can take months to dry.

On the surfaces Bond paints several layers of terra sigillata, a suspension of fine clay particles applied as a slip, then scratches through the layers with a sharp tool. This ancient technique pre-dates glazes and produces a sheen—the tactile quality he seeks—and integrates the surface design with the body of the work. The sgraffito marks are often zoomorphic figures—strange conglomerates of humans and animals, some with religious connotations. Links between male and female suggest sensuality, sexuality and love, and figures hide behind masks that evoke demons.

The interiors of these vessels contrast with the smooth, controlled exteriors. The insides are much more organic and textural, like intestines. For some viewers they evoke body orifices. It is a way of 'getting inside the skin', exposing human and, as a consequence, his own vulnerability. Bond is reaching beyond the domination of technical and aesthetic aspects of ceramics to more challenging concerns.

Over the years the surfaces of these pieces have become more figurative and graphic. The early vessels have evolved into waisted pieces that imply a torso, and the mysterious interiors remain as important as the external imagery. An opening at both ends became more obvious to him, like a human with two openings, functioning as a passage more than a vessel. Another group of works, a series of sculpted paper clay figures, approaches the theme more literally.

Bond has been included in a number of Fletcher Challenge Ceramics Award exhibitions, and received a Judge's Commendation in 1996. He has won a number of other awards since 1993, a highlight being the 1997 Cleveland Art Award. He was also invited to participate in *Papatuanuku*, the 1997 Stone Sculpture Symposium in Christchurch, and has work in the 1998 *6ème Biennale de la Ceramique* in Andenne, Belgium. He works on a number of pieces at any one time, never specifically for exhibition or competition, and he supports himself primarily through teaching drawing, and handbuilding in clay. His driving force is to intrigue viewers with content, not with process, which is nonetheless based on strong crafting values. This is firmly grounded, provocative work which stands to one side of much of New Zealand ceramic practice.

Sign to Pursue a Promise
Ceramic
170 x 110 x 105 mm
Private collection

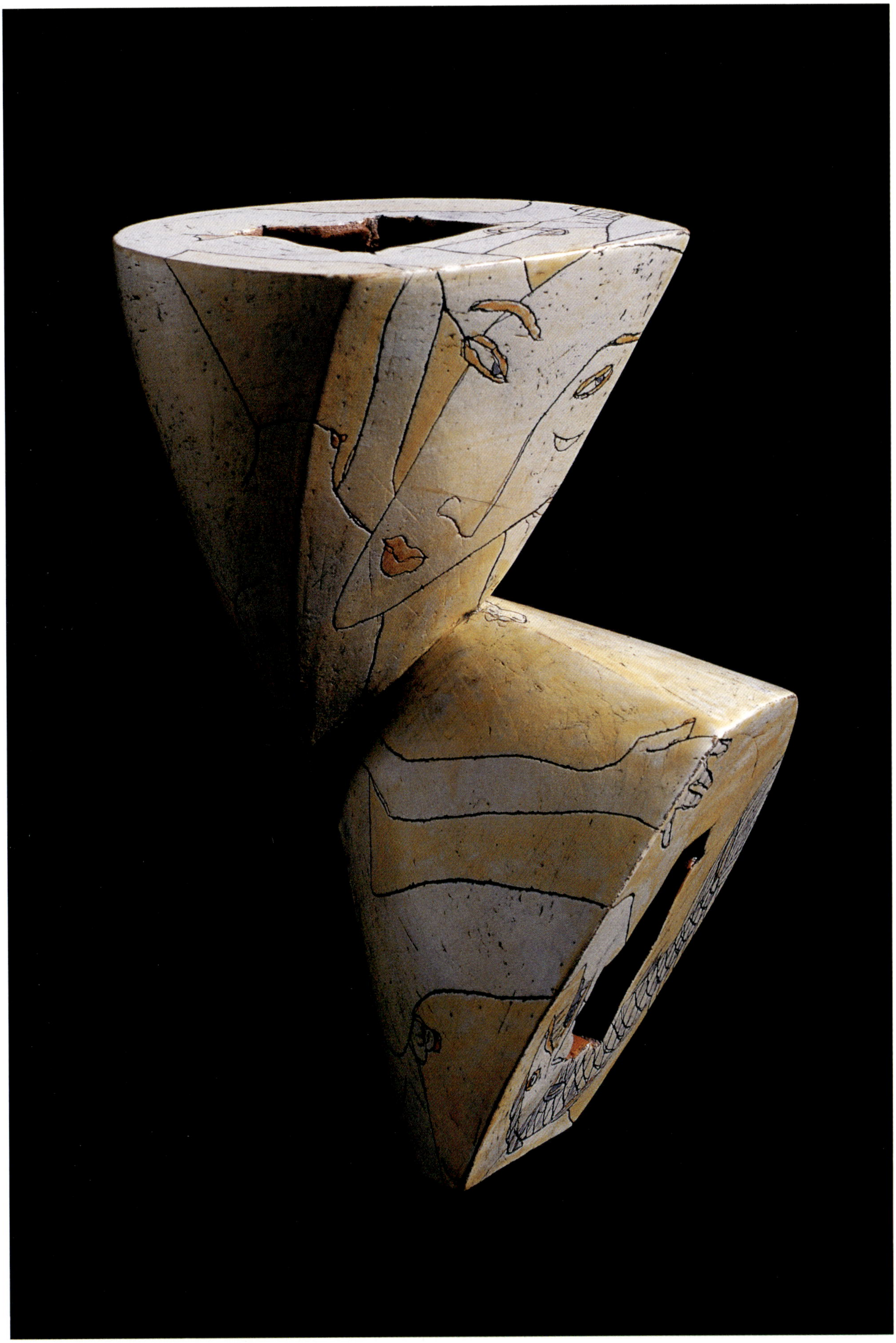

8

KOBI BOSSHARD

Born Uster, Switzerland 1939.
Apprenticeship with Burch-Korrodi, Zurich, Switzerland,
and School of Applied Arts, Zurich 1956–61.
Moved to New Zealand 1961.
Lives in Dunedin.

A long-term, fluctuating association with minimalism and modernism characterises Kobi Bosshard's jewellery. This is hardly surprising given that his European training was influenced by early Bauhaus ideas. Bosshard's interest is in function, and the resolution of construction with the physical processes is of primary importance. Generally, any social or personal meaning is incidental rather than imposed. He places a high value on craftsmanship, and his work is informed by life and its events, geometry and the making process.

Bosshard is a third-generation goldsmith. When he came to New Zealand he worked as an alpine guide at Mt Cook, and his early New Zealand work included setting hand-polished pebbles for tourists. Like Jens Hansen (33) from Denmark and Guenter Taemmler from East Germany, he had come to a country with no studio jewellery tradition as they knew it: they were the pioneers. They were all committed modernists whose work had parallels in music, literature and painting, from which Bosshard found much stimulus. From the outset of making jewellery he took on apprentices, initially on an exchange system with Hansen. In 1983 he established Fluxus as a co-operative workshop with Steve Mulqueen, and in 1984 he co-founded the Details Group, a national jewellery body.

In 1993 Bosshard created his *Souvenir Series*, which he perceived as a break from the impersonality of the minimalist approach. By making specific references to the external world he was communicating some sentimental meaning in his work for the first time. Some of these works were reminders of his Mt Cook days, others were about specific holidays in Australia and New Zealand. Yet they were also part of the modernist continuum, exploring shapes, voids and solids, while also playing with the word and the concept of 'souvenir' as memory. Brooches were made in pairs, one as a memento of a place, the second one with the stone absent, as if removed or lost. The series toyed with the triggers that unlock our memories.

His newest work, composed of triangles, has reclaimed the geometry and formalism of earlier work. Evidence of how these pieces have been made is apparent and, in true modernist style, the construction is an integral design component. Unmanipulated file marks on the surfaces add warmth to the coolly elegant silver, and fittings and clasps are unconcealed. The patterns which emerge reflect the need to join elements, and technical decisions determine the aesthetics of a piece. Conversely, Bosshard places no real emphasis on construction; the emphasis is on integrity, uncontaminated by trends. He believes that the senses are acknowledged after the design process is complete.

For Bosshard, aesthetics emerge from the integrity of idea, function, execution and form, but he acknowledges that he now accepts external references where once he rejected them. A purist he may have been on arrival in New Zealand, but he has adapted to circumstances, influencing and being influenced by those around him. The final response is with the wearers of his jewellery. The abstract modernist objects become enriched with layers of personal experience and association.

**Brooches
Sterling silver
48 x 48 mm,
30 x 30 mm,
35 x 18 mm,
Bracelet
Sterling silver
210 x 30 mm
Collection of the
artist**

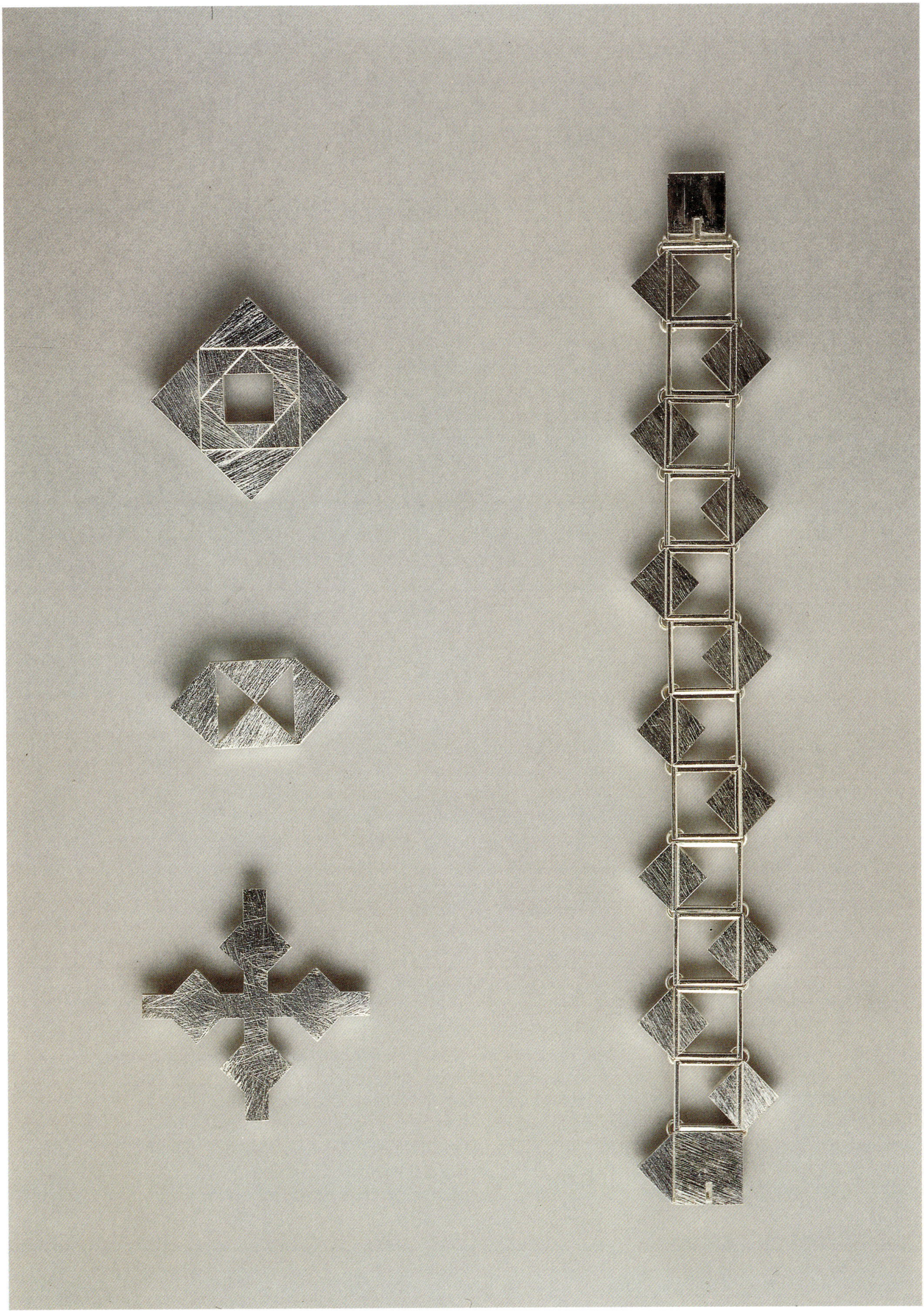

9

CHRISTINE BOSWIJK

Born Christchurch 1939.
Ceramics Certificate, School of Fine Art, Otago Polytechnic 1977;
Post Graduate Certificate, National Art School, East Sydney Technical College 1988.
Lives in Nelson.

There is a haunting beauty and spiritual quality in the highly acclaimed ceramics of Christine Boswijk. Singly or in groups, her abstract sculptural images have a presence which evokes feelings rather than a specific narrative. They act as triggers for viewers who bring their own personal experiences and stories to them.

Clay is fundamental to Boswijk's work—she enjoys its three-dimensional capabilities, its tactility and versatility. There always seem to be new discoveries about clay, despite its having served humans since prehistoric times. She handbuilds her work, intuitively working in a symbiotic relationship with her material, searching for an inexplicable quality that she recognises when it happens.

In 1988 Boswijk went to Sydney for post-graduate study on a QEII Arts Council grant. Until then she was known for creating handbuilt vessels. During this period her thoughts turned to her roots in New Zealand: the horizontal lines and verticals in the landscape, Mt Cook, the sea, the geology of the country. She began to acknowledge the aging process and that the resultant image appeared less than perfect. Her search was for underlying stories to which she could allude. She sought the intrinsic beauty of an idea—its essence—rather than applying a superficial layering. She thought, too, about issues surrounding being a woman—bandaging processes, nurturing and nourishing. She began to use clay in a way that acknowledged these issues intuitively rather than academically. Her respectful involvement with her material informed what she made, mistakes were seen as solutions, and she created work that evoked geological structures.

In 1991 Boswijk was one of a group of ceramic artists commissioned to make work for *Treasures of the Underworld* at World Expo in Seville. Encouraged to create to a large scale, she worked from transparent images of a stand of nikau palms. She drew large, expressive charcoal drawings that focused on the bulbous bellies rather than the fronds of the trees. It seemed as though the energy of the trees emanated from there. Boswijk's response was to work in the space between the photographic images and the drawings, the real information and her response to it. What she created was a magical nikau forest—wrapped, bandaged forms that reflected the fragility and vulnerability of the forest. As in other commissions and exhibition work, she created an intensely personal abstract expression, distilling the brief to its essence and allowing the work to develop a life of its own.

A commission for the Joint Women's Caucus at Parliament for Suffrage Year in 1994 was developed in a similar way. Her research sought the essence of the female principle and she looked to women as the vehicles for human life. Working with unglazed, unadorned white clay, she searched for a feeling of strength and a subliminal understanding of white. The collective information was translated into a torso-like piece, a response from the gut and the back of the brain.

Other recent commissions have included state gifts and a private commission, *Icon for Women,* which satirises a war memorial and again seeks to capture the essence of women. With each project one becomes aware of Boswijk's extraordinary affinity for the organic, expressive and poetic qualities of clay.

**Icon For Women
Ceramic
700 x 520 mm
Collection of
Edith Ryan**

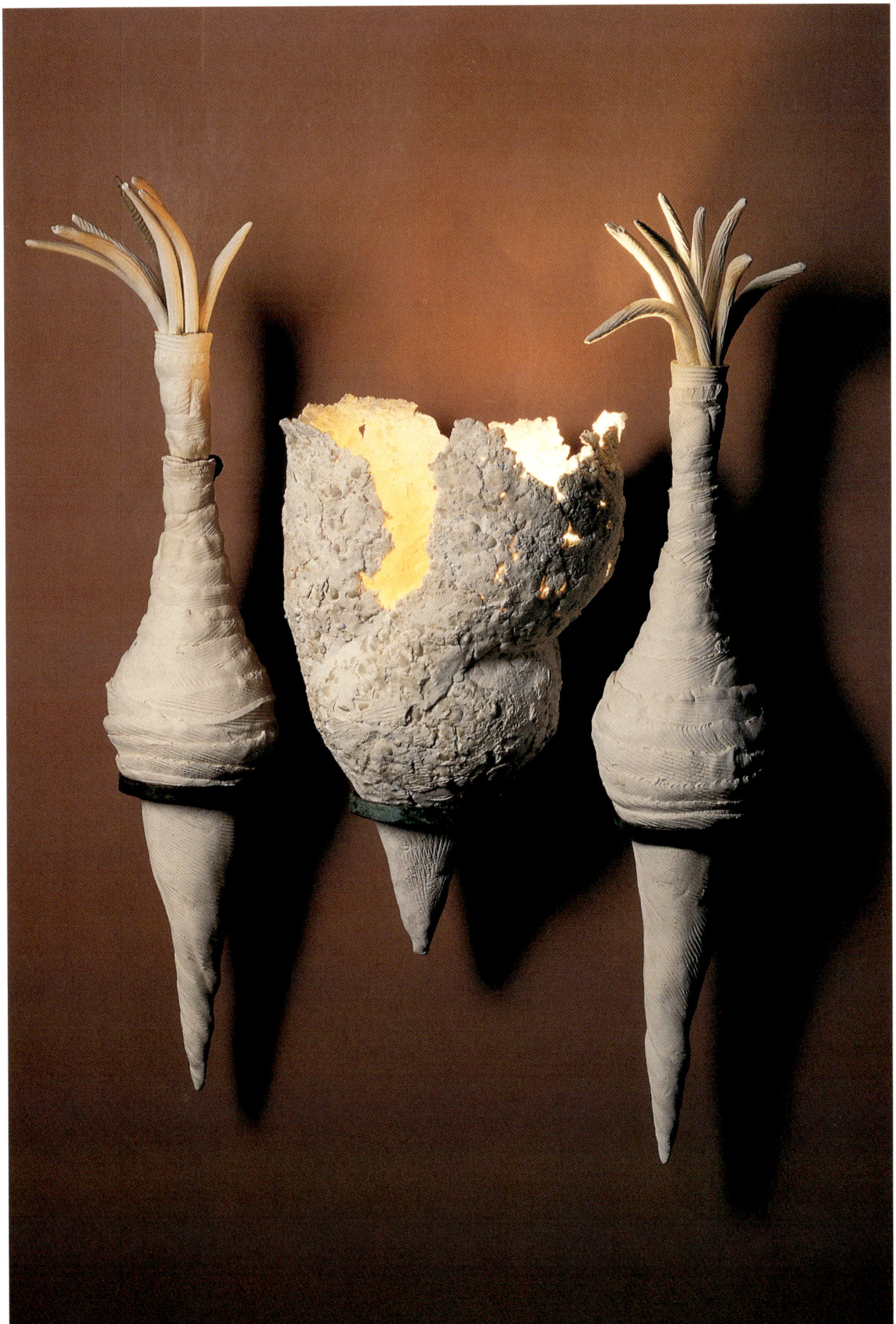

10

BARRY BRICKELL

Born New Plymouth 1935.
BSc, University of Auckland 1960; Auckland Teachers Training College 1960.
Began potting full-time 1961; awarded OBE for services to pottery 1987.
Lives in Coromandel.

'It is not the thing but how.' This is the way Barry Brickell, one of New Zealand's best-known potters, sums up his philosophy. A pioneer and self-proclaimed eccentric, he has an elemental affinity for clay and fire as well as for his environment. His passions for art, conservation and engineering have translated into a unique lifestyle that includes making clay sculptures, creating and managing the Driving Creek Railway and Pottery, and developing a native forest project.

Brickell discovered pottery as a thirteen-year-old when, not far from the family home at Devonport, he found the local gas and firebrick works. Kilns, furnaces and steam engines became a source of fascination. He credits Len Castle (14) with teaching him to throw on a wheel; from Keith Patterson he learned the principles of coiling clay; and Bernard Leach's *A Potter's Book* became his Bible. A good mind for engineering led him to make many experimental kilns. Creative stimulus came from evening painting classes with Colin McCahon (Vol. 1, 50) and conversations with artists like Toss Woollaston (Vol.1, 99) and Theo Schoon.

When he began to pot full time at Coromandel, a prolific output of domestic ware earned him a living. In 1974 he moved to his present property at Driving Creek, where he accommodated numerous young trainee potters, many of whom were seeking an alternative lifestyle. Pioneer potter Helen Mason also moved there, as did Wailin and Tom Elliott. Many students worked beside him, observing and learning. Brickell is adamant that students learn—he 'never teaches'. QEII Arts Council grants in 1962, 1974 and 1986 assisted his projects, but more importantly he received a number of commissions. These included mural projects in the 1980s, and participation in *Treasures of the Underworld* at World Expo, Seville, in 1992. In 1985 he published *A New Zealand Potter's Dictionary* and in 1998 he published the booklet *The Story of Driving Creek*.

Despite the communal aspect of Driving Creek, Brickell has remained fiercely individual and solitary. He has always shunned clubs, societies and competitions, and rejected fashion and trends. He built New Zealand's first wood-fired stoneware kiln at Driving Creek. Although he had a ready supply of clay and pine wood fuel, he soon realised he needed to access them with minimal environmental impact. Thus was born his narrow-gauge mountain railway. This and rejuvenating native forest became a major visitor attraction, absorbing much of his time and energy. Nonetheless, making large clay sculptures and throwing small vessels on the wheel have continued to be an important part of his life. He has had many exhibitions, and has cautiously accepted invitations to teach and demonstrate his work in Australia, Canada, Vanuatu and Finland.

His often untitled sculptures are built up slowly into unglazed coiled terracotta forms that are voluptuous, sensual and often human scale. He groups them within invented generic titles derived from his biology and geology studies at university, like *Spiromorphs*—his spiral forms. These abstracted pieces, which often refer to human bodies, appear to act as an escape valve in the face of Brickell's ostentatious virginity. He seems to pour all his sexual energy and sensuality into these sculptures, a number of which are intertwining forms. Clustered on his property, they are like groups of 'offspring', integrated into the landscape.

**Spiromorphs I & II
Woodfired terracotta
1260 x 560 mm,
1430 x 450 mm
Collection of the artist**

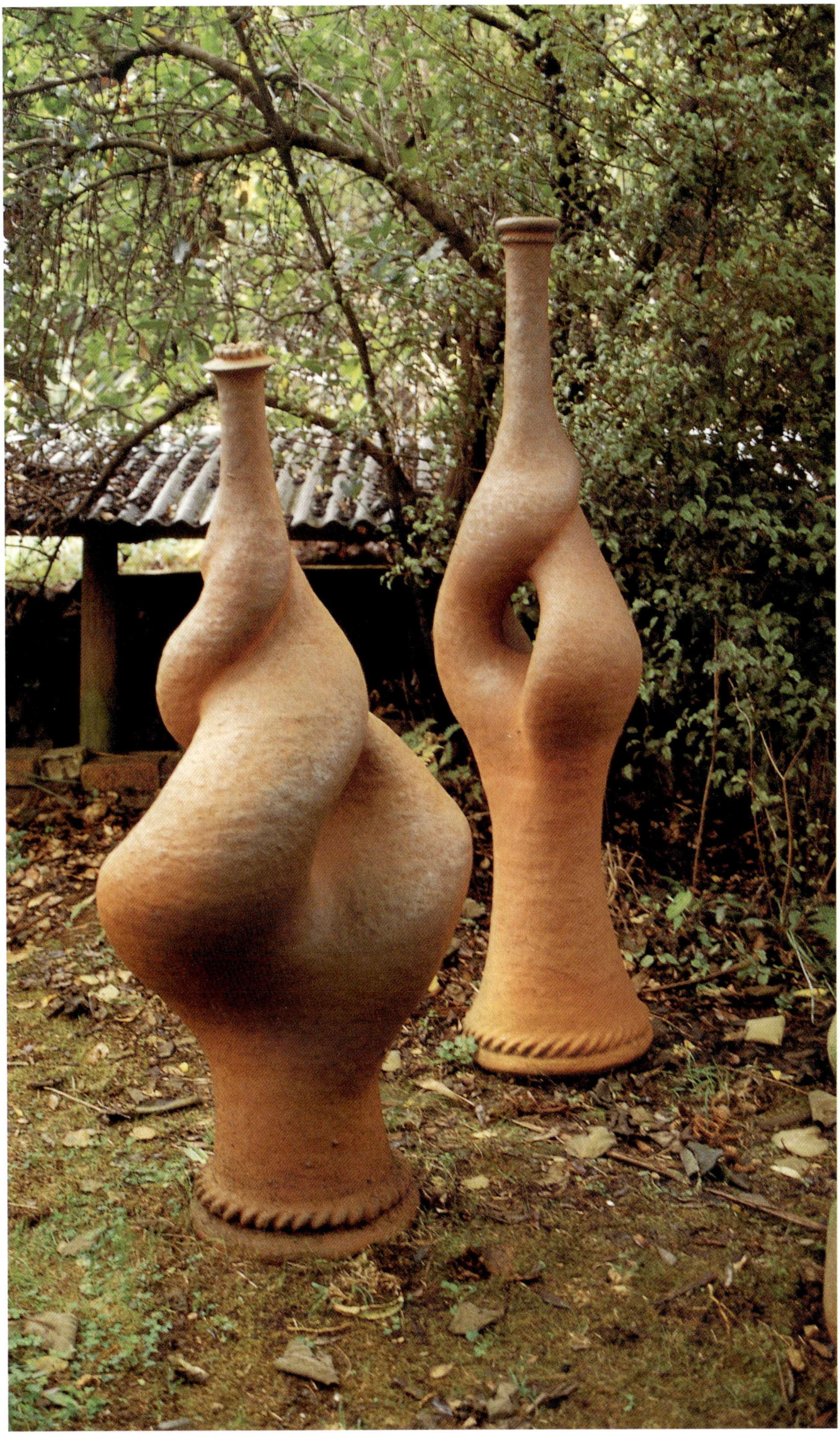

11

FREDA BRIERLEY

Born Dundee, Scotland 1942.
Migrated to Auckland 1982.
DFA, Whitecliffe College of Art and Design 1993.
Lives in Auckland.

Emotional rather than intellectual maps guide Freda Brierley's stitched works—works which are narratives more likely to be told by the viewer than the maker. She sees herself as someone who likes to be inside, looking out, rather than outside, looking in. Her works are frequently set in interior spaces—strange abstracted places she hardly recognises. She stitches from instinct after doing many drawings to guide the way, aiming to challenge viewers with visual puzzles and perhaps a title and visual clues. Interpreting the work becomes the prerogative of the viewer.

Machine embroidery is her preferred way of working. She relishes the richness, textures and depth she can achieve with stitchery rather than with drawing, and the tactility of threads becomes an important ingredient. The eloquent raw edges of fabric appeal, as do the distortions and undulating surfaces created by altering thread tensions. These stitched works take time to build up, challenging her to retain the spirit of the idea. In her newest works she is content to partially cover the surface, thus reclaiming the fabric as an integral visual component. The seduction of stitching for its own sake is a thing of the past for Brierley.

She works spasmodically rather than continuously. Her sketches and paintings are preliminary ideas, not finished art works but a means to an end—her 'clearing shed', which includes figures loosely sketched from memory rather than from life. The images are invariably about people, and are often quite personal; they mirror emotions, almost like letting an outsider read one's letters or diary. To distil her ideas, she likes to work in concentrated bursts on these sketches, searching for a situation, a drama that might alter the equilibrium of a situation, the layered meanings expressed through layers of thread and fabric.

Brierley regards the high point of her professional life, which includes a number of awards, as a ten-day residential symposium for embroiderers held in 1994. The encouragement and the freedom of expression she developed were a prelude to an exhibition by the participants at the Barbican in London in 1995. Equally significant for her was the associated trip, a turning point after being a reluctant immigrant to New Zealand. It inspired her poignant work *Which Way Home*, with its anguished face and separate compartments, one alluding to the clear bright light of New Zealand, the other to the enveloping blanket of Scotland. The work acknowledged the many years she lived in New Zealand before she could consider it her home.

On the Edge, a more recent work, is more ambiguous, but no less autobiographical. Three mysterious figures fill the work, constrained in their allotted bands of colour. There is still richness in the built-up threads, which are permitted to spill out of their allotted area, and the sketchiness of the piece is retained despite the painstaking process. Brierley has harnessed her techniques to produce a work that speaks to the viewer with eloquence yet restraint, simultaneously revealing and concealing aspects of her inner self.

**On the Edge
Machine embroidery
500 x 400 mm
Collection of the artist**

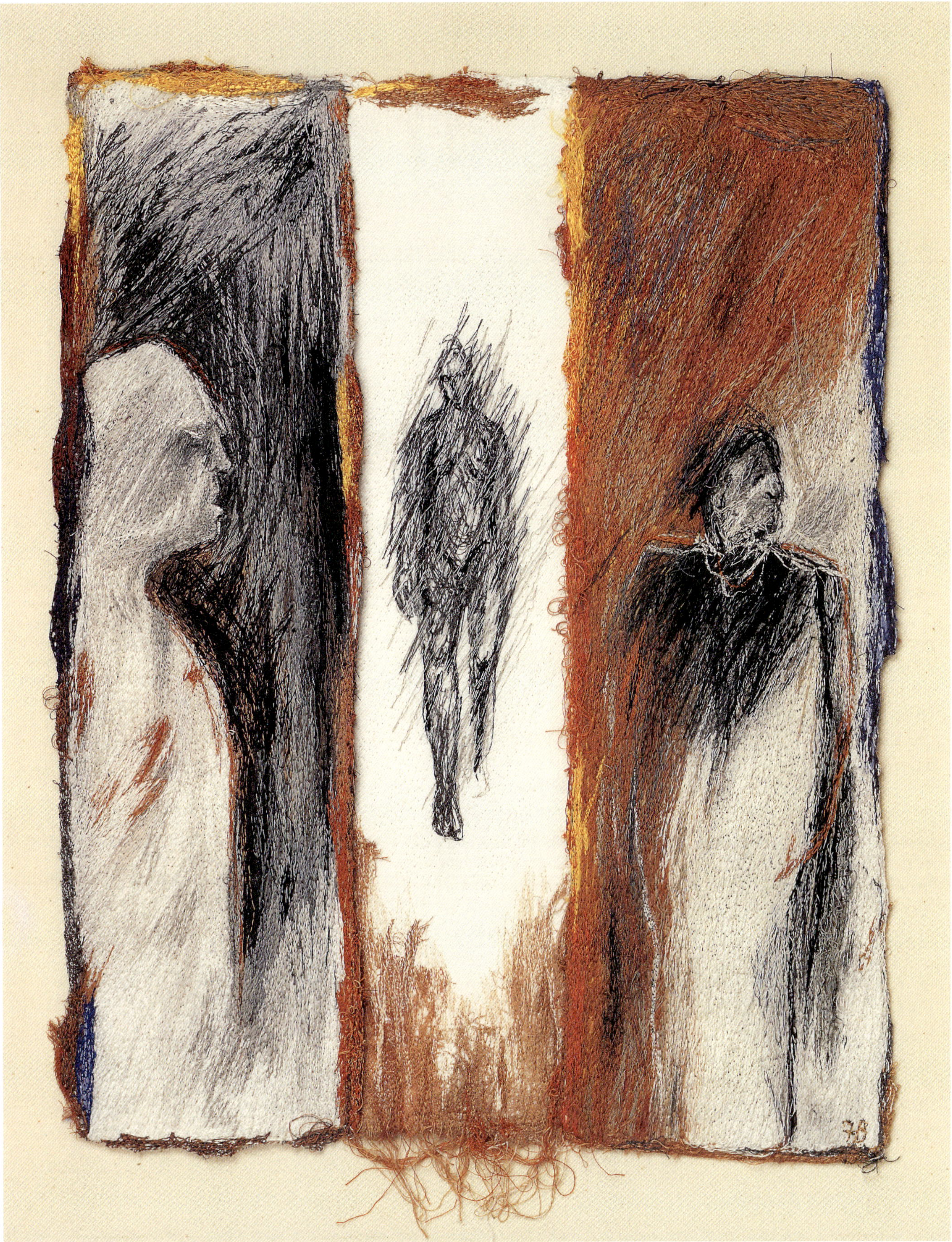

12

ALAN BROWN

Born Raetihi 1951.
Ati-Hau-Nui-a-Paparangi.
First exhibited knives in Auckland 1982.
Lives in Napier.

A lack of formal design training has never held Alan Brown back, and the years of experience in farming, building, landscaping and furniture-making were the training ground for his art-making. He believes that an innate sense of design cannot be taught and this belief has been validated by the recognition of his talent at several stages in his artistic career.

The landmarks in Brown's career are easy to identify. He won the international Winstone's Craft Biennale Award in 1989 with a beautifully sculpted contemporary waka huia filled with finely crafted treasures. He had been exhibiting fairly regularly since 1986, but this award opened doors to national and international exhibitions as well as to commissioned works. In 1991 Athfield Architects commissioned Brown to make thirty pieces of furniture for the Wellington City Library. In 1993 he received a Major Development Grant from the QEII Arts Council. Another significant event was being Artist in Residence at the Eastern Institute of Technology at Taradale in 1994. Since then he has been based on campus, visible to students, and continuing to create finely crafted work for exhibition and commission.

A recent sculpture symposium in Wellington provided Brown with the impetus to expand the scale of his works. By doing so he appears to have crossed a threshold. In 1997 he commenced a major commission to create large bronze works for an Auckland inner-city refurbishment project that involves working with architects, landscape designers and a property developer. Making large sculptural work has become important. It extends the design and crafting skills he has developed over the years, and enables him to make salient comments on the times in which he lives.

Brown continues to make jade and silver jewellery, corporate gifts and commissioned pieces, including the annual Supreme Tourism Award trophy. As before, he works across a range of scales in different media. Parallels can be drawn with the work of carver John Edgar (24), whose large carved stone sculptures grew from concerns at a jewellery scale. Brown is driven by a personal philosophy, one in which spirituality, family and peer support underlie his decision to change direction. He pays tribute to peers and mentors who include Edgar as well as Owen Mapp (48), Paul Mason (49) and Donn Salt.

Creativity is all-important to Brown, who sees it as a positive, healing act which is able to counteract the destructive forces in our society. He draws with equal ease on his Maori and Nordic heritages to feed his content and nourish his philosophy, and he integrates cultural aspects into a number of his pieces. His Maoridom gives him a feeling of connection to the true nature of the earth. There is joy in his use of wood and stone which he considers to be the finest of materials. He seeks dialogue with his viewers through his works, and these become a means of expressing his love of the land and his culture. Brown sees his works acting as markers of the present for future generations.

Makotuku—Where White Sails Once Waded
Bronze
1900 mm
Private collection for public display

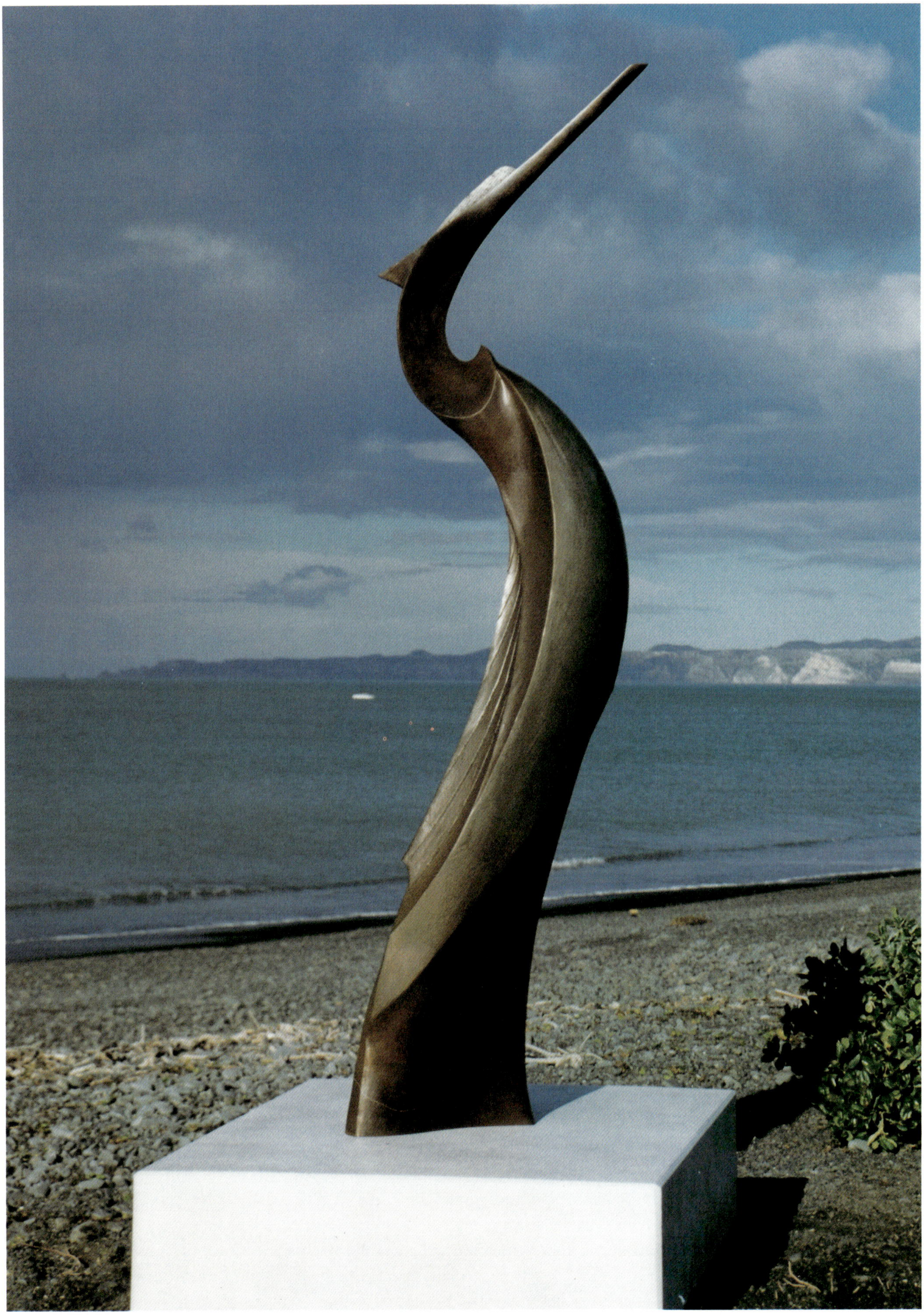

13

EMMA CAMDEN

Born Southsea, England 1966.
Southampton Institute of Higher Education 1985;
BA (Hons) (Glass with Ceramics), Sunderland Polytechnic, England 1990.
Moved to New Zealand 1991.
Lives in Auckland.

Softly whispered words float through Emma Camden's most recent red glass boxes—words about love and sex, strong direct words of street culture. In these works, assertively titled *Boxing a Lover*, the words can be discovered in a certain light. Perhaps the words are a logical sequel to her tearaway student days, but now there is an ambiguity—the bravado seems at odds with the quiet presence of the words which lurk beneath the surface of the glass.

Light is what Camden plays with: light that strikes and penetrates her glass vessels. Her forms are smooth, richly coloured and translucent. She understands how rays travel through fused granules of glass, where they appear to become trapped, reflecting and refracting until the object becomes saturated with light. She plays with angles as well—jaunty angles that make some of her works appear slightly off-balance and momentarily disturbing. The angles fit with a philosophy that grew out of an admiration for the metaphysical concepts of Giorgio de Chirico.

Being an immigrant makes Camden very focused about place, and her work documents her response to living in New Zealand. She is clear that this work could never have happened in England, where she absorbed history, used Pompeiian symbols and worked directly with surrealist concepts. New Zealand offered her new ways of seeing and being, and she perceives this country as being 'soft at the edges': land masses surrounded by water, land dotted with small houses.

The recently completed *Immigration Series* was about moving in and out of New Zealand by aeroplane and boat, and acted as a visual diary. Big city spaces were described by patterns of soulless windows and monochromatic towers. References to the Pacific at times appeared in her work, as commentary and descriptor rather than appropriation, but the dominant themes in the series were based on stylised Western images, referring to modes of transport and to her environment.

Underpinning the narratives has been a continuation of her homage to surrealism. Her images have been tied to the metaphysical dream—crooked, tilted, upside down, the angles 'all wrong'. The dream state has given her licence to play with the balance of the objects, to exaggerate, to add a dynamic quality and to lift the icons onto a plane suggestive of a state of transportation.

Casting glass was largely self-taught, as Camden's studies had focused on flat glass. A grant enabled her to attend a workshop with David Reekie in Canberra, and she has spent valuable time at the glass studio Pilchuck in Seattle. Her casting processes have become more refined, and she achieves a high level of finish through sand blasting, acid etching and hand sanding with diamond pads.

This sophisticated work is now moving onto the international stage. It is well conceived and beautifully executed, hard edged and 'urban'. A protective shell seems to enclose the inner space and, on occasion, Camden allows the light to seep into her work to reveal its heart and vulnerability. Those are moments worthy of discovery.

Tower of Secrets
Cast glass
730 x 140 x 130 mm
Private collection

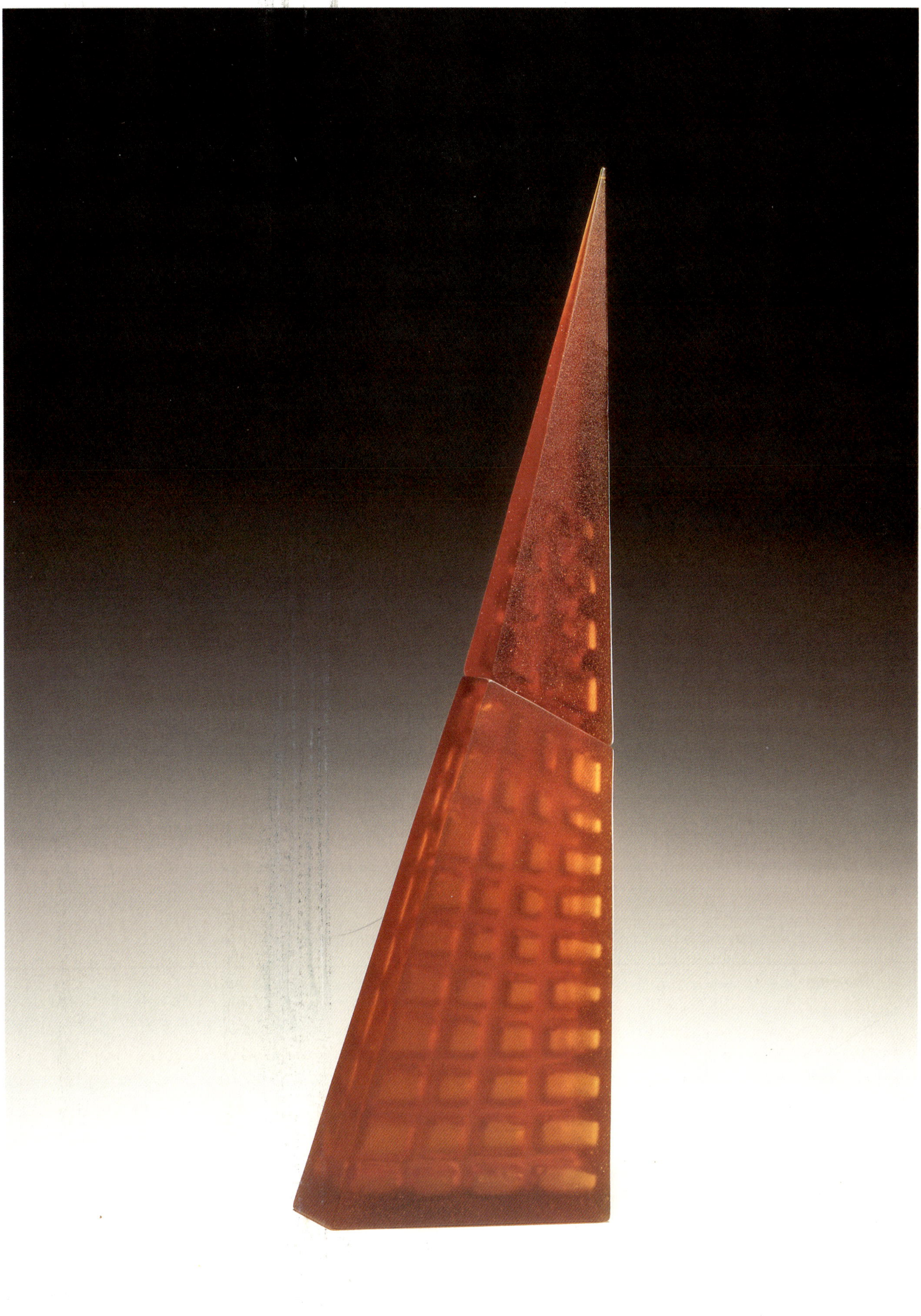

14

LEN CASTLE

Born Auckland 1924.
BSc, University of Auckland 1946; Teaching Certificate, Auckland Teachers Training College 1947.
Began potting professionally 1962.
Lives in Warkworth.

Len Castle has worked with clay for over fifty years. A pioneer, innovator, teacher and mentor to many, he is a legendary figure, known nationally and internationally. Clay represents his love of the land, and provides the link between his major interests in art and science.

When he first started working with clay, he was drawn to the refinement and elegance of the work of Scandinavian studio designers which was based on Chinese pots of the Tang and Song dynasties. Castle also discovered the spontaneous, less 'well-behaved' peasant pots of Northern China in Auckland Museum. Very early in his career he read the seminal *A Potter's Book* by Bernard Leach, and in 1956, on a scholarship from the Association of New Zealand Art Societies, he spent a year making production ware in Leach's studio in England.

However, it was the spontaneity, assuredness, direct earthiness and 'truth to materials' approach of Japanese potter Shoji Hamada, who had worked with Leach, that touched him most. The ancient traditions of China, Korea and Japan appealed strongly to Castle, and he realised that Hamada's pieces were modern examples of these traditions. Hamada and Leach became the greatest influences on the contemporary ceramics movement in New Zealand, with Castle leading the way. It was the beginning of the development of his own unique style. Today his work is a consolidation of all the earlier influences, which included an interest in Zen Buddhism. He acknowledges that artist Theo Schoon taught him how 'to see', as well as the principles of pattern making. With friends like Barry Brickell (10), Helen Mason and Mirek Smisek he shared potting discoveries.

Castle continues to be prolific and experimental, working simultaneously across a number of series. Recent work, the *Earth Movement Series*, consists of small, intimate, sculptural pieces: joyous celebrations of material and texture. He uses the energy of both hands to prise open a block of clay that has been wirecut, creating fluting that resembles limestone country. He pulls the clay open until it tears and a deliberate 'fault line' in the clay provides the interplay he seeks. The unglazed, occasionally pigmented works are about earth movement but also evoke open books, or readings of the interior of the landscape.

Parallel to this work is the *Secrets of the Sea* series. Castle is fascinated by the radial forms of echinoderms, the perforated exoskeletons and creatures that move with tube feet. Making these satisfies his love of handbuilding. Many larger works are press moulded. Throwing on the wheel is a spasmodic activity, rather like sketching, and he enjoys it most when he has to make quick, intuitive decisions.

A passion for rich texture has been in evidence for many years. Notable examples are the very large pots made for *Treasures of the Underworld,* shown at World Expo, Seville, in 1992, the crusty rims of which contrasted with the smooth interiors that gleamed like lakes. In his exhibition *The Restless Earth Touches Me* at Rotorua Museum of Art and History in 1992, the forms and textures reflected his interest in the geothermal landscape. His endless fascination for all aspects of the land and clay continue to inspire him to new work, to gain further understanding of his material, to probe beneath its surface and seek its essence.

**Earth Book, Volume 1
Ceramic, earthenware
240 x 250 mm
Collection of the artist**

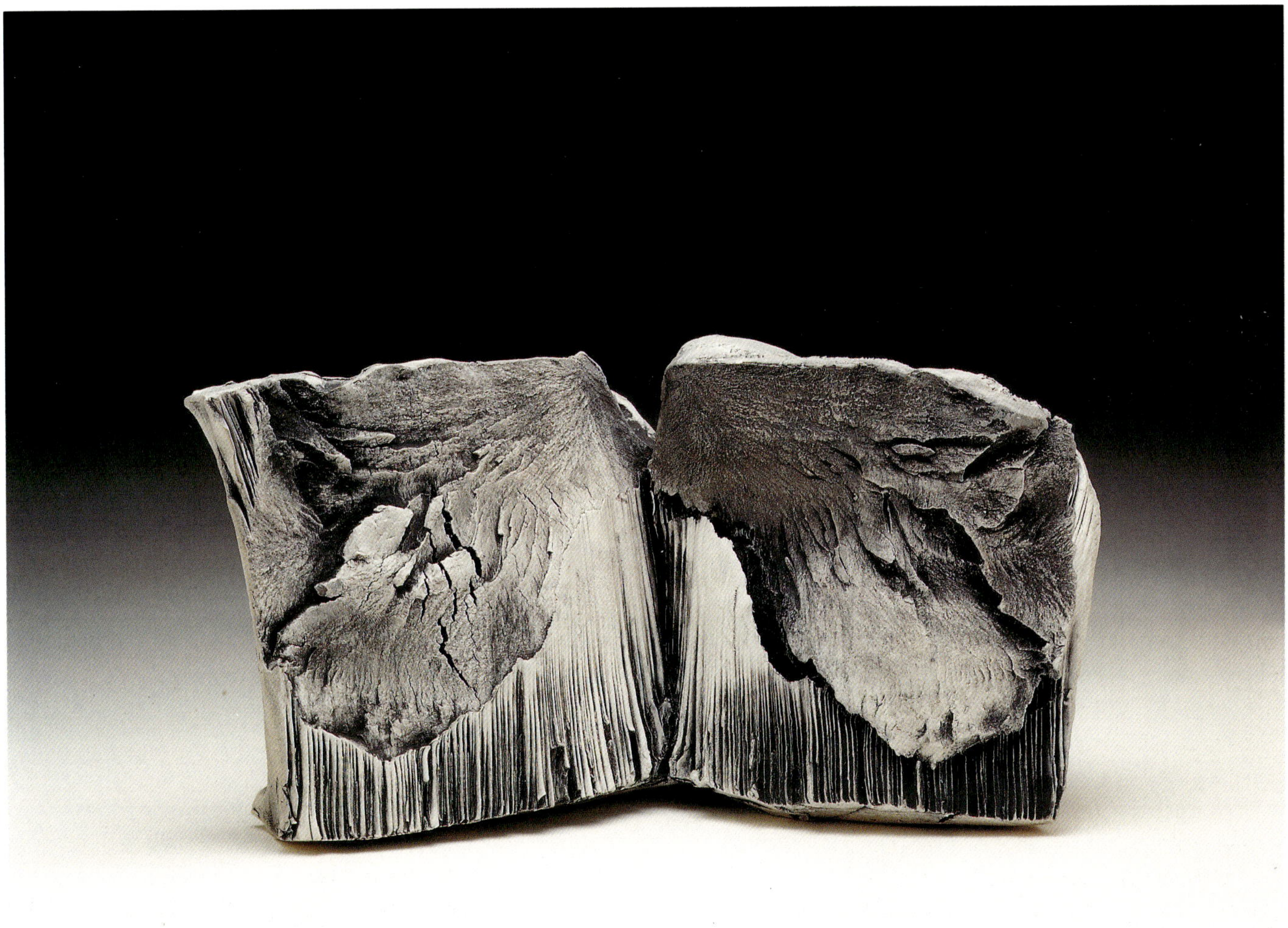

15

MADELEINE CHILD AND PHILIP JARVIS

Born Sydney, Australia 1959.
Moved to New Zealand 1968.
Ceramics Certificate, Otago Polytechnic 1978;
BA (Hons) Ceramics, Camberwell School of Art & Craft, London 1990; MA, Royal College of Art, Ceramics and Glass 1992; Advanced Studies 3D, Central Saint Martins College of Art, London 1993.
Returned to New Zealand 1994.
Lives in Dunedin.

Born Winchester, England 1968.
BA (Hons) Ceramics, Camberwell School of Art & Craft, London 1990; Royal College of Art, Ceramics and Glass 1990–91.
Moved to New Zealand 1994.
Lives in Dunedin.

Complementary skills mixed with compatible aesthetics and philosophies have produced a dynamic collaboration between Madeleine Child and Philip Jarvis. Their output consists of lively individual and collaborative works in clay, as well as graphic work under the label of Madpanic.

Child's appreciation of contemporary ceramics was heightened when she saw an exhibition of English studio pottery brought to New Zealand by the Crafts Council in 1982. Twelve years based in England followed, including six years studying ceramics, a residency in Lisbon and a scholarship to New York. After completing his studies Jarvis worked at the Victoria and Albert Museum where he came to appreciate, more than ever, decorative ceramics collections. The pair travelled to New Zealand via Mexico in 1994. The pottery and tiles they saw in Mexico became the main inspiration for their exhibition of 'tile platters' and vases at the Dowse Art Museum in 1995. The exhibition was well received and the freshness of their approach seemed a long way from local ceramics.

In 1996, with a Creative New Zealand grant, Child and Jarvis returned to Europe and worked at the European Ceramic Work Centre, The Netherlands. This was followed by a research period in Portugal. The wonderful facilities and technical support at the centre made very large work possible. Child threw large rims of clay on two-metre-wide bats, and the resulting hoops of clay were manipulated into different shapes like drawn outlines or 'loopholes'. These highly original pieces made their way into collections at the European Ceramic Work Centre as well as in New Zealand. Child and Jarvis exhibited them at a joint exhibition, *Sculpture for the Home*, at the Canterbury Museum on their return.

The *Tile Dress* Child and Jarvis exhibited at the New Zealand Wearable Art Awards, Nelson, in 1996, required a coat-hanger which they made from clay using the same 'loophole' technique. That inspired a playful series of clay works and a personal collection of coat-hangers. Jarvis also developed a series of 'pillow bricks' and tiles which he exhibited in *House Jewellery* at Fluxus and Masterworks in 1997. This was a fruitful period when separately and together the pair exhibited and won a number of awards.

In 1997, during a residency at the Millay Colony for the Arts in upstate New York, Child and Jarvis worked directly with autumn leaves as a source of colour to make large two-dimensional collage works. These were inspired by Andean feather textiles they had seen in the Metropolitan Museum of New York, and incorporated patterns created from flattened cardboard boxes and fellow residents' clothing.

Currently they produce cards, tiles and glazed bricks as small production works. References to printing and textiles inform the surfaces of their collaborative clay works, and they take ideas from graphic design to clay and back, as positive and negative images. Their ceramic work includes figurative sculptural pieces. The torsos are made from moulds taken from tree trunks and become vehicles for surface decoration—these are works that are innovative, exuberant and very skilled.

**Pair of Trunks:
left My ♥ pants 4 U,
right Bermudas
Ceramic
ca. 590 x 270 mm each
Collection of the artists**

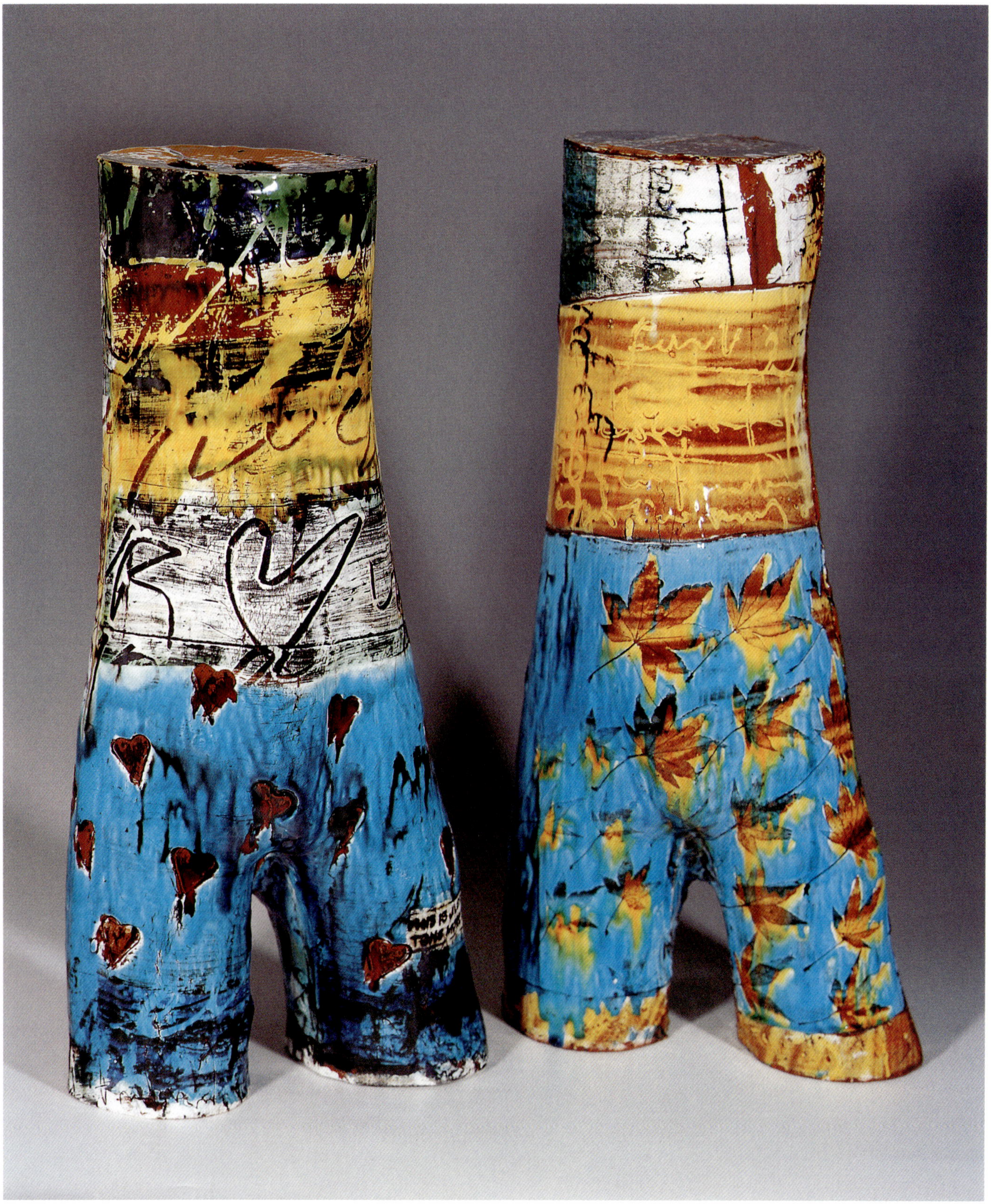

16

PETER COLLIS

Born Auckland 1951.
BA, Auckland University 1975;
Dip Teaching, Auckland Secondary Teachers College 1976.
Lives in Auckland.

In 1978 Peter Collis began potting full time and established his home studio nine years later. He has been committed to the medium in a number of ways, including taking executive and consultative positions in a number of organisations for craft and ceramics. He has taught widely in the medium, was Artist in Residence at Wanganui Polytechnic in 1984, and has exhibited nationally and in Japan, Canada, Singapore and Taiwan. He has been the recipient of a number of grants and awards.

Known for his work as a production potter, Collis has become adept at throwing well-formed vessels for domestic and commercial interiors. When he looks to overseas counterparts, he sees a longevity of design solutions that cannot be sustained in New Zealand. The local market wants frequent changes. For Collis those changes are at times incremental—the development of new glazes and lustres to alter his palette, variations of the gestural brushed enamel lines that sweep around his pots or additions of gold- or silver-leaf fragments. These pieces are instantly recognisable, whether in the form of miniature vases and bowls or enormous urns and platters. They are about technique, elegant form and resolved surface treatment—smooth, decorated, highly glazed and intense colours on classical shapes.

Collis's inspiration comes from other media. Invitations to exhibit and give lectures in Japan and Singapore since 1993 have helped to clarify his ideas and encouraged him to consolidate his work while finding additional new directions. Despite his proficiency in throwing clay, and his need to earn a living, he understands the importance of experimentation. A significant addition to his repertoire in recent years has been a series of simple forms with granular surfaces. These vessels, which are assembled from cast components, have been sprayed with an Egyptian paste applied as single colours. Collis's palette became lighter for this series, with yellows, blues, pinks and turquoise—colours associated with the Pacific. Unlike the highly glazed works, which might be in editions of up to fifty, these pieces are in smaller editions of no more than ten. The forms are generally more open and sculptural than the thrown pots. They are often 'double-skinned' pieces that imply mass and solidity but are, in fact, hollow shells.

The Egyptian paste vessels have led to the most radical departure to date—a series based on Pacific nets. Using galvanised wire mesh, Collis created sculptural forms which he covered with paper clay. Applications of Egyptian paste, followed by firing then dipping the pieces in acid and water baths, produced intriguing crystalline surfaces. The forms are loosely defined, occasionally with reference to vessels, but that is no longer an imperative. By removing the obvious functional references, Collis is taking unprecedented risks and inviting new responses to his work. For the first time an element of content beyond that of vessel-making is introduced. The forms and their shadows are provocative: his tall black spires are almost malevolent. This is a direction which is unlikely to replace Collis's production ware, but it is an exciting addition to a solid body of work.

Pacific Net Stalagmites
Wire, paper clay, Egyptian paste
750–1100 mm (h)
Collection of the artist

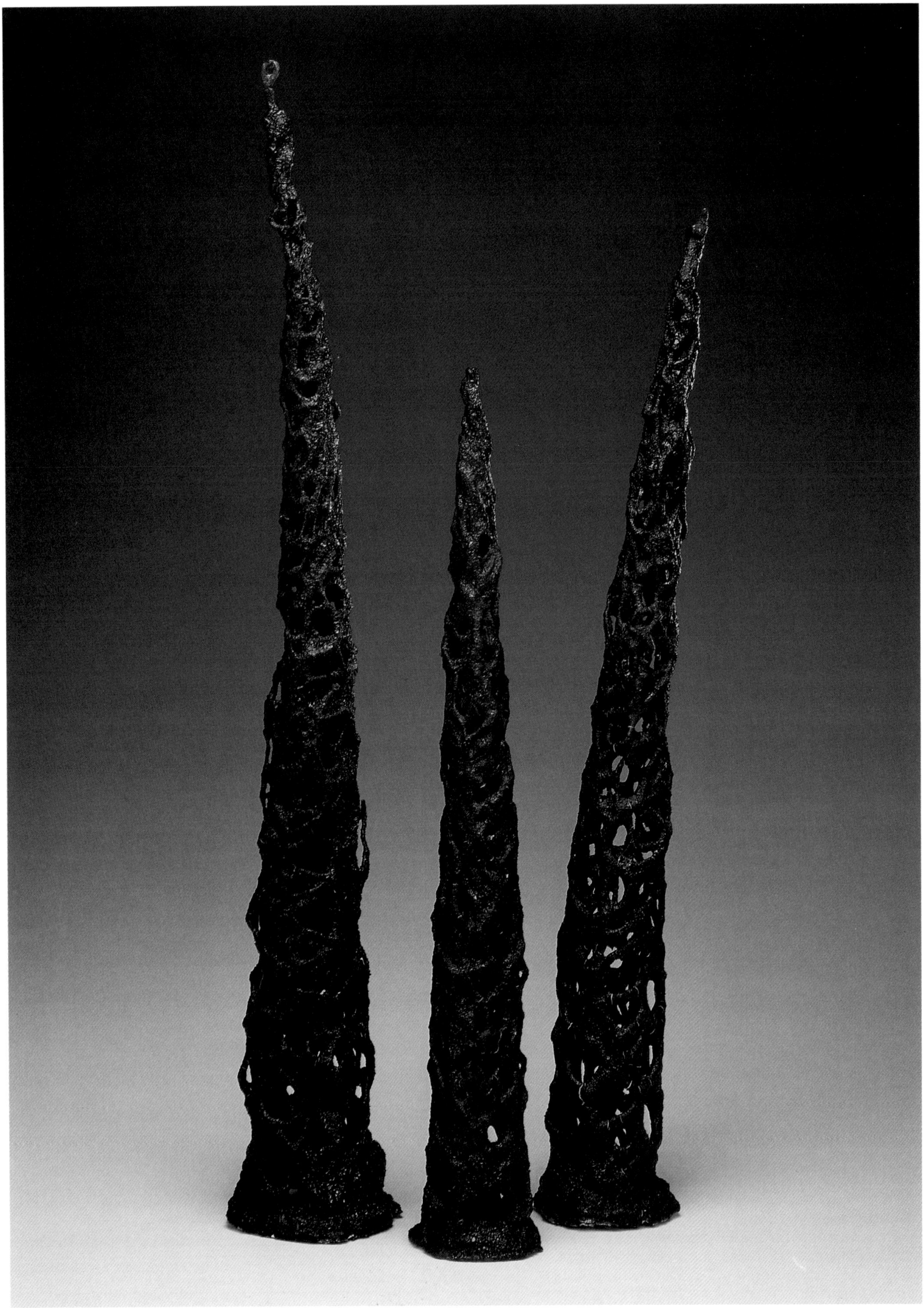

17

JIM COOPER

Born Westport 1956.
Otago Polytechnic School of Art 1984, 1989.
Lives in Westport.

The rugged West Coast of the South Island has always been home to Jim Cooper, and the isolation has made possible a freedom of expression that probably could not have occurred anywhere else. His ceramics are vital, energetic, figurative pieces contextualised by an active mind, flashes of insight, a sense of humour and a sense of tragedy. His work could be seen as naive or folk art but there is a richness of knowledge as well— of Picasso's drawings, Colin McCahon (Vol. 1, 50), West Coast American ceramics, cartoons, rock music lyrics and, most importantly, self-knowledge. Expressionism might be a more accurate descriptor: his is a wild, emotional and unique way of working.

His earliest clay works in 1982 were vessels, but Cooper felt constrained, unable to express his ideas effectively. He started painting on slips, cutting away areas, moulding parts and encasing the works in clay boxes. He acknowledges Neil Grant as his teacher and mentor while he was a student at Otago Polytechnic. This was when he made the leap to handbuilt pieces which emerged as passionate, confronting and sometimes surreal statements. First they were heads which developed into torsos, then whole bodies and relief sculptures. He felt that a solitary, free-standing figure would be too exposed; it needed a setting, a way of being encased. The reliefs were often about more than one person—human interactions contained in their own environments.

The vulnerability is his own. His work expresses anxiety—about the times when, a few years ago, it was difficult to work, about everyday life and his relationships. Stabilising factors also appear in his work, but with a quirky touch. Extraordinary images appear as visual flashes of ideas, like organs squirting blood. Titles like *She's a Cold Fish*, *She Shouldn't Be with That Guy* tell stories, as throwaway lines or clichés. Figurative works seem an ideal way to express himself. Cooper talks about avoiding the front part of the brain—the cerebral part—and deals with emotions. If the artistic statement isn't always pleasant, then that reflects life.

Many of his images are raw and confronting. He uses glossy colour on heavily grogged terracotta clay which adds an earthiness to the colour. Sometimes he makes unglazed terracotta works which are like working drawings. They follow from prolific drawings and paintings—fast, uncontrolled works on paper to solve ideas, proportions and size. Upside-down pieces appeal to him, like *Portrait of the Artist's Mother Standing on Her Head*. He enjoys the disorientation and precariousness of the world being turned upside down. At times figures fall off their plinths while he is building them—the battered look remains, as in real life. In some works he fills the frames until the narrative appears to be bursting out of its seams.

Cooper has exhibited in a number of centres lately, and he always surprises his viewers. The ideas are flowing and he is producing a large number of works. They are becoming more articulate, less chunky—sometimes as child-like visions of his beloved dog, his dreams and his reading matter. Now he is more familiar with process and with the risks he is taking, he knows he can pull it off. It's a bit like riding a bike.

My Dog as an Egyptian God
Low-fired clay, polychrome glazes
800 mm
Collection of Pat and Marilynn Condon

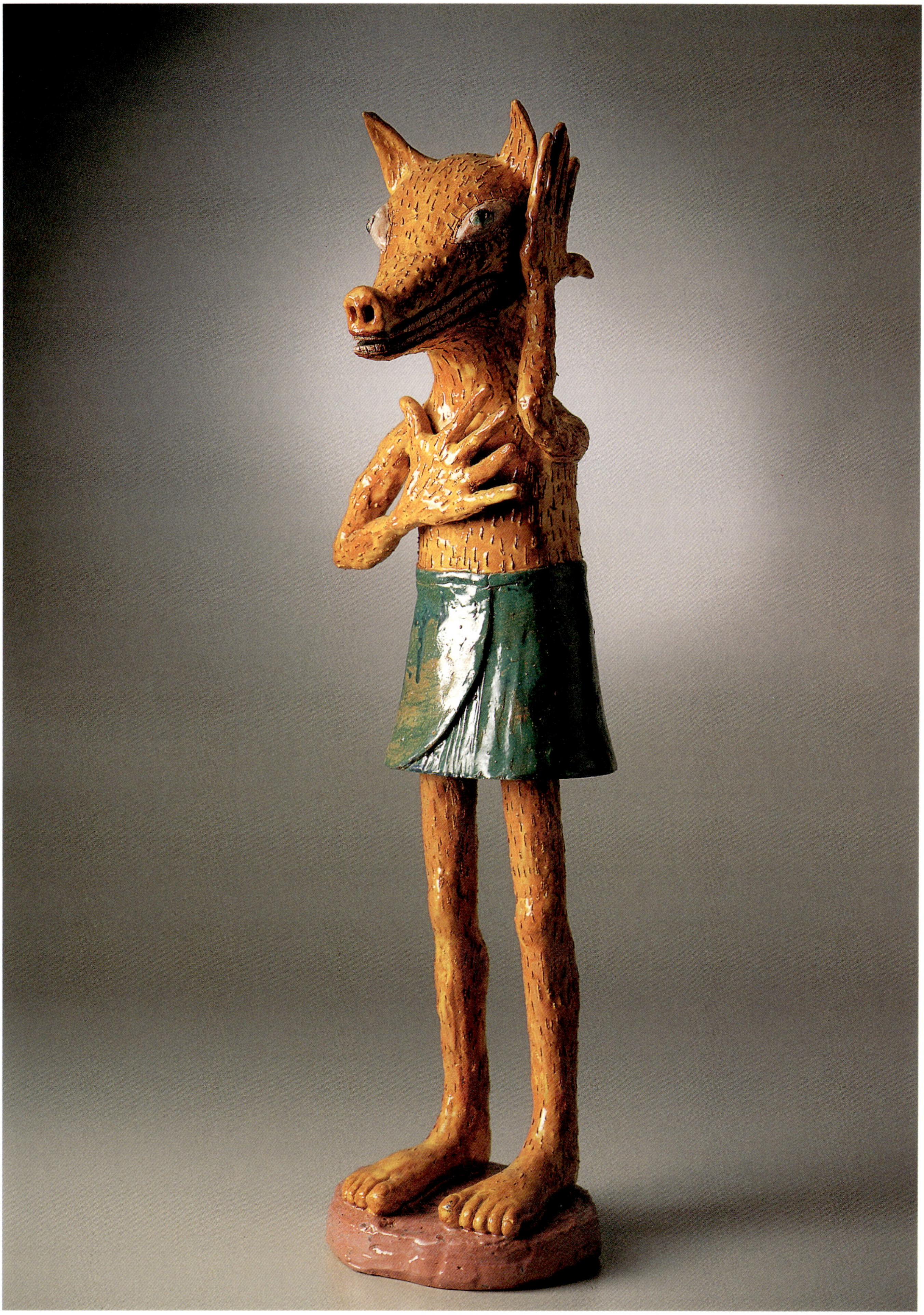

18

PAERAU CORNEAL

Born Rotorua 1961.
Ngati Tuwharetoa, Te Ati Haunui a Paparangi.
Certificate Craft Design Maori, Waiariki Polytechnic 1988;
Dip Craft Design Maori, Waiariki Polytechnic, Rotorua 1991.
Lives in Hamilton.

A dual exploration of clay and fibre gives Paerau Corneal's work a very personal style. She started to work with both media as a student at Waiariki Polytechnic, and pays tribute to Tina Wirihana (96) and George Andrews for their support at the time. Since then she has established a relationship between clay and fibre that is based in the mixed-media tradition of Maori art.

Although clay is a non-traditional material for Maori, Corneal does not see this as a limitation, nor does she see her clay sculptures as a non-Maori art form. She is a member of Nga Kaihanga Uku, a national Maori clayworkers' group that perceives the absence of a formal clay tradition as an advantage in developing distinctively Maori contemporary work.

Corneal's work is based on revisiting traditional Maori art forms, creation stories and issues concerning Maori women. The first major acknowledgement of her work was an invitation to participate in *Treasures of the Underworld* at the World Expo in Seville in 1992. She created seven large clay *Waka Huia*—treasure containers set in totara plinths and embellished with fibre. These ambitious, distinctive, handbuilt forms were designed to be gender specific, to position women as retainers of knowledge yet, at the same time, to allude to seafaring.

She makes clay sculptures based on creation stories of powerful women. They consciously shift the emphasis away from women as sexual objects, and address the general lack of sculptural images of Maori women beyond the marae. For *Uku! Uku! Uku!*, an exhibition by Maori clayworkers at the 1998 International Festival of the Arts in Wellington, she created *Hinemanu*, *Wahine Atua of Forest Birds* as an extension to the story of Hinenui-te-po. Her piece suggests a relationship between the two fantails representing the life force—the atua—as indicators of human mortality. The work is also about responsibility to the physical, personal and working environments. It makes connections with Maui and Hinenui-te-po, and the story of mortality becomes a relevant contemporary message while acknowledging women's status.

Working with fibre, Corneal tells different stories, some as more abstracted notions. *Patupoi*, shown at *Te Uha*, an exhibition at Te Taumata in 1996, was an installation of suspended forms representing weapons. Technically innovative, and lethal in use, these were based on the long poi, with kiekie woven around a stone. Another series was created over clay forms which were then removed. They reflected an interest in structure and technique, simplicity and repetition, appearing as open structures where the exterior and interior spaces merge and the function of the form becomes irrelevant. *Taki Tahi*, exhibited at *Whakatu*, Bishop Suter Gallery, Nelson, in 1997, was a group of three such open-weave structures. By opening the weave Corneal creates beautiful, ethereal works that challenge the notion of containment.

The newest clay and fibre works reflect a growing maturity and confidence, merging Corneal's interests in figurative and abstracted works with a strong, celebratory acknowledgement of being a Maori woman.

Harakeke Pot
Flax/Australian raku
180 (h) x
200 mm (diam)
Collection of the artist

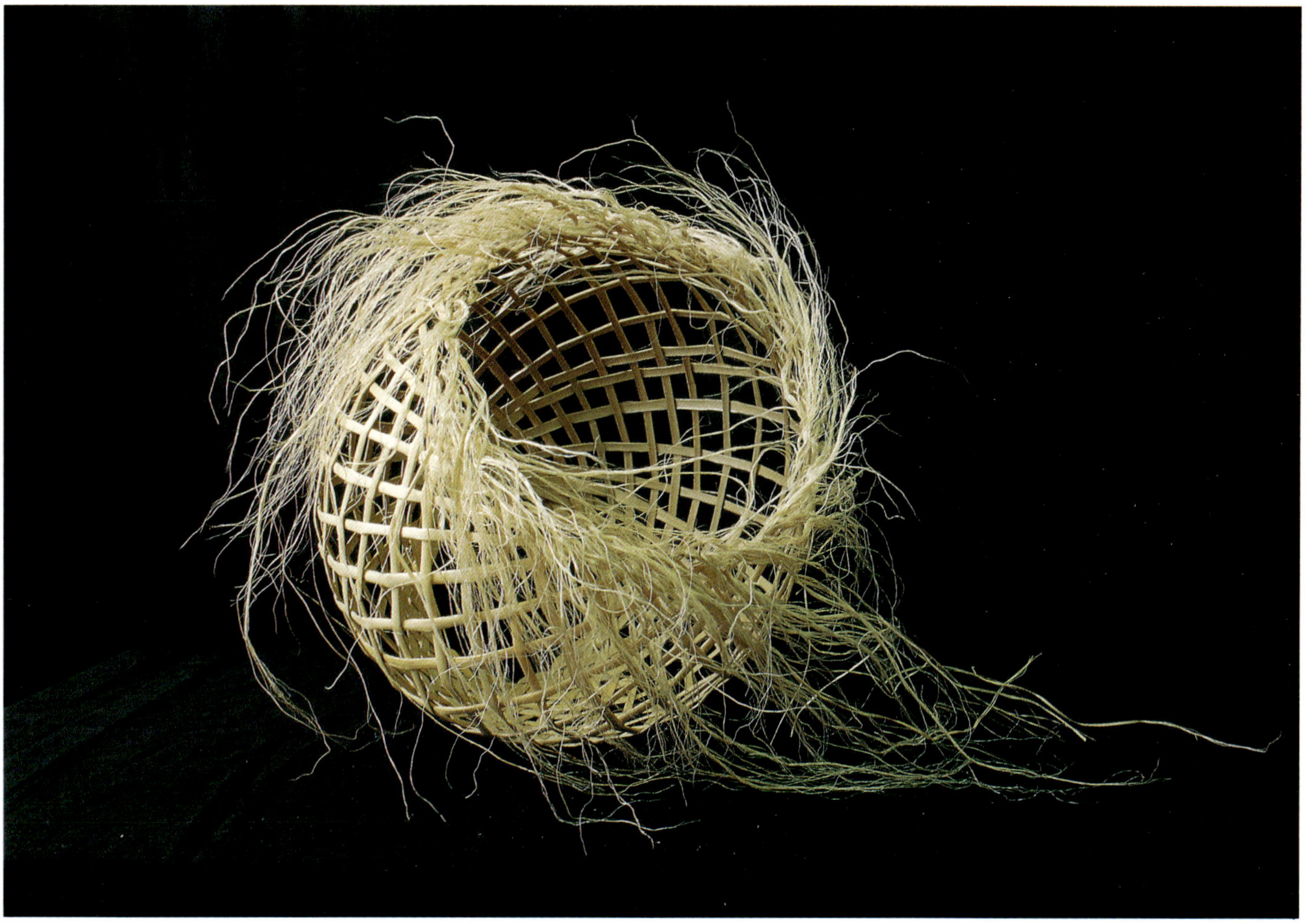

19

JOHN CRAWFORD

Born Greymouth 1951.
Trained at Waimea Craft Pottery 1968–74.
Lives in Ngakawau.

When John Crawford created his installation *Hung out to Dry* at *The Garden Exhibition*, Suter Gallery, Nelson, 1998, he worked with the same philosophy that he brings to much of his work. He set out to show objects in context.

The conceptual basis for *Hung out to Dry* was domestic ritual. Thirty-five square images on paper were hung on five clotheslines. In front, as symbols of hope, were three seedtrays with orderly rows of pinched clay 'seeds', reminiscent of food offerings like bakers' trays; to the sides were 'maps' consisting of bound porcelain and earthenware, as visual clues. On first acquaintance the work seemed a long way from the more usual tableware and clay sculptures for which Crawford has become known. However, colour, space, texture and establishing order through grids are familiar issues in his work; in the installation they are intensified.

His day-to-day work is tableware, which he creates in collaboration with his wife Anne. Both were trained at Waimea Craft Pottery, a traditional Bernard Leach-style workshop, and learnt to appreciate that making things is part of the human condition. Their teachers, Jack Laird and Carl Vendelbosch, provided them with production skills and an appreciation of balance, symmetry and strong forms. The sound technical base provided them with a springboard for their own personal style of ceramics, which they decorate with majolica glaze.

Since childhood Crawford has drawn on paper and enjoyed the narratives that ensue. Many drawings are of personal experiences—horse riding, the offering of food, vessel-making, self-image, desires and dreams. They are non-literal and spontaneous, and he enjoys freedom from the ceramic process. The images on paper feed into his ceramic work and he has developed an interaction between the different media.

His sculptural work based on horses and figures in particular originated from his drawings. Initially inspired by a horse that was brought to graze beside the studio, these works have developed a life of their own. A fascination for the relationship between horse and figure evolved into a metaphorical statement and an exploration of emotions. The images, expressed with enamels and glaze crayons and sometimes cut as silhouettes, were applied to slabs which were produced by cutting open wheel-thrown cylinders without bases. The theme was explored with the assistance of a QEII Arts Council grant in 1989, and the results were shown at a solo exhibition at the Bishop Suter Gallery, Nelson. The early works were illustrative and used a range of colours, but recently Crawford has stripped his sculptures to monochromatic colour, as in *People I Have Known*, 1998. These newest sculptures are about form and the relationship between components rather than surface.

Crawford's work has travelled to Australia, Canada, England and USA, and he is currently preparing his third solo exhibition in Munich, Germany. He has been a frequent exhibitor throughout New Zealand, and was included in several Fletcher Challenge Ceramics Awards in the 1980s. He occasionally teaches workshops, has been the recipient of a number of awards, and his work is held in many collections.

**People I Have Known
Ceramic
850 x 200 mm
Collection of the artist**

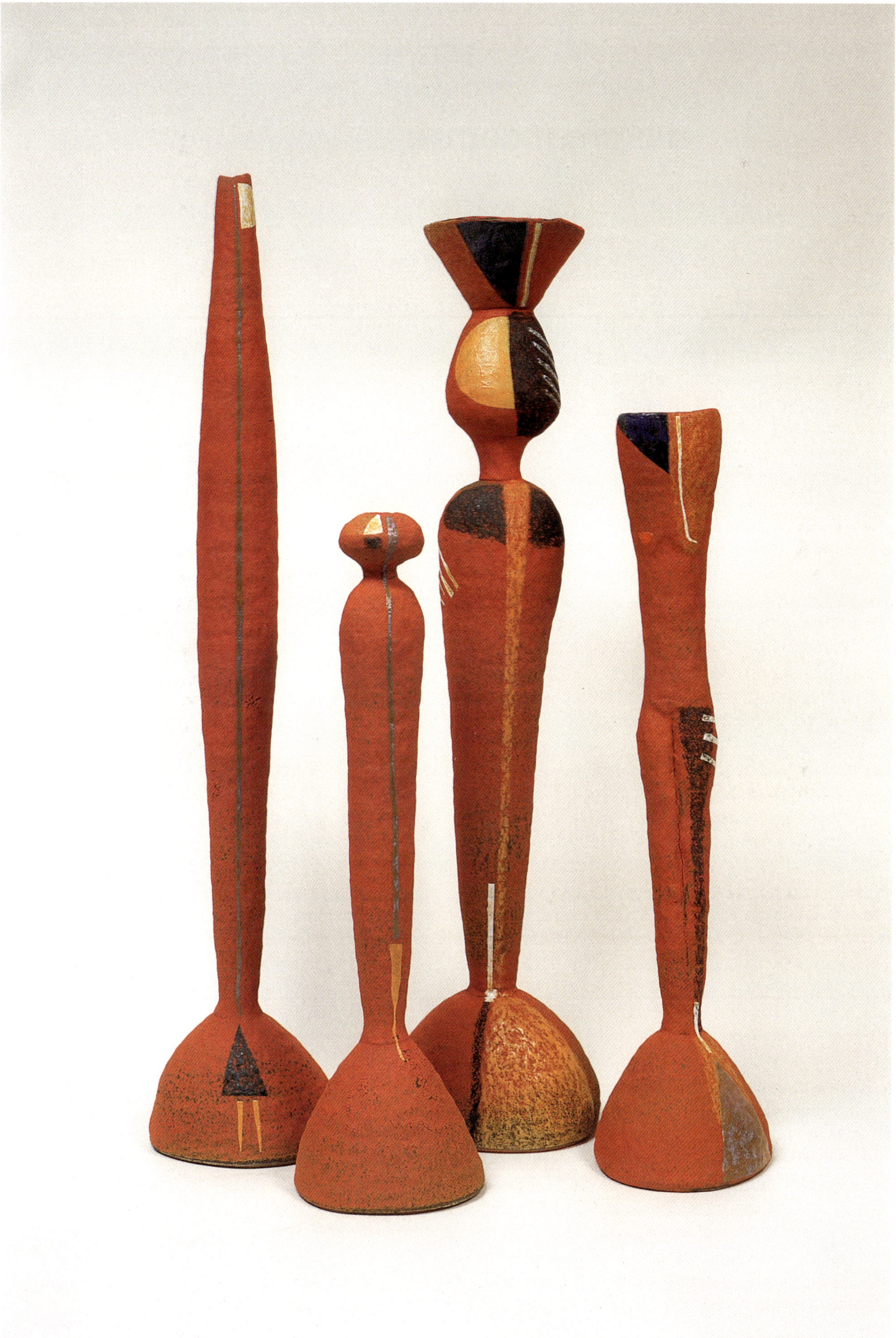

DEBORAH CROWE

Born Dundee, Scotland 1963.
BA (Hons) Design, Glasgow School of Art 1985;
Postgraduate Dip Embroidered and Woven Textiles, Glasgow School of Art 1986.
Moved to New Zealand 1986.
Certificate of Adult Teaching, AIT 1992.
Lives in Auckland.

Deborah Crowe considers herself to be an artist working from a textile base, and this typifies the attitudes of a number of practitioners associated with fibre art. Like many contemporaries in Australia, the USA and Europe, Crowe entered the genre through weaving, but her work now encompasses concerns that have as much to do with sculpture and fashion as crafting.

Crowe's early works were concerned with the nature of fabrics and with transforming two-dimensional cloth into three-dimensional forms. Her initial experimentation explored the relationship between traditional processes of weave and stitch using non-traditional materials like wire and nylon monofilament woven in twill and herringbone patterns. Further exploration came from observation of architectural and nautical structures, and an examination of the contrasts between internal and external spaces. The use of open weaves and resulting transparency provided a barrier while still engaging the viewer with the space beyond—a continuing feature of her work.

Underpinning all her work, which has won a number of awards, is a methodology based on woven and stitched textiles. The manifestations are drawings, woven sculptures and, more recently, garments. They are works that refer to the body, where the garment is seen as both object and metaphor for containment, enclosure and protection of the body and self. This textile sensibility informs her teaching and her artistic output: stitched rather than glued connections, thread-like drawings and machine embroidery are part of her visual repertoire.

In 1994 Crowe created a series of three-dimensional woven works, and painted and drawn images relating to the tortuous qualities of corsetry. Her more recent works refer to security, wrapping and protecting the body against the indignities of corsetry. By physically enclosing the human form she was able to explore other aspects of the relationship between the internal and external self. This exploration culminated in wearable work created in collaboration with fashion designer Kim Fraser, confirming that her sculptural and wearable works are strongly related, each genre seeming to comment on the other. Winning the prestigious Supreme Award at the New Zealand Smokefree Fashion Awards in 1997 with a collaborative work provided them with the impetus to create wearable pieces under the fashion label Fraser Crowe. They went on to win two sections of the 1998 Smokefree Fashion Awards.

Crowe recently started working with handmade paper, and the ideas continue to develop. Issues of absence and presence are characterised in the work *in absentia*, which explores the concept of objects floating in space. The hard metallic shell is a found material, a departure from her more usual approach to fabricating all her work. The white cast paper shawl behind it represents her interest in the effects of light and the way fabrics fade. It suggests the degenerative qualities of some works, like the sagging and distortion of textiles under their own weight. These newer works are more subtle but no less exciting than before, and the issues have been edited and simplified. They move gently in space—ethereal, beautiful in their detail, the familiar three-dimensional shawl forms evoking mysterious presences that may have once filled them.

**in absentia
Wire mesh,
embossed handmade
paper
ca. 1500 x 650 x
1500 mm
Collection of the
artist**

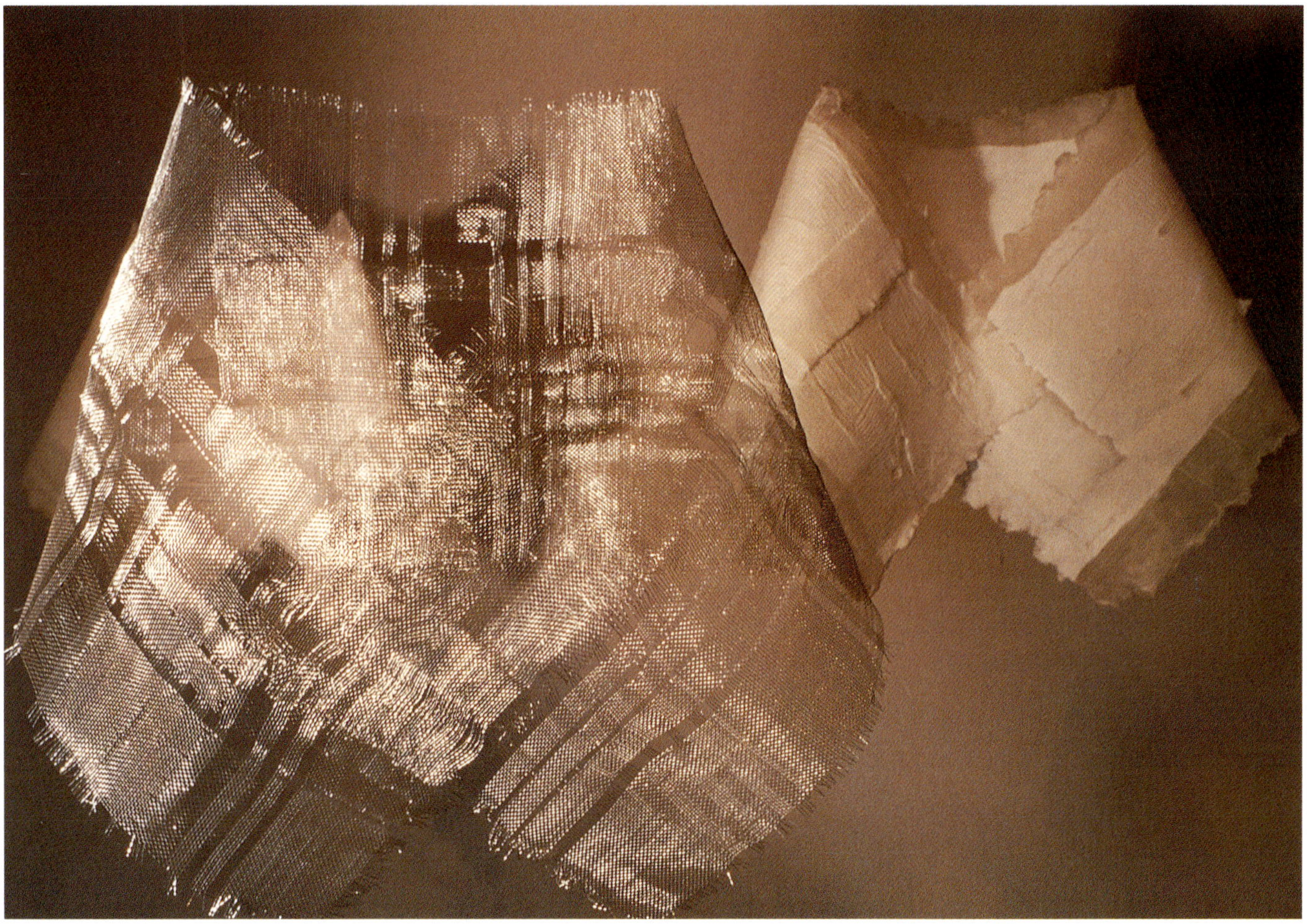

21

ANN CULY

Born Lower Hutt 1952.
DFA, Ilam School of Fine Arts 1973; graduated Teachers College of Education, Auckland 1975;
Certificate in Craft Design, Otago Polytechnic 1990.
Lives in Dunedin.

For Ann Culy making jewellery is making portable art. She really enjoys making objects of beauty that function physically and have their own liveliness by being attached to the human body. She applies the same formal elements of proportion to her jewellery that she formerly brought to her sculptures, and has the same commitment to producing good work. Yet she feels freer working as a jeweller, and is happy to relinquish ownership of the pieces—to see the work worn. Making body adornment somehow seems less precious than making sculpture.

Her background is in painting and sculpture, and she taught art intermittently at secondary and tertiary level from 1976 to 1991. Making jewellery became a natural progression from the tiny figurative bronze castings she made from modelled wax in the late '70s. In 1990 she studied jewellery at Otago Polytechnic, then became a full-time jeweller exhibiting nationally. In 1995 she established her own business, Lure Jewellery Workshop, as a shared workspace, gallery and retail outlet for contemporary jewellers.

Her recent production is a reworking of very simple ideas, like the organic finger rings which vary slightly every time she makes one. They are often playful in concept, like a ring over a ring or a wind-up coil. The primary concern is how they will be worn and the interaction with the wearer. This becomes evident when she makes sturdy catches on brooches and bracelets, and when she creates loosely defined, rich surfaces that reveal carefully worked details on close examination.

She records what happens in her life as drawings, paintings and sculpture, and the drawings become a source for her jewellery. The miniature cast sculptures have translated into tiny leaping and dancing figures cut out of the metal as negative images. Culy often packs a number of figures into a shape, allowing her viewers to interpret the narratives. The visual concerns of the individual pieces are related, and in close proximity with each other establish a lively interaction: the collection appears as an art work.

Culy works mainly with silver, but she also uses gold and precious stones. She enjoys gold for its malleability, gorgeous colour and its ancient history—a primeval instinct. She believes that she shares the same delight in the sensuous properties of a material as people did aeons ago. In one series of work she fused a thin layer of gold to silver before proceeding with the intricate cutouts. Her processes are varied—she enjoys etching, constructing, casting, cutting and forging. She likes to contain stones by cradling them, rather than drilling through them or holding them in rigid claws. The softness of line she aims for evokes a comfortable human quality, as though the piece could already have a history.

Sometimes she takes prints from her jewellery. The cutouts become embossings—three-dimensional works on paper. They are all part of a lively, coherent body of work that gives the wearers room to interpret and make the work their own.

**Series of brooches
Silver, pure gold,
precious stones
30 x 25 mm each
Collection of the
artist**

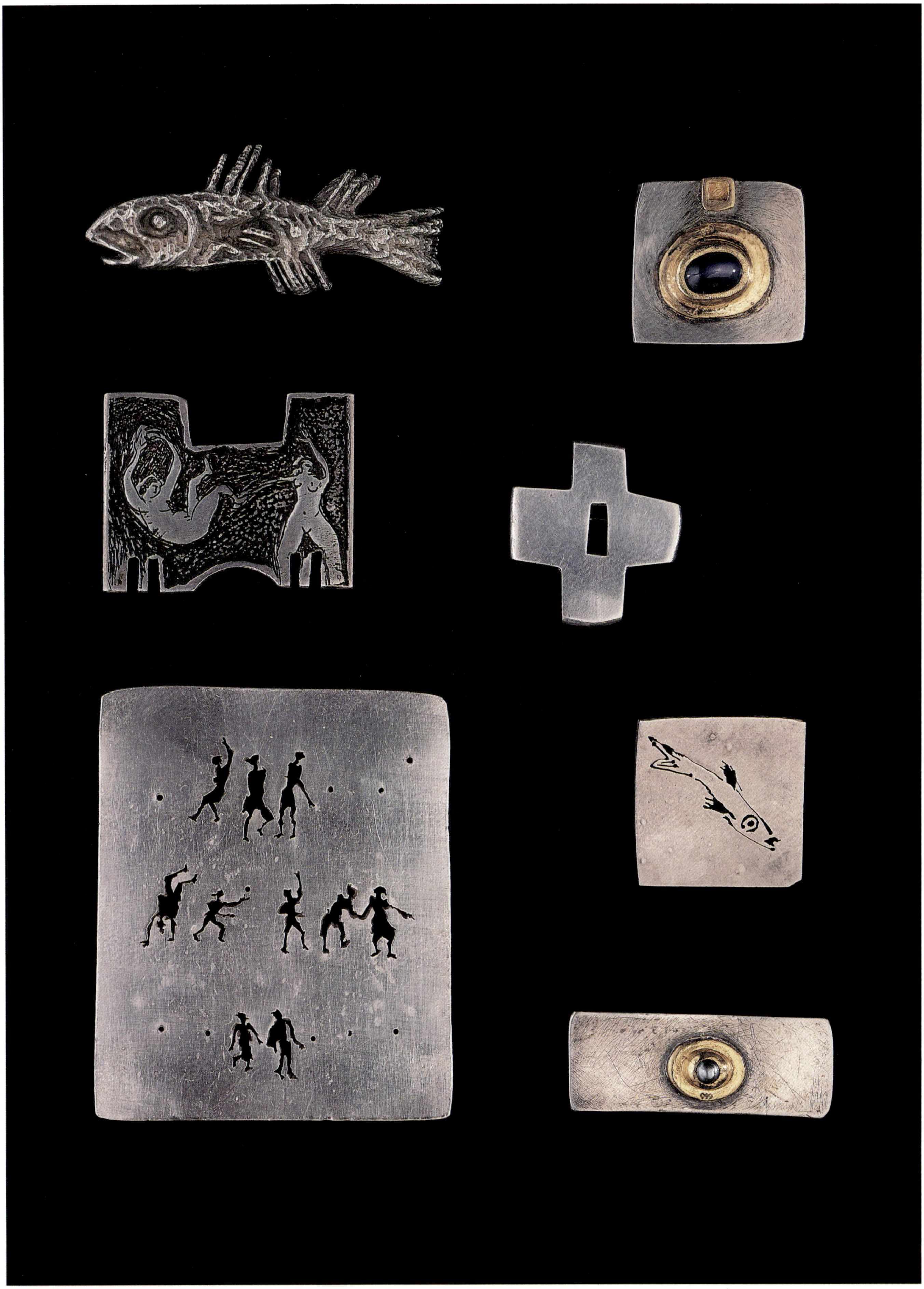

22

ANDREA DALY

Born Wellington 1965.
B Visual Arts (Contemporary Jewellery), Sydney College of the Arts 1987;
Post Graduate Dip Visual Arts (Contemporary Jewellery), Sydney College of the Arts 1988;
completing MPhil Art History, University of Auckland 1998.
Lives in Auckland.

For Andrea Daly, looking at women's role in society is more about questioning her own position than making a feminist statement. She is of a generation which has relinquished the term 'feminism' but retained the ideas. She aims for integrity in her jewellery by seeking to make social commentary based on her own experience of a Catholic upbringing, and wants the ideas to ring true because they are more than superficial observations. She uses humour, not to cause offence but to make the ideas and her jewellery more approachable.

Daly currently teaches at Manukau Institute of Technology and is a partner in Fingers contemporary jewellery gallery. She has had three solo exhibitions, and has been included in a number of significant jewellery exhibitions throughout the country. Her work has also been exhibited in Australia and the USA.

She observes that jewellery expresses distinct ideas in different cultures. It can be a reflection of society and express social position. It can also convey information about site, while occasionally commenting on the mingling of cultures. Daly is interested in the function of jewellery as a signifier of the ways in which the body is understood and positioned in society. She recognises that the meanings conveyed through jewellery can be ambiguous when de-contextualised and thus removed from the culture from which it is derived.

Early work included icons of Madonnas. Daly was interested in situating the Kiwi Madonna—sometimes with paua halos—in the environment of the packed lunch, muffins and the great New Zealand barbecue. It was a way of observing her own culture within the domestic domain. Her perception was that the Madonna was a confused figure—for some a powerful one, officially acknowledged, yet without power within the Catholic hierarchy. She made many images of Madonnas as brooches and pendants. The materials varied from gold leaf representing precious icons to collages on paper representing the inexpensive—like the Virgin Mary mass-produced on holy cards.

Daly's attitude to aesthetics is based on a desire for her jewellery to reflect a history of being wearable rather than negating that history. She is aware of 'grunge' jewellery coming from Europe, especially Germany, and recognises the differences between her work and 'grunge'. Her aim is to be accessible, and neither too reactionary nor alienating. She wants her work initially to attract, then for underlying levels of content to emerge—a lighthearted statement more than an earnest one.

An example is *Merit Badge*, one of a series of four works. Made of dish sponge, ribbon, fake diamond and gold-plated copper, the badge has a recipe for pavlova on the back. The work is about the domestic kitchen as an unacknowledged site of production, and the badge of honour is for work achieved at that place. By working with materials other than metals, Daly leads viewers to discover her ideas through the unexpected and to find a new kind of beauty in the prosaic.

Merit Badge
Dish sponge, ribbon,
fake diamond,
gold-plated copper
20 x 45 x 60 mm
Collection of Dowse
Art Museum

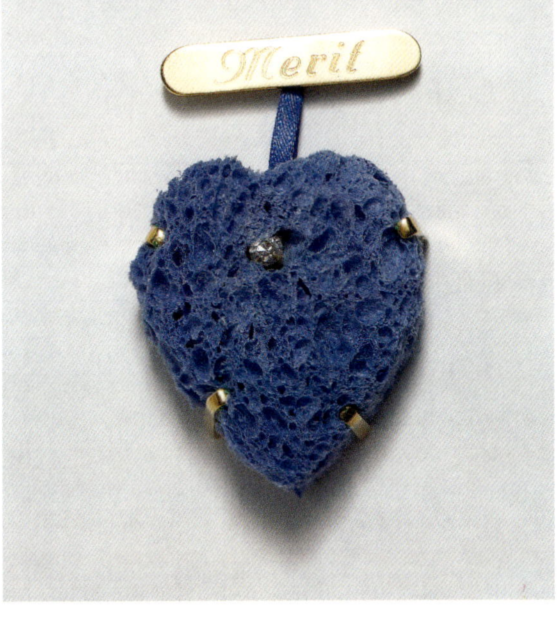
Merit

PETER DECKERS

Born Rotterdam, The Netherlands 1953.
MTS Vakschool Schoonhoven (jewellery craft school) 1973–77;
teachers' course, Academy of Fine Arts, Rotterdam 1980–81;
Free Academy (Sculpture), The Hague 1980–81; Fine Arts Course, Academy of Fine Arts 1981–82.
Emigrated to New Zealand 1985.
Lives in Upper Hutt.

Peter Deckers' jewellery training was very traditional. However, his fine arts education introduced him to conceptual thinking, and his work now merges the two strands. His diverse work experience was in The Hague and Nepal, and on arrival in New Zealand he and his wife Hilda Gascard established a jewellery workshop where they produced mainly production jewellery.

Migration proved to be liberating, intellectually as well as physically, and Deckers describes himself as 'a cold war and environmental refugee'. His first solo exhibition in New Zealand was *Environmental Distortions* at 33 $^1/_3$ Gallery, Wellington, 1989. He made 'off-beat tokens' which were designed to reflect society and its natural and man-made disasters. That year he started teaching part-time at Whitireia Polytechnic.

Deckers often starts with found or bought old pieces of jewellery. He recognises a value in them that is at odds with their categorisation as unsophisticated or tasteless in terms of contemporary studio jewellery. His jewellery has parallels with that of Australian Pierre Cavalan, and their common process is bricolage which is based on discarded images or materials—the cultural indicators of the past—reassembled in new ways with different meanings.

The challenge for Deckers is to imbue these pieces with value by altering perceptions of them. He wants to understand the layered mysteries he believes exist in the values we place on each other. This notion of values—real, pretentious, imitated and distorted—becomes the starting point for his jewellery. He recognises that pieces of jewellery have traditionally been symbols of wealth and status. However, there has been a shift in the symbols of status, and money, human sentiments, national pride and technology appear to have replaced precious stones and valuable metals.

Deckers has had a number of solo exhibitions and has participated in many group exhibitions. In many ways his work stands to one side of New Zealand contemporary jewellery. He is unafraid to engage with kitsch and to use fakery to explore his ideas. Colourful, cheap glass stones viewed through perforated screens of metal take on a new life. When he builds up layers over existing jewellery, it is about covering up, and Deckers sees this as a metaphor for life. In some new work, in beautifully constructed wire cages, he has encapsulated real stones—representing the core of society. Once again the viewer is encouraged to think about values.

As an immigrant, Deckers became an observer of New Zealand culture, and he recognised that by exploring other cultures he also began to understand his own. He has challenged stereotypes of immigrants by probing issues of cultural consciousness. In the ring *Two Worlds in One*, he placed two objects side by side within a single cage. They represented Deckers' observations of the Pakeha world developed through machines and the 'paua pureness' of Maori culture. These intellectual explorations are supported by carefully crafted work that speaks with a unique voice.

**Various titles
Nickel silver and
sterling silver
Various sizes
Collection of the
artist**

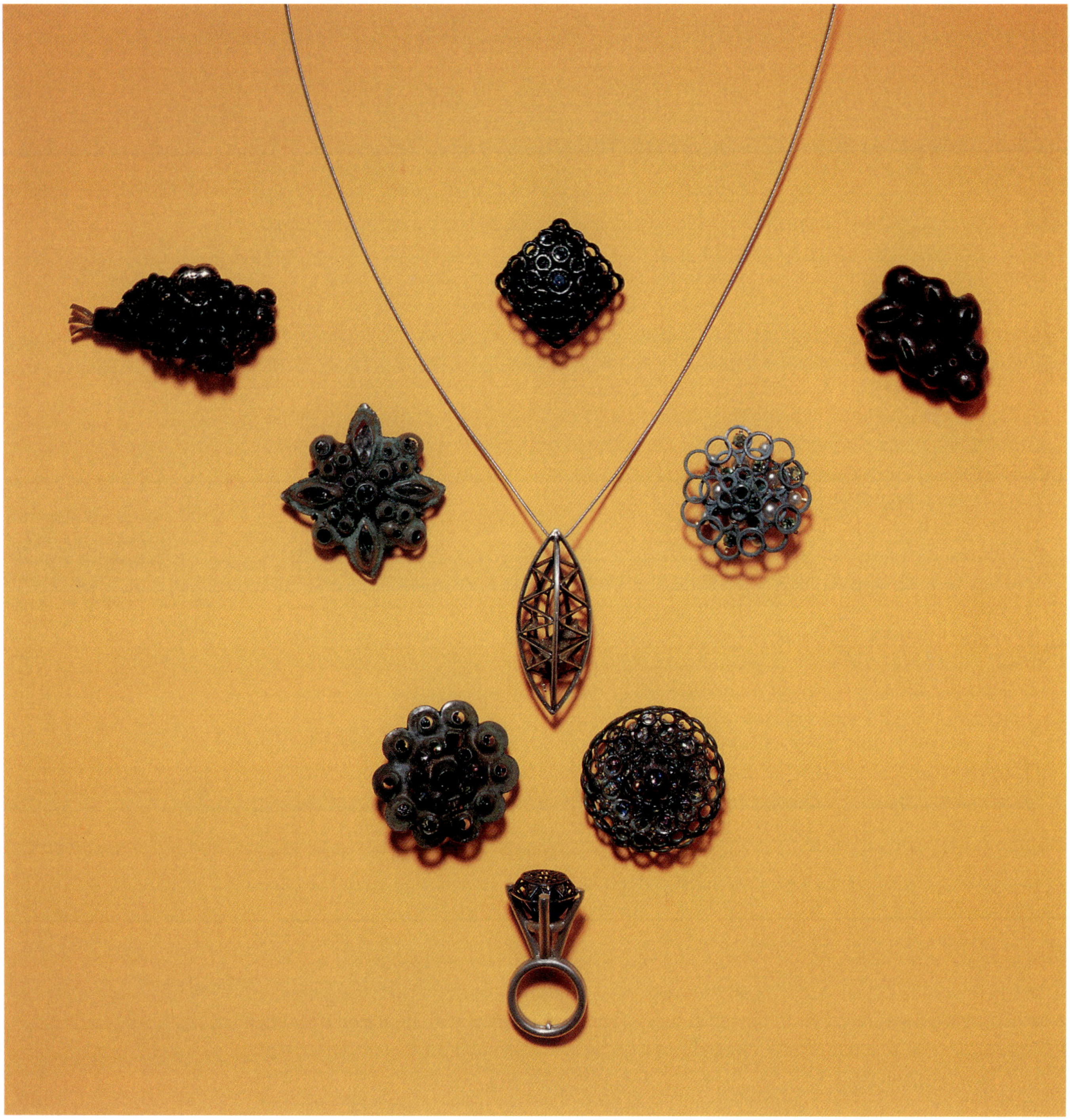

24

JOHN EDGAR

Born Auckland 1950.
BSc (Hons) University of NSW, Sydney 1972.
First established jade carving workshop, Auckland 1977.
Lives in Karekare.

John Edgar works as a fine artist, yet his creative journey has been through the crafts movement, and this creates some ambiguity in positioning his work. His stone sculptures are defined first and foremost by ideas and secondly by materials and process. In 1992 he began making large constructions of granite, marble and glass, while only occasionally creating jewellery. He has produced many solo exhibitions since 1979, and his works have been seen widely in New Zealand as well as in Australia, Japan and USA.

When he started carving Edgar looked to Chinese as much as to Maori traditions for inspiration. He developed a personal style of minimalist works—icons in the form of pendants, medallions and small sculptures with an elegance of form and exquisitely fine detail. He has worked with pounamu, but an awareness of its scarcity redirected him to less precious resources like argillite, basalt and greywacke, which he sought to imbue with preciousness through his crafting. He prospected for stone in the South Island during the 1970s and '80s, and over the years many of his works have made reference to geological as well as social concerns.

He became known for pendants with enchantingly detailed edges to accommodate their cords, and medallions like the series *Coins of the Realm*. The latter were divided horizontally with undulating lines evoking the landscape, and they nestled in perfectly formed wooden boxes. A simple stone acquired a magical quality when he layered the centre with alternating slices of glass—a concept he later developed to a very large scale. The transparency of the glass, reflecting and refracting light, contrasted with the solidity of the stone. In his more recent works tiny glass fragments inserted into landscape slabs evoke glimpses of the sea or jewels.

Double titles and double meanings are the stuff of *Lie of the Land*, Edgar's 1998 travelling exhibition of stone sculptures. 'Lie' of the title explores the physical nature of the land while questioning false notions about it. The ten superbly crafted granite and marble pieces are larger than anything he has previously made. The ideas are larger, too, as Edgar probes notions of land and identity through fractured images. His works question what it is to be a New Zealander and whether there are defining characteristics of this nation.

Symbols abound, like flags, stars, flagstones, a broken boundary stone and bones of ancestors. The tall columns, *Loom—Kaitiaki*, are at once threatening and protective, acting as an identifying mark, a pair of guardians. They contrast with Edgar's more usual horizontal images that refer to the landscape. This work produces an interface between black and white, an abstracted profiled face, a sense of unease and an idea of dislocation.

He works with slabs of stone, cutting through rather than chipping at them. Most are to be viewed frontally rather than in the round, are three-dimensional in their form but function as two-dimensional images. The ambiguity seems appropriate, and the solidity of the materials he uses—stone, glass and metals—firmly anchors the concepts physically, visually and intellectually.

**Loom—Kaitiaki
Granite, marble
2600 x 1000 x 25 mm
Collection of the artist**

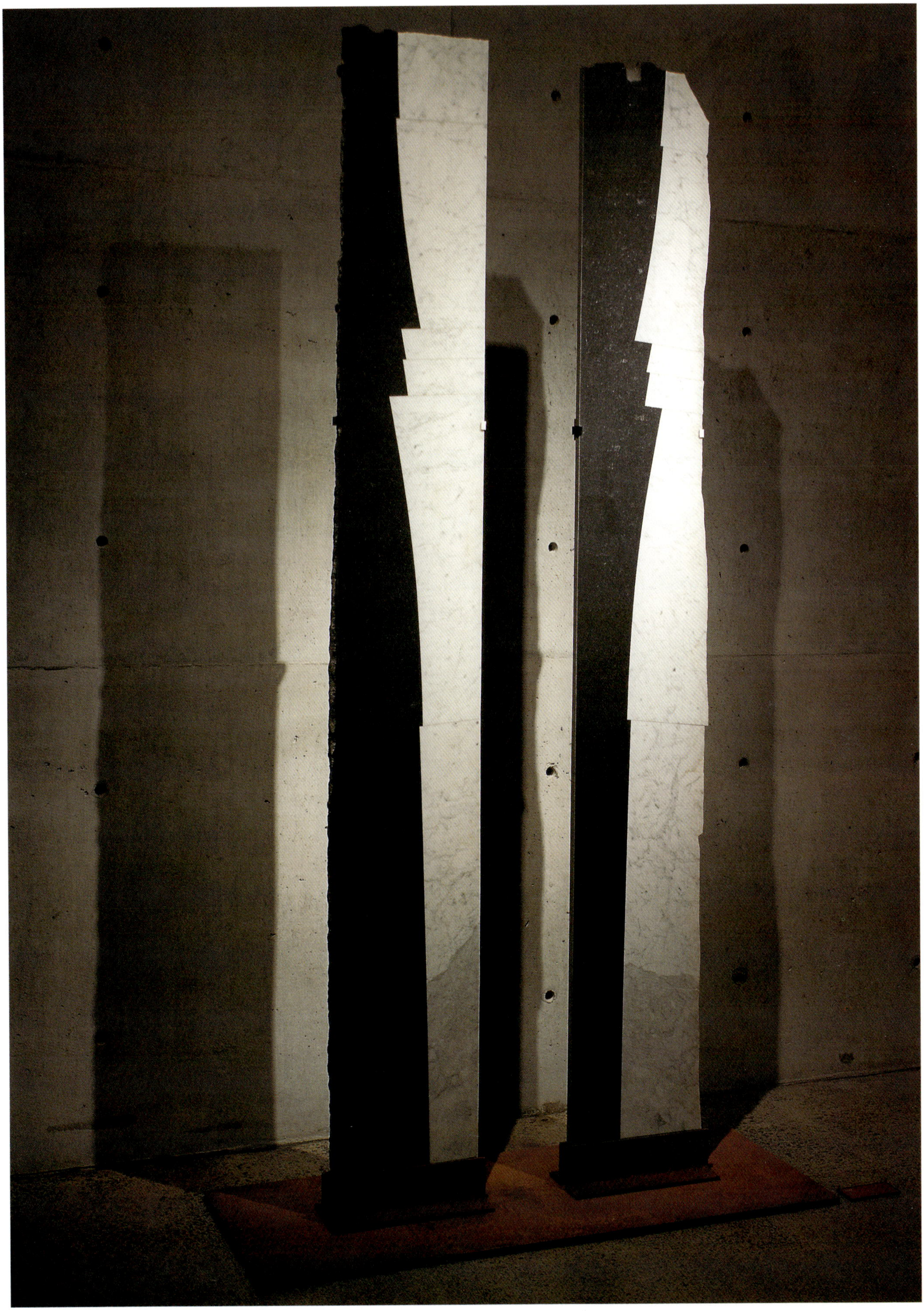

25

MOYRA ELLIOTT

Born Bristol, England 1947.
Came to New Zealand 1959.
Camden Institute of the Arts (Sculpture, Ceramics), London 1971–72.
Lives in Auckland and Wellington.

In the autumn of 1990 while on a Fulbright Scholarship in New York, Moyra Elliott experienced a strange sense of dislocation that was to trigger her most significant work. The perfume of imported spring flowers seemed strangely out of place, and she was struck by the idea of displacement, the differences between home and New York. She decided to look no further than twenty metres from her back door for inspiration, and thus grew her *Garden of Unearthly Delights* series, which became part of her *Plant/Transplant* series.

The ceramic works she created were primarily a statement about her New Zealand garden, which she saw as a metaphor for the local neighbourhood—a mix of English 'granny's garden' and indigenous, tropical and Asian plants. From her studio overlooking the garden she saw the colours of purple jacaranda against a bright blue sky. The volcanic soil would explode into life in spring and summer, and Elliott would, like many binge gardeners, at times prune vigorously.

The image bank grew and eventually was distilled into striking, over-sized leaf forms growing straight out of rock-like formations. Elliott created wonderful rich surfaces evoking lichens on rocks and bark, molten lava in the sunlight, and light filtering through trees. Her experimental glazes were based on large quantities of lithium—poisonous, expensive, magical and able to produce extraordinary mottled colours. There were structural problems to solve—how to strengthen the rocks but reduce their weight and mass and find a means of joining the components. The results, exhibited since 1992, were stunning sculptures with strong profiles, unlike anything seen in New Zealand.

The *Cast Series* of small, fragile works grew out of the *Garden of Unearthly Delights* as pieces which evoke the fine skins that cicadas leave on rocks and trees. She captured the way cicadas cling to surfaces as semi-translucent, three-dimensional protuberances. These pieces seem a long way from the work that preceded the *Garden of Unearthly Delights*.

Elliott's early work looked more outside her own environment for inspiration. Seeing Pueblo women burnishing pots with their babies beside them in the south-west states of USA was instructive to this young mother, who was impressed by the relative safety of their process. Rather than sand the clay and release particles into their children's environment, they pushed the silica into the clay. Initially Elliott made round pieces that evoked those of Zuni, Navaho and Pueblo cultures, and these soon evolved into tall cylindrical works. Upside down they became helmets and, as a result of her research into archaic cultures, she developed a series about armour and, later, Japanese-inspired bells. Her output also included decorated, handbuilt terracotta platters. She acknowledges that strong cultures in clay cannot be ignored and she needs to know about them, but what became important was the need to define her own place.

Directorship of the Fletcher Challenge Awards from 1990 to 1996 coincided with Elliott's strongest work, which received many accolades nationally and internationally. Her current job as Curator at the Dowse Art Museum in Lower Hutt gives her the opportunity to crystallise her ideas through curating and writing about craft art, and, once again, concepts for new work are developing.

**Plant/Transplant XXI
from Garden of
Unearthly Delights
series
White earthenware,
terracotta, bronze,
steel
430 x 470 x 300 mm
Corporate collection
(Fletcher Challenge)**

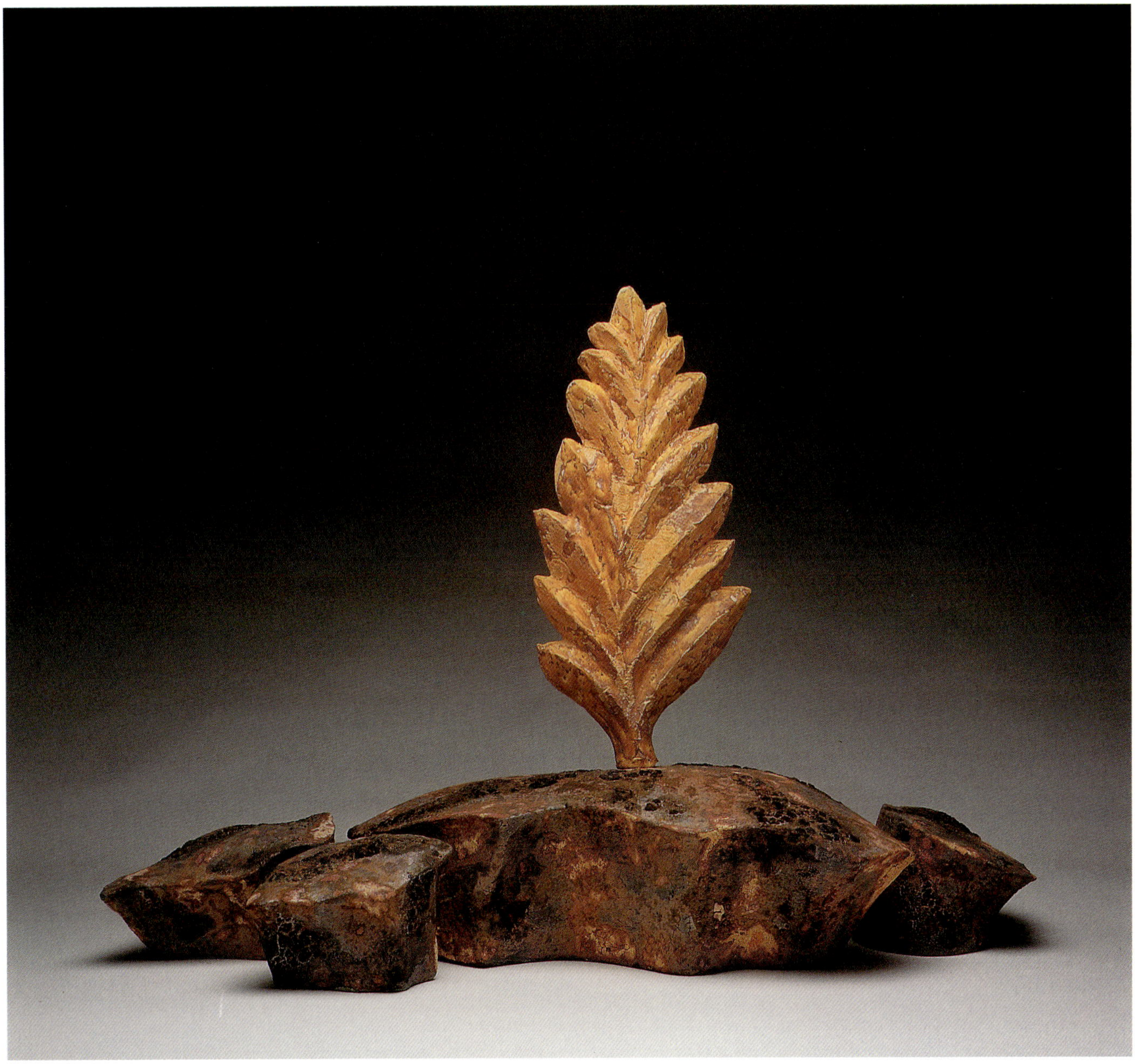

26

PENNY ERICSON

Born Auckland 1952.
Teachers Certificate Diploma, North Shore Teachers College 1972;
Graduate Diploma of Visual Arts (Ceramics), Monash University, Melbourne 1997.
Lives on Waiheke Island.

There is an endearing simplicity to Penny Ericson's newest ceramics. She has created a series of mounds, many quite small, like islands or hills. The inference is apt—Ericson lives on Waiheke Island, and her environment has had considerable impact on her work. These rock-like works, which beg to be seen as a cluster, form a harmonious landscape/seascape which acquires an almost spiritual quality. Perhaps this is because of the repetition of the gentle form and the subsequent relationships between the pieces. The serene *Landforms* have a distinctive characteristic—at their widest extremities they lift slightly like a prow rising out of the water, creating a hint of ambiguity, a shifting balance, even a slight sense of movement.

These forms are consciously understated, and form a backdrop for the exploration of surfaces that are smooth, rough, glossy and matt. They express the many moods of the land and sea within Ericson's view. In addition, they are an opportunity for experimenting with the interaction between slips and glazes as well as with the effect of different sands and clays under the glazes. The scientific process of trial and recording becomes loose and organic in its expression. It is as though Ericson is dressing the rocks in all their variations. Some look as though they have been struck by shafts of light, and exhibit vibrant hues; others are dark and mysterious, or softly muted.

The *Landforms* appeared as an inversion of earlier pieces. Although Ericson's work has always been sculptural and never had more than a passing reference to pottery traditions, previous work evoked vessels more consciously. They were generally larger than later, simpler forms and were made of paper clay—clay slip with paper pulp added for strength. At times she exaggerated the presence of the paper—its importance seemed to equal that of the clay.

These were rough, 'organic abstractions'—a gutsy expression of the coarse textures and surfaces of Ericson's everyday world—and she built them from pre-rolled or poured slabs of clay. Hers was a process of assembly, of layering and combining a number of elements. The vessel made reference to her life-long interest in the sea—its beaches and rugged coastlines. The boat form—sometimes conceptual, at other times literal—has always slipped into Ericson's work. She recognises a range of interpretations and enjoys the sense of completeness the boat evokes. It becomes the means of transportation to the rocks, landscapes and seascapes with which she is so familiar, as well as to her childhood memories.

Ericson has found clay to be a gentle, forgiving and accessible medium which she discovered during teacher training, initially from Chester Nealie (61). For a number of years she taught at primary school; she then worked as a full-time art specialist teacher, and taught part-time at Auckland College of Education until 1991. She first exhibited in 1979, but it was not until 1992 that she held her first solo exhibition at Fire and Form Gallery, Hamilton. Since then, as a full-time ceramist, she has continued her studies and exhibited frequently throughout the country.

Landscape
Clay
1000 x 400 x 600 mm
Collection of the artist

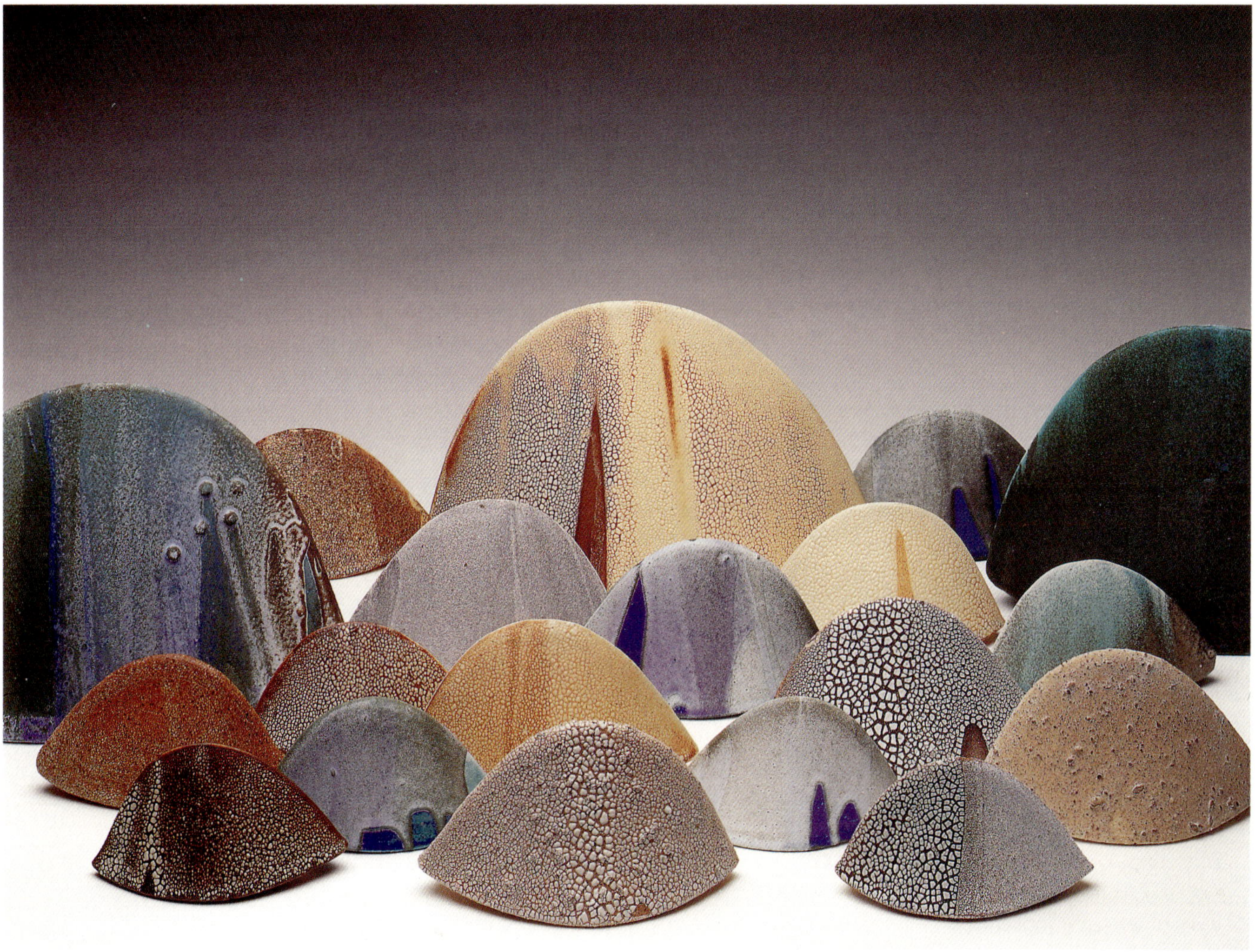

WARWICK FREEMAN

Born Nelson 1953.
Started making jewellery with Peter Woods (Perth) 1972; worked in a number of workshops including Lapis with
Daniel Clasby (Auckland) 1977, and Jens Hansen (Nelson) 1977–78.
Became a partner of Fingers Contemporary Jewellery Gallery, Auckland 1978.
Lives in Devonport, North Shore City.

There is an intellectual, lyrical elegance to Warwick Freeman's jewellery, work that is quietly resolved, exquisitely crafted, and that belies the buzz of ideas behind it. He is known for his thoughtfulness, as someone prepared to confront issues of appropriation and identity from a post-colonial point of view. His early training included working in the manufacturing jewellery industry as well as in a number of studios in the early 1970s. He is now seen as a pioneer of the contemporary jewellery movement in New Zealand, and has earned the respect of a number of graduates of polytechnic craft design courses as well as the wider public.

Freeman identifies the Pacific as an appropriate starting point for his work, and he and other members of the Fingers collective consciously chose, in the 1980s, to look to the Pacific region rather than to Europe for inspiration and materials. Auckland, a city that houses a significant museum collection of Pacific Island jewellery, had become home to a large Maori and Pacific Island population, whose cultural influences stimulated jewellers like Freeman and Alan Preston (68).

Freeman makes no apology for the way he looks to these cultures when he refers to his homeplace. They are part of the urban culture that surrounds him, and he uses the role of the artist as commentator to locate himself in this culture. He probes, head on, the relationships between Maori, Pacific Island and Western imagery, and the different ways of working, and also enquires about the concepts of uniqueness and originality. He finds it interesting that since the 1980s his works have become objects of cultural identity, not through a deliberate articulation of his intention but through commentators and his audience, the wearers of his jewellery.

Freeman's work is seen internationally. His solo exhibition *Insignia* was shown in Melbourne as well as in New Zealand in 1997, and a group of pieces from that show were purchased for the collection at Schmuckmuseum in Pforzheim, Germany. The work is modernist, with simple abstracted forms, and ideas reduced to their essence. In *Insignia* he used symbols that acted as hieroglyphics, collectively becoming a narrative—a visual sentence. The exhibition consisted of cultural symbols, like road signs or a sign language. Some symbols were quite literal, like a leaf; some evoked heraldic imagery, like the shield; others referenced the domestic, like a key. Many were objects found in his studio, already part of his visual vocabulary: simple objects engendering a sense of familiarity. Yet there was also ambiguity; some of the signs could be interpreted in more than one way, depending on how the viewer engaged with the work. He shifted the meaning by his use of materials, by his reinterpretation of the familiar, and by the juxtaposition of the pieces.

That juxtaposition is a continuously changing one. Freeman produces work as small editions. Exhibitions are 'snapshots' of current interpretations of his concerns rather than individual projects. They are part of a continuous process, part of his development as a significant figure in contemporary New Zealand jewellery.

Insignia—Brooches
Greywacke, quartz, jasper, greenstone, pearlshell, turtleshell, bone, silver
Set: 270 x 70 mm
Schmuckmuseum, Pforzheim

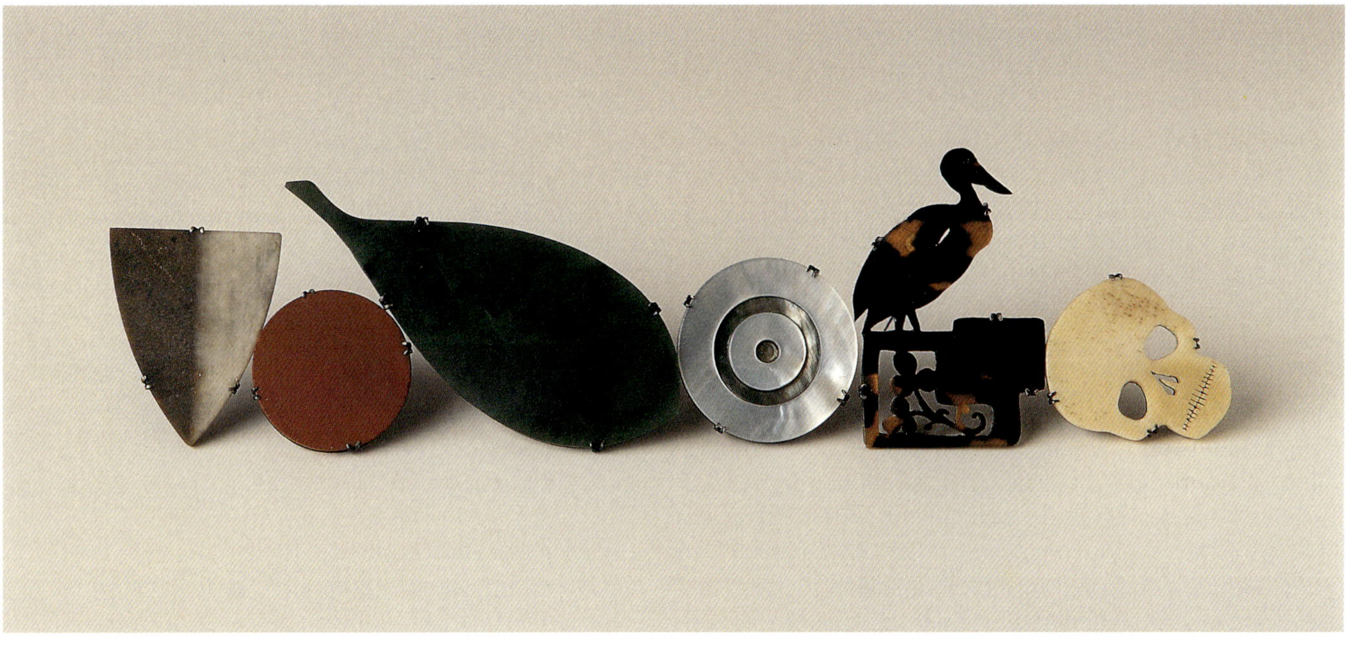

28

STEVE FULLMER

Born Portland, Oregon, USA 1946.
Commercial Arts Course, Mt San Antonio Jr College, California 1964–65;
Commercial Arts and Pottery Courses, Long Beach Jr College 1971–73.
Arrived in New Zealand 1973.
Lives in Nelson.

Steve Fullmer was never particularly aware of mythology when he lived in South California. He dealt in real things, including two years drafted to the US Army. It was not until he came to New Zealand that he realised the South Pacific was alive with mythology.

He didn't deliberately set out to make mythological creatures—they just evolved. Most of his output has been domestic ware, to which he pays as much attention as his sculptural work. In the mid-1980s he made a series of *Pilots*, vessels that, unlike vases or bowls, implied movement. The *Pilot* pieces typically had a single huge wing, decorated with marks that evoked passage through space. They appeared to have travelled through great heat and many gases, as though they had been through Hell, then emerged lean and battered. They were deliberately rough, quick and spontaneous-looking forms, provocative, fantasy images that suggested Halley's Comet and outer space.

In 1985 Fullmer won a Merit Award at the Fletcher Brownbuilt Pottery Award with one of these pieces; in 1986 he won the Supreme Award; and in 1987 he was a joint winner of the Supreme Award. His work was represented in a number of international exhibitions after that, and in 1991 he was commissioned to produce large-scale work based on the *Pilots* for World Expo in Seville.

For Expo Fullmer re-invented the concept and created three works named after the sailing vessels of Columbus. After consulting with Maori, he created nine eels representing the waka that made nine great Polynesian voyages and referred to a legend of several waka being led by a group of eels. Controversy and difficulty surrounded this concept, and differing opinions about eels as food led Fullmer to remove the names from the pieces. The experience, which he had undertaken with integrity and no intention to be inappropriate, was a sobering one. Less contentious were the tuatara and 2000 pebbles, rocks and boulders for the exhibition. The tuatara, the oldest living reptiles on earth, enchanted viewers, reminding them of ancient toads and skinks. Fullmer continues to make these occasionally, and they are in worldwide collections from Singapore to New York.

The next theme, *Mudfish*, was based on mythological ideas. The endearing image, based on a slab body supported by legs that appear to be in motion, has a quirky, cartoon quality which appears again in the more recent *Reefheads*. Some of these are being developed at a very large scale. The pieces epitomise Fullmer's approach to all his work, both domestic and sculptural. He likes them to be individual and robust, to have a certain masculinity.

His process, which he discovered by accident, now has quite sophisticated results that he can control. Fullmer sponges and drips on layers of coloured slips, followed by a layer of white slip, which he allows to dry slightly or completely. He then hoses the work, removing layers of colour with water and his hands—an eroding, etching process. It is as though time, wind and rain are acting on the piece. He looks for accidents—angels, aquatic images, mountains, floating dogs—and finishes the process with playful, judiciously chosen marks or human features.

Reefheads
Clay
230 x 220 mm each
Collection of the artist

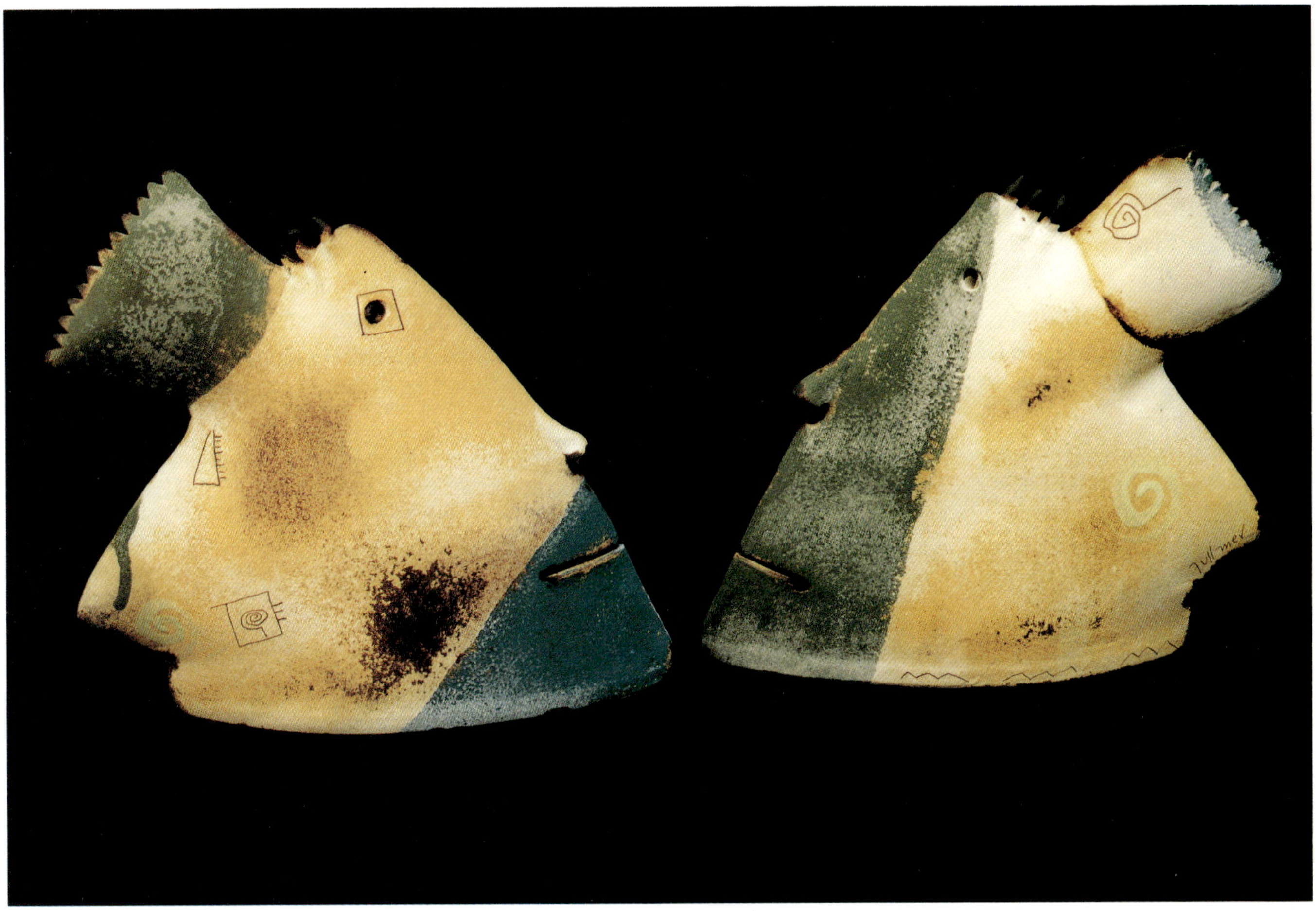

29

ELÉNA GEE

Born Auckland 1949.
Worked for manufacturing jeweller 1968; largely self-taught.
Lives in Auckland.

Through the medium of jewellery Eléna Gee seeks to pass through the conscious mind to discover the unconscious. Hers is intensely personal work which has an organic grace and beauty that goes deeper than merely depicting the sources of her images. Those sources could be debris from her favourite beach; the shape of a silhouetted mountain; or the blue, red and gold plaster saints that once graced the local church. The church she refers to is one from childhood, and her memories include painted plaster stones, bleeding hearts representing self-sacrifice, a dove symbolising the Holy Spirit, and golden-winged angels. Those memories are in contrast with the contemporary art which replaced the saints when the small church was rebuilt.

Gee believes that the conscious part of her mind alone produces forms that are too tame, elaborate and controlled for her liking. She strives for a raw simplicity of colour and form, but resists the urge to refine and tame—an urge that pulls her like a magnet, like a societal pressure, a way of being that was taught. Her attitude to children's drawing and their freedom to create signs is reminiscent of Paul Klee's envy of children's innocence and directness.

Her images tap into, evoke, but never emulate reality. The symbolism emerges from purely abstract shapes, like a pentagonal piece of stone that evokes a child's drawing of a house, which in turn requires a splash of paint to represent a door. However, the house is not really a building, rather a metaphor for security. Similarly, a sky-blue piece of wing-shaped lapis lazuli symbolises freedom more than flight, and a heart can represent love or sacrifice.

One way Gee works is to make moulds for casting from existing forms, often natural objects, like shells. The moulds allow her to make multiples, and the process of working with soft wax, then making a fired clay mould, helps to abstract the images. She aims for looseness, letting the edges of the wax take on their own characteristics. The element of chance is appealing—is about releasing control.

There is a lot of brilliant contrasting or complementary colour in Gee's current work. It is perhaps a reaction to a previous group of works which seemed starved of applied colour, and was often limited to the grey of a found stone, with maybe a splash of gold leaf. Her use of colour appears cyclical, periodic and slightly unpredictable. The way she finishes her pieces is more constant. The work may have a rough presence and its form be loosely defined, but everything is carefully honed, with a fine finish so as not to irritate the wearer. The finish retains the source of the material, maybe a rock or a worn shell, and she seeks the rugged and the worn more than the perfect example she might have sought when she was younger. Each piece is invariably wearable but can equally be seen as a tiny sculpture, a talisman to ward off evil thoughts, an enchanting treasure for contemplation.

**Brooches and Pendants
Stone, paint, gold leaf
ca. 50 x 45 mm
Collection of the artist**

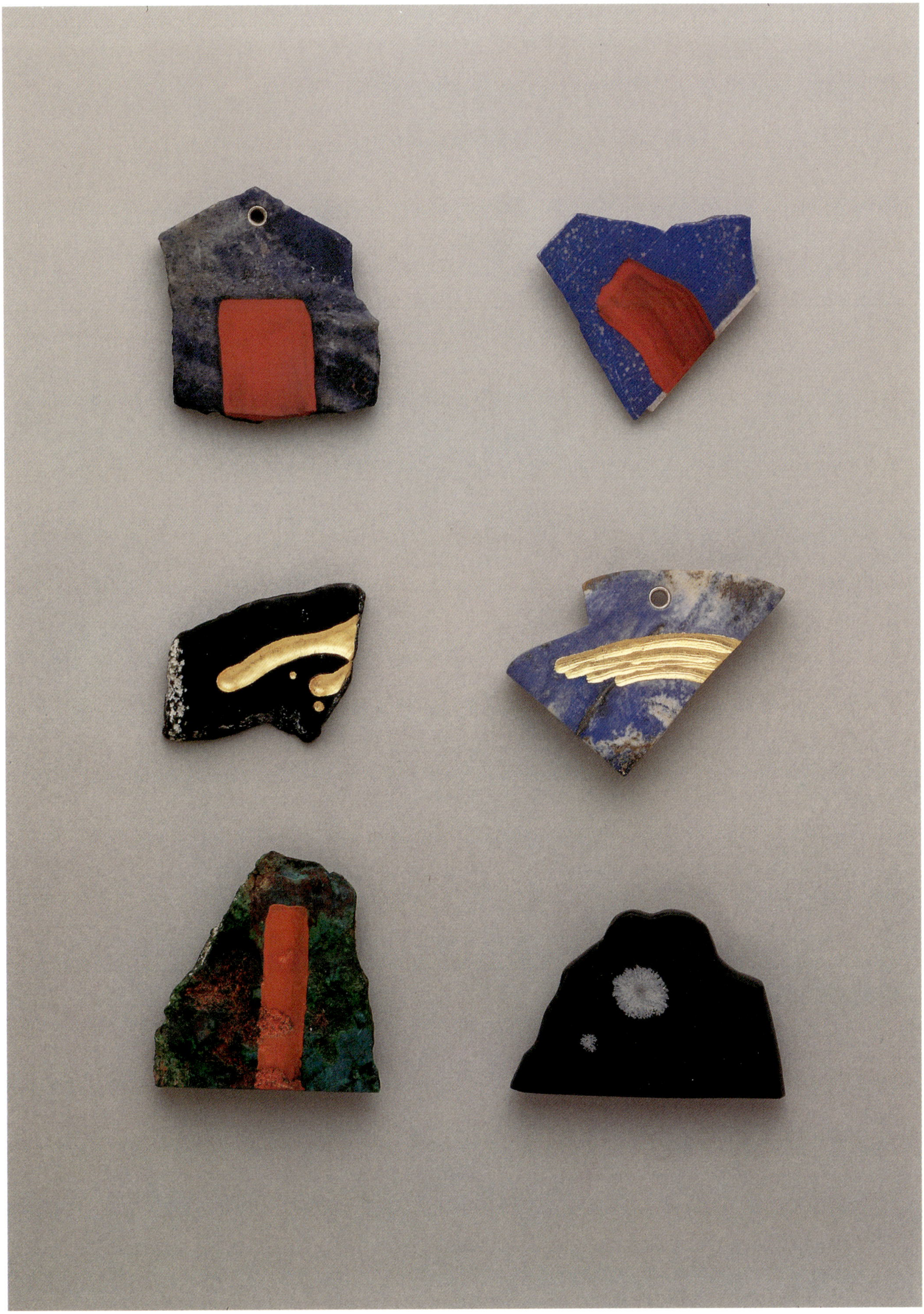

MATARENA GEORGE

Born Pukapuka, Cook Islands 1935.
Self-taught since age 16.
Came to New Zealand 1958.
Lives in Manukau City.

Matarena George saw her first tivaevae when she was a teenager living in Rarotonga, having moved there from Pukapuka when she was nine years old. She was so enchanted by its beauty that she resolved to make one herself. That was the beginning of a lifetime of appliqué and patchworking. Her first work was an appliquéd tablecloth in two colours, but she soon went on to make bed-size tivaevae, which she continues to make for her family, friends, community and occasionally for exhibition.

Her father had been a tailor and made clothes for community needs. From him she learnt how to look, create stitched works and cut her own patterns. The heritage of sewing in the Cook Islands dates from when the missionaries arrived in the eighteenth century. They brought fabrics and taught the Cook Islanders some simple stitches. The women soon adopted the medium as their own, often working collectively on a single piece. The brightly coloured tivaevae were generally made as bed covers—to be used, and frequently given to loved ones, as heirlooms and often to be buried with their owners.

George hand-makes tivaevae in this tradition—sometimes alone, at other times in the company of other women. The patterns are her own and she makes bold, symmetrical works in unorthodox colour combinations. They are cut and overlaid on a contrasting background, and all loose edges are stitched down. A variety of stitches is used in tivaevae, and George enjoys working with a range of effects. Blanket stitch is traditional for appliquéing one layer of cut fabric to its background. In another favoured stitch, otita (oyster) stitch, the process includes twisting threads around the needle. (The name is an anomaly, as oysters were not known in the Cook Islands; like the process, the name was probably imported by a traveller.) Often variegated cotton thread is used to add to the richness of effect.

George credits her Pacific Island heritage for her love of flowers and for her use of a multiplicity of vibrant colours, as in *Orchid*. Many designs are based on flowers she remembers from her childhood, although she is starting to incorporate some New Zealand flora. She was particularly inspired by the beautiful flowers she saw in 1986 while on holiday in Tahiti. Accuracy is important to her, so she prefers not to mix a breadfruit leaf with a frangipani flower, unless it is in a vase of mixed flowers. Her imagery generally comes from her personal experience, so she never looks to tapa for inspiration—that tradition was lost from the Cook Islands and she didn't see any tapa until she lived in New Zealand. She is more likely now to look at the use of fabrics in quilts by palagi for inspiration.

At times her tivaevae are based on biblical stories. *Joseph's Dream*, for example, depicts wheat sheaves, the sun, moon and stars. Some are figurative and include text, maybe the names of the loves in the owner's life. These could also be Cook Island legends, like *The Eel and the Coconut*, which George has interpreted with humour and energy. That energy, and an innate design sensibility, are visible in all her tivaevae, which are vibrant evocations of a culture that has had considerable impact on New Zealand life.

**Orchids
Tivaevae
Cotton
2000 x 2000 mm
Collection of the artist**

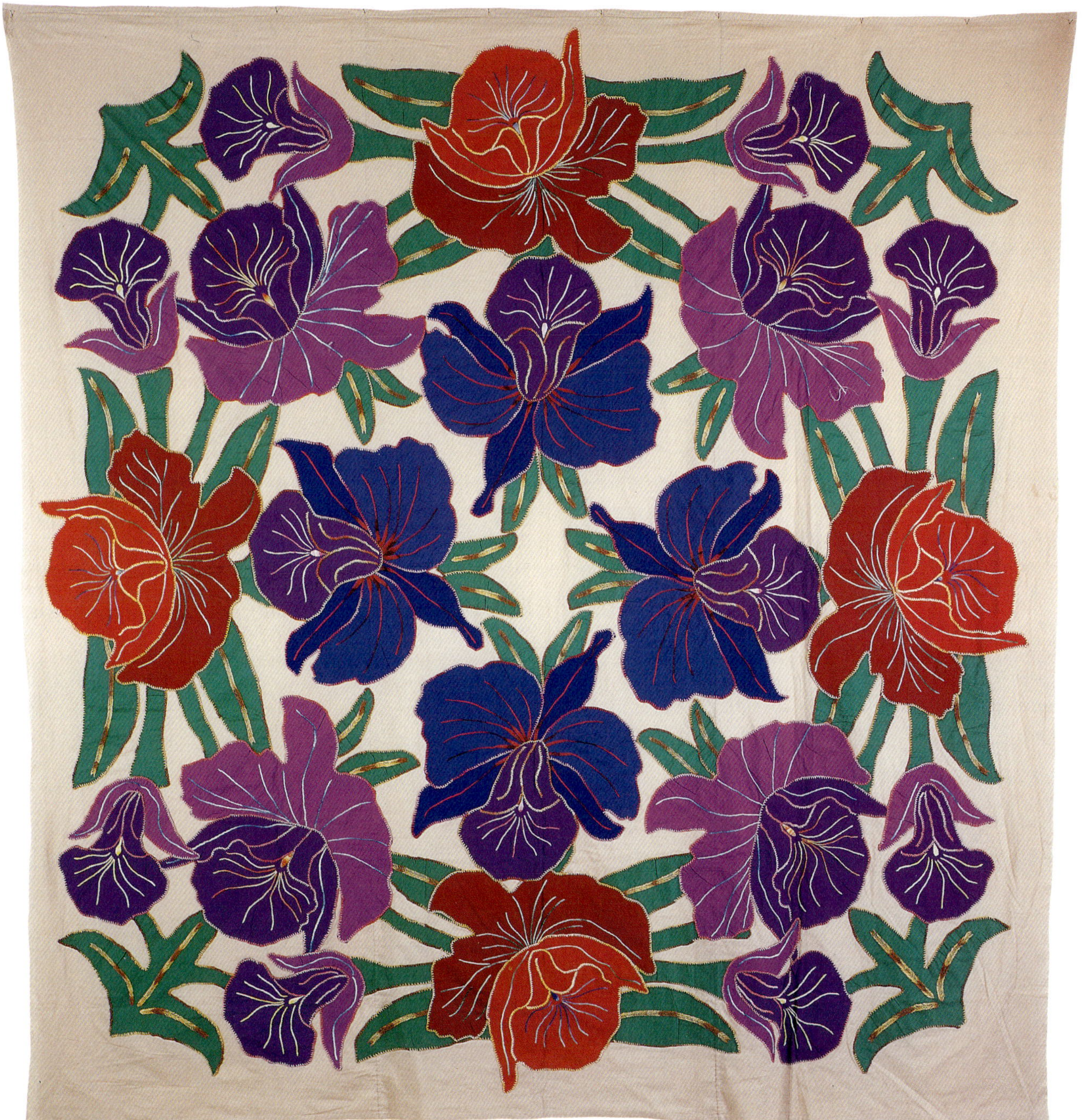

31

JUDE GRAVESON

Born Auckland 1941.
Certificate in Craft Design, Waikato Polytechnic 1989;
Dip Design for Craft, Carrington Polytechnic 1991;
Certificate in Adult Teaching, AIT 1993.
Lives in Auckland.

When Jude Graveson makes paper she combines contemporary conceptual thinking with an ancient low-tech process. She came to paper through her love of textiles and mark-making, and from respecting the centuries of human use of fibre in many cultures. There is a sense of the archaic in the textures and surfaces of the paper she makes. For Graveson, paper is the signifier for the inventiveness of the mind, the medium by which we record ideas, as evidenced centuries later by those who interpret the marks made on its surface.

Graveson is inspired by paper's tactile qualities, and finds the medium an appropriate vehicle for exploring issues about thought, language and making meanings. Academic study is an ongoing process for her, and the intellectual ideas inform her artistic output, which is characterised by a distinctive use of rich, earthy, aged, weathered colour. Her subject matter encompasses observations, memories and personal experiences, and reflects a sense of place, both of her travels and where she lives. It is informed by diverse sources like the pages of her mother's cookbook, or the scratchings on the walls by inmates at what was Oakley Psychiatric Hospital and later Carrington Polytechnic.

She has a fascination for the seemingly irresistible human desire to layer things, events and people with meanings. The notion is expressed literally in the form of artists' books, and with wall works that evoke archaeological findings spread out to discover meanings and links. She seeks intellectual connections or invents some where none are to be found, and interprets the connections graphically, seeking to convey anthropological evidence and the wonder of the human hand, nature and human thought.

Her imagery reflects a search for clues of the presence of process—by hand, tool, machine and mind—much as an archaeologist might search, and her mark-making evokes the traces of human and natural processes. Those marks could be bandsaw marks, the weathering effects of wind and rain, thread on a quilt, or the bark on a tree. Her surfaces are rich with repeat patterns, like water on sand, wire gratings and grilles. These works are at their most beguiling when the viewer discovers unexpected connections between the process of the hand and the process of the mind.

At times Graveson makes reference to cultures other than her own, as in *The Path is Made by the Walking*, a piece she made as a graduating craft design student. The sculptural work made reference to Nepalese prayer flags as well as to Buddhist meanings, and reflected the broad range of her research into philosophy and into the processes of material culture. She continues to use technologies that relate to tapa making and hand paper making in China, India and the Philippines, as well as to Western traditions. In her studio, The Paper Press, she conducts workshops, makes paper to commission, and makes art works that have won her a number of awards.

Cultural Artefact III: Vertebrae
Handcast paper, harakeke fibre, pigment, paste and dye
1540 x 500 mm
Collection of the artist

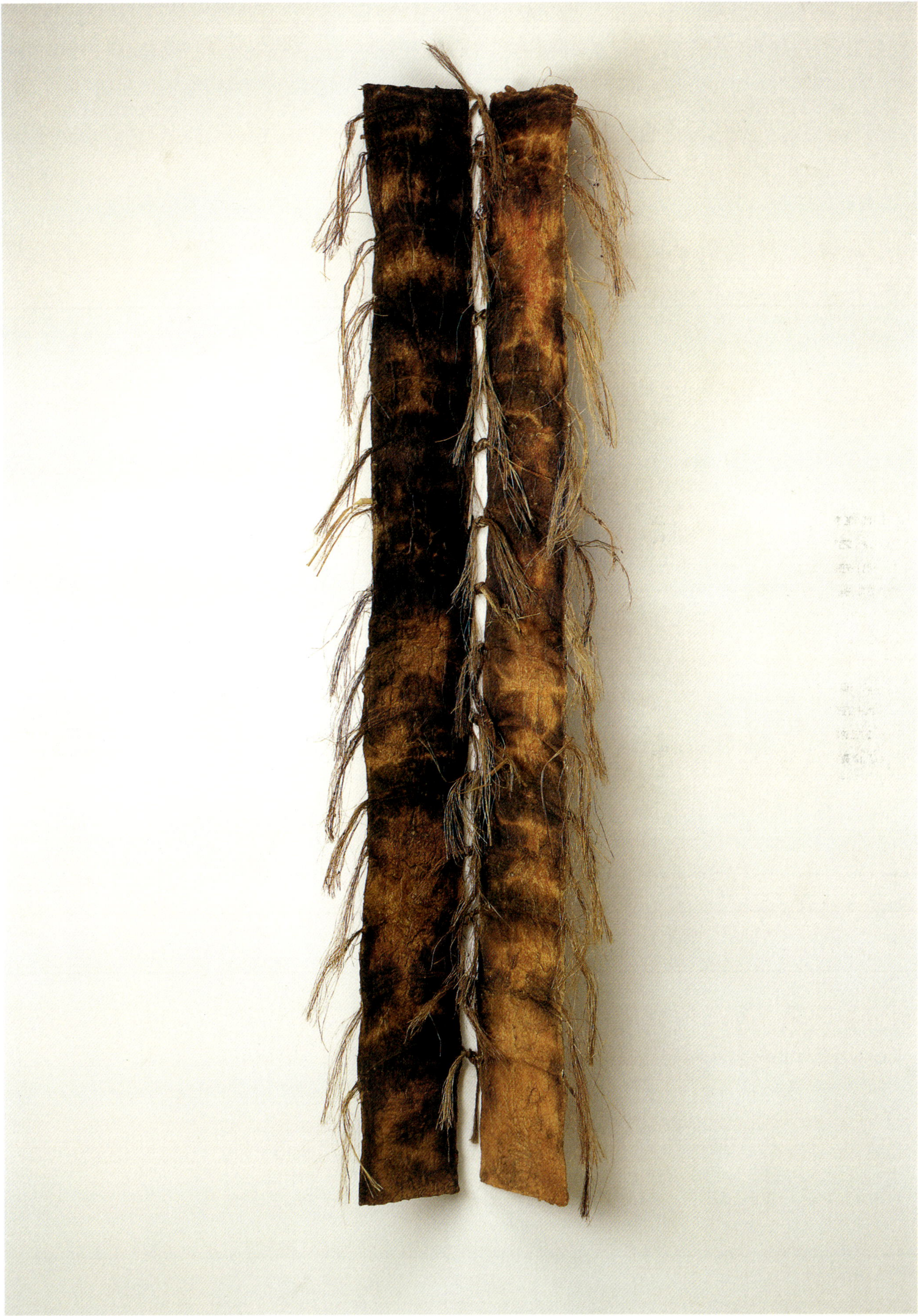

32

ROSE GRIFFIN

Born Matamata 1957.
Dip Fine Arts, University of Canterbury 1978;
Dip Teaching, Auckland Teachers College 1979.
Lives in Nelson.

For three years Rose Griffin filled her workbooks but did not create any new work. It was an introspective period, a time for teaching and processing ideas, a gestation period that permitted new beginnings when she returned to making in 1997.

Griffin has spent time looking at family history and domestic stories as well as garments and samplers in museums, and she has become excited about the richness of imagery and concepts in her culture. Her current work, about the way clothing tells a story, was made with her grandparents in mind. She based her pieces on garments from the 1920s—the period when they were first married—desiring to communicate some of their values about pastoral farming and life. The life-size machine-stitched collars and yokes—a man's and a woman's—are made of dried grass representing agricultural materials. They form an eloquent statement about sewing and its place in historical narrative.

Although she had sewn in traditional ways during her childhood it was not until 1981, when she began designing and making silk garments, that Griffin came to textiles as an art form. By 1988 her ideas had shifted, and she approached textiles more conceptually, producing work that revealed a dual commitment to textiles and mark-making. In her works she used stitch and thread in addition to graphic marks on flat surfaces of paper or canvas. Marks on surfaces and marks hanging off the surfaces were her interests, and she enjoyed challenging the line between the domestic and 'art'.

In 1994 she spent six months in an informal textile programme at Canberra School of Art. During that period she questioned her focus on textiles, and spent considerable time drawing and painting. On her return to New Zealand her works revealed an absence of thread, occasionally represented by rows of punched holes produced by a sewing machine. She was still thinking in terms of textiles.

Griffin is less interested in recreating historic processes than in talking about historic activities from a contemporary point of view. She questions attitudes she encountered throughout her art education which ignored textiles and processes using a sewing machine as valid artistic expressions. She developed an interest in exploring the way textiles are part of our individual or collective creativity. She acknowledged that fabric and thread satisfy a human need, and that there are large numbers of women in the community who stitch as an expression of their creativity. By examining the lives of her ancestors and how stitchery fitted into them, she is contrasting the level of acceptability then and now. If enthusiasm and dedication to sewing for family is regarded as an inferior domestic activity, Griffin seeks to reclaim that while questioning what has changed, why and how.

She works spontaneously now. Part of the challenge of working with textiles, unlike drawing, is the difficulty of making changes during the process. It seems important that the work not appear forced. Textiles have become gestural 'drawings' for Griffin and she seeks the essential mark in her work and the humanity the gesture contains. For the viewer there is a sense of familiarity and enchantment.

A Full and Useful Life: Clothing for Lewis & Nettle
Grass, thread, buttons
140 x 460 mm; 280 x 260 mm
Collection of the artist

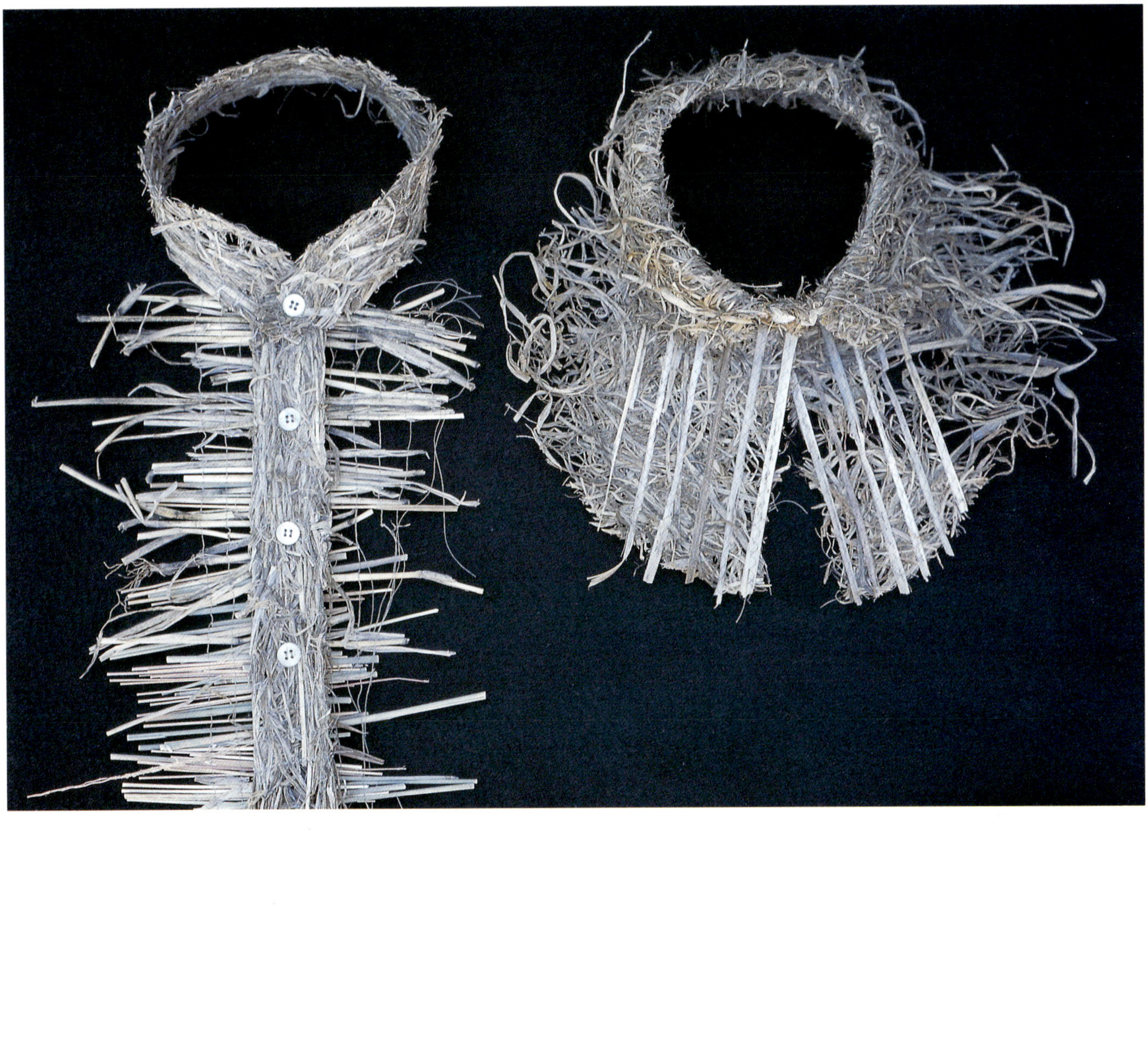

JENS HANSEN

Born Gram, Denmark 1940.
Came to New Zealand 1952.
School of Applied Arts and Industrial Design, Copenhagen 1961–64.
Returned to New Zealand 1965.
Lives in Nelson.

Mies van der Rohe's dictum 'less is more' is enthusiastically embraced by Jens Hansen. Simplicity and purity of form have been his goal since he had his first exhibition of jewellery at New Vision Gallery, Auckland, in 1960. At that time, jewellery was not perceived as an art form, so this was a bold move. Soon after, having completed a traditional jewellery apprenticeship, he returned to Europe where he studied jewellery and silversmithing for four years.

In 1966 he established his first jewellery studio in Auckland and had high ideals of making one-off pieces, but necessity led him to making production work which he continues to this day. In 1968 he moved to Nelson, a place that was becoming more known for its potters. Those were artistically solitary times, and Hansen had no jewellery peer group; his workshop, like that of Kobi Bosshard (8) in Dunedin, became renowned as a training ground for a number of studio jewellers. He sought classes in painting and lectures on design theory, as he had done in Europe, and discovered the work of modernist sculptors Hepworth, Moore, Arp and Brancusi, whose simplicity of line and generous forms continue to be his inspiration.

Hansen, who comes from a long line of blacksmiths, remains unapologetically European in his approach, although his work does not strictly follow Scandinavian traditions. A modernist and traditionalist, he gravitates to stone, gold and silver. He identifies differences between his workshop, which focuses on silversmithing, and that of the traditional jeweller: he is more likely to use a hammer than pliers and files to shape the metal. The results are fuller, more massive forms than the traditional. He develops an intimate relationship with the metal, and frequently returns it to the fire to keep it malleable and receptive to the shaping blows of the hammer.

Hansen's experimental departures are exemplified by the work he did during a residency at Otago Polytechnic in 1989. While the reaction from his peers to this looser, less formal work was encouraging and he thought the ideas had merit, he wanted the results to be more refined. In 1990 Hansen was one of a small group of jewellers invited to an Arts Council-funded symposium headed by Otto Kunzli and, again, he looked to develop work in new ways.

There is often little difference between his one-off and production pieces. Enduring values, consistency of form and sophisticated crafting are always important, and some of his designs have changed only incrementally during the past thirty years. He believes that the strength and durability of metal sets up its own harmony. Most of his works have highly polished surfaces which create an ambiguity of form through reflection. Rather than dulling the work with machine matt finishes, which he dislikes, Hansen leaves it to the wearer to impart a personal patina—then the work is complete.

His work has been seen throughout New Zealand, in Australia, USA and Europe, and he has had twenty-five solo exhibitions. He has been the recipient of a QEII Arts Council grant which allowed him to study jewellery in Copenhagen; co-founded Details, the organisation for New Zealand craft jewellers, and has taught extensively.

Three rings, three brooches
Silver
Various sizes
Collection of the artist

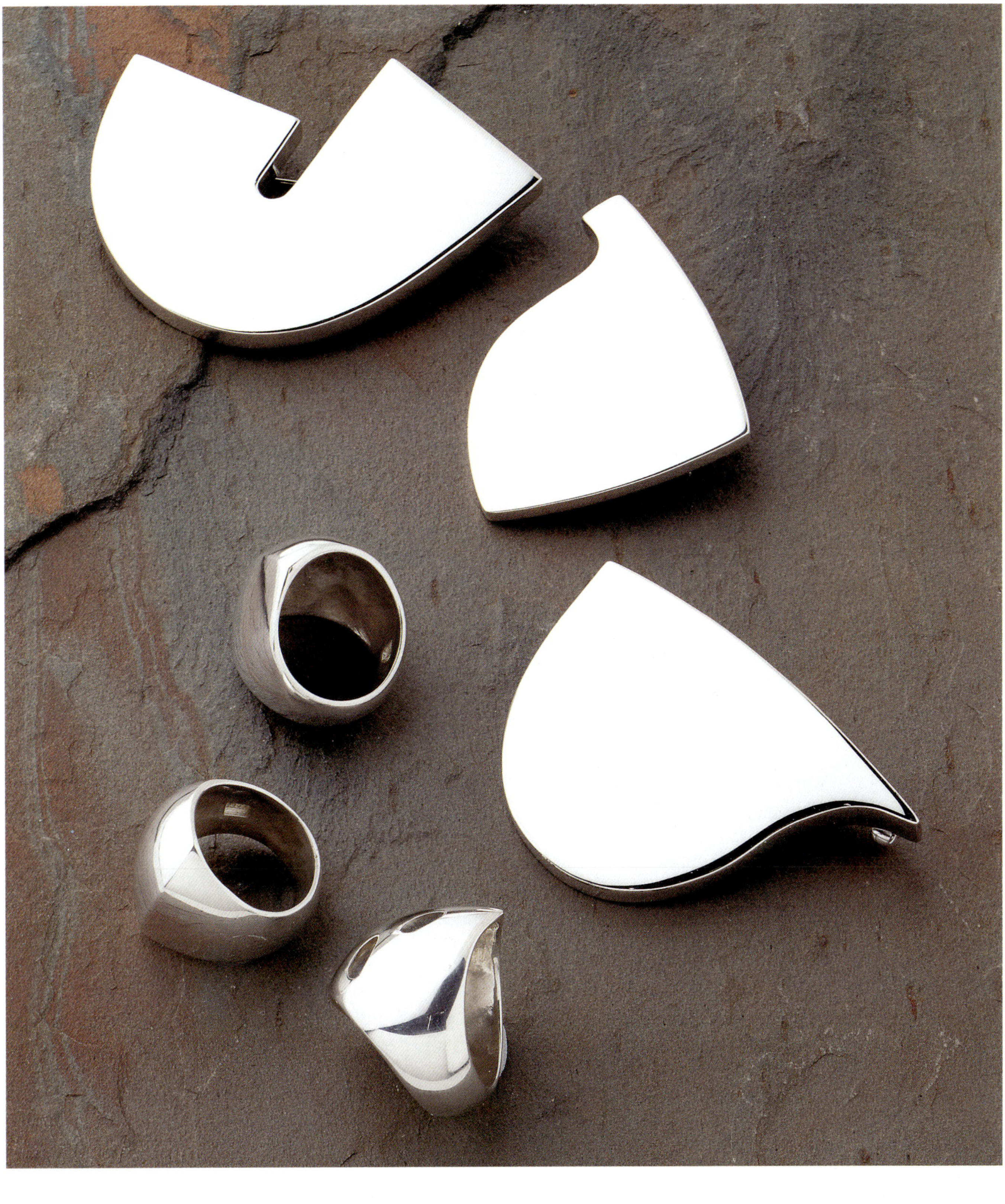

34

NIKI HASTINGS-McFALL

Born Auckland 1959.
Certificate in Contemporary Jewellery, Manukau Institute of Technology 1993;
Dip Visual Arts, Manukau Institute of Technology 1994.
Lives in Auckland.

Niki Hastings-McFall is one of the few practitioners represented in this book who have a short history of craft production. She started making contemporary jewellery in 1992, and her work is exceptional in the way it signifies her Pacific Island heritage.

Hastings-McFall explores the notion of ethnic hybridity in her work, and it is for her a personal journey of self-discovery. It combines freshness with a developed personal visual language. When she met her father shortly before he died in 1993, she was exposed to a range of heritage issues she had never considered before. His background was predominantly Samoan, with German, French and Irish ancestry, while her mother's heritage was English, Irish, Scots and Welsh. For Hastings-McFall there were discoveries and connections to be made from the realisation that there was a huge legacy of images, legends and customs, and more than one way of life that she could draw on as her own.

Exploring her Pacific Island heritage developed its own momentum, as did seeing it in relation to being born in New Zealand. Identity became a complex issue, and in her work she dances around, rather than succumbs to, stereotypical perceptions of what is Pacific. Against a backdrop of Fa'a Samoa, siapo and tattoo, she creates jewellery from an image bank that expresses, with integrity, living in New Zealand—a Pacific island. There are sometimes religious references in her works, acknowledging the belief system she was raised with, while commenting on the impact of missionary zeal in the Pacific.

Some of her works are neckpieces, juxtapositions of shells, glass beads and bone with fragments of metal, coins, computer disks, perspex, money cards and film strip. They point to time and place, and to the society in which she lives. In her exhibition *Past Pacific* in 1997 she showed a number of neckpieces. Many were large, as expressions of honour, for placing on the head and shoulders—symbolic gestures and signifiers that directly reference the Samoan practice of creating upper body ornaments. The traditional kapkap, a pectoral ornamental found in the north-west Pacific region, is a form that influences and inspires her. Typically it was made of giant clam shell overlaid with finely pierced tortoise shell. Hers might be made with metals and pearl shell, or with a computer disk. Using contemporary materials recognises the tradition of using whatever was available for ornament. Any rare ornament could become a form of currency or a badge of chiefly rank.

Metal reflects a European material culture and is basic to Hastings-McFall's repertoire. She often uses alloyed metals—amalgamations—which reflect the way she perceives herself. Simple techniques are an active choice, as is the use of repetition. Bright colours appeal, interpreted through the use of titanium, copper, silver, gold and brass. She acknowledges the influence of Fatu Feu'u and Jim Vivieaere on her thinking, and is inspired by the layers of meaning she reads into the work of Warwick Freeman (27), Eléna Gee (29) and Alan Preston (68). But ultimately her work is a very real personal expression that takes its primary inspiration from her diverse cultural heritage.

**Siapo I, Siapo II
(8 brooches)
Silver, niobium,
titanium, copper,
brass
(square) 35 x 35 mm,
(oval) 65 x 25 mm
Various collections**

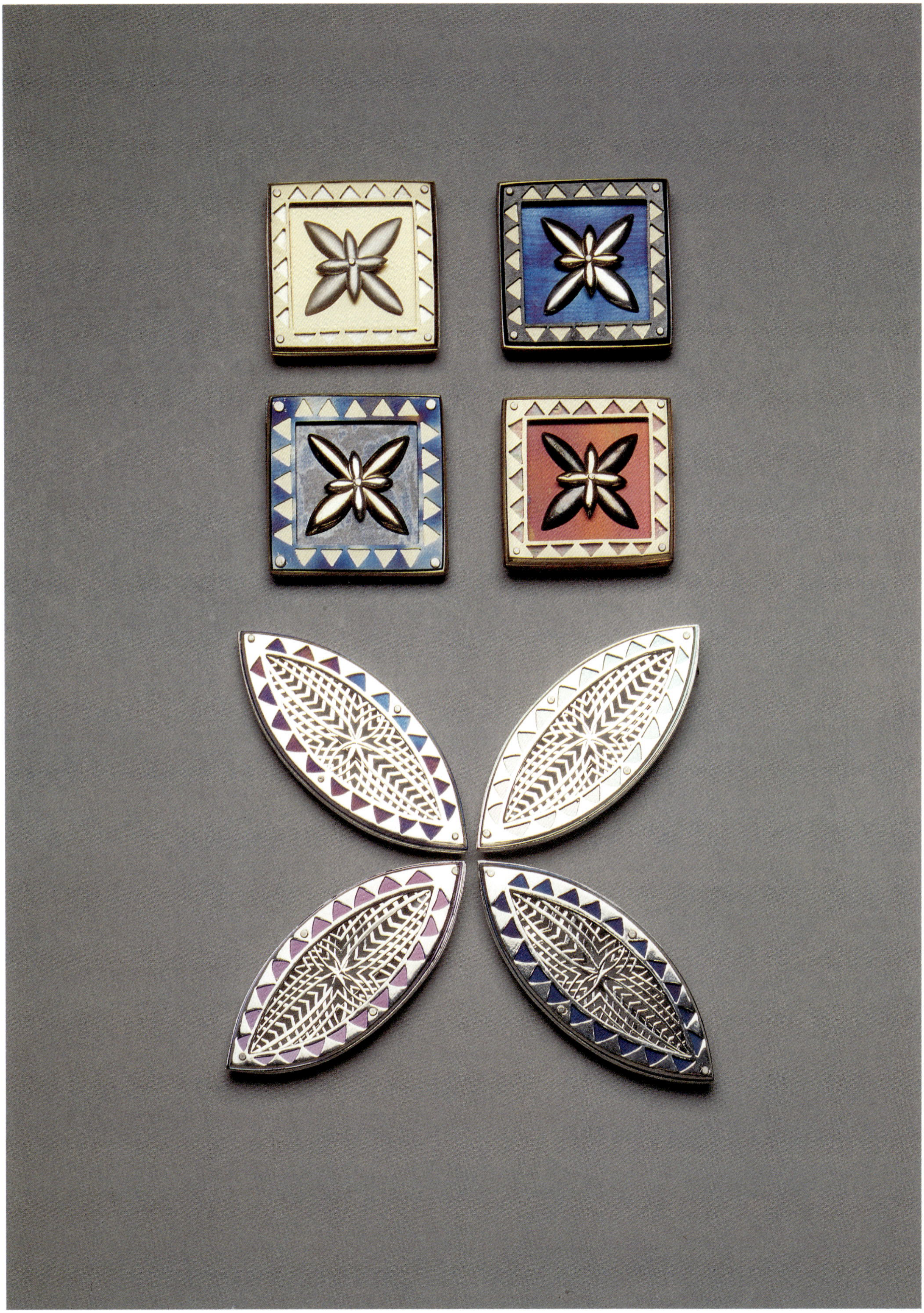

35

GAVIN HITCHINGS

Born Woolwich, England 1937.
Emigrated to New Zealand 1965.
Trained as goldsmith/jeweller 1970;
partnership in Jens Hansen Ltd Gold and Silversmiths, Nelson.
Lives in Nelson.

Gavin Hitchings has been blurring the lines between sculpture and jewellery for a number of years. He tutored in jewellery and metals at Nelson Polytechnic from 1986 to 1995, has won a number of craft awards since 1977, and has been the recipient of two QEII Arts Council grants.

His works sometimes seem large as jewellery yet are miniatures in a sculptural context. They can also act as maquettes for larger works. Scale is actually of little importance in some works, exemplified by *Boulder Sculpture*, a large steel work in Miyazu City, Japan designed in 1997. The pieces are generally made of silver, occasionally of patinaed brass and titanium. Although he is not governed by material, Hitchings knows silver well—it is integral to his thinking.

A collaboration—a unique meeting of interests—occurred between Hitchings and sculptor Graham Bennett (Vol. 2, 4) in 1988 following Bennett's *Boulder Bank Project*. Hitchings' interpretation of Bennett's large-scale installation was a miniaturised response, and this began a visual dialogue. Both had a strong interest in the relationship that develops between architecture and land, in a visual and imaginative sense. A decade later, Hitchings continues to develop this theme in his jewellery and small sculptures.

Since 1991 he has taken imaginary tangents to abstract thought and, using the same elements of boulder and architecture, has explored them in a metaphorical sense. His *Boulder Brooches* were characterised by marks that refer to the land—the organic flow lines of long-shore drifts, crossed with formal impositions on the landscape.

Some pieces were about dislocation—the tectonic plates that keep Earth constantly on the move. Others were fragments overlaid with an open-ended system and linear elements projecting into open space. They made reference to time, and some, as linear drawings in space, distorted perspectives. At times they shifted to axonometric or isometric renditions. Hitchings found the succinct writing of Robert Smithson to be congruent with these ideas, and acknowledged this in his work titled *Stones of Unknowing*. This influence is paralleled by an interest in the ideas of Marcel Duchamp.

He continues to base his work on the boulder, a strong ovoid form. The boulder defines a specific place and its unique qualities. Hitchings makes reference to personal places and structures, modifying them, letting them disintegrate. At times they return to a former condition—a form of entropy—and he discovers a sense of growth as well as disintegration. These ideas manifest themselves in his work in a number of ways: as drawings, prints, sculptures and jewellery.

In his work, curves define solids, voids and arches. In the *Bridging Series I*, 1996, Hitchings retained the curvature common to his boulder works. The architectural paraphernalia remained as references to structures in trusses, ladders and frameworks. He implied a fourth dimension as a band of time and thought of bridging in terms of time and substance. These works led to *Bridging Series II*, 1997, which made further reference to the triangulation of architectural and engineering structures. The *Void Series*, 1996, implied boulders and was filled with references to buildings and structures. The outlines became memories of the boulders and the land they signified.

**Three brooches
Sterling silver
75–90 x 45–55 mm
Collection of the artist**

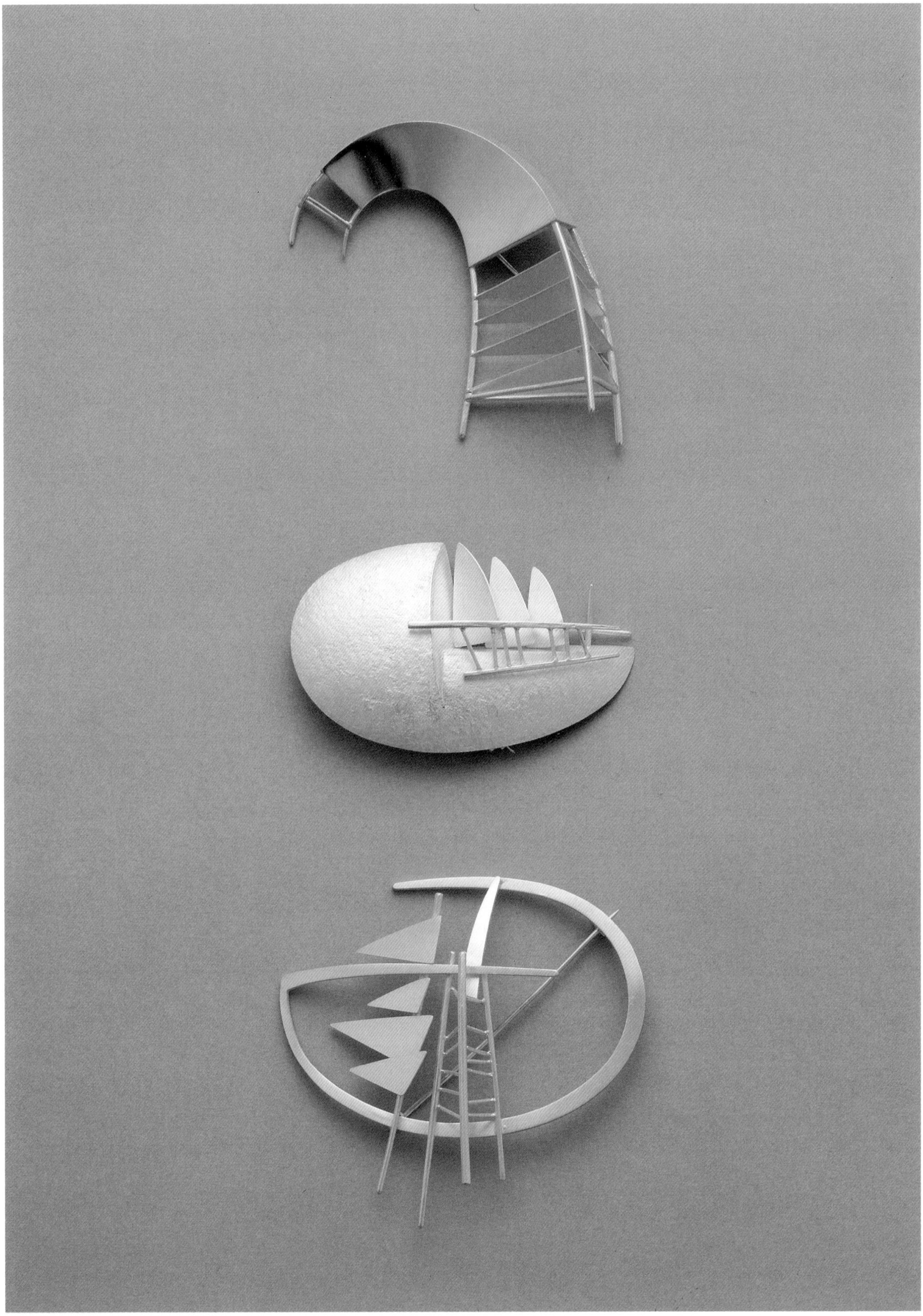

OLA AND MARIE HÖGLUND

Ola Höglund
Born Stockholm, Sweden 1956.
Trained at Kosta Boda and Orrefors
glass studios 1972–77.
Arrived New Zealand 1982.
Lives in Nelson.

Marie Höglund
Born Gothenburg, Sweden 1955.
Trained at Kosta Boda and Orrefors
glass studios 1972–73, 1975–77.
Arrived New Zealand 1982.
Lives in Nelson.

When Ola and Marie Höglund came to New Zealand and established their first glass studio in 1984, they relished the isolation from European and American glass studio trends. They saw it as an opportunity to develop a personal style. They arrived after three years of glass blowing in Swaziland, bringing the skills and disciplines of glass blowing and hand-finishing they had acquired at the influential Swedish glass colleges of Kosta Boda and Orrefors. Their experience had taught them how craft could be allied to industry, and it fostered the high standards they demand of themselves.

Theirs is a team effort that is a balance between virtuoso performance, consistency of product and an understanding of the unique properties of the medium. They eschew 'mistakes disguised as art' which they believe are prevalent in studio glass. These days, although both are involved in designing the pieces, Ola Höglund blows glass with the help of an assistant and Marie Höglund develops the surface treatment. Ola believes that vessel shapes have a universal vocabulary, and that changes in his work are the result of his growing expertise and control of the seductive medium.

His ideas are driven by form, colour and technical goals, and a desire to produce a broad spectrum of objects that people enjoy using. He acknowledges that no two pieces are ever the same, yet he aspires to uniform quality. In a set of goblets he aims for them to be as identical as possible, and believes the personality is in the set rather than in the individual pieces.

Marie Höglund's background was in textile design and weaving, and she admits that her aesthetic is tempered by living in New Zealand. The overlays of raising a family in this environment come through in her work—in the colours and the loose style she has developed. She does the time-consuming decoration—carving, engraving, sand blasting, and painting with enamel paints.

Together the pair have mastered the difficult graal technique first developed in Sweden in 1916. Precise decoration within the glass is possible in this process, which involves layering colours on a bubble of glass, cutting the imagery through the layers while still on the blowpipe, then reheating and shaping the piece. The mixed colours become one layer and the decoration becomes distorted during blowing, which gives fluidity to the imagery. The painted graal process involves applying finely ground glass mixed with an oil medium to the glass bubble before final shaping. The images are often figurative, abstracted and painterly, at times almost naive, the faces seemingly pressed against the glass surface. Others are linear patterns that comfortably encompass the vessel.

In 1994 they established the Höglund Glassblowing Studio, a studio complex that has become a significant visitors' attraction in Nelson. Here they produce work in a rich palette of colours—a far cry from their early works, limited to two colours—and they make their own glass with sand from Mt Somers. Their work is widely distributed in New Zealand, and is exhibited in Australia, USA, Japan and Europe. They have won a number of craft awards, and have work in private and public collections. Importantly, they have contributed greatly to the development of hot glass in New Zealand.

**Ladies with Blue Hair
Painted graal with freeblown incalmo glass
290 mm
Collection of Isobel Rose**

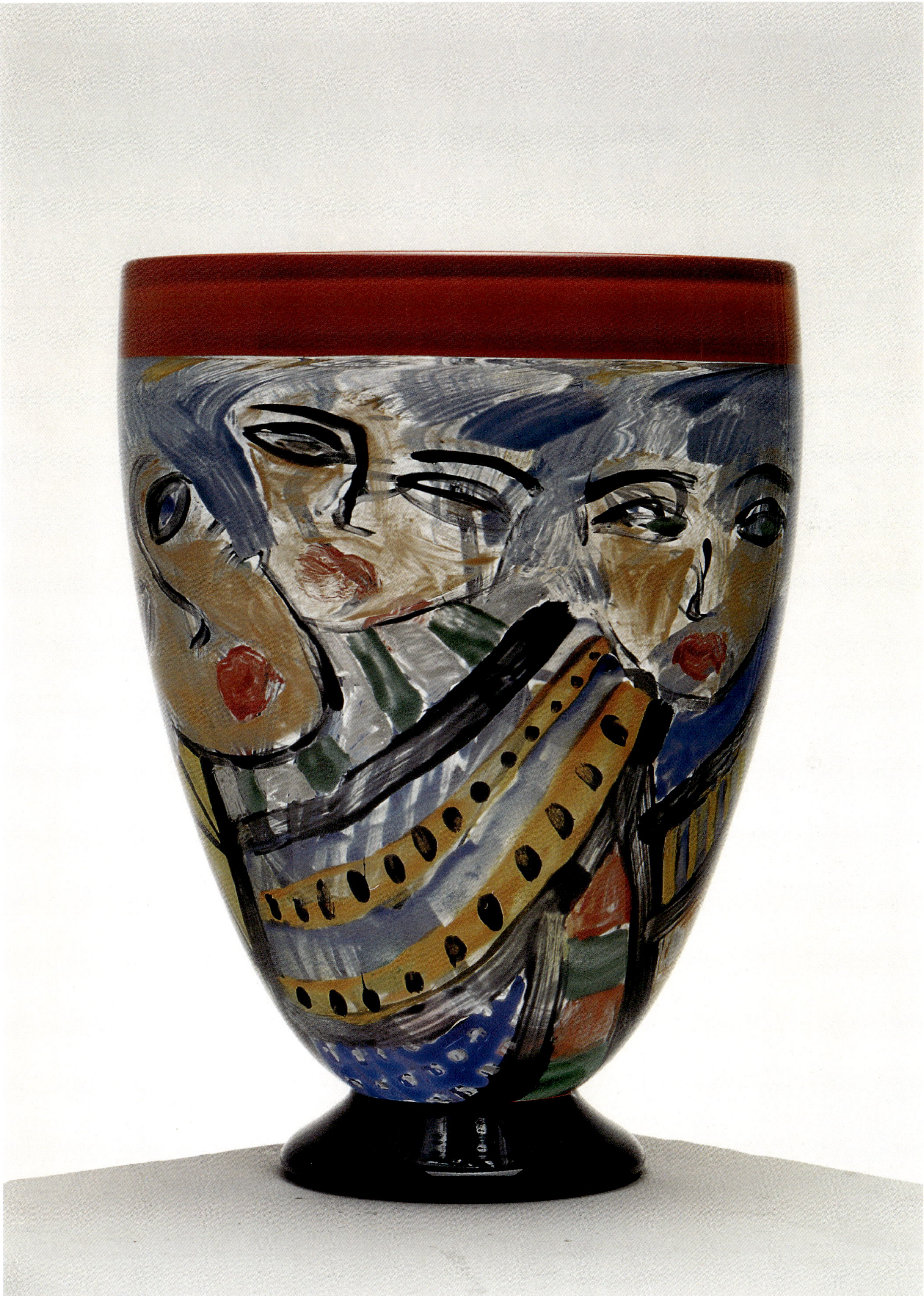

37

SUSAN HOLMES

Born Auckland 1941.
MHSc (Nutrition), University of Otago 1965.
Lives in Auckland.

Fantasy and flamboyance characterise wearable art from the hands of Susan Holmes. Her special skill is in making garments that have personality and movement. Her forms billow and flow from the body, not as a self-conscious device, but as a celebratory characteristic of the fabrics she chooses. Holmes' work is not really about fashion, although her many awards include the Fantasy Award in the Benson and Hedges Fashion Award in 1978; it is more about a spirited journey exploring a wide range of fabrics, dyes and an eclectic mix of supporting materials.

She responds well to an imposed brief and enjoys devising unusual visual ideas, like the quirky commissioned *Montana Duck* in 1997 to celebrate the silver jubilee of Montana Wines. *Dragon Fish*, which won the Supreme Award at the Nelson Wearable Art awards in 1996, was made to the brief for the silk section titled 'Underwater'. Holmes took a lateral approach to the theme after finding a spiky bundle of split cane which inspired her design. Baskets provided the material for the fins; silk, a favourite material, was added to the spine, and she was on the way to creating a graceful, magical female fish.

The process for Holmes is a celebratory one. Many of her materials have come from the beach or from foraging at garage sales and fleamarkets, the source of a wealth of baskets and tapa. The tapa seems appropriate when she works on a Pacific theme. She has had long flirtations with wool, and has used spinnaker cloth for commissioned sculptural work, but her love of the fluidity of silk in all its forms is the most consistent feature of her work, dating back to 1970. There are no limitations to her use of materials: she has even included black shade cloth for the wings in *Rainbow Warrior*, and flexible fibreglass rods to restrain the curved edges of her three-dimensional shapes.

The work evolves from a good deal of loose drawing in which she aims to capture movement and energy. From there she moves to the body form, the tailor's dummy, pinning, draping, exploring the idea. She needs to resolve the design before she can start colouring her fabrics. Holmes' early efforts at applying colour to fabric were by block-printing scarves and tunic shirts. When she started making dresses she was loath to cut into the printing—and that was the beginning of her distinctive process of printing and colouring after cutting out. Since then she has mastered many dyeing techniques, and she uses dyeing, printing and painting as the mood takes her. The dyes are used like watercolours, and she tunes her lively colours by eye rather than formula.

Her skills are now being used for the television series *Greenstone* and *Hercules*. New ways of working to duplicate and replicate, while aiming to achieve a worn look, stretch her vast knowledge of dyeing and printing. Most importantly, she still creates her wondrous, individual, one-off pieces for commissions and wearable art events.

**Dragon Fish
Wearable art,
recycled baskets,
silk, split cane
2 x 2 x 2 m
Collection of New
Zealand Wearable Art**

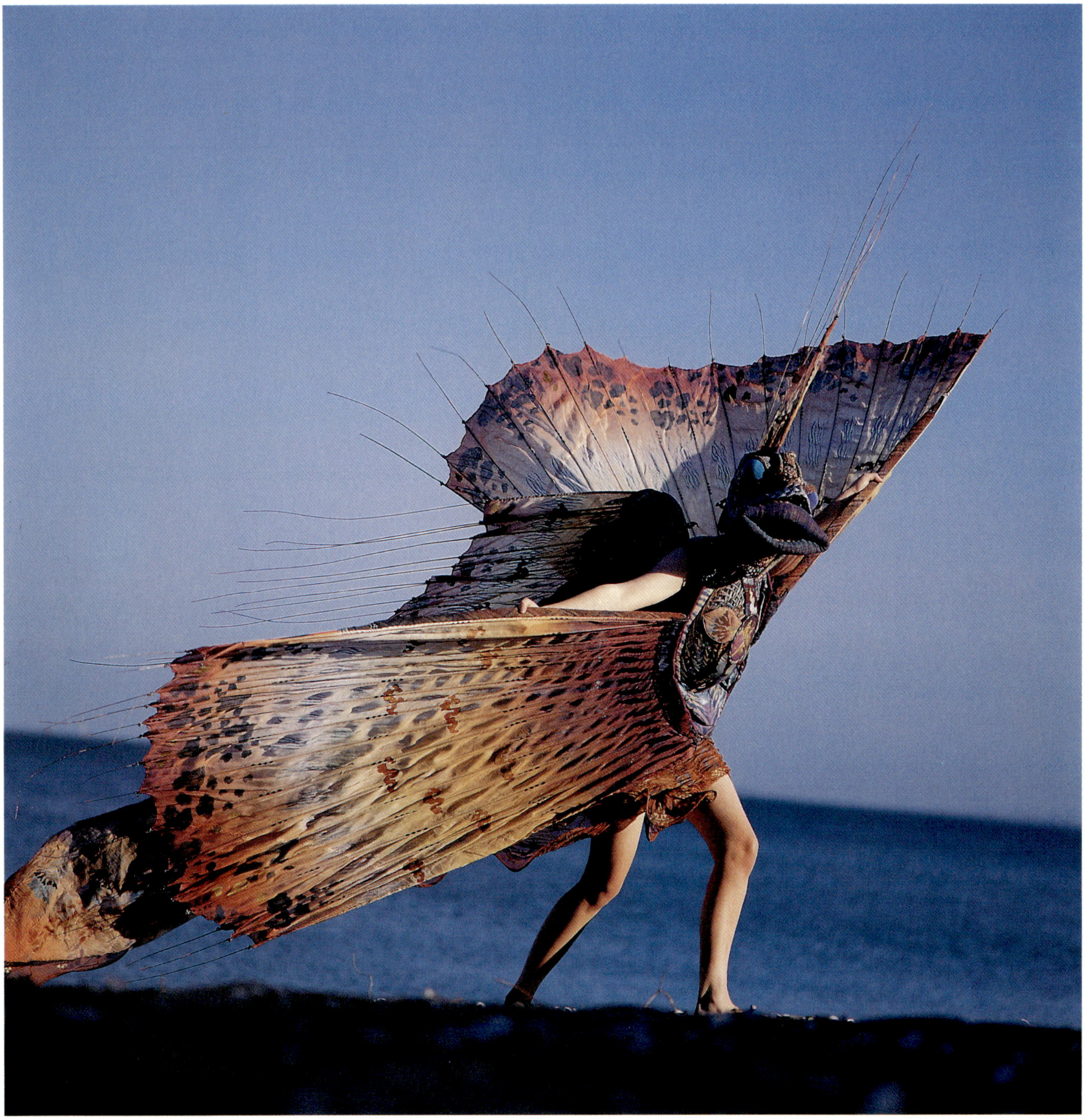

38

MEGAN HUFFADINE

Born Invercargill 1955.
BA, University of Otago 1977; Postgraduate Dip Archaeology, University of Otago 1978;
BFA, Canterbury University 1987.
Lives in Nelson.

Domestic activity and the small rituals that are part of everyday life are the focus of Megan Huffadine's mixed media work, and she brings a questioning, thoughtful analysis to her highly individual pieces. It may be overstating it to say that she addresses human rights abuse and environmental issues through her art, but a humane thread of understanding and caring underpins what she makes, and she looks at ways of making incremental yet significant shifts in people's awareness through her work.

Huffadine is first and foremost a sculptor and a teacher. She creates furniture as a form of functional sculpture—a way of enriching lives in a domestic context and of being accessible to a broad viewing audience. Her work can be perceived as fitting simultaneously into craft art, fine art and design, breaking down the barriers between the genres while firmly focusing on issues of function in its broadest sense. The functional elements become familiar points of reference through which Huffadine explores notions of function, form and content. Her work is layered with meanings and always carries a message, and she combines drawings and sculptural furniture in a single work, allowing the two-dimensional concerns to merge with the three-dimensional.

The composite nature of some of Huffadine's work puts it in the realm of installation. A dialogue between components is established and a human space is defined—to be viewed from outside and to participate in from within. She juxtaposes literal and abstract representations of her ideas which are informed by feminism and sociological concerns. There is a lively interplay between her loose drawing and the endearing, small, constructed details. Painterly colour and surface treatment are important and, for all the serious intent, there is a real joyousness in her approach to detailing. The lovingly created details are part of a conscientious attitude to crafting that mirrors her wider concerns.

Huffadine often makes cabinets; she enjoys the raft of meanings and associations attached to them, including that of a shrine. Doors close over some works, wholly or in part; they function equally well open or closed, revealing or concealing the activity within. Often complex in structure, their purpose extends beyond mere containment. There is a certain playfulness to the relationship between her organic forms and the box-like nature of a cabinet, and the way she handles that relationship and colour becomes the lure to attract closer scrutiny. Chairs, which are sometimes part of her installations, are designed to function well. Huffadine amplifies their purpose, seeing the chair as symbolising stillness, an antidote to busyness, meeting social as well as physical needs.

Her materials are diverse, but an affection for wood is apparent, and she enjoys the diversity of effects possible through carving, painting and other mark-making. The direct involvement with her materials is important, and she includes collage, papier mâché, metals and ceramics in a rich visual vocabulary to produce her unique, slightly quirky compositions of furniture and drawings.

Compassion
Mixed media
Drawing
1300 x 550 mm
Cabinet
1500 x 360 x 230 mm
Courtesy of Judith Anderson Gallery

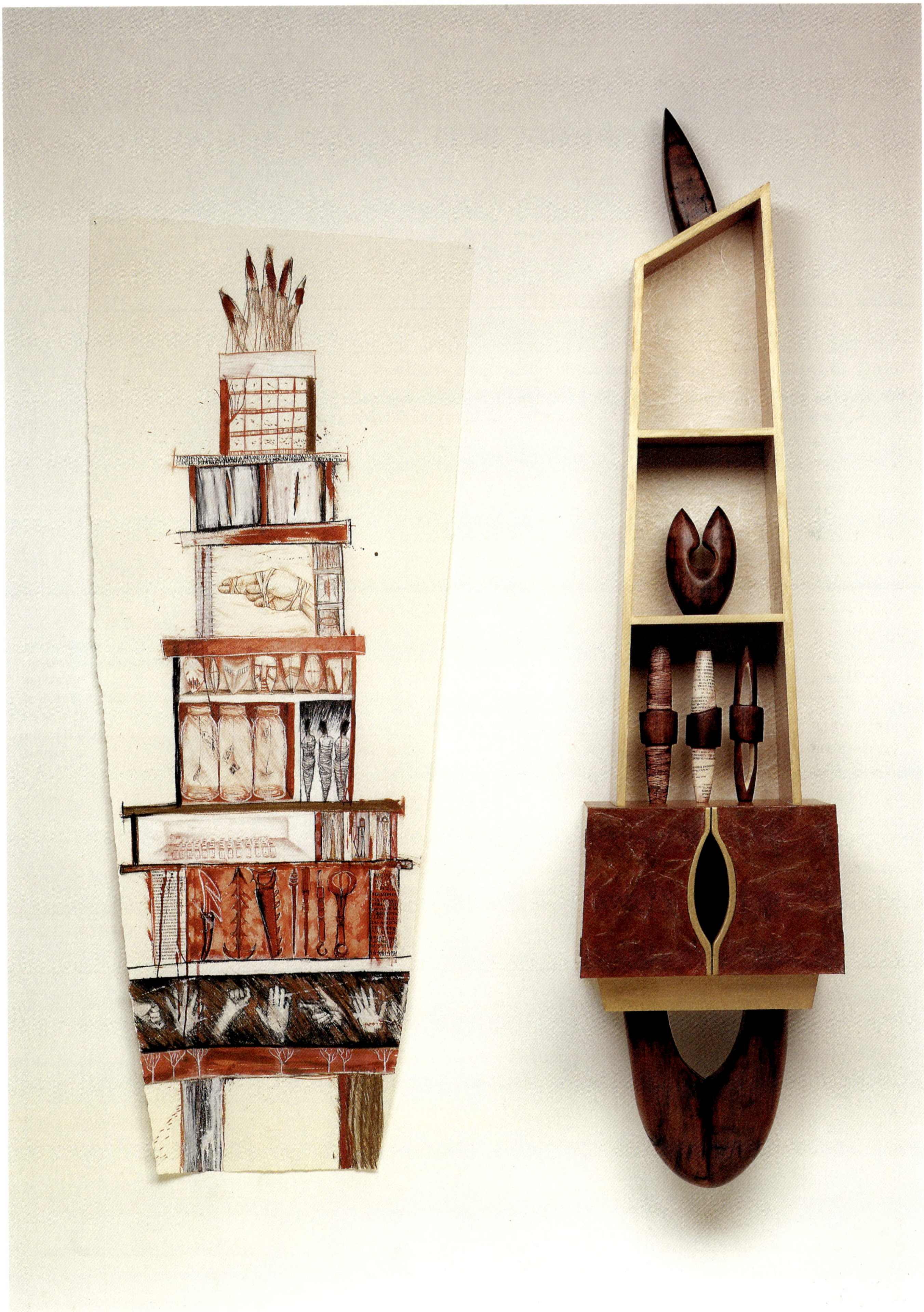

39

HUMPHREY IKIN

Born Lower Hutt 1957.
BBS, Massey University 1978;
School of Architecture, University of Auckland 1981.
Lives in Auckland.

Basic considerations of structure and function are the starting point for Humphrey Ikin's elegantly resolved and superbly crafted chairs, tables and cabinets. He likes to return to first principles, to redefine the 'how' and 'why' of stable construction; to define the components simply and durably, using subtly modulated surfaces and uncluttered forms and details, while treating each piece he makes as a prototype for production. Structural integrity is a major concern for Ikin, and it goes hand in hand with creating visually satisfying work. His works are crisply articulated, and ideas are reduced to their essence.

The notion of modernism is very much alive for Ikin, who believes one can always progress with making functional objects. Exploring the sociology of furniture, who we are and the way we live, he starts with a sense of place, culture and history as essential components of functionalism. His inspiration comes from several sources, but the ideas underpin his work rather than provide direct visual links. He talks of being inspired by the natural world, light on the landscape, the land itself, Rietveld's 1918 *Red Blue Chair*, the benches carved from single tree trunks for Melanesian chiefs, and The Group architects of the 1950s whose aim was to define visually a New Zealand design identity.

Ikin is articulating an emerging New Zealand identity in his work—one that celebrates the materials, the process and the end user. It acknowledges its Pacific location and rejoices in being practical. *Facing North*, a travelling solo exhibition originating at Wellington City Gallery in 1997, was a significant marker in his development. Through his furniture, he defined the phenomenon of living in New Zealand as outward-looking, north-facing and self-confident.

There have been occasions when Ikin has made sculptural works, as stepping stones to new ideas for furniture. He is attracted to processes involving carving and reduction as well as to construction, and has responded to the need for mobility in furniture by reducing its weight through hollowing. Thus a table or cabinet, as exhibited in *Facing North*, becomes a hollow box or channel—a development of his earlier substantial canoe-like serving tables, the weight of which was reduced with sculptural curves and hollowing. The newest works are superbly assured, spare in their forms and classical in composition, while implying a sense of place.

Ikin has a real understanding of the characteristics of wood, and believes that it ages gracefully if treated well. While he regards wood as being without equal, he prefers to retain visual clues to the material rather than to rely on its seductive qualities. Currently his concern is for solid colour—the white wood of American ash, red paint on oak or textured plywood, and black stain on a number of timbers. He also likes to use materials like stainless steel, aluminium or white zinc for their practicality. Using materials with restraint is important to Ikin. He resists using too many materials in any one piece, and believes in building up a room with a number of pieces of furniture, rather than trying to put a whole room into a single object.

Tall Red Shelves
Plywood, eucalyptus, paint, steel
2200 x 600 x 290 mm
Collection of the artist

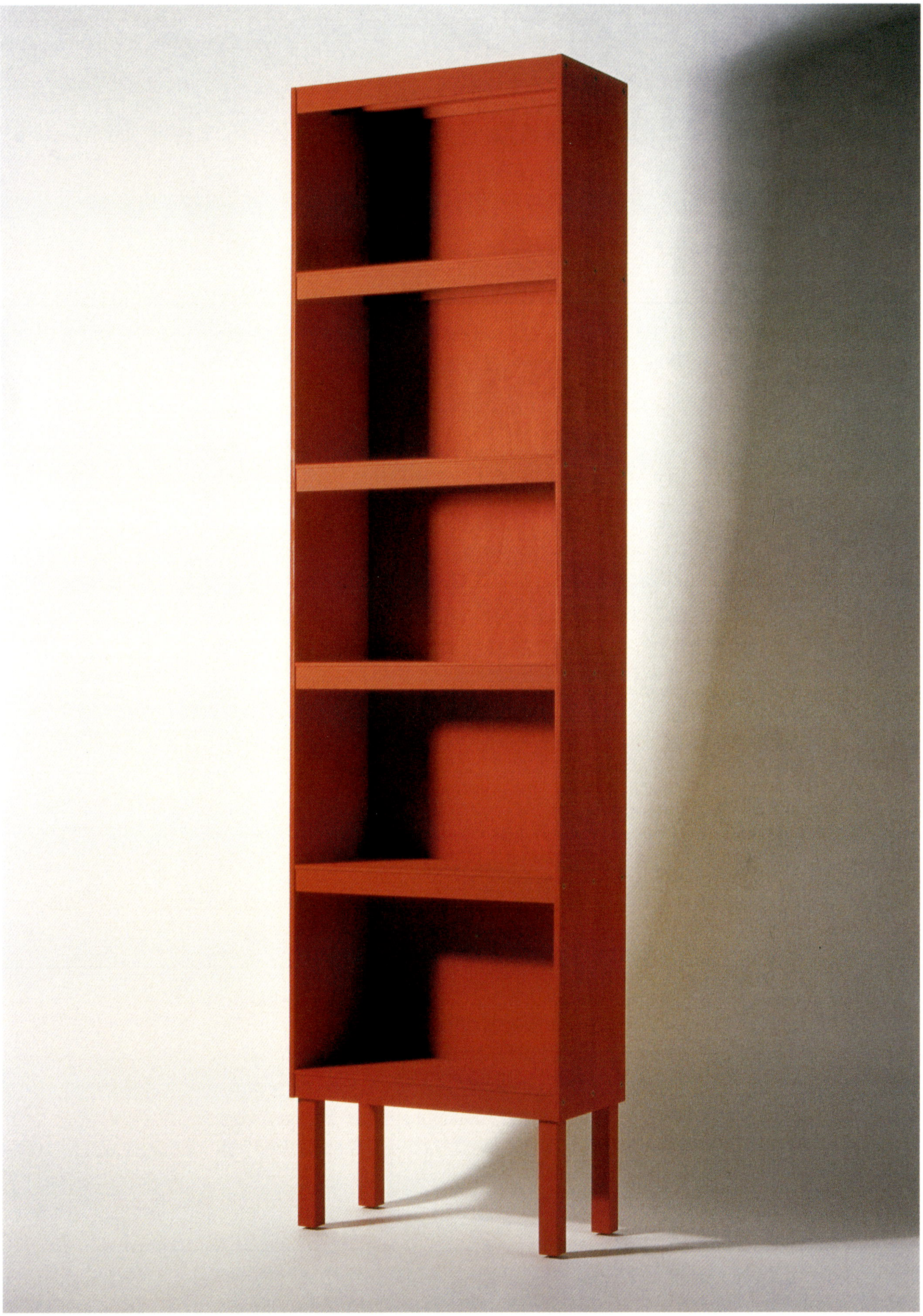

LYNN KELLY

Born Wellington 1957.
Wellington Teachers College 1975–77;
studied for Certificate in Horticulture (by correspondence), Lincoln University 1978–82;
Certificate in Craft Design, Wanganui Community College 1987.
Lives in Dunedin.

Superstition, good luck charms and a sense of humour are part of Lynn Kelly's Irish heritage and her jewellery. The combination produces satisfying, delightful results that make people smile rather than ponder seriously. Kelly uses sayings like 'pinch and a punch', 'loves me, loves me not', 'touch wood' and 'good as gold' as titles which provide fruitful sources of imagery. They are sayings from her childhood, and the images in her newest work have the same easy flow as the words.

She started making good luck charms during a period when her mother was ill in 1996. They were charms given lovingly from daughter to mother—minor humorous works with a serious intent. These charms are sometimes in the form of horseshoes, wishbones or crossed fingers.

The enjoyment of making charms led to her making a bracelet titled *Pohutukawa Flowering before Christmas Leads to a Long Hot Summer*, which combines her current concerns: a sense of being a New Zealander and a longstanding love for horticulture. Her interest in gardens has been both a source of paid employment and a major source of inspiration for her jewellery. She has always produced many drawings based on plants, and has spent a considerable amount of time gardening.

Kelly's jewellery training and her ability to work with silver grew not only from her course of studies but also from working for a manufacturing jeweller and, later, at Fluxus. The early work experience seems very removed from her recent adventures with coconut shell, tap washers and shells. Her use of coconut shell has been challenged for its Pacific Island connotations, but for Kelly the use of the material was pragmatic. She used discarded material from her kitchen as a frugal way to work—a way of accessing inexpensive materials from everyday life. In her eyes the material was an expression of her own domestic environment rather than another culture.

The year 1997 was an important one for Kelly, during which she believes she made considerable progress, creating work unlike anything she had previously made. It began with a three-month residency at Nelson Polytechnic—a period of reflection, intensive production and a chance to explore a very personal means of self-expression. By taking time out from the Fluxus studio where she has been a partner since 1988, she was able to build on the strong crafting base acquired during her apprenticeship. With Kobi Bosshard (8) leading the way, jewellery from Fluxus has been strongly influenced by European modernist design values. This has not necessarily led to a homogeneous style—the emphasis has been more on making things well, and those working in the studio moderate each other's work. Kelly's work has evolved in this environment, but it was time away from the workshop that allowed her to develop a stronger persona, more humour and new self-confidence. More than ever before, her work now bears a personal stamp, one that reflects her heritage and her passions.

**Loves Me, Loves Me Not necklace
Sterling silver, freshwater pearls
820 mm long
Collection of the artist**

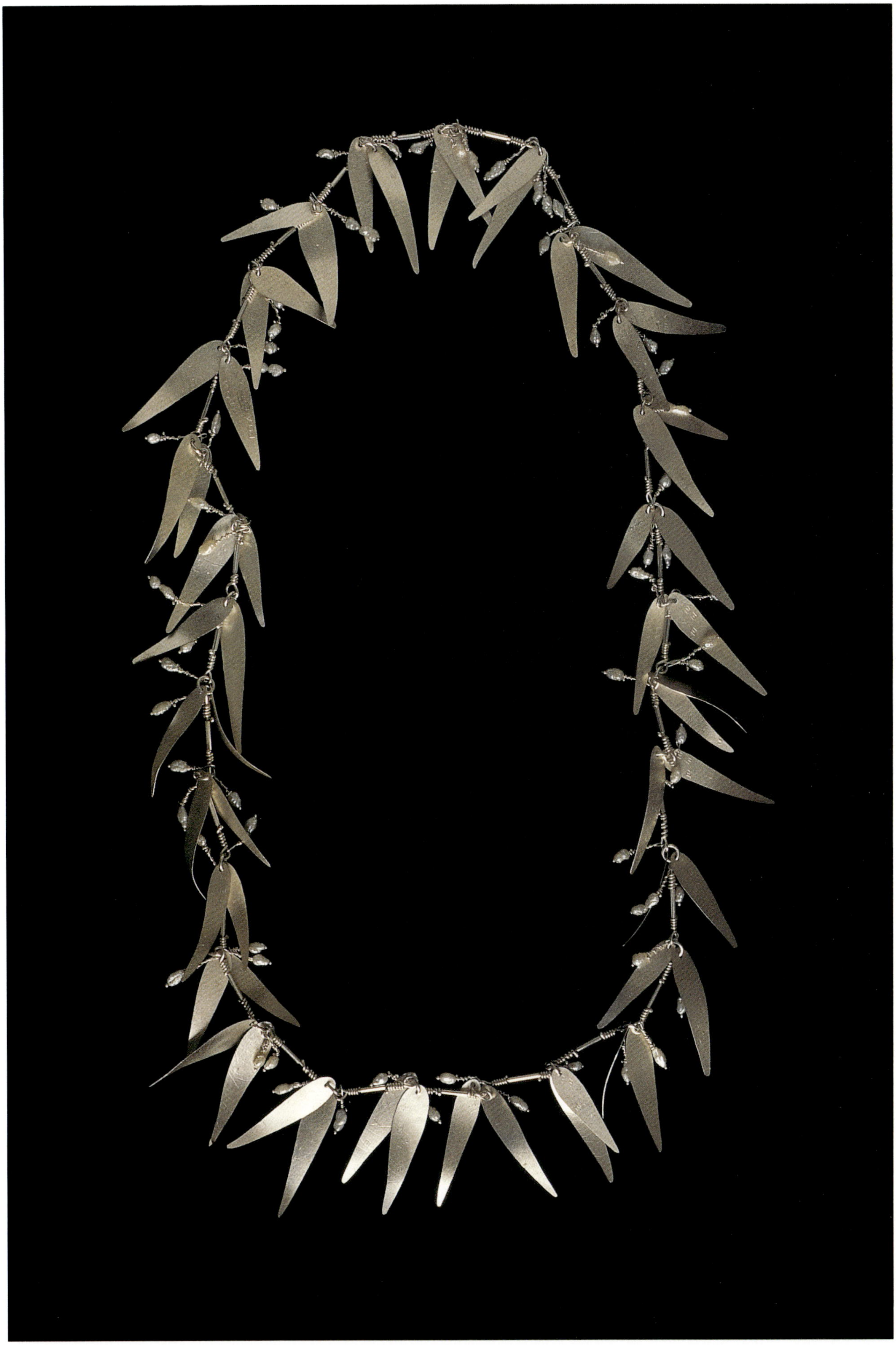

HILARY KERROD

Born Darlington, England 1946.
Educated Kiribati, Tuvalu and Waiheke Island.
Auckland Teachers Training College 1966; Dip Craft Design, Carrington Polytechnic 1990.
Lives on Waiheke Island.

Family narratives in the form of screen-printed images feature on a number of Hilary Kerrod's clay works, several of which have won awards. Making these works is part of her way of collating and integrating differing views and images of her parents after their recent deaths.

For the past decade Kerrod has been handbuilding what she calls 'quasi-functional' vessels which reflect life events. Her forms reveal her process, and she likes the idea that one can see how the clay has been wrapped and where it has been joined. Using ceramic ink she has made herself, she screen-prints on to thin slabs of moist clay, then joins the slabs. By this process the photographic images become integral to the clay rather than sitting on the surface, and give the work a depth of surface and a layered, slightly degraded appearance.

Clay hasn't always been Kerrod's preferred medium. When she went to Carrington Polytechnic in the 1980s, it was to work with fibre. She already had considerable knowledge about weaving, colour theory and percentage dyeing. She acknowledges the important part Bronwynne Cornish (Vol. 2, 19) played in introducing her to clay while she was a student. The fibre processes soon appeared in her clay work—as rope-like tops on her vessels, as fabric-like surfaces using resists and printing, and as textures reminiscent of weaving patterns.

Kiribati weaving was a part of Kerrod's childhood that she needs to claim as a cultural connection, capturing, honouring and celebrating it in her work. Integrated with her printed figurative images are fragments of text: some feminist writings and, more recently, precise information about fishing from an English/Gilbertese dictionary. On her works she wants to record events and stories, to tell truths which are revised when new ones are discovered.

Symbolic figures of women as vessels have been another theme in Kerrod's work, which invariably includes the human form in some way. Dancing in Kiribati is a precious memory, and with it goes an interest in bodies and in the way the dancers moved. She has also wanted to understand anatomy, and found her involvement with a life clay group gave her an understanding of volume and of the body in space. With this knowledge she felt free to play with the proportions, to enlarge the bodies and portray the heads as tiny. Her figures, often women wearing headdresses and carrying handbags, are personal statements. She sees handbags as a rich feminine symbol, fulfilling women's desire to conceal, reveal and contain, to be separate from the outside world—a similar metaphor to her vessels.

One group of work was about the non-human proportions of Barbie dolls and the archetype of ideal woman. Kerrod made dolls which were surreal in their proportions, anti-ideal and anti-Barbie, and they included a group of Egyptian Barbies. Another series was about male figures seen as hunters, gatherers, explorers and handlers of the TV remote control. An ongoing series of enchanting clay whistles is incidental yet integral to Kerrod's work.

Tamnei
Slab built from screen-printed slabs of white clay
190 x 100 mm
Collection of the artist

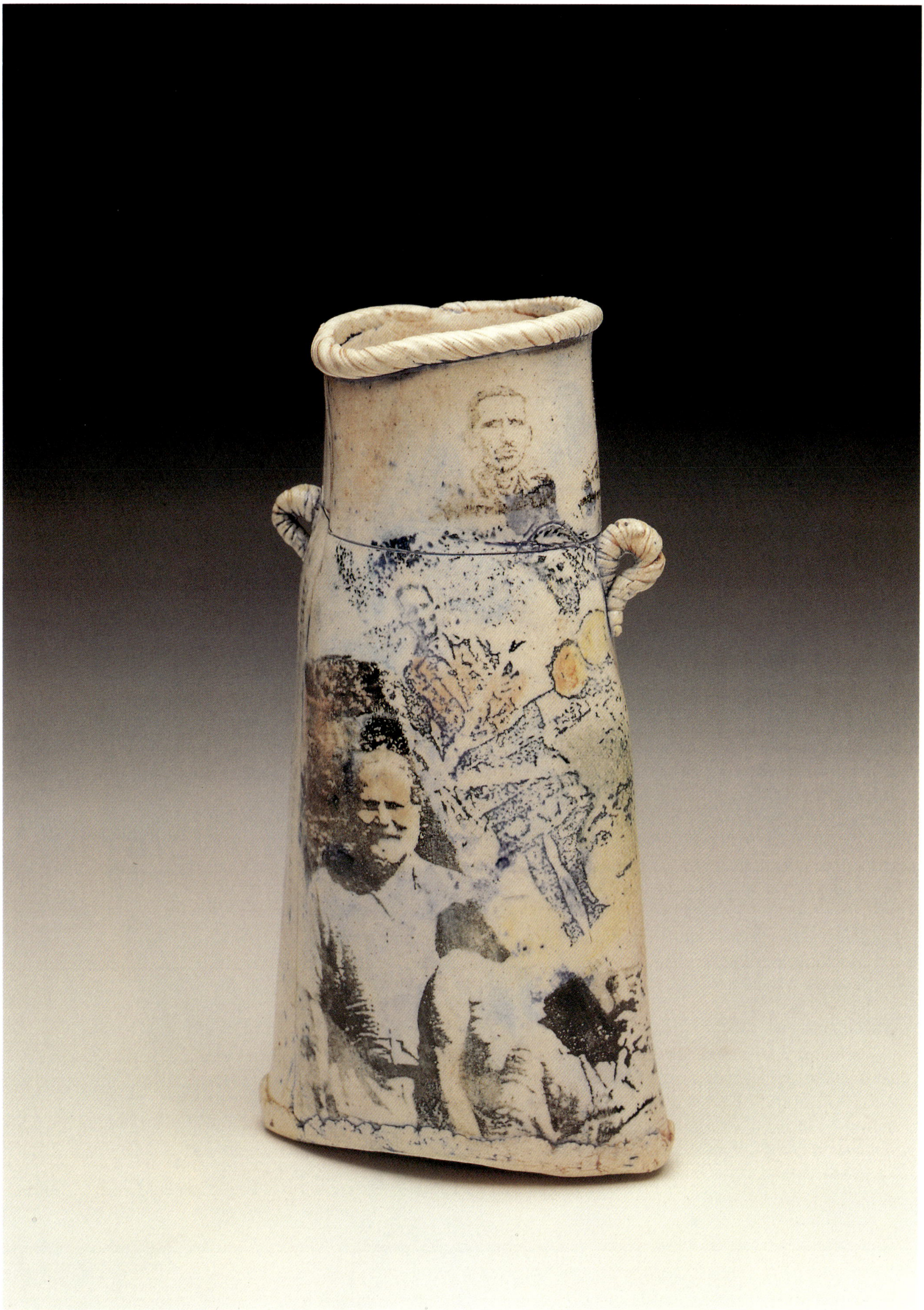

HEATHER KILGOUR

Born Hamilton 1969.
DipFA (Sculpture), Otago Polytechnic School of Fine Arts 1990;
Arts papers, University of Otago 1991, 1994, 1995; currently completing MFA, RMIT, Melbourne.
Lives in Dunedin.

Using traditional craft techniques like crochet, weaving and forging steel is Heather Kilgour's way of subverting the art/craft dichotomy. Although she comes from an art background she enjoys moving between the two genres, blurring the boundaries of functional and non-functional objects like chairs that cannot be sat on and clothing that hangs in a gallery. Her work tends to be ideas-based rather than in a single medium. She makes political posters, but specially relishes working with steel, despite its inherent health risks.

There is an element of rococo in Kilgour's work. Her aesthetic preference reveals swirls and curls, but recently she has pared down her forms. She has moved from visualising work in a two-dimensional fashion—reducing a chair, for instance, to separate planes. Her forged pieces have an organic quality and are formed by black lines in space, the spirals and curves taken from nature.

Kilgour's most ambitious project is a forged steel gate. It has been part of her life, on and off, for the past seven years. She started working with steel while at art school, after which she gained access to a forge at the Dunedin Early Settlers Gasworks Museum, and has recently moved to the Chestnut Tree forge. The process appealed because of its directness. She had been casting paper from plaster moulds and had created metal armatures to support the life-size cast-paper figures. Frustrated by the reduction and distortion of the cast paper, she decided to create not just the armature but the whole work from steel. The gate is the first of a pair. The human figure has been painstakingly created to human scale—a guardian which functions as readily alone as it will when accompanied by its partner.

In another project, as a celebration of harakeke, Kilgour created a large throne-like seat in collaboration with fibre artist Robyn Webster. She created the curved steel structure of the chair, basing her design on the form of the flax plant, while Webster wove the seat and back of the chair. The weaving pattern also became a motif in the steel frame and in the seat, reflecting Webster's work. Kilgour was inspired by the expansiveness of churches in her youth and their large scale contributed to the generous size of many works, including the seat. The form of the chair is also used in a number of pieces made in reference to gender issues. The throne was conceived as a seat for women who had reclaimed their power. Kilgour likes playing with stereotypes and creating ambiguous expressions. Her work on gender issues includes a set of androgynous shields.

In contrast to her work in steel, Kilgour created a very delicate work woven from her own hair. Flax seeds were placed inside the tiny woven vessel, making a political statement about pharmaceutical companies appropriating seeds—a large issue expressed in minute form. Between the extremes of expression and size she makes domestic objects—pokers, candlesticks and lamps; ornate, decorative, one-off pieces. They make reference to details observed in churches as well as to forms found in nature, and are a means of developing a lively visual vocabulary.

Gate panel
Forged plate steel
1870 mm high
Collection of Anne Kilgour

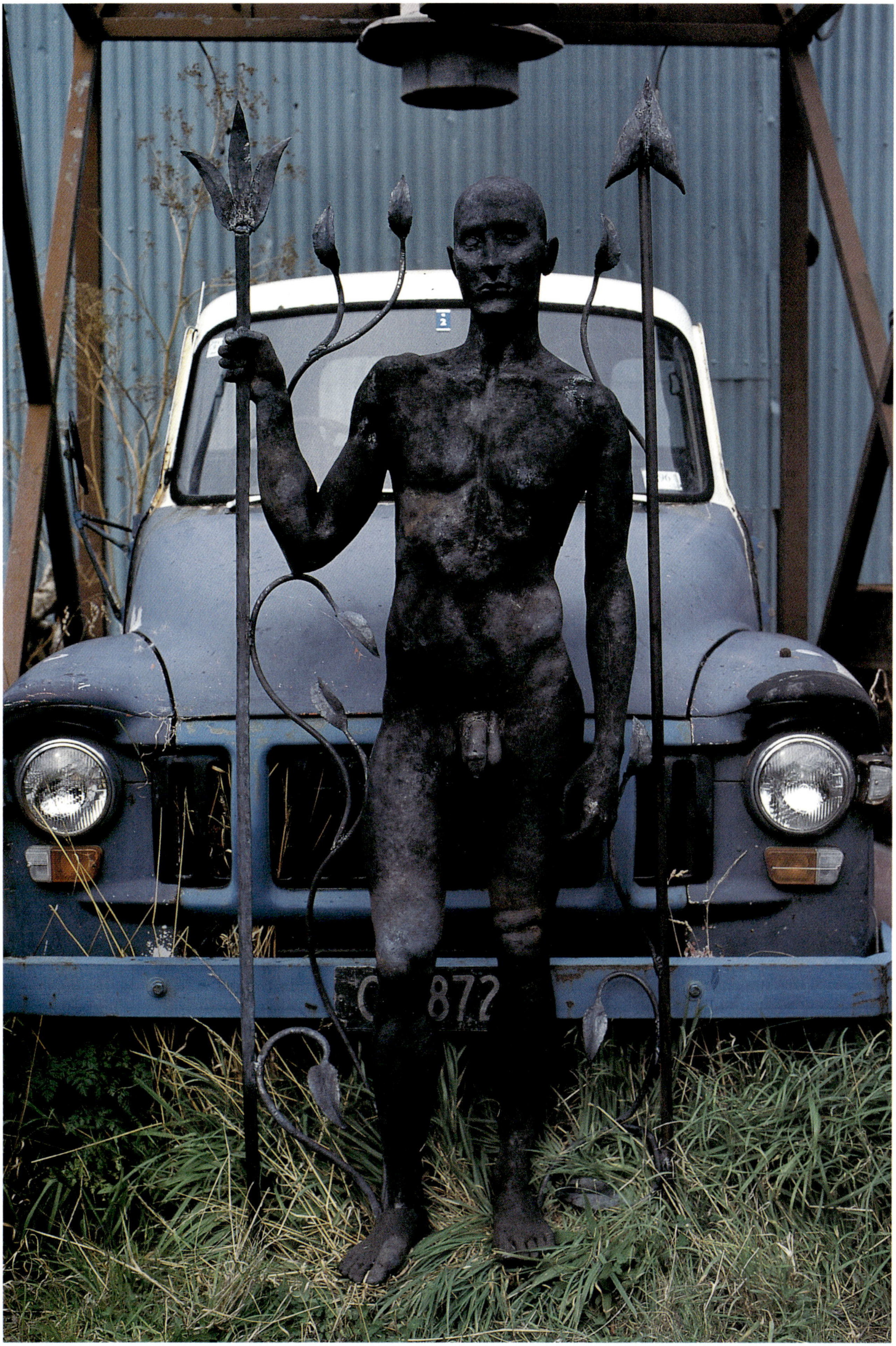

43

RANGI KIU

Born Wairoa 1968.
Ngati Kahungunu.
Craft Design Certificate 1987.
Died Havelock North 1998.

Rangi Kiu had his first and only solo exhibition at Hawke's Bay Museum in 1997. It marked, for him, the end of the apprenticeship he considered necessary after completing his studies. That decade had seen him learn about the history and traditions that informed his use of harakeke. He taught part time at several polytechnics during this period, attended workshops to develop his repertoire of skills, and showed work in a number of exhibitions throughout the country.

His early work was mainly in the form of ink drawings and paintings informed by kowhaiwhai, whakairo and tukutuku. The sculptures that followed were in wood and bone, inspired by the work of Fred Graham. Birds have been a recurring theme in his work, representing messengers, weavers, spirit carriers and taonga.

His most significant work has been in harakeke, with issues of whakapapa as a background. Eddie Maxwell, also a Maori weaver, was one of his mentors. Kiu became known for kete using exceptionally fine strands of harakeke, and some spectacular sculptural fibre works. He perceived links between fibre and wood, the traditionally gender-defined media in Maori culture, and chose to work with both, thereby creating a highly individual creative path. He recognised the relative newness of contemporary fibre art, and his decision to work experimentally was to break down barriers to innovation and change perceptions of Maori flax work.

A period of study and research at Auckland Museum in 1996 taught him a great deal about cloaks. He was inspired by their beauty and qualities of fine crafting. His response was to undertake a cloak similar in style to those that were to be seen when Cook first arrived in the country. Kiu created border panels that owed as much to European traditions of twill as to taniko weaving. He chose not to work with the soft, processed muka of the old cloaks, preferring undyed, unbeaten harakeke strands which became a characteristic of his weaving. The material he used had body and sheen, and he loved the play of light moving across the finely woven areas. He chose to work in a labour-intensive way, and the fineness of his weaving meant that his cloak was destined never to be finished.

The most dramatic of Kiu's works are skeletal forms that hang in open spaces representing the space between earth and sky. They relate to the body, and to structures of houses, their heke and pou—rafters and posts. His interest was in developing the techniques of constructing these works, the changeable shapes and planes they form. There was pleasure in the way they collapsed and were portable, enabling different interpretations in different environments. To give the works weight, some parts were left to curl like piupiu when they dried, and only the ends were stripped to the inner fibre. Compared to the extraordinarily fine work of the cloak, these were relatively quick to produce.

The most recent recognition of Kiu's talent came when he was awarded the 1998 Hawke's Bay Craft Award. His unexpected death, days after this, halted a career that was in full flower.

**Hono/Wehe/Hono
Join/Separate/Join
Harakeke/flax
1000 x 600 x 600 mm
Collection of the artist's family**

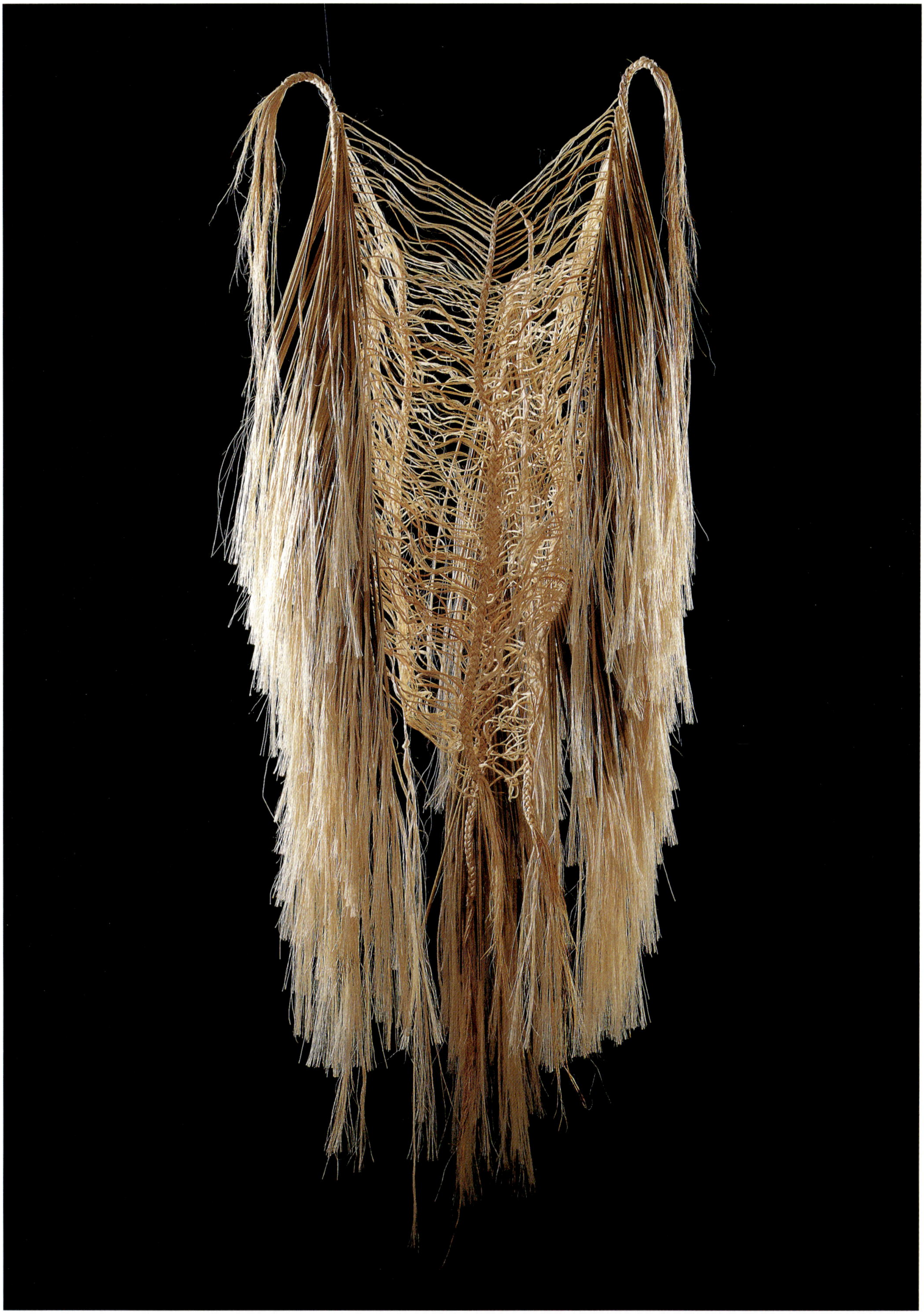

MAUREEN LANDER

Born Rawene 1942.
Pakeha, Ngapuhi-Te Hikutu, Hokianga.
BFA (Photography), University of Auckland 1987; BA (Maori Studies), University of Auckland 1989;
MFA 1st Class Hons (Sculpture), University of Auckland 1993.
Lives in Devonport, North Shore City.

Maureen Lander's art is connected to craft traditions through fibre materials and process. She creates large mixed-media installations—beautiful, ephemeral, sculptural works about fibre, light and space. Many installations have incorporated silky muka, extracted from harakeke leaves, as well as other parts of the flax plant, used in new and traditional ways. There is, in her work, always a sense of her direct manipulation of the fibre, as well as a love and respect for it. Lander came to art through sculpture and photography, and both continue to be significant.

Dual heritage plays an important part in Lander's work, and many pieces explore and extend the traditions of Maori fibre art juxtaposed with Western art practices and contexts. From Maori weavers—Diggeress Te Kanawa (83), Hinemoa Harrison and Eddie Maxwell—she learnt to work with indigenous fibres like harakeke, kiekie and pingao. She has a strong commitment to the conservation and sustainability of pingao, one of the materials traditionally used to 'dress' the walls of a new meeting house. She also turns to nylon monofilament, plastic netting and fine wire where appropriate. By creating installations in public galleries she feels she is working in a Pakeha way, but she honours her Maori heritage through links she makes to whakapapa, land and natural resources. She also takes inspiration from the work of Marcel Duchamp. Many of her installations have been formally resolved, their multi-layered content distilled to a simple visual statement with a pithy title.

Lander is fascinated by new media, including light-sensitive finishes and moving images. *String Games*, her most dynamic installation to date, was installed early in 1998 for the opening of Te Papa, the Museum of New Zealand. It is rich in meaning and visual pleasure, with changing light rhythms playing on the structure in a magical way. Video clips are linked in content to the luminous strings in space, which form patterns surrounding the large Maori figure 'Whare Kehua' in the centre of the work. The video includes traditional and contemporary Maori string games, some taken from films by James McDonald in 1919 and 1920. In the centre of the installation is a replica of Duchamp's *Boite en Valise—The Portable Museum*, which is held in Te Papa's collection. Her reference is to Western art practices and museum contexts. A second video depicts Duchamp's images being unpacked and the box repacked with photographs of string figures collected by James McDonald and Johannes Andersen for the Dominion Museum (now Te Papa).

A lecturer in Maori material culture in the Maori Studies Department at the University of Auckland, Lander also undertakes a very full exhibition programme in galleries and public spaces. Her work has been featured in a number of publications and exhibited widely throughout New Zealand and in Australia. Through various gallery projects she has received Arts Council/Creative New Zealand grants. Significantly, she has worked collaboratively on a number of projects, sometimes with other artists and sometimes with members of the community. This remains an important aspect of her work.

**String Games
Multi-media
8000 x 8000 x 4500 mm
Collection of Museum of New Zealand, Te Papa Tongarewa**

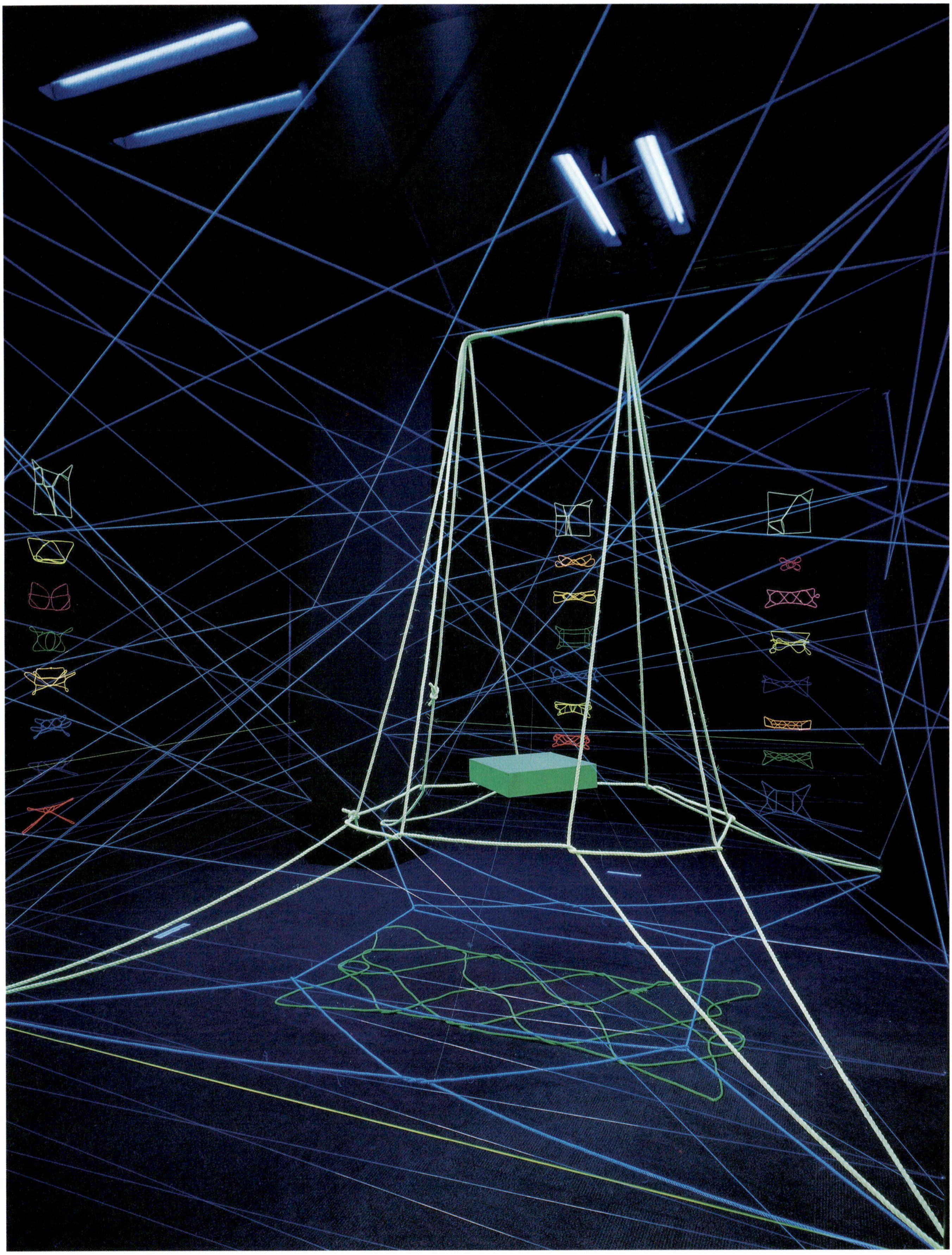

PHILLIP LUXTON

Born Whakatane 1959.
Worked in family production pottery 1980;
collaboration with painter Max Gimblett 1990–93.
Lives in Auckland.

Phillip Luxton's life has revolved around clay since he began working in the family production pottery. He had worked briefly as a landscape contractor prior to that and developed a love for gardens that has informed his work. For fifteen years he has made formal, functional works like birdbaths, fountains and urns. He looked to Japanese ceramics for inspiration for a number of years, then turned to small, funky domestic ware. He started to define his own personal style when he started making larger, more earthy vessels. His signature pieces became very large, heavily grogged terracotta clay works that seemed to defy the limits of working by hand. Developing these works was encouraged by a substantial QEII Arts Council grant in 1988.

He spent considerable time developing his studio at home. Once he had facilities for large works, his dilemma became how to combine the desire to work to this scale and yet retain an immediacy and spontaneity in the pieces. A number of works became sculptural, but a realisation that they were driven by technical considerations rather than aesthetic ones pushed him to re-evaluate his work. From 1990 to 1993 he collaborated with the painter Max Gimblett (Vol. 1, 29) on a number of projects. During this period Luxton developed techniques of loose, uncluttered, painterly applications of colour and a new sense of self-awareness.

Luxton's abstracted sculptures have been evolving steadily since that period, sometimes with oblique autobiographical references which reveal a layer of vulnerability and humanity. The theme of the life cycle—from birth to death, celebration and loss—underpins these works. Many pieces are now human scale—generous and organic, occasionally with reference to the body or, more frequently, the plant world. The glazes he has developed are often brushed on like paint.

His main body of work continues to be large vessels. Designed for longevity, these carefully crafted works are as considered and labour intensive as the sculptures. They express the more ordered aspect of his personality, and are made for galleries and commissions. His organic approach is conscious rather than self-conscious, often embellished with architectural motifs and ornamentation that have more than a passing reference to the nineteenth century. Details, occasionally as additions of clay, are generally carved, and his palette is restrained.

Recent work includes three large bas relief murals which assemble a number of different components. These are proving to be an exciting challenge. Parallel to this work are also new developments in his free-standing sculptures. He has always worked with steel, mainly for making machines associated with his studio or as armatures for large works. The attraction of steel in its own right has led him to explore works that incorporate it as an aesthetic component, not just for structural strength. Luxton acknowledges the limited life of rusted steel, but it appeals as a sympathetic companion material to clay. With the visual introduction of the new material, connections between components have become important. However, his commitment to clay and the clay community is fundamental, and he never strays far from it.

Urn
Terracotta
1300 x 650 mm
Collection of
G. Brookfeild

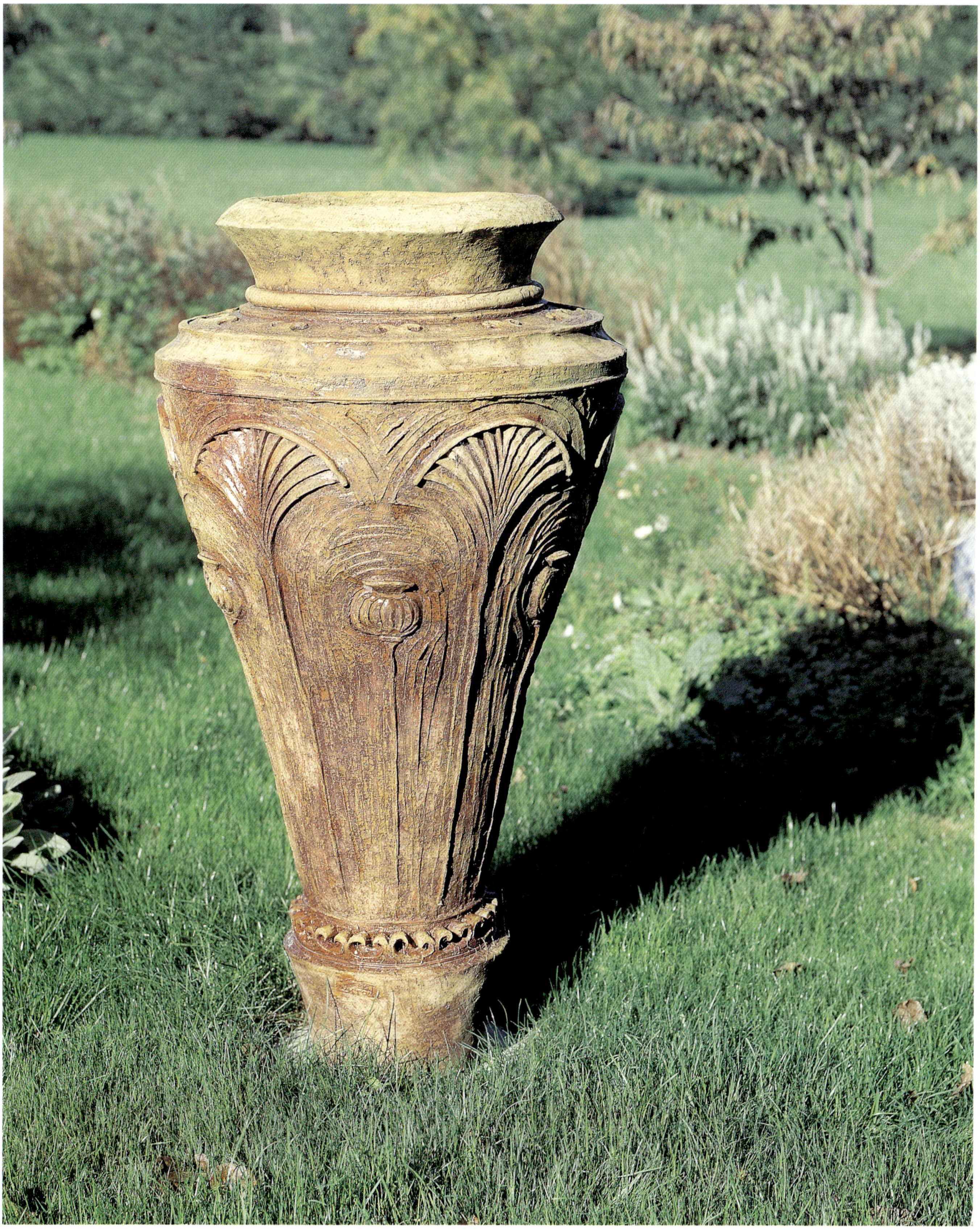

46

TOI TE RITO MAIHI

Born Hastings 1937.
Ngai Te Ipu, Ngai Te Apatu of Ngatikahungunu, Ngati Hao of Tai Tokerau, Bland family of Yorkshire.
Primary Teaching Certificate, Auckland Teachers Training College 1954; lifelong education in Maori art.
Lives in Kaikohe.

A fascination for kelp goes back to Toi Te Rito Maihi's childhood. She remembers gathering kai moana with her father, filling sacks to share with other families. With the last sack filled, her father sliced an opening in a long broad ribbon of kelp with a knife, put his fingers inside to break the spongy interior, made a fist, then pulled the sleeve of kelp up his arm like a wrinkled stocking until the whole length opened. The kelp sack was filled with paua. Maihi's memories of kelp are associated with plentiful, beautiful food and she remembers, too, how muttonbirds were preserved in their own fat in the kelp containers. Her fascination for traditional Maori fibres led her beyond these traditions about the land. In 1986 at the exhibition *Karanga Karanga*, shown in Wellington, Auckland and Gisborne, she began to express her love of the sea by using kelp. She created small pockets that she filled with stones and shells, and plaited the 'tails' of kelp. They became some of her most distinctive images, and she created a very large work in this genre for the Wellington City Library, in 1987.

Maihi's parents were storytellers and she grew up surrounded by art. Her mother drew and painted, and gave her a love and understanding of the power and beauty of words. Her father wove kete, carved and knitted, and gave her a love of music. Maihi longed to weave, but her father taught her sister instead, leaving Maihi to fight for the knowledge, thus ensuring that she would treasure it. As a teenager at Queen Victoria School for Maori Girls she began to research taniko and raranga, and since then has drawn, photographed and recorded different fibres and techniques, and the articles made from them. She has never had any formal art tuition and started making art intuitively as a young mother. Some of her earliest paintings in 1976 were of interlacings of harakeke—the raranga patterns that she knew. Over the years she has moved from one medium to another, referring to weaving and kowhaiwhai to tell her stories.

When Maihi produces work in fibre it is often contemporary in expression, but she follows tradition in that she creates visual metaphors and analogies to tell the philosophies and stories of her culture. Using her knowledge of fibre and the stories surrounding it, she draws parallels between fibre structures and how society functions. She believes that by applying a visual format to social aspirations she can create new understanding of social policy. For Maihi it is more important to use art forms in the wider community than in galleries, and she enjoys working communally and collaboratively. In 1990 she designed the Maori component and helped to make the Commonwealth quilt which was conceived and designed by Carole Shepheard. In the same year she wrote and illustrated *Pakahe! Pakahe! Whalesong*.

She has exhibited extensively within New Zealand, and internationally in Australia, USA and Germany. Her work includes teaching, which is very important to her: she describes herself as a 'provocateur of creativity'. Maihi continues to be involved in curating, consulting, ambassadorial roles, and networking with other indigenous cultures.

Circles
Kelp and water pebbles
2500 x 500 mm
Collection of the artist

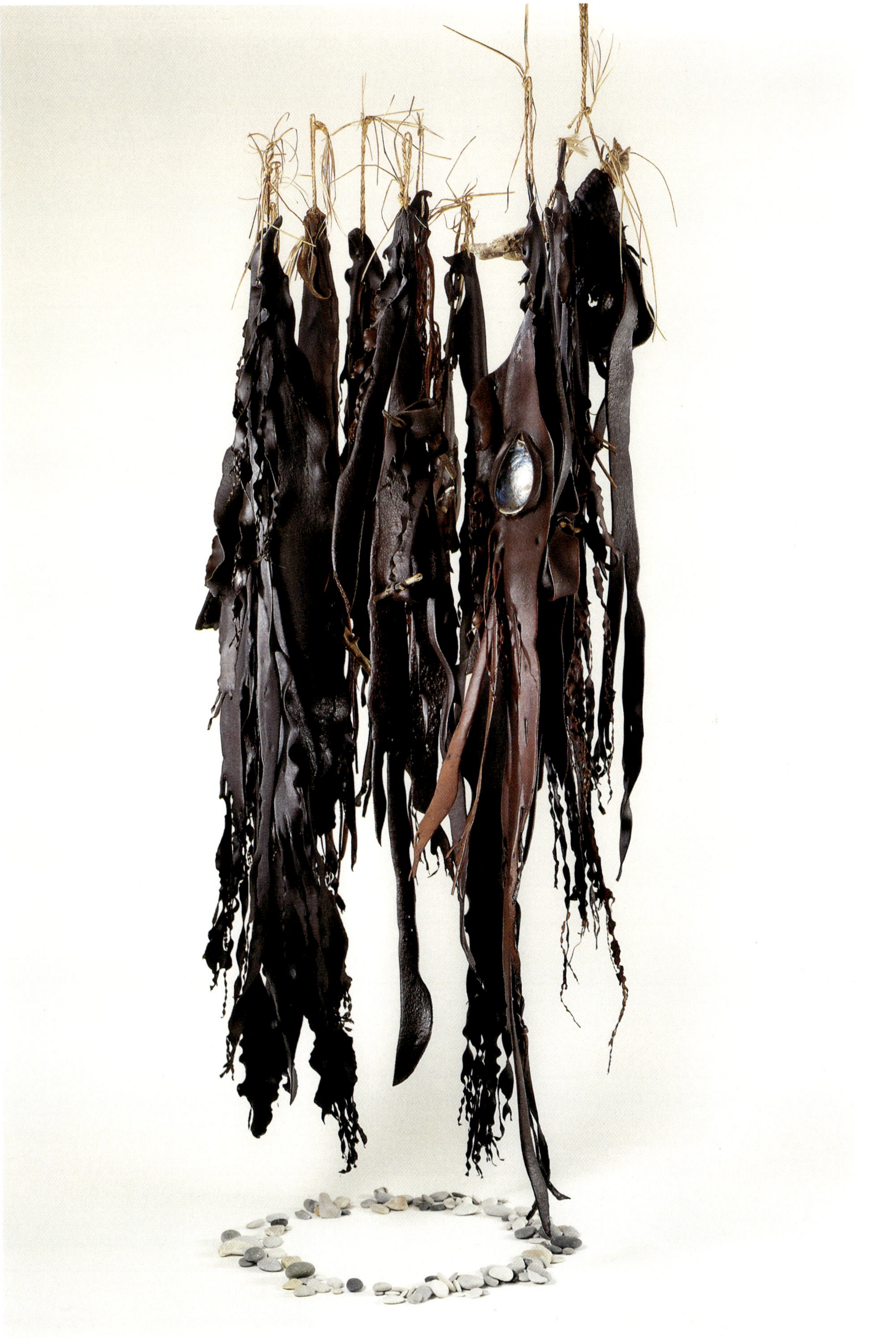

LINLEY MAIN

Born Auckland 1949.
Studied architectural glass at Derix Glass Studio, Kevelaer, West Germany 1986;
studied architectural glass at Chartres Cathedral, France 1990.
Lives in Auckland.

Linley Main's passion for glass started in 1978 during the early stages of the studio glass movement in New Zealand. Her earliest successes included exhibiting in *Young New Zealand and Australian Glass*, which toured Europe in 1984, and winning the Craft in Architecture Award in 1985 with a collaborative entry created with Douglas Roberts, a graphic designer.

With the assistance of QEII Arts Council grants in 1986 and 1990 she went to Europe to learn more about the medium. She observed in the work of German designers an emphasis on structural elements and a strong focus on the architectural qualities of the window. At the workshop at Chartres, the focus was more on restoration and contemporary painting. Both of these strands became strong influences on Main's development and as a result her work gained in confidence, revealing an interest in structure combined with a painterly quality.

An awareness of interior design and architectural features provides a background to her commissioned work. Main encourages the involvement of her clients, as individuals or committees, in developing the brief and in the selection of glass—a process that creates trust and rapport. Rather than limiting her, this gives her a frame of reference and a starting point for her designs.

A private commission in 1996 for the owners of a restored bach at Piha encapsulates Main's process for the development of ideas. The interior design, references to art deco, the external environment with its nikau palms and tree ferns, and a scrapbook of images provided by the client were her starting points. Resolution was simple and effective: using stylised imagery she combined sandblasting the glass with a painterly approach to applying colour.

A number of marae projects, working beside Maori master carver Paki Harrison, have been important commissions. Most significant was a commission in 1996 at Harrison's own marae at Kennedy Bay, Coromandel. That work, which was mainly sandblasted, evoked the destruction and regeneration of the Coromandel bush. Ever sensitive to cultural issues, Main consults when using Maori narrative and motifs in her work. Ecclesiastical commissions have confronted Main with contrasting architectural challenges. Recently she has completed work for two Anglican churches, the historic St Peter's in the Forest, Bombay, and the new Christ Church, Papakura, designed by Professor Toy.

Most of Main's work is site specific and commissioned by private clients. The economic crisis in 1987 adversely affected commissioned architectural glass, which was readily classified as a luxury, and many of her colleagues working in this way left the country or undertook other work. Main continues by combining her interests in working in flat glass with other design activities. She was a founding member of the New Zealand Society of Glass Artists, and has been actively involved in its work through conferences, workshops and exhibitions. Glass still inspires her and she remains passionate about it as a medium for enhancing architectural spaces.

Living at Piha
Glass and lead, glass
paint and silverstain
600 x 620 mm
Collection of Tracey
and Steve Skidmore

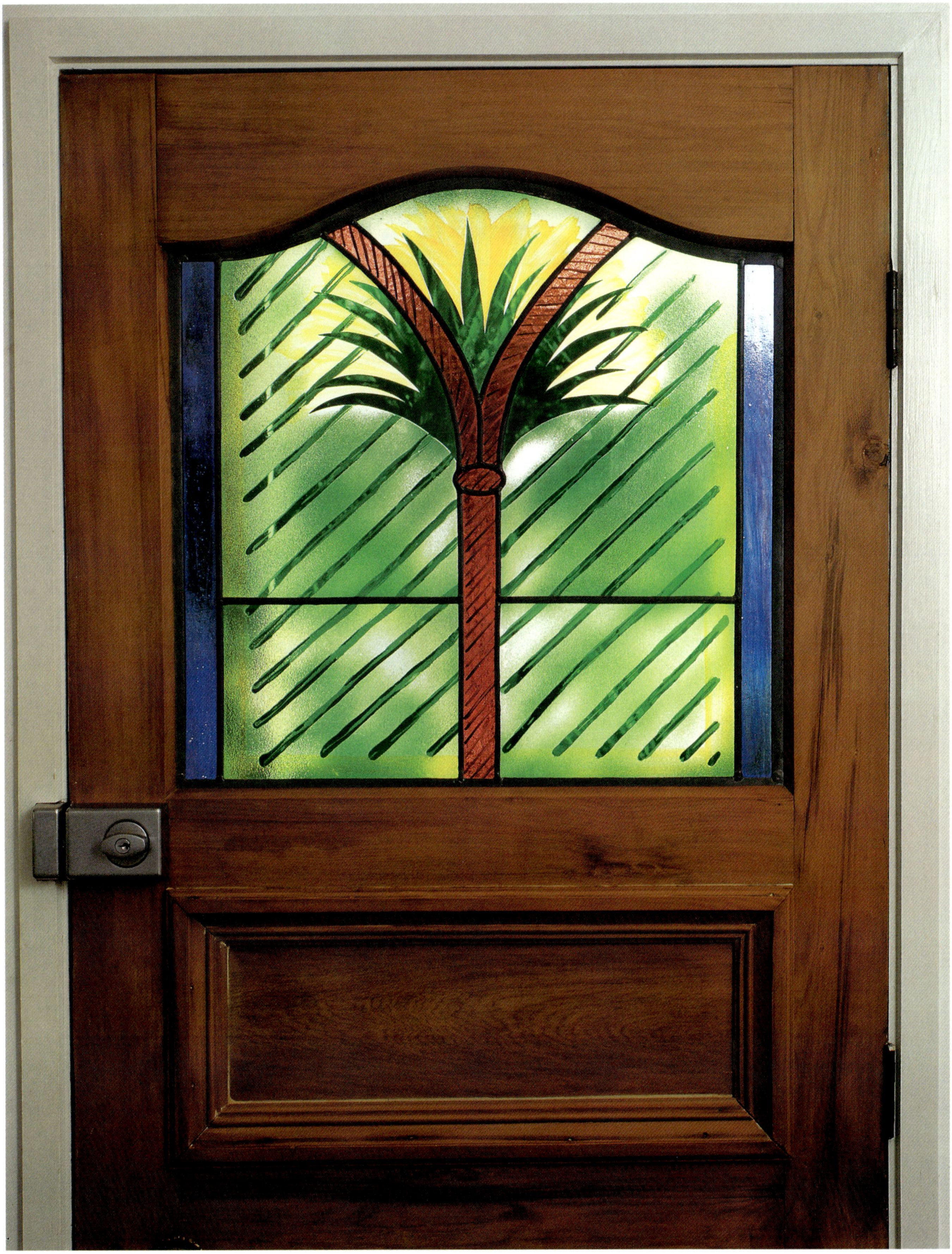

48

OWEN MAPP

Born Blenheim 1945.
Student archaeologist, Canterbury Museum 1956;
museum assistant, National Museum 1964; ten years of travel, study and research in many countries.
Lives in Paraparaumu.

Owen Mapp's early interest in archaeology introduced him to Maori amulets of jade and whale ivory, which stimulated his interest in carving. He undertook intensive research into carving during his extensive travels. In the 1960s he worked in museums in Sweden and England, and at the Masada excavation in Israel.

His earliest bone carving in 1969 was with a pocket knife, rasps, files and drills. He became the first contemporary professional bone carver in the country at a time when most Maori carvers worked with wood and few people worked with jade. His biggest breakthrough, in 1970, was the discovery of steel hand gravers used by an Australian jeweller to produce controlled engraved marks. This simple technology, which later became a subject of his teaching, was the same as that used by Scandinavian stone or flint gravers 10,000 years ago.

Initial influences were Maori and Polynesian and, later, Scandinavian and Asian. In 1979 he exhibited internationally and researched netsuke collections in Denmark and Sweden. He adopted the format but not the imagery of the Japanese netsuke as a vehicle for his ideas. Netsukes by definition are three-dimensional works to be held in the hand, unrestricted in process or material. Originally they were made from a natural wood root, and were designed to act as toggles above an obi (sash). A double cord attached to the back of the netsuke is passed under the obi and is held together by a small bead (ojime). A small box (inro) is hung from the cord.

In 1990, with a QEII Arts Council study grant, Mapp established a connection with the Japanese netsuke carvers and since then has exhibited with the Japan Carvers Association. In 1994 his work was included in *Treasured Miniatures: Contemporary Netsuke*, a Japanese curated exhibition for the British Museum and Los Angeles County Museum of Art.

Mapp's interests extend to making utensils, small sculptures and body adornment. Like the netsuke, which is carved on its base as well as on its visible surfaces, his knives have surprises like carving on their ends as well as on the handles. In some works he makes reference to sexual balance by the depiction of genitalia. He likens these to European works dating to 6000 BC. He is best known for his exquisite bone carving but also makes silver 'landscape' brooches from cuttlefish castings, influenced by William Sutton (Vol.1, 86), a Canterbury painter who makes use of the natural attributes of cuttlefish bone.

Mapp uses spirals which have been likened to Maori imagery. He believes that he has interpreted many influences, including Maori, rather than appropriated them. It is significant for him that a number of his works have been commissioned by Maori and, in 1976 and 1977, he was a guest artist at exhibitions of Nga Puna Waihanga, an organisation for contemporary Maori creative artists.

Mapp teaches at Whitireia Polytechnic and continues to exhibit nationally and internationally. He has worked in television production, and has designed for the New Zealand National Film Unit. His work is held in international collections and he has been commissioned to create gifts for the New Zealand government. He eschews the term 'master carver' but is nonetheless one of the most proficient carvers in the country.

Melting Snow, Mountain Stream Running, Fallen Feather—Sake cups and feather netsuke
Cowbone
sake cups 90 mm (h); feathers 130 x 50 mm
Collection of the artist

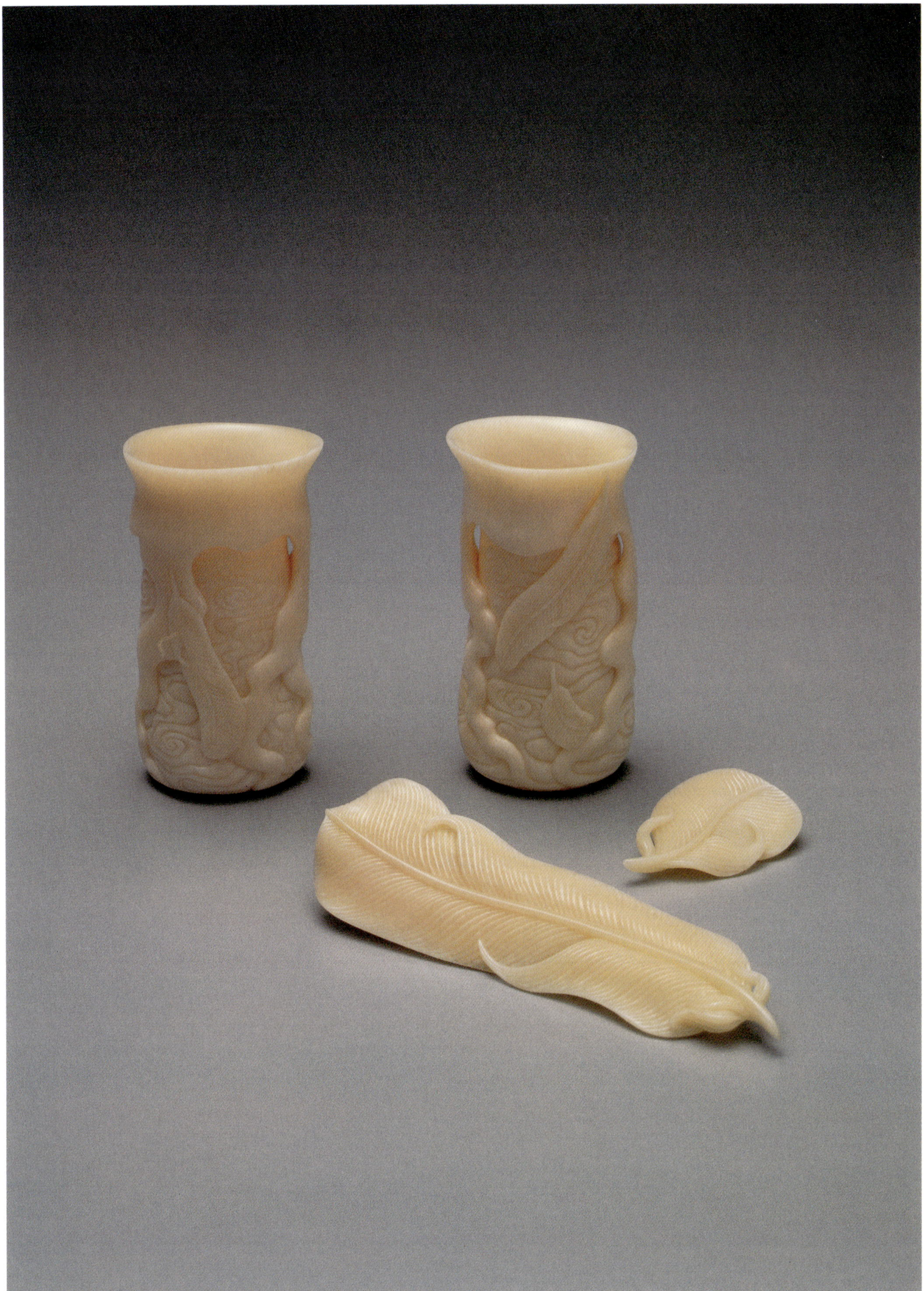

PAUL MASON

Born Marton 1943.
Self-taught.
Lives in Kaeo.

Paul Mason's work has always been unashamedly minimalist. His recent, very large stone pieces, several made in India in 1996, are linked to earlier works in that many still allude to the vessel. He believes that vessels are his last connection to the Crafts Movement, in which he has played a significant part.

When Mason started creating jewellery in the mid 1970s, he did so intending to earn his living this way. He never saw himself as a jeweller, rather as a maker of objects. He worked in an advertising agency after leaving school and spent time in Australia. His father had been an engineer, and like him Mason developed an affinity for machinery. An innate artistic sensibility, an appetite for reading and an interest in Zen Buddhism led to an exploration of Japanese culture, aesthetics and attitudes to materials which influenced him for over a decade.

He soon developed a reputation for superb craftsmanship in wood, bone, shell and metal, and incorporated precious resources like ebony, hardwoods, jade and precious stones. He made earrings, pendants, cufflinks, rings and necklaces, but what specially caught the public's imagination were the small, Japanese-inspired, exquisitely inlaid wooden boxes originally designed to contain jewellery.

In 1980 Mason moved to Mangaweka, where he created very detailed, tightly conceived works. He made less jewellery; the boxes became larger; and from these evolved a series of inlaid bowls. In the heady, pre-crash days of the 1980s he was also commissioned to design furniture and fittings, including some for the National Library in Wellington.

With a move to Whangaroa in 1990, Mason's personal work became self-confident and expansive. He relinquished the Japanese influence, defined his own style and no longer wanted to be seduced by beautiful materials. His interest in tools was for how they performed. Subtly finished stone forms, expressing volume, mass and density, became his main interest—purer, more sculptural forms than ever before. He identified with the work of the French Dadaist Jean Arp, Japanese/American sculptor Noguchi, and Greek/American Dimitri Hadzi. He also started to make simply formed, richly coloured, cast-bronze bowls and platters. He enjoyed finishing them with patinas, which he compared to putting colour on canvas. The recipes for the patinas were his own, and he found pleasure in the dangerous exploration of volatile chemicals.

Accolades have included being sent by the Crafts Council to teach in India in 1979. He taught at Elam School of Fine Art in the early '80s, and in 1985 was appointed cultural ambassador by the New Zealand government. He has received several QEII Arts Council grants and many commissions, and has exhibited widely, nationally and internationally. In 1998 he was nominated for the prestigious Seppelt Contemporary Art Award in Australia. Recent royalties from designs for a series of manufactured door handles have liberated him from financial constraints. With that has come new freedom to create from stone what he most enjoys. This takes him into ambiguous territory that is at odds with contemporary fine arts practice yet also beyond his craft roots: as always, Mason is creating his own place.

Adrift
Granite
2760 x 600 x 300 mm
Private collection

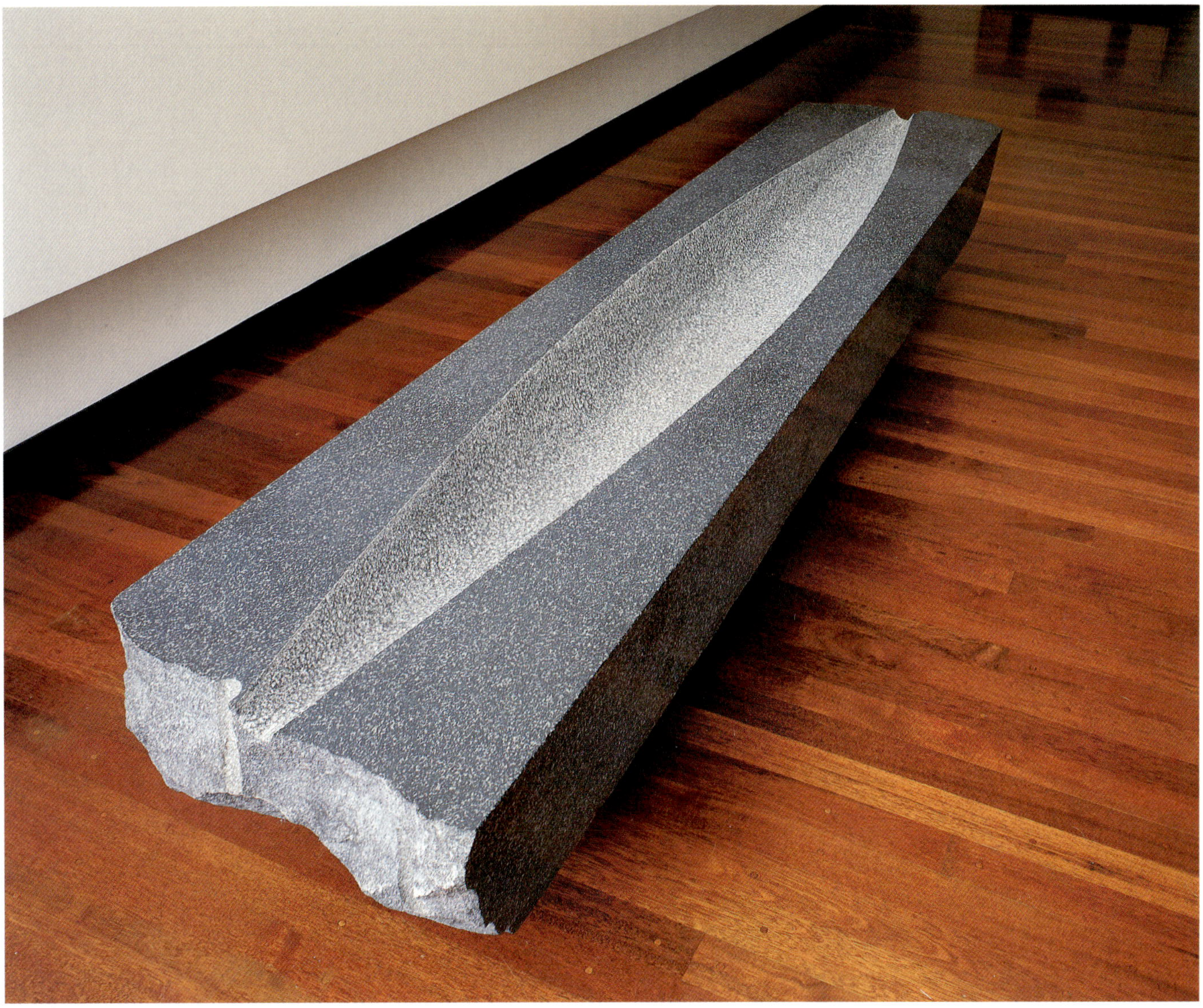

ELIZABETH McCLURE

Born Lanark, Scotland 1957.
Dip Art (Glass Design), Edinburgh College of Art, Scotland 1979;
Postgraduate Diploma, Edinburgh College of Art 1980.
Lived in New Zealand 1987, settled in New Zealand 1993.
Lives in Auckland.

A life of travel and a rigorous art education in Scotland form a rich backdrop to Elizabeth McClure's glass. Work experiences include a British Crafts Council project with Wedgwood Glass, and production work in various studios including Dent Glass in England and Isle of Wight Glass. She worked as a designer for Senami Industries while living in Tokyo and has taught in England, Eire, Japan, Australia and New Zealand. She has received a number of awards and residencies, her public profile is considerable, and her work has been represented in a number of prestigious international and national exhibitions and publications.

McClure's glass reflects her diverse background, and reveals a broad vocabulary of skills including blowing and casting. This technical expertise is a primary attribute of her work, but she aims to retain techniques as her servants. It is difficult to believe that when she started working with glass, colour was not the most important element. Her student involvement in weaving was significant, and informed her later work, particularly in the use of colour.

In 1984 McClure was invited to teach in a private glass art school in Japan. She stayed there until 1986 and exhibited on a number of occasions. The first invitation was to participate in an exhibition of bottles, a new vehicle for her ideas and a chance to analyse the unique properties of bottles. She created some that were like drops, akin to test-tubes, which made reference to Egyptian amphorae. They were suspended between a solid base and top, in a link with her earlier weaving interest, and tied to the structure with fibre. Her desire was to show the bottles as small precious objects, about the scale of a woman's compact in a handbag. The later *Marui* (round) bottles developed from this time in Japan.

McClure also worked on architectural glass projects in Japan, using a lot of sandblasting. This was a far cry from her miniature bottles. It took some time before she reconciled the different strands in her work and recognised that the common thread was mark-making. That mark-making continues to be a significant characteristic: at times within the glass; currently, penetrating the surface.

She spent 1987 working in New Zealand, and from 1988 to 1993 lived in Australia. There, while continuing to work with bottles, she experimented with large incalmo bowls, the multiple parts of which were joined while hot, allowing her to trap brilliant colour inside the glass.

McClure reduced her scale of working to a more intimate one while on a fellowship at the Creative Glass Center of America in 1997, when she experimented with small open bowls and blew a number of blank forms ready for surface decoration. Back in New Zealand she has been applying diamond and stone-cut marks to the bowls, engraving, sandblasting and adding painted colour. The work has changed, revealing a richer palette than the sometimes agitated primaries which characterised earlier work. She attributes the shift to the colours of Samoa she encountered at the South Pacific Arts Festival in 1997. Motherhood, the American residency and the Samoan experience have contributed to her present direction. They have introduced a new softness, less obvious virtuoso performance, more inner strength and tranquil beauty.

**Ipu Laulä'au—
Leaf Bowl
Blown glass, green underlay colour, black overlay colour, intaglio wheel cut using diamond wheels. Machine and hand ground and finished
140 x 100 mm
Private collection**

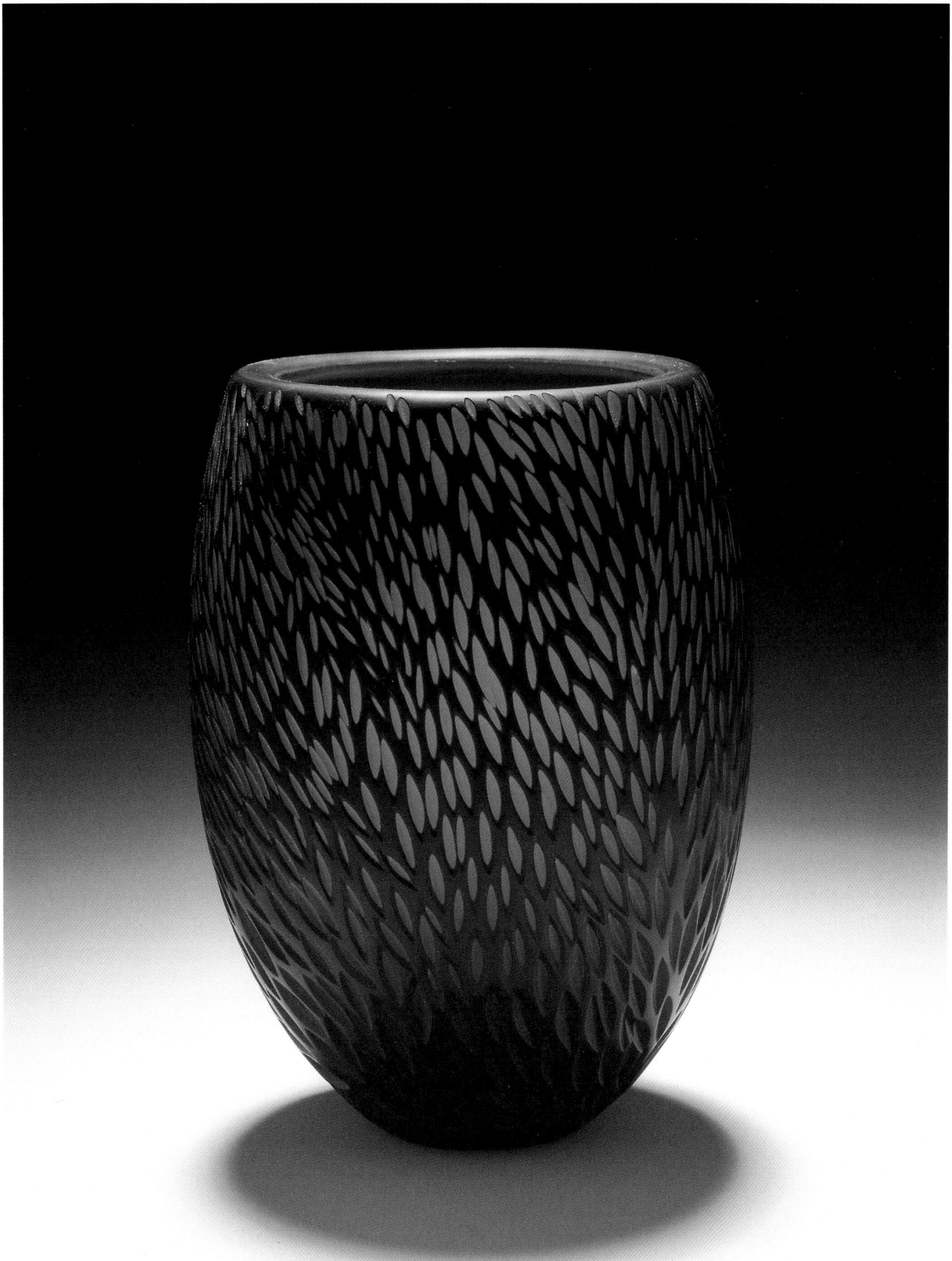

51

ROYCE McGLASHEN

Born Nelson 1949.
Apprenticeship at Waimea Pottery 1966–71; qualified as Master Potter.
MBE for services to ceramics in New Zealand 1989.
Lives in Brightwater, Nelson.

Nelson is known as a centre for ceramics, and Royce McGlashen is one of the best-known exponents from the region. For more than thirty years he has worked with clay, and exhibited widely in New Zealand, Australia, England, USA, Singapore and Seoul. An impressive list of achievements includes Merit Awards at the Fletcher Brownbuilt Pottery Award in 1983, the Fletcher Challenge Ceramics Award in 1987 and the Winstone's Craft Biennale 1989. In 1989 he was awarded an MBE for services to ceramics in New Zealand.

He has combined working as a craft artist with related business ventures. In 1984 he established Mac's Mud Company, producing stoneware and porcelain clays. In 1989 he started designing for Temuka Pottery and he was part of a team that in five years changed the pottery from a declining, non-decorated pottery operation to a thriving industry of colourful hand-decorated ware. He sees this domestic manufactured work as reflecting a New Zealand lifestyle—the way we live and serve food. The vessels and plates are designed to complement our flavours and aesthetic sensibilities.

Currently McGlashen produces mainly domestic ware and works on paper. The teapot has been the focus of his attention for a number of years. In the 1980s he became known for a number of innovative, witty, sculptural, non-functional teapots. They were symbols—icons of New Zealand life—and had grown out of practical domestic forms. Lately he has reclaimed the functional teapot. Clay sculptures now take a different form. Some have become tributes to friends and their lifestyles and passions. They are handmade rather than slipcast, with titles like *Sea of Houses* and *Toolbox*.

Another group of works has evolved into hill-like vessels with tall chimneys. Inspired by time spent at D'Urville Island, they represent the ruggedness and isolation, the real blue of clean air and sea, and nights with brilliant stars 'boring into his head'. He has experimented with images that refer to the environment, galaxies, and the reflections of stars in the water. On the island nothing shines except on the water, so his work is roughly tactile, created by brushed-on coloured slips with abstract motifs scratched into the surface. Any stream of thought is superseded by the need to make and to let the imagery evolve from his hands in an intuitive, practised approach.

The process for these sculptures gives very different results from earlier work. In the 1980s his finishes were inspired by watercolours, and he created effects like washes, with overlays, wax resists and painted lines. He used sulphates and salts of metal which oxidised and burnt off in the kiln. McGlashen's mother was a watercolour artist who encouraged him to work on paper, and he worked in similar ways on paper and clay. He liked the vibrancy of gouache, using big brushes to create bold strokes, and was interested in working with colour and painting flowers—simple, uncluttered ideas with energy rather than story lines.

Occasionally he applies the same imagery to both paper and domestic clay objects, and an interaction develops as the images move backwards and forwards. The volume of the often small clay works invites human involvement, a certain intimacy—perhaps a quality he discovered when he was originally taught by Jack Laird at Waimea Pottery.

Shepherds Delight
White clay/dry slip
450 x 300 mm
Unknown ownership

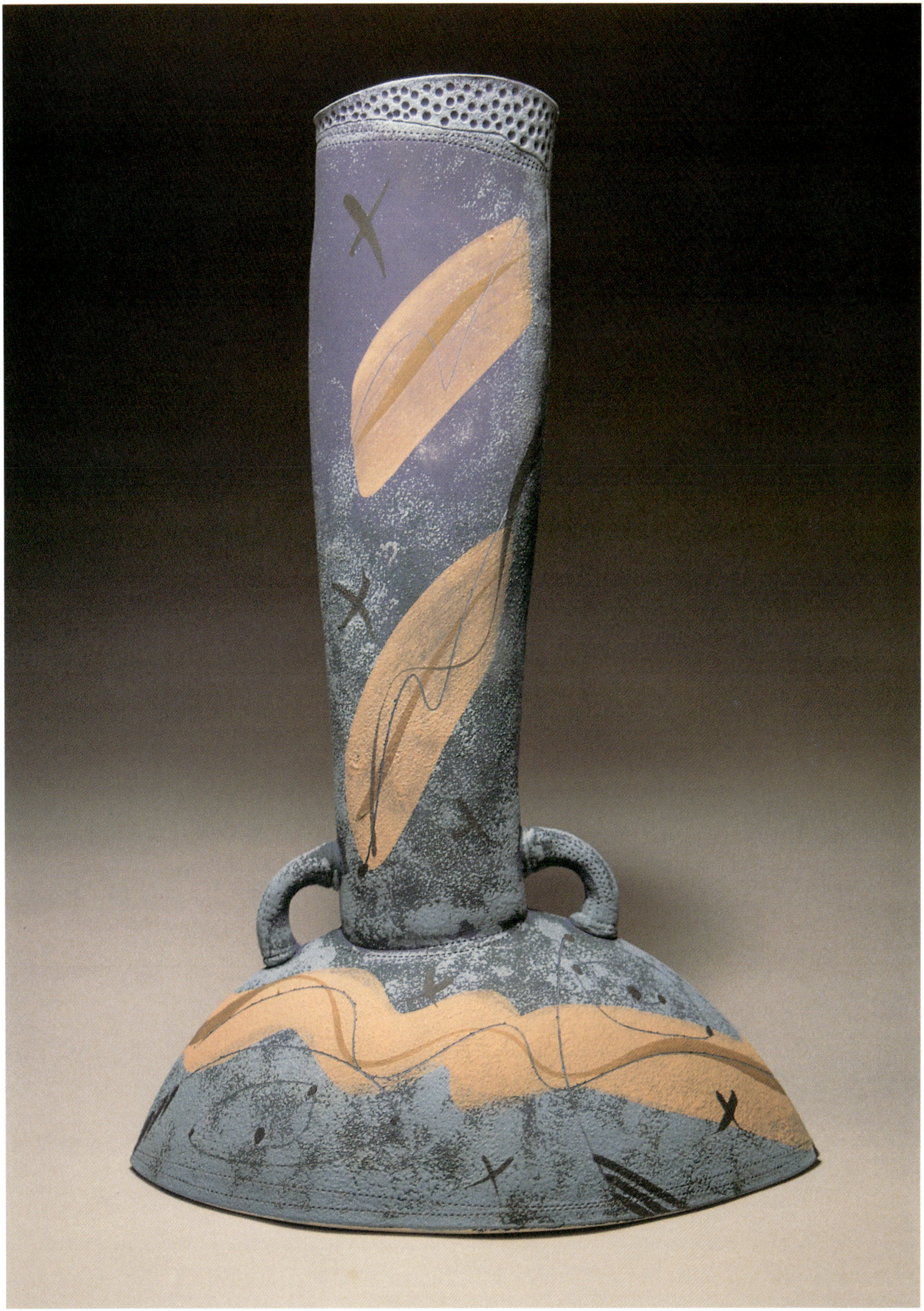

MIKE McGREGOR

Born Whakatane 1963.
Dip Applied Art, Northland Polytechnic 1990.
Lives in Auckland.

Glass blowing, the most seductive of all media, captivated Mike McGregor when he was a student. His studies included painting and printmaking, but the process of blowing glass and an opportunity later to work full time in a production studio in London pointed him strongly in the direction of glass. His early experiments as a student saw him pushing limits, including creating wine glasses with exceptionally long stems, but always with an eye for good form.

McGregor spent three years in London in the early 1990s, blowing glass and assisting English glass artist Patrick Stern. It was a major formative experience and Stern's techniques inspired McGregor's current work. He also worked in the London Glassblowing Workshop, and the experience of long production hours was invaluable. On his return to New Zealand he worked for Burning Issues Glassblowing Workshop in Whangarei, building the hot-glass workshop with Bevan Taka and Keith Mahy, and later blowing glass.

An awareness that the public look for individual one-off works is undaunting for McGregor. He wants his work to be saleable, but primarily he seeks consistent, uncluttered, well-resolved forms and is happy to produce the same objects repeatedly to perfect them. The works retain subtle differences, but the goal articulated by veteran glass blower Garry Nash (59)—the need to master and control the process—is echoed by this younger practitioner.

He enjoys making production ware—domestic utilitarian objects for daily use. It is an intuitive process, whereby he designs as he makes. Evaluation occurs during the slow, meditative period of cold finishing, while he is cutting the rims for subtle effect or grinding the glass. The individuality he seeks makes him shy away from Italian influences which are strong in New Zealand and to look to his experience in England as his starting point. There is also pleasure in making tools and devices specifically for his own needs, like the curling tongs with which to create the spouts of jugs.

McGregor limits the surface decoration of his works to a few simple techniques, the special touches that give the works their distinctive characteristics yet remain subservient to the forms. Bowls are trailed with coloured molten glass, rolled on chips of contrasting colours, and dipped into a ridge mould to create lines and spots that ripple over the curved surfaces. Occasionally the surfaces are frosted. On some of his platters and bowls he applies a resist to the inside before dipping the piece in acid, thereby retaining a clear surface through which to view the surface decoration.

In 1997, in Ashburton, McGregor held his first solo exhibition. In the same year he received an invitation to participate in an exhibition organised by the London Glassblowing Workshop. The exhibition subsequently toured England and Europe. The acknowledgement was well timed for this young artist whose talent and commitment deserved such encouragement.

**Hand blown bowls
Hand blown glass
(orange)
ca. 300 mm (w);
(green)
ca. 300 mm (h)
Collection of the
artist and Gordon
Ferguson**

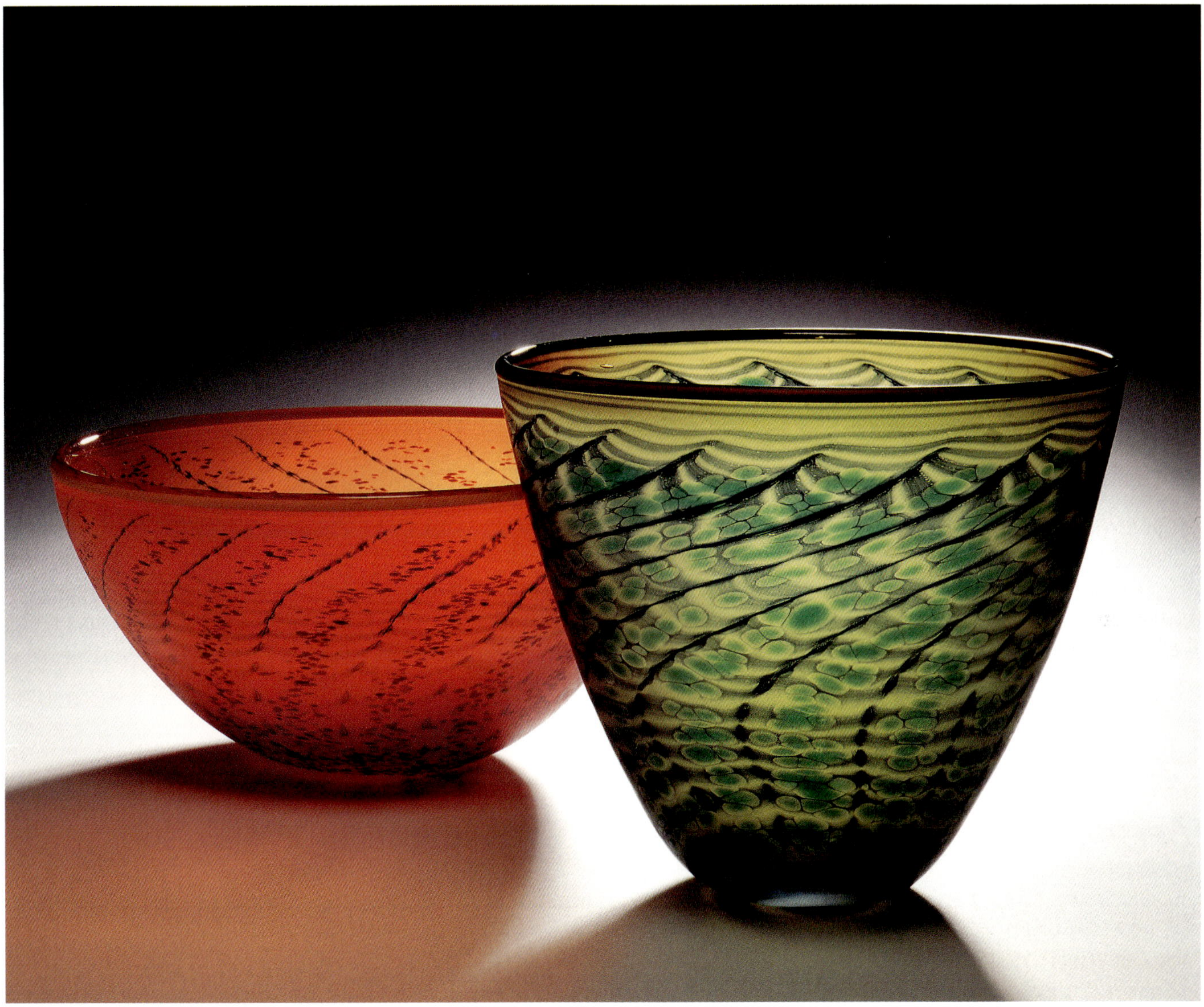

PETER McKAY

Born Akaroa 1951.
Apprenticeship with Kobi Bosshard, Akaroa 1968–73.
Lives in Akaroa.

Peter McKay seeks to make jewellery that has substance. He wants to create pieces based on more than pure aesthetics—the work deserves layers of meaning, given the many hours of uncompromising attention to fine detail. He believes that it took him more than fifteen years to find a personal direction different from the minimalist work with which he was in close touch. McKay shares a number of basic precepts with jewellers like Kobi Bosshard (8) and Warwick Freeman (27), like attitudes to wearability and appropriate fastenings, but he was never able to connect emotionally with modernism as they appeared to do. He sought a more spiritual quality—a different soul.

Although he completed his apprenticeship in 1973, he established himself as a jeweller in 1985, and the first of a number of solo exhibitions at Fingers gallery in 1986 marked the resumption of his interrupted career. Since then he has exhibited nationally and in USA, and has occasionally tutored. A need to earn a living raised his awareness of the relationship between manufactured jewellery and his work. Fish became a frequent motif, a readily understood and appealing universal theme, and some works referred to landscapes. The question 'Do souvenirs have to be tacky?' arose, a similar question to that posed by jewellers like Bosshard and Alan Preston (68). Like Preston, McKay explored the kiwi as a souvenir, but the high cost of making it defeated the purpose of the inexpensive memento.

In 1992, with the assistance of a QEII Arts Council grant, he was Artist in Residence at Waikato Polytechnic. The period gave him time to develop his most personal and beautifully resolved work. Art historical references to religion offered McKay a fruitful direction. He enjoyed the postmodern approach of borrowing from another time to give his work 'guts' and content. He felt free to romanticise and wallow in nostalgia, and made art historical references to archways, birds and hearts—the latter as a conscious jewellery cliché and already part of his repertoire. Defining the external shapes of his pieces gave him a philosophical as well as a physical framework. They became architectural references—like formal, static arches, illustrated in *Corvus Mortuus*, which depicts a golden bird under an arch.

Some of McKay's newest works, with titles like *Veiled Threats* and *Shrouded House*, are based on draped fabric. These small brooches are distinguished by their architectural references—a device that accommodates the fastening and gives structural strength. Henri Magritte's heads draped in metal are the springboard for these illusionist pieces. Jude Rae's paintings (Vol. 1, 71) of draped fabric also come to mind, and, like Ann Verdcourt (89), who works in clay, McKay's use of art history, and especially the work of Magritte, is a rich source of imagery.

Some works grow from a single word that inspires an idea. McKay plays with words and re-enlivens clichés and platitudes like *Two Birds with One Stone*. Although he has travelled a different journey, and his imagery is very different, the way he visually plays with clichés is not unlike the approach of jeweller Lynn Kelly (40). For McKay it is part of a new consciousness in the way he works. What doesn't change is the way his iconographic brooches, pendants and beads are always exquisitely detailed.

**Nine pieces of jewellery
Sterling silver and gold
ca. 50 x 50 mm each
Collection of the artist**

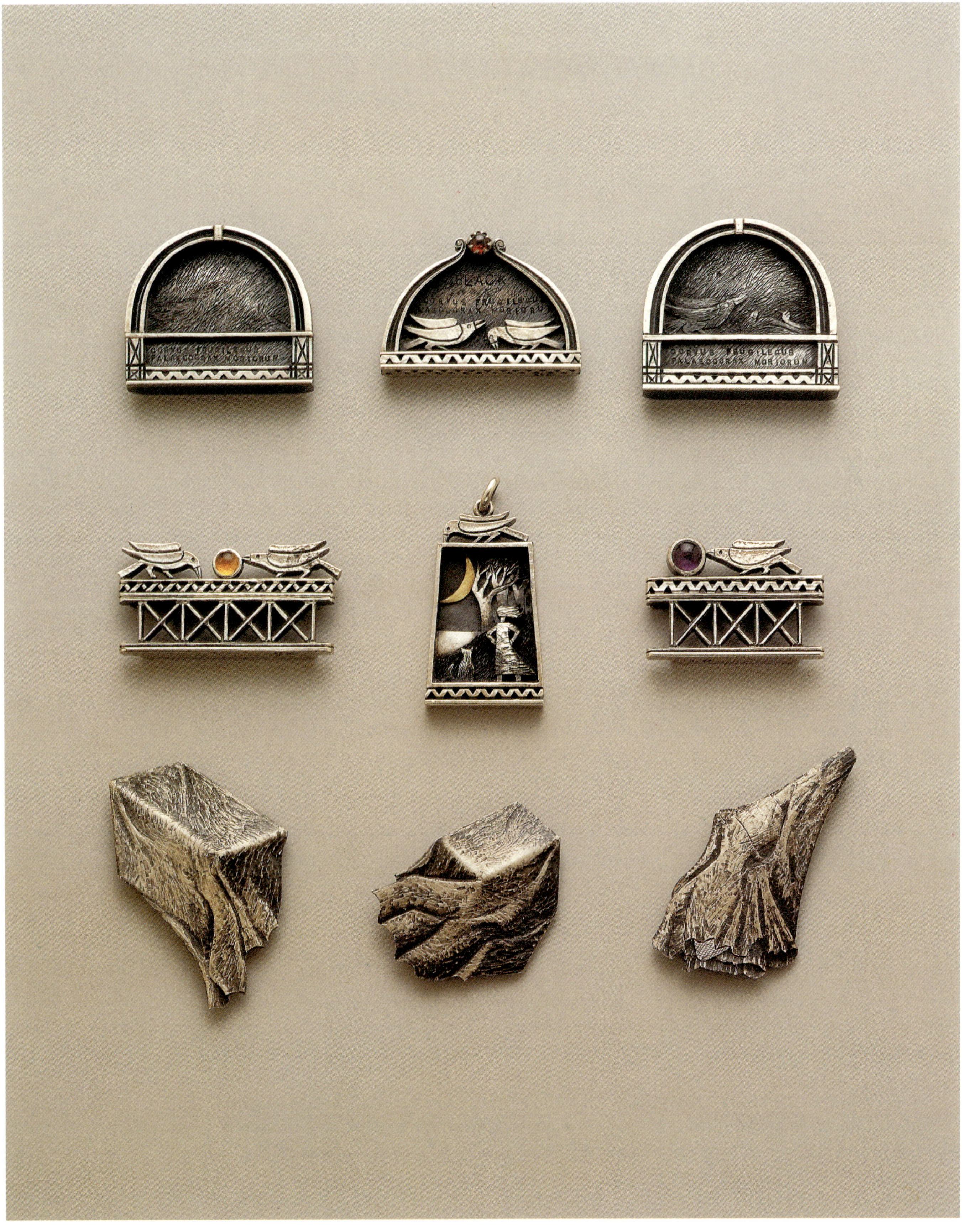
BLACK

MATT McLEAN

Born Hastings 1954.
Dip FA, University of Auckland 1975; Dip FA (Hons), University of Auckland 1976.
Lives in Auckland.

Matt McLean's clay sculptures are large, spectacular works that are often poised on their points—like dancers. The analogy is appropriate: as a student, McLean was involved in choreography, dance, theatre and short-film making. The stage presence of these works is explained, as is his proclivity for precarious structures that imply movement.

Stability of these sculptures comes from the relationship of the parts rather than from the individual components, so the works retain an element of insecurity—a device that invites engagement with the work. The pieces function as metaphors for the interdependence of communities—the physical equivalent of a musical ensemble creating a unified sound. They are about relationships—discordant or harmonious—and the need to co-operate in order to form a working structure.

His is a meditative building process that requires careful planning and evolves over a period of time. He often processes his own clay but isn't limited to this. New pieces feature red earthenware and white slab clay, as well as the terracotta he has formerly used, and recently he has tried to move away from his preoccupation with wood-firing. The work is created in the horizontal plane, built up like a puzzle, then given depth. Its final assembly in the vertical plane occurs after firing, and the way the pieces interlock is masterful.

Each component has its own personality and, occasionally, an iconographic function. The large scale of the components is determined by the limitations of the kiln, but McLean seeks to relate the weight of the individual parts to human scale in order to create the appropriate tension. He tends to use glaze in broad areas of strong colour, often frontal, as a distancing device. The effect is deceptively two-dimensional, somewhat like signwriting. These works, in fact, are at their most potent when placed in a landscape and viewed in a broad context, yet they easily withstand an intimate viewing experience.

McLean makes another more spontaneous series of works which functions as a recording device about events and the society in which we live. They are often massive, tile-like pieces that express the plastic nature of clay. He uses these loose slabs like a printing process, recording tyre marks—the marks of a mobile society. These pieces express a sensory relationship with his material and movement.

When McLean left art school he spent a number of years making utility items in the form of large garden pots. There seemed little scope for creative development, but it was a training ground for working with clay. He travelled and worked overseas for a year and, in 1988, decided to explore his sculptural ideas solely, interspersed with occasional teaching and commissions. In 1994 he received a Creative New Zealand grant, and he had a solo exhibition at the Dowse Art Museum in 1997. He has been a regular exhibitor at the Fletcher Brownbuilt Pottery Award and the Fletcher Challenge Ceramics Award, and has received a Merit Award (1992), a Judge's Commendation (1993) and a Double Merit Award (1994)—all of which recognise his ability not just to work to a large scale but to do so with rugged finesse.

**Openings
2000 x 1000 x 1200 mm
Collection of the artist**

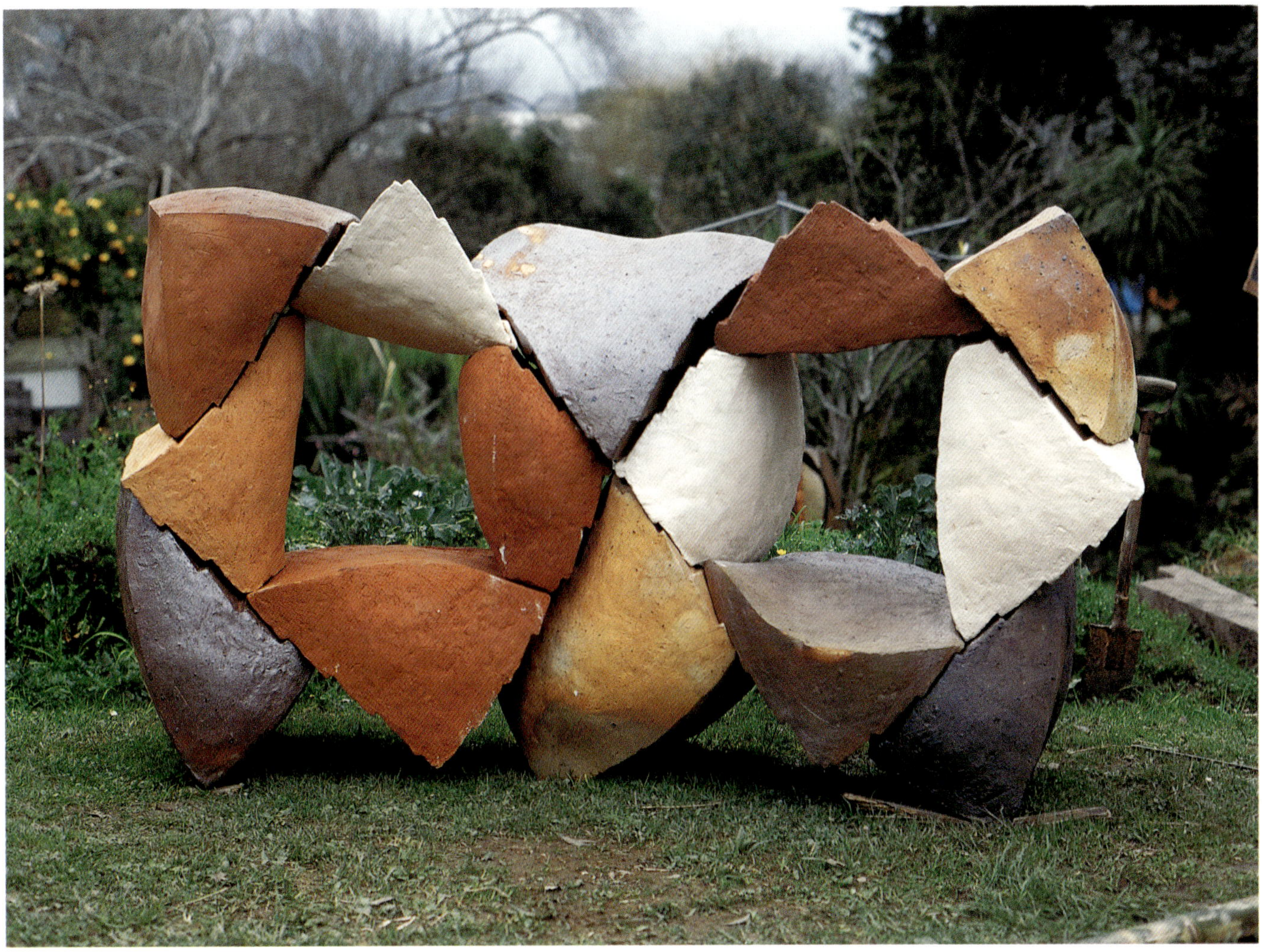

55

HAMISH McWHANNELL

Born Akaroa 1960.
University of Canterbury 1980–83.
Trained in jewellery at Daniel Clasby Workshops 1985–86.
Lives in Auckland.

Letting his eloquent, beautifully crafted works tell their own stories is important to Hamish McWhannell. The narrative is not always easily comprehended, but the images are engaging and provocative, and invariably include a layer of visual humour—a personal, quirky style.

His works are tiny and mainly figurative. They sometimes take the form of jewellery, but really function as miniature sculptures. McWhannell doesn't see himself as making jewellery that necessarily beautifies or adorns. Some of his work is wearable sculpture, and other images are definitely unsuitable to wear. These tantalisingly obscure pieces owe a good deal to comics and cartoons stylistically, but they go further because of their three-dimensionality and the way McWhannell plays with perspective. In the past he has often worked less sculpturally, implying rather than creating environments for his figures, but more recently he has taken his work into a more literal three-dimensionality.

McWhannell has always started by drawing the comics and cartoons of his imagination. Sometimes the inspiration is a drawing by Ralph Steadman. A wry sense of humour and a slightly mischievous take on an idea soften the intensity of some of his subject matter. The quirky demons have a hard edge of reality and self-knowledge—a disturbing unease. The work seems intensely autobiographical.

A sprawling figure wearing flippers in an open two-sided room seems caged in, unable to rise to his feet, evoking a touching helplessness despite his oxygen tank. Or a graceful female figure like an Yves St Laurent model from the 1960s features on a brooch, sending out signals of unavailability. Some works are in the form of animals, and the viewer is again left to imagine their contexts. McWhannell offers few illuminating titles. He has no desire to distract viewers from really looking at the works and prefers to let them draw their own conclusions.

Until recently his work was generally fabricated from silver and brass sheet, with an intricacy of detail that makes the work so appealing. McWhannell has enjoyed this process, but now he is also working with casting, which offers more scope for developing his work in the round. For him the technology is never an end in itself, just as making jewellery is not important as an end product. His newer works are heavier and less appropriate as jewellery. Some are becoming small framed wall works, retaining the scale of jewellery if not the spirit of it.

There is a strong thread of continuity in this work, and McWhannell's experimentation involves figures, humour and cartooning. It is the humour that offers the viewer a glimmer of optimism and a way to engage with the work. Perhaps understanding the work might be too painful; maybe comprehension is less important than participating visually and inventing one's own narrative.

1917 and China
Sterling silver
57 mm (diam) x
11 mm;
59 x 32 x 32 mm
Collection of the
artist

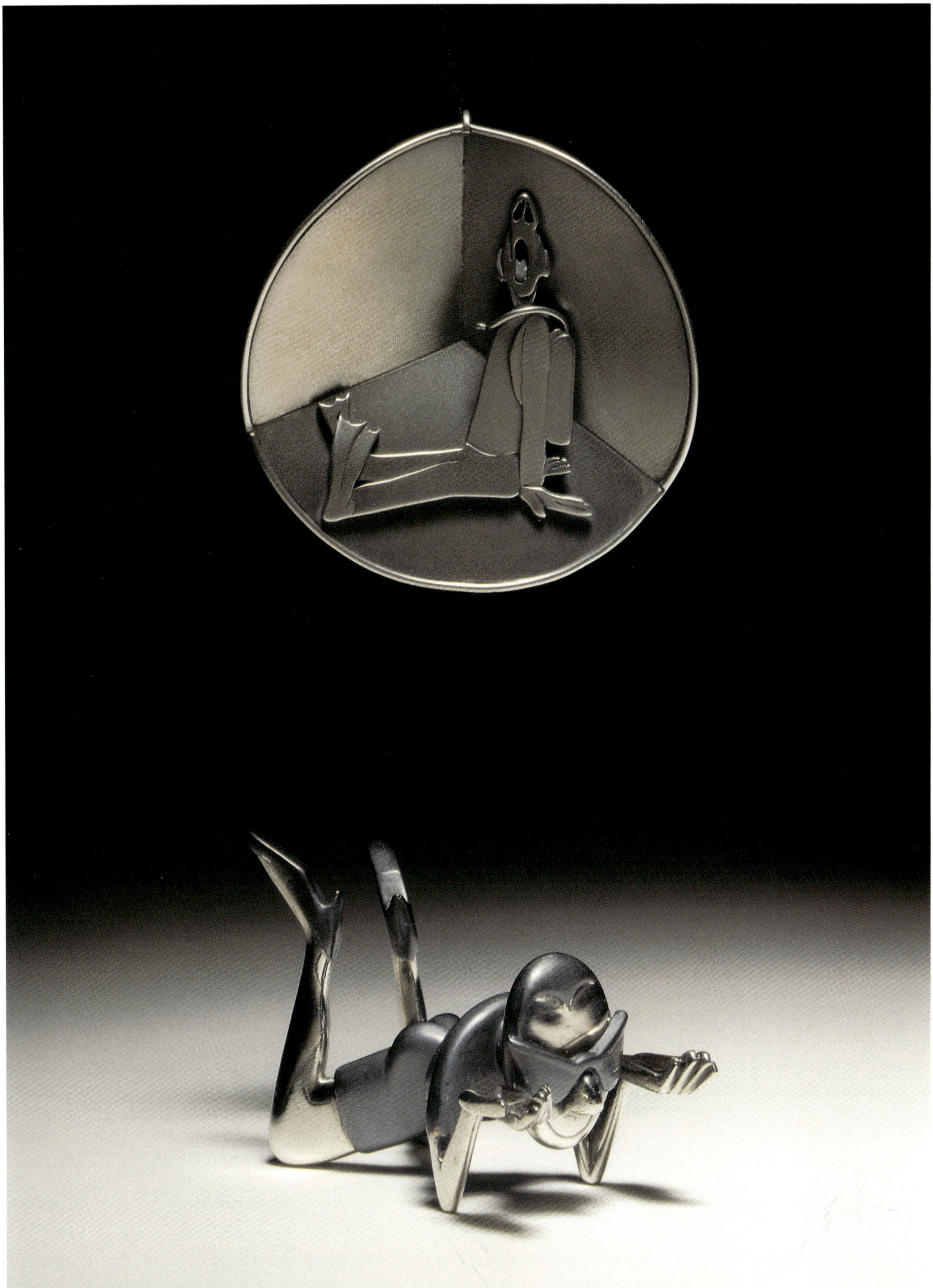

ROSS MITCHELL-ANYON

Born Orange, NSW, Australia 1954.
Settled in New Zealand 1964.
Teachers College Diploma, Palmerston North Teachers College 1975.
Lives in Wanganui.

A good pot needs to be experienced and judged by much more than just appearance, according to Ross Mitchell-Anyon. It doesn't need to be flamboyant or a display item to be an integral part of life. Mitchell-Anyon believes that many potters are preoccupied with wanting to fit into a fine arts formula, and his view is that art is made when makers engage with materials and forms with passion. For him, the deliberate intention to 'make art' may, in fact, preclude its making.

When he began working with clay at teachers training college he wanted to make practical pieces with a heart and a function. Education in clay in New Zealand in the 1970s was in the Hamada–Leach tradition which looked to Japanese culture, but Mitchell-Anyon was also inspired by English potter Michael Cardew, who wrote *Pioneer Pottery*, and was more comfortable with the way Cardew looked to his own English tradition. Inspiration also came from New Zealand pioneer potters Len Castle (14) and Barry Brickell (10). Mitchell-Anyon wanted then, as now, to make good things that people come to love through using them.

Mitchell-Anyon makes objects with love, care and integrity. His process begins with digging clay from Pahiatua. He values collecting his material—he is more attached to it, and consequently more respectful, recycling rather than wasting it. He works minimally with glazes, and he enjoys the process where clay and glaze become one—become part of the body. He uses clear or shino glazes on stoneware or earthenware clay, and the pieces are subjected to woodfiring and salt in the kiln.

Traditions, materials and process inform his work, which takes the form of jugs, teapots, bowls and cups—basic objects designed to contain liquid and food. The forms are the product of the process, with no trickery or cunning. Teaching and demonstrating to students has shown Mitchell-Anyon the value of breaking some of the rules of pottery. The teaching situation often requires rapid process from a pragmatic point of view, and this discovery impressed on him the value of directness and working as much as possible while the pieces are wet.

Repetition is important in his work. There is pleasure in making and seeing the production process occur—a workshop full of boards bearing clay pieces at various stages of the process. In a session making a large number of coffee cups, for example, he lets the forms evolve and mutate rather than looking to impose 'quality control'. His solo exhibitions contain large groups of works, indicating the context in which they are made. In 1989, at his exhibition at the Fisher Gallery, Pakuranga, he exhibited along with the vessels the containers in which the works were transported, as well as hands made of clay, thereby contextualising them further.

Over the years a number of his works have become larger, and some of his outsize teapots and jugs have outgrown their function, merely making reference to it. Mitchell-Anyon makes these without preciousness or artifice. They are an extension of what he has always made—the same genre of work he has in his kitchen, and that won him a Merit Award at the Fletcher Challenge Ceramics Award in 1993, as well as numerous other awards.

Jug and lidded jar
Ceramic
260 x 125 mm;
150 x 125 mm
Collection of
Lyn Hurst

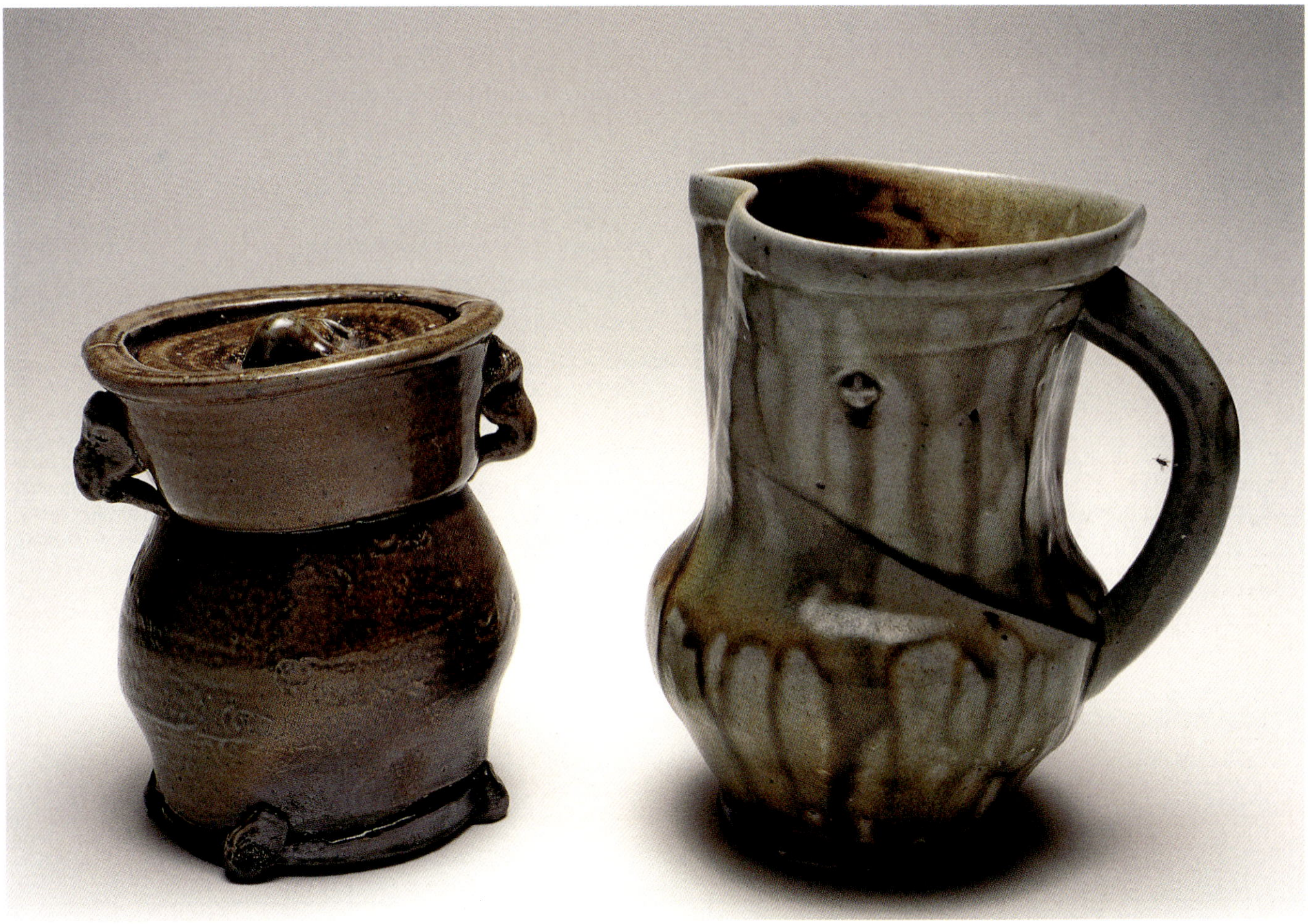

GAEL MONTGOMERIE

Born Martinborough 1949.
BA, Victoria University, Wellington 1971; School of Architecture, Auckland University 1974.
Lives in Nelson.

The speed and spontaneity of wood turning are appealing features for Gael Montgomerie. She loves being able to work directly without measured drawings or a completely finished idea in mind. She came to the medium through studying architecture and working in building and furniture making. However, her interest in working with wood and machinery stems from growing up on a farm where doing hard physical work went side by side with learning 'female crafts'.

Her beautifully formed bowls have a distinctive female aesthetic—the use of gentle applied colour and necklace-like adornment around the rims as well as carving and calligraphy. The garland of found materials like bamboo, willow, silver birch, eucalyptus and vines is more than mere decoration. Montgomerie often makes reference to the life of the whole tree from which the wood for her bowl has come, in which case the twigs she uses are the tips of the tree—evidence of the changes that occur while it grows. She seeks a balance between the formal symmetry of the turning process and the exuberance of the living tree. The inclusions on the formally turned pieces are visually softening, as are the tiny lugs which were originally turned on the lathe. Recently she has been making these from copper.

Montgomerie often uses less than perfect pieces of wood: the knots and bark feed her with ideas. She enjoys making objects from undervalued species like sycamore which was so readily available when she lived in Dunedin. She had wanted a white wood to paint on, and found the sumptuous sheen and good cutting quality suited her needs. Sustainability is of major concern to her, so she acquires her wood from sustainably managed forests, demolition sites, windfalls and tree surgeons.

Being a passionate gardener has taught Montgomerie about the colours of trees, like the dark bare branches of winter, the acidic green of new growth in spring, and the flame colours of autumn. In her turned bowls and vases, which are always superbly proportioned, she wants to evoke the whole tree and the annual cycle. It was in 1990, at the Wanganui Polytechnic symposium 'Out of the Woods', that she started applying colour to her pieces. She initially aimed for subtle effects, trying painting, rubbing in oil colour then washes of acrylic colour. The colours were an enhancement, never a barrier between the viewer and the natural texture, and over the years they have become brighter and more confident. More recently she has experimented with tissue paper and dyes, and a patina of liquid bronze, fragments of gold leaf, texturing and hammering. The painterly effects are always handled discreetly, even minimally, never obliterating the wood grain. They are the magic, the sparkle that distinguishes Montgomerie's objects from the work of many other woodturners.

A number of acknowledgements have come her way, including acceptance for a master class in Philadelphia in 1998. Such opportunities are important for the critical debate Montgomerie craves. She occasionally teaches, and has her own gallery attached to her studio. A frequent guest exhibitor throughout New Zealand, she has also exhibited in Australia, Japan, Germany and USA.

Growth Ring Series
Sycamore, acrylic paint, copper, bamboo
230 x 120 mm
Collection of Ruth and David Waterbury, Minnesota

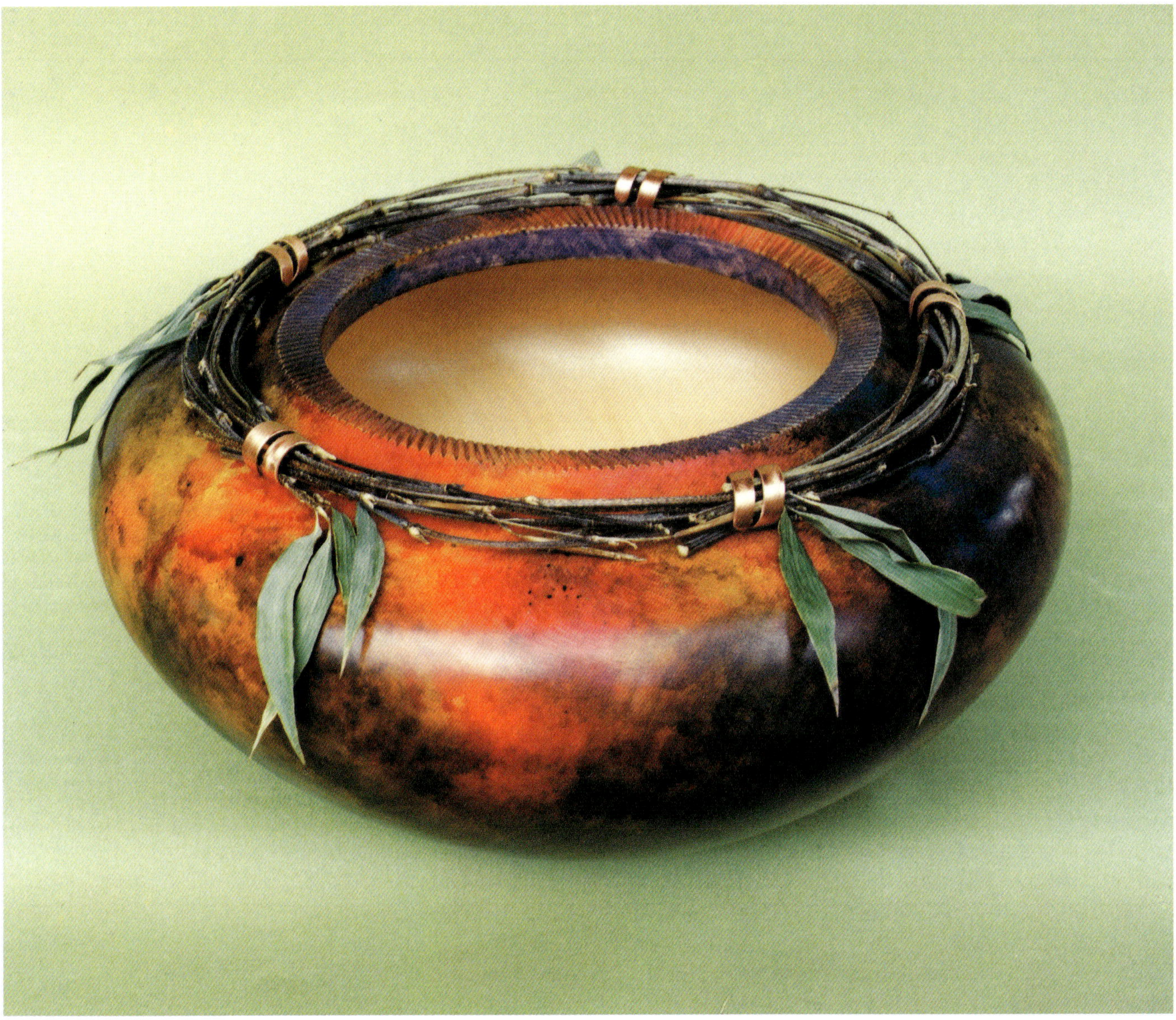

GAELEEN MORLEY

Born Tokomaru Bay 1941.
Qualified as nurse, Napier 1962;
first introduction to clay by Bob Huck of Fulford Potteries, Havelock North 1969;
attended clay workshops at several summer schools.
Lives in Taradale, Hawke's Bay.

The solitude of a childhood on a back-country sheep station is echoed for Gaeleen Morley in the long quiet periods of working with clay. She has a strong commitment to the medium and, after three decades weathering the changing market, she continues to support herself this way.

Her earliest work was wheel-thrown tableware. She recalls the first workshop conducted by Peter Stitchbury, the encouragement of John Parker (63) and the early pleasures of making pots. Largely self-taught, she has over the years developed considerable expertise with clay and glazes, and conducted much experimental work in a small American test kiln. She has taught glaze technology at a number of workshops, and has been a technical adviser to Hawke's Bay Polytechnic (now Eastern Institute of Technology) since 1978. Colour and texture play an important part in Morley's work, and an adventurous spirit has led her into experimenting with many unusual substances. A QEII Arts Council Development Grant in 1992 gave her the opportunity to develop new forms in her work and explore further richly textured and uniquely coloured glazes.

Making tableware was the starting point for Morley's most distinctive work. She started by making teapots as functional objects because they were saleable, but the same enquiring mind that wanted to explore chemical reactions under heat prompted her to start pushing the limits of the form. Her teapots evolved—their shapes changed, different glazes were applied, and handles were created in a number of ways. Her quest became to see how far she could extend the concept of the teapot.

Seeking answers continues to occupy a considerable part of Morley's production, although she continues to make everyday objects like clocks. The teapots have become parodies, retaining the identifying characteristics of handle, spout and lid. However, the handle might be a twisted ribbon of clay, the spout solid rather than hollow, and the lid might be firmly fixed to the body. Significant changes also occurred in the body, which might be not only elongated but also hollowed at the base, evoking china figurines. Containment in a traditional sense is no longer an issue, but there are new characteristics, most notably a figurative quality and a sense of movement and dance.

Her lively *Dancing Teapots* are often created in playful pairs, establishing a dynamic, eloquent composition with a strong negative space between them. The relationships between pairs could be perceived as unequal but balanced—about the dominant and the submissive. Current works have a new sophistication and less exuberant surfaces than some of the earlier works. They are still graceful, although less about dance, and have led to a series of bowls and spheres with similar finishes.

Since 1991 Morley has also collaborated with artist and educator Jacob Scott in making tiles for a number of projects for the Napier inner-city development and at the Eastern Institute of Technology. She has exhibited widely and received several awards, and her work is in collections in New Zealand, Britain, Australia, USA, Japan and China.

Teapot Forms
Clay
350 x 140 x 80 mm;
280 x 120 x 70 mm
Collection of Helen Schamroth and Michael Smythe

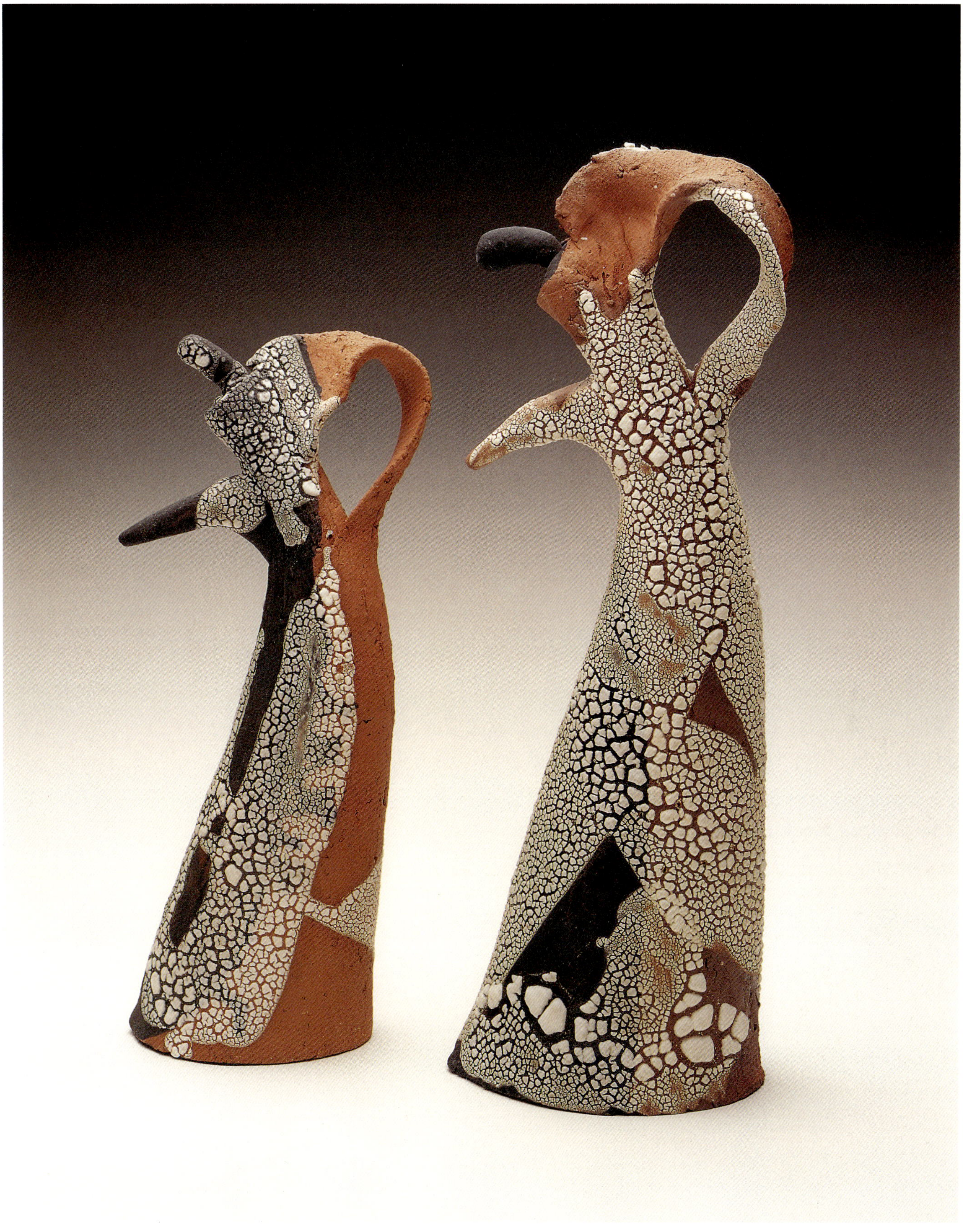

GARRY NASH

Born in Sydney, Australia 1955.
Moved to New Zealand 1973.
Began working with glass 1978; joined Sunbeam Glassworks, Auckland 1981; acquired ownership 1988.
Lives in Auckland.

Twenty years after he started, Garry Nash still talks about the magic of the glass-blowing process. It is the molten state that captivates him, the process of creating a form and retaining it—that brief period when a team wrestles with the hot liquid mass that collapses so easily under gravity. Once the work has cooled he no longer feels the same attachment to it, and this allows him to sell the work. He used also to be fascinated with building the tools and equipment, but that attraction has faded and he is now content to import tools. Technique which used to be appealing has become a means to an end—a way of capturing a feeling or a form.

There is pleasure for Nash in working with a permanent material. He is driven by wanting to leave artefacts that record the experience of living in our time for future generations. When it comes to recording history, he sees objects as so much more eloquent than words. He enjoys working to a large scale which is challenging to produce but has a certain presence. Making tiny delicate objects also has its attractions. For Nash the work stays fresh by experimentation and pushing limits. Blowing glass is a sociable activity compared to many other crafts, and he enjoys his involvement with young talented team members. He uses his studio for teaching as well as production, and as a base for significant visiting practitioners. His commitment is an acknowledgement of his place in a continuum, of passing on skills that date back hundreds of years.

There are no short cuts to the sophisticated pieces Nash makes. He is driven by ideas, seeks elegant forms that best express those ideas, and regards the vessel as a noble form which can carry emotion and message. The inner and outer surfaces offer different ways of seeing and interpreting, enhanced by light passing through them. His current work is possible because of new cutting wheels and the use of lustres. Etching, sandblasting and diamond cutting wheels are used to enhance elegant, controlled forms. Dancing motifs are deeper than surface decoration: they seem to penetrate the works, allowing light to move through.

Nash doesn't like to create the 'happy accident' as a single work. Those pieces may point to new directions but his interest is in mastering and controlling the process, producing a piece that is fluid and fluent, and that carries his message. Despite the volume of work produced in his studio, he has never totally identified with production craft. He is more interested in the development of the work, seeking new factors to excite and inspire him. The next piece is always the best one.

Nash used to sell his major sculptural pieces overseas, and his work is in a number of public and private collections. The best pieces were highly sought after and hard to make, and he received considerable recognition in Australia, USA, Japan and Europe. However, he believes it is important that some major works are retained in New Zealand, and with the growth of the local market many more now remain in the country.

Flotsam
Opalino, free-blown glass, diamond wheel intaglio cut and frosted
500 x 100 mm
Collection of the artist

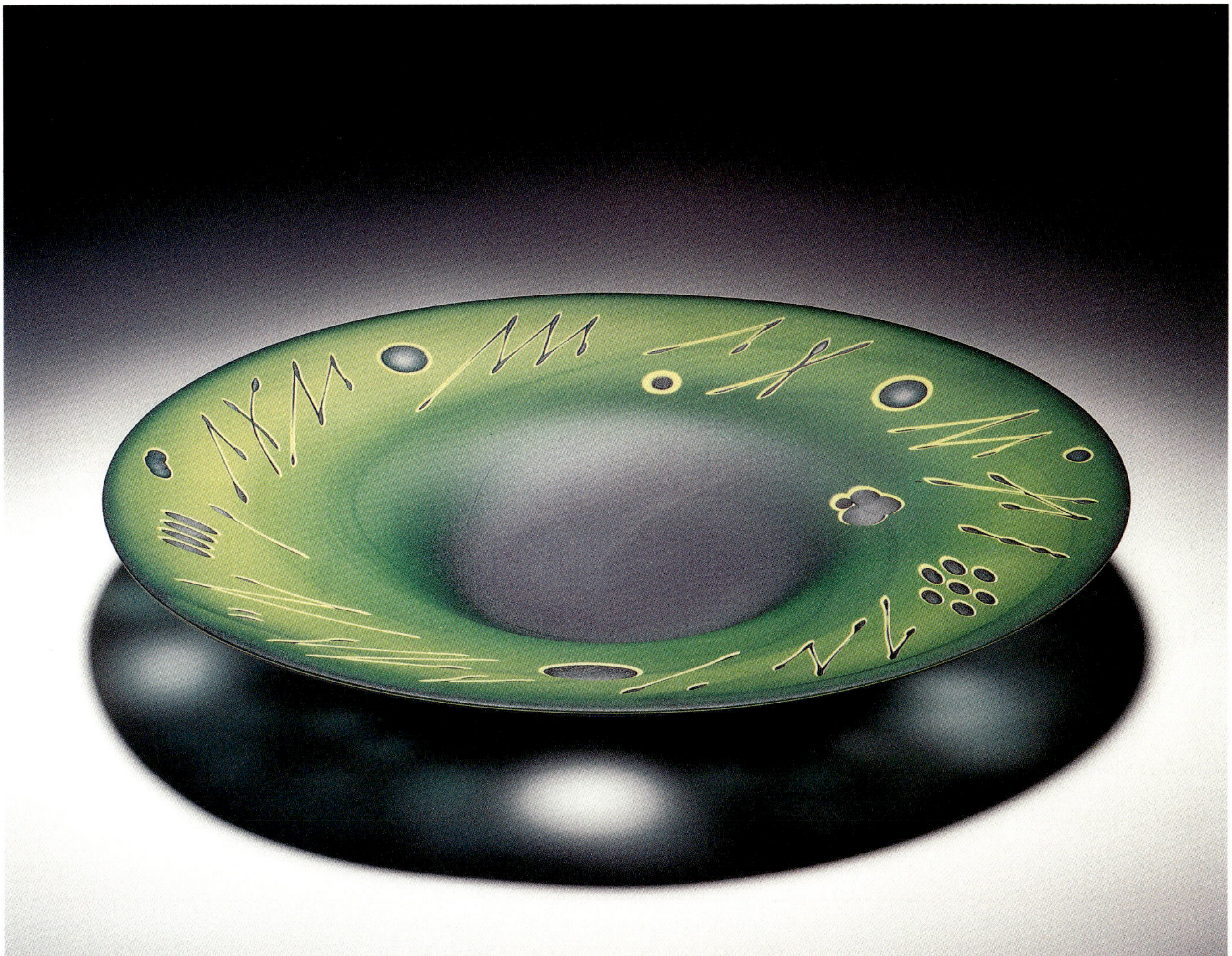

60

MANOS NATHAN

Born Rawene 1948.
Te Roroa, Ngati Whatua, Nga Puhi.
Dip Textile Design, Wellington Polytechnic School of Design 1968–70.
Lives in Dargaville.

Maori carving tradition has been one of the strongest influences in Manos Nathan's ceramics. It was an obvious source, with no Maori clay tradition as a reference. In 1982, after being away for some time, he returned to Northland to carve and decorate Matatina Marae, Waipoua, at the request of his elders.

He became interested in clay when he met Robyn Stewart (78) and appreciated the low technology she employed when handbuilding, burnishing and pit firing in the manner of Pueblo Indians. At first he took his influences from many sources. Like Stewart, he was impressed by the black pots of Maria Martinez, and he also looked at pots from Fiji and Papua New Guinea. His iconography was Maori, but his form language straddled carved Maori vessels and those seen in his travels.

Nathan established a number of fruitful links with fibre artist Toi Maihi (46), teacher and potter Colleen Waata Urlich, pioneer potter Barry Brickell (10), and Baye Riddell (70), the rangatira of Maori ceramics. He gained knowledge about clay as well as support for Maori youth programmes, and soon became a serious advocate for Maori clay work. Nga Kaihanga Uku, a Maori clayworkers' collective, was formed in 1986 by Nathan and Riddell, who organised a hui at Tokomaru Bay in 1987 followed by another at Matatina Marae, Waipoua, the following year. In 1989, on a Fulbright Cultural Grant, Nathan and Riddell visited and studied with native American potters and artists. He has exhibited and curated extensively in New Zealand, Australia, England, USA and Germany.

When he started working with clay, Nathan was challenged by his elders who wanted to see the relevance for them. In order to win them over, he had to link his work to the narratives of his culture and to talk about a whakapapa for clay and fire. He made works about the creation story and adhered to traditions from other media—like spirals—in his surface treatment. The first works that truly fitted into a Maori cultural context were the *Waka Taurahere Tangata* (placenta bowl) and the *Waka Pito* (umbilicus pot). It seemed logical to use clay containers for the traditional practice of burying the placenta and umbilicus on ancestral land. Nathan saw how these pots could forge links with Maori custom and values, and they affirmed and acknowledged genealogical connections with the land.

The newest work, created for *Uku! Uku! Uku!* at the International Festival of the Arts, Wellington, 1998, honours the creators of the sacred burial chests of his Te Roroa people of Waimamaku. These very large pieces make reference to the historical receptacles for bones. They also make sorrowful commentary on the looting of the burial caves on the Kaharau Wahi Tapu at the turn of the century, and the removal of the taonga to museums throughout New Zealand and overseas. These are the most potent of Nathan's images—impassioned and eloquent.

Part of Nathan's heritage is Cretan, and he has a real affection for Minoan ceramics. He recalls clay ornaments from Crete around the house during his youth, and these may have influenced his aesthetics, but his conscious thinking is definitely about Maoridom.

**Whakapakoko
Clay (raku body),
oxides
650 x 400 x 280 mm
Collection of the
artist**

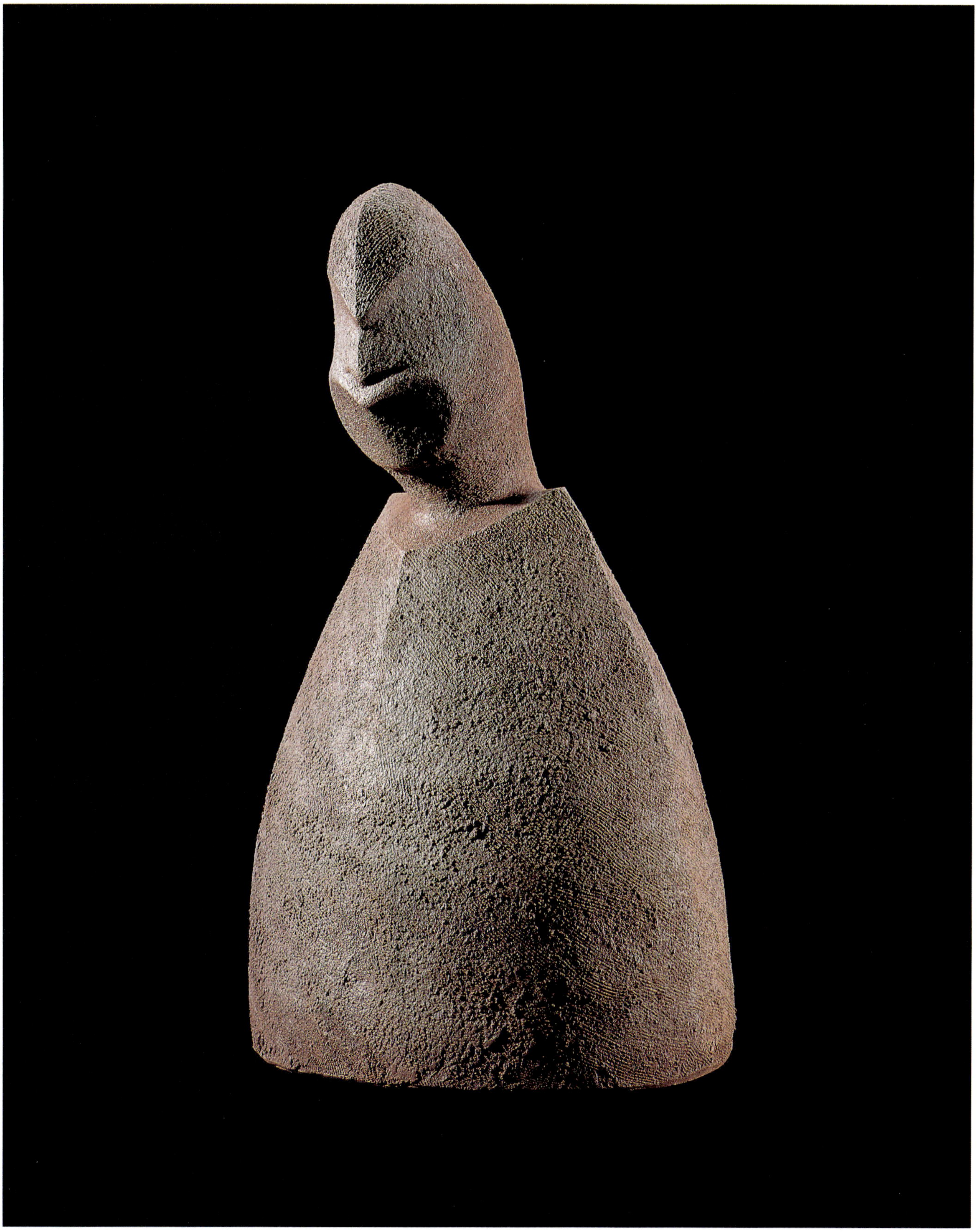

CHESTER NEALIE

Born Rotorua 1942
Teachers Certificate, Auckland Secondary Teachers College 1963.
Began potting in 1964. Moved to Australia 1991.
Lives in Gulgong, NSW.

Chester Nealie likes to engage with the elements when he creates his pots—it is an empathy for the craft philosophy that developed in the 1960s and '70s. After teaching science at secondary school he became lecturer in ceramics at North Shore Teachers' College from 1972–75. Since then he has had an impressive career as a full-time potter. This includes grants, and many residencies and awards, notably the Premier Award at the Fletcher Challenge Ceramics Award in 1982 and 1987. His work has been widely exhibited in New Zealand and internationally, and is held in many collections. In 1992 he was a member of the *Artists in the Sub-Antarctic* expedition to the Auckland Islands, and he participated in the subsequent exhibition as well as in *Treasures of the Underworld* at World Expo in Seville. In 1993 he was a Research Fellow at Monash University.

Len Castle (14) was a great inspiration to Nealie, helping him to understand the freedom of clay. Like Castle, he looked to Chinese and Korean pots and to Japanese process. He admired the work of the Japanese potters Toyoza Arakawa and Toyo Kaneshige, and took inspiration from a small photograph of Arakawa's wood-fired anagama kiln buttressed by boulders. Developing a personal philosophy was encouraged by visiting English potter Michael Cardew.

Nealie's organic forms are thrown on a slow-turning wheel and reveal the essence of making—the finger indentations, the gentle squeeze and the pressure of applying a lug or handle. The pieces need to be strong to withstand the rigours of his firing process. The sensuality of clay is translated into slightly waisted forms evocative of human torsos—pieces that beg to be hand-held. His vessels are infused with emotion, and are personal in their evocation of antiquity and ritual. He has no desire to follow trends but has worked for long enough to observe the cyclical nature of aesthetics.

Although the wood-firing process is to a great extent unpredictable and there is an element of alchemy, Nealie has developed considerable control over the variables. He has learned the painter's skill of layering colours, and Chinese Soung pots have taught him that chips, cracks and scars expose a soul which has little to do with symmetry and predictability. The wads of clay and shell he uses to separate pots during firing act as windows to fluxed layers of ash deposits. Prising them off exposes layers of time and colour, as well as scars and fossil-like imprints—a narrative akin to the weathering of rock.

In 1991 Nealie moved to Australia where he has a group of peers who share his philosophy and aesthetics. He maintains links with New Zealand, and frequently conducts workshops and exhibits on his return. His palette has altered to include the burnt, dry and dusty hues of his new environment, but there is still a place for the subtle tones developed from his New Zealand experience of living with the mangroves of the Kaipara Harbour. He now feels more confident to express these roots, and recognises the subliminal effects of wandering the shorelines—the colours of limpets and anemones, rocks, pebbles, shells, sea and seaweed. His placement of shells when he separates pots in the kiln is a considered action—it reflects his sense of being a person of the Pacific.

Patu
Anagama woodfired,
clay
120 mm
Collection of Peter Masters

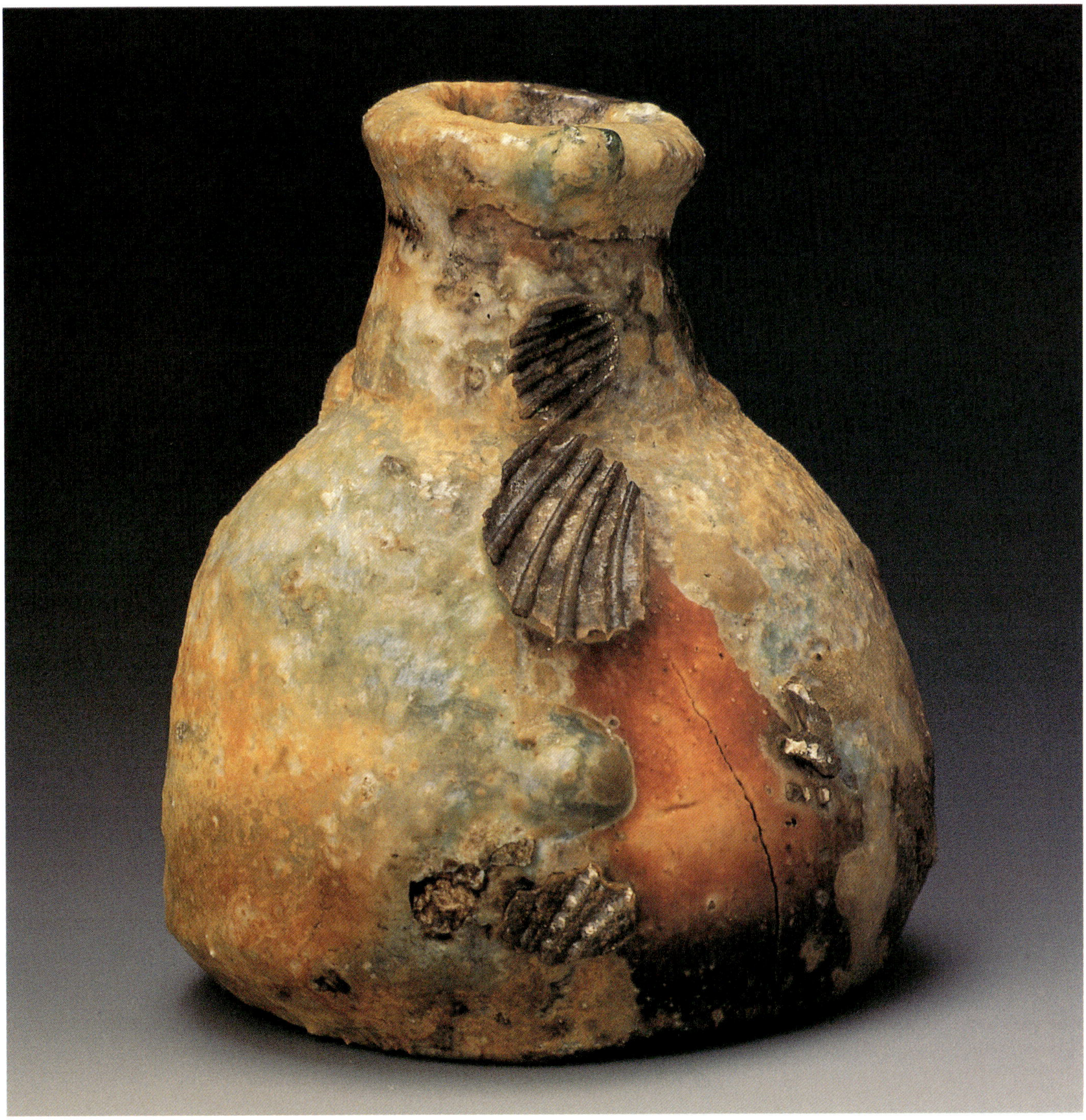

62

MICHAEL O'BRIEN

Born Auckland 1963.
Bookbinding Trade Certificate, ATI 1985; Advanced Certificate, ATI 1986.
Lives in Oamaru.

For Michael O'Brien handcrafted books are not a way of turning back the clock. He believes that the issues he addresses are contemporary—environmental and social as much as aesthetic. He nonetheless evokes the past in his persona and lifestyle, and his crafted book bindings have a certain timelessness.

A strong interest in the British Arts and Crafts Movement is the basis for O'Brien's work. He likes to recall the principles of the movement and its emphasis on the dignity of making by hand as well as the integrity of the craftsman. He also looks to the writings of the Powys brothers for inspiration. When he first started to bind books, O'Brien was primarily focused on their structure. Now he believes that a book is a four-dimensional art form, the intellectual information within the covers providing a significant dimension. His pleasure comes from engaging with the text in order to create a relevant and coherent design. He wants the book to be more than covers, end papers, spine and pages—rather a sculptural object designed to be handled, yet maintaining a form language that fits within the conventions of a bound book.

O'Brien enjoys the fact that books are not flat. He emphasises the tactile, three-dimensional quality of expressive bindings. They are most likely to be in bas relief and not necessarily confined to the rectangular plane. His use of scale drawings and prototypes to resolve design issues is balanced by occasionally letting the design evolve intuitively. Generally he uses traditional bookbinding materials—good-quality acid-free board, vegetable tanned leather, leather stains, Irish linen thread, balsa wood, archival paper and glues. Occasionally his covers are constructed of PVA glue mixed with leather shavings, leather dust and stains.

A period spent in London in 1986–87 revealed to O'Brien a small community of bookbinders and collectors—this was an inspirational time for him. While there, under expert instruction, he developed skills, pushed boundaries and competed successfully in an annual competition for novices. That support was lacking on his return to New Zealand, but he nonetheless established a lively workshop and made craft bindings, commissioned work and occasional exhibition pieces. In 1994 he moved from Auckland to Oamaru, attracted by the town's superb Victorian architecture and magnificent landscape. In 1995, with the assistance of an Arts Council grant, he went to Yorkshire, and was once again stimulated by the environment. There he worked with bookbinder David Sellers who, like him, had come to bookbinding through the trade but was also influenced by contemporary art and music. That passion was infectious.

A number of O'Brien's books have been accepted for exhibition in Australia, England, USA and Italy. Several have been purchased for public and private collections. O'Brien has been included in a number of significant international exhibitions, including the Tregaskis Centennial Bookbinding Exhibition in London, Sheffield and Bath, 1995; Twenty-five Gold-Tooled Bindings: an international tribute to Bernard C. Middleton's Recollections, London, New York, San Francisco, 1996; and the rigorously selected Leopardi's *The Infinite*, Ricanati, Italy, 1998. This recognition is not just of his considerable crafting skills, but also of an emerging personal style based on a strong philosophy and response to his beautiful environment.

The Book of Nature (book box)
Card, paste, paper, moulded paper, found objects, stain, paper, glue, paste (archival materials)
260 x 215 x 85 mm
Collection of Donna Demanté Ogilvy

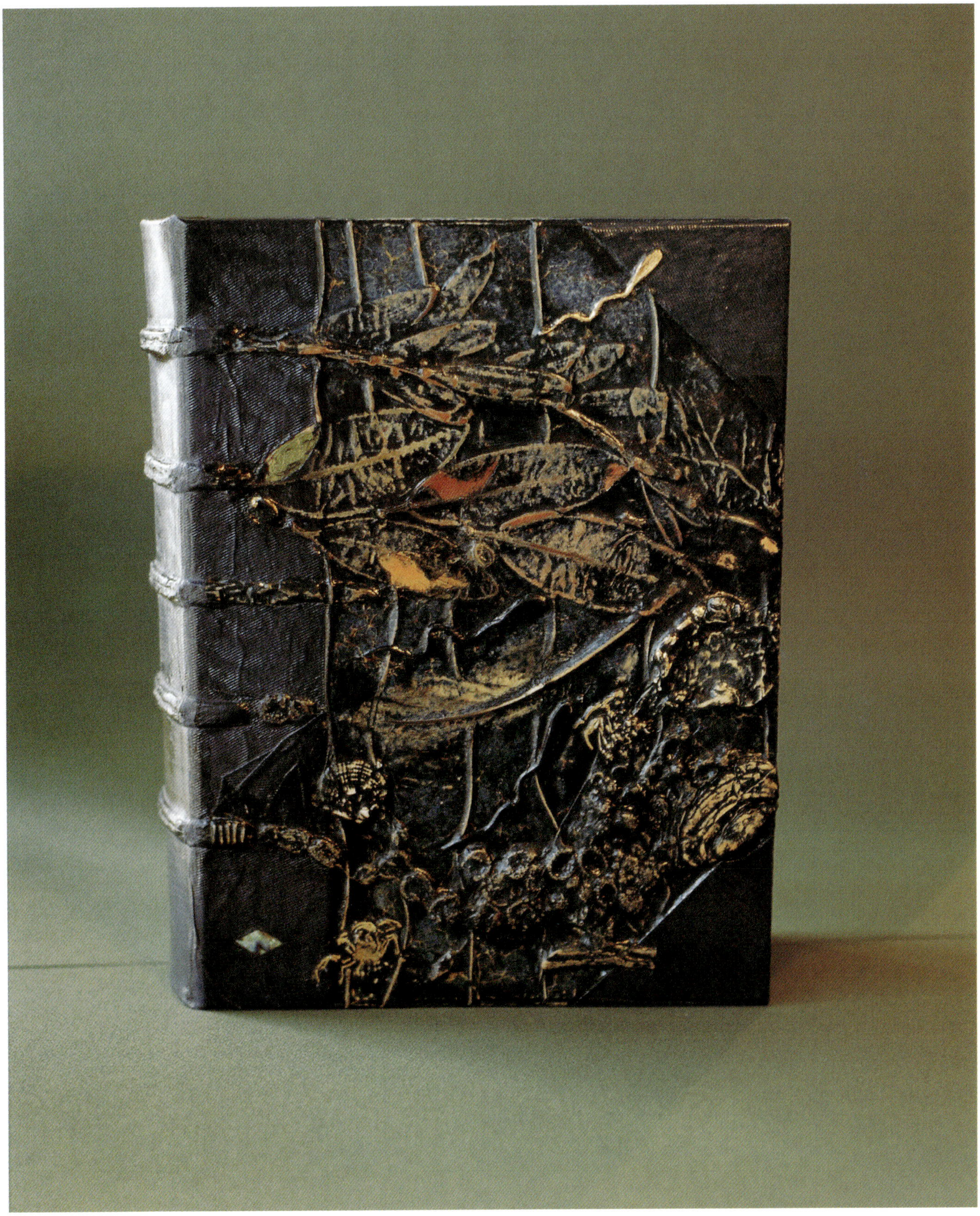

JOHN PARKER

Born Auckland 1947.
Graduated Auckland Teachers Training College 1970; MA, Royal College of Art, London 1975.
Lives in Waitakere.

'If you haven't got anything to say, don't open the bag of clay' might sound a bit dramatic, but dramatic theatrical displays are John Parker's forte. He works as a writer, a designer of exhibitions, theatre sets and costumes, and a maker of exquisitely formed pots, and brings the same philosophy and approach to all he does. In 1988 he and Cecilia Parkinson wrote *Profiles: 24 New Zealand Potters*.

Parker works with three-dimensional images in space. Take the design of *The Pharaohs* exhibition at Auckland Museum in 1997. He had a real affinity for the objects and brought an appreciation of the makers to his design of the space, which was conceived as a series of vistas with individual backgrounds. By creating an unusual context for the works, with an element of risk, surprise, drama and theatricality, he was able to reflect some of the qualities he perceived in the Egyptians. So it is with his pots, when he sets up similar dynamic presentations.

Parker's pottery output is project based. Working to deadlines provides the adrenalin rush on which he thrives. Rather than feeling fragmented, he perceives a pause as a gestation period, one that gives him time to stand back from his pots and re-evaluate them. He used to feel guilty about these blocks of time not working with clay, but soon realised that he was taking his potting more seriously by not churning out huge quantities of work. This way he experiences a certain freedom to make work that pleases him but that might not be commercially viable.

Stark, minimalist and referencing the industrial, the pots in his exhibitions are dramatically lit still-life clusters of practised, precise shapes. His pots are beautifully formed, strongly based on simple geometry; they are elegantly glazed and crisply detailed. They tease out notions of functionalism, and seem to bear no relationship to the mainstream of contemporary New Zealand ceramics. His aesthetic sensibility and philosophy are more related to the European design movements of de Stijl and the Bauhaus than to Bernard Leach and Hamada, who influenced a number of his peers.

Recent work is white—an arbitrary choice that coincided with painting his house white. Maybe it was no accident: white seems to dominate his environment and apparel, so why not his pots? It fits with his philosophy of wanting to pare away the inessentials, of taking risks and, he says, expresses a certain bloody-mindedness. He wants to remove unnecessary tricks to get closer to understanding the concept of the bowl as the container, the vessel, and keeps finding new things to do and new simplifications. That very paring away becomes a masterly trick and an intensely personal visual device.

Parker decorates some of his pots with holes. Immediately there is a play of light—theatrical, penetrating, reflecting, creating playful shadows, evoking the architectural features of his theatre designs. He loves the idea of fakery, of playing intellectual games, and enjoys making clay look as if it could be plastic or powder-coated aluminium. That playfulness never denies his mastery of clay and his ability to create beautiful works.

**Ridged Sphere; Gobo Bowl; Gobo Vase; Gobo 'V' Bowl; Ridged Sphere; Gobo Bottle; Gobo 'V' Bowl
Ceramic
240–310 mm (h)
Collection of the artist**

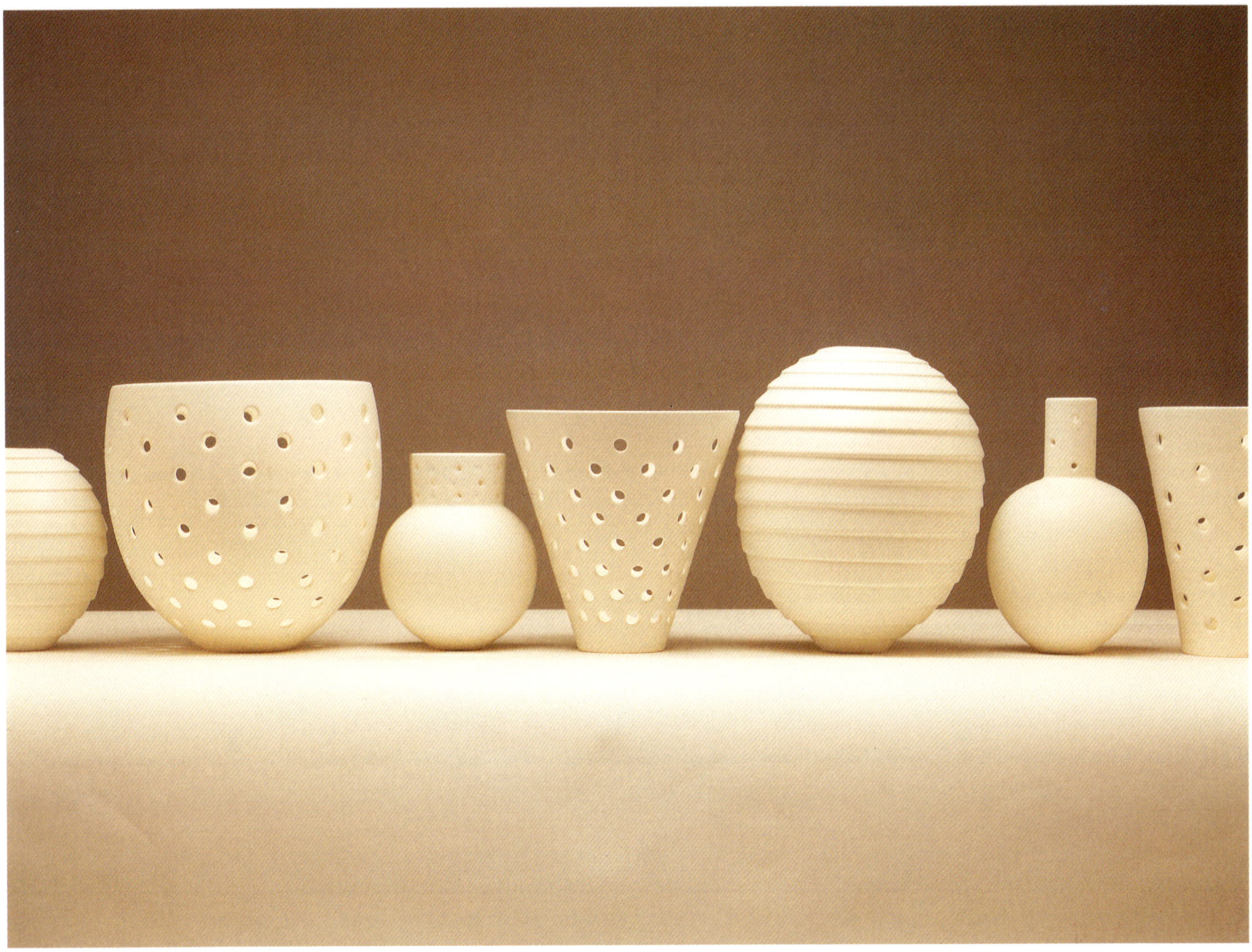

RICHARD PARKER

Born Nelson 1946.
Teachers Certificate, Christchurch Teachers College 1967.
Lives in Kaeo.

Richard Parker's pots have a mischievous, theatrical quality, so it is not surprising to discover that the maker has a background in teaching art, drama and music. All the qualities Parker encouraged in his students in the early 1970s now emerge from his pots as a lively aesthetic sensibility, a flamboyant presence and energetic, rhythmical movement.

Parker started potting full time in 1973 after spending some time teaching and working in theatres. He had developed an interest in clay while teaching in Nelson where there was a strong pottery culture. A summer school potting with Yvonne Rust was the turning point for him and he speaks fondly of Rust, and later Peter Alger (3), who encouraged him.

In the mid 1980s he embarked on what would become his signature work. He took a very old idea—wire-cutting into a solid block of clay—and shaped his works as three-dimensional drawings with strong, winged silhouettes. The immediacy and audacity excited him, and the new works attracted considerable critical acclaim nationally and internationally. The wings of these pots are important features, often making reference to human form—playful, strongly defined, yet not macho. Parker perceives the pots as people with lines to deliver, like actors on a stage. His production suggests a narrative quality, with dialogue developing between family groupings.

Parker continued to make domestic ware while he explored the 'drawing pots'. After several years the two genres merged and he now creates a range of pieces using the same design philosophy and surface decoration. His domestic ware—platters, bowls and vases—has the same impudent personality as his less physically functional pieces. He believes that to establish a working rhythm he has to keep making—to break a lot, dispose of them, sell them and keep making them until they flow easily. His low-fired terracotta works have a practised fluidity and a restrained palette. He likes working with clay roughened up with coarse particles for texture and a single basic glaze. New work is invariably informed by preceding pieces, giving a sense of family and lineage.

In 1991 Parker was commissioned to work to a very large scale for *Treasures of the Underworld* at World Expo in Seville. Some very large works currently being made are part of a long progression since that time. The process is different from that used for the more intimately scaled works, and Parker finds it difficult to maintain their spontaneous spirit and energy. The large pots appeal to Parker for reasons beyond the technical challenges, and they have been realised since workshop facilities and machinery have become available. Parker is aiming for a resonance between the viewer and the pot—a sense of matching the volume of the pot to the volume of the human body. The development period has been so long that there is a danger of losing the initial spark, but for the persistence and personality of the maker. Meanwhile there is the joy of his smaller pieces—the definitive style that enchants, entertains and wants to be centre stage. His pieces are award winners—distinctive, joyous works with upturned toes, splashed colour and a delightful human persona.

Vase—striped pattern
Terracotta
300 x 310 x 165 mm
Collection of the artist

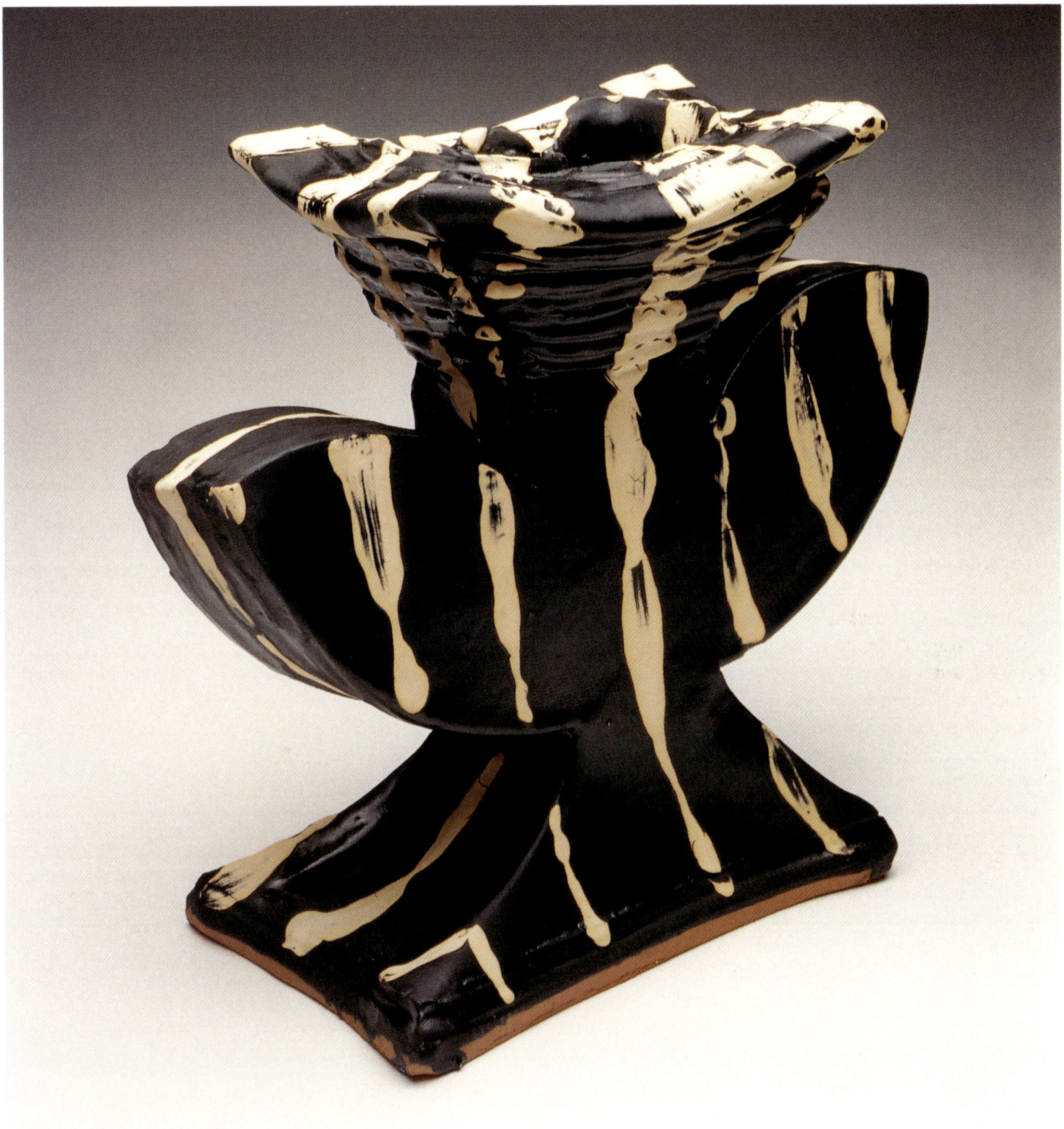

DIANA PARKES

Born Hawera 1944.
London City and Guild's Embroidery Examination 1981;
Dip Craft Competence in Embroidery, Assoc of Embroiderers' Guilds Inc 1990;
Adult Learning Papers, Dip Teaching, ASTU 1991–92.
Lives in Lower Hutt.

The New Zealand flag frequently appears in Diana Parkes' stitched works. It is a spinoff from a commission in 1991 to create the Queen's Colour for the Navy. This was the first time that this ceremonial flag had been commissioned locally; previously it had been made in England. It was also Parkes' first contact with the defence forces, and it opened up a new world of protocol, a hierarchical system and a fresh perspective on war. For the first time she saw the defence forces in human terms.

A number of ceremonial commissions have come her way, and recent ones include the Girl Guides Association Chief Commissioners' flag, the Maori Battalion flag and a ceremonial flag for the Signal Corp. She has responded well to the formality of these projects—they fit with her ability to create exquisitely stitched, carefully composed textile works within rigorously defined constraints.

When she is not creating commissioned work or teaching, Parkes makes small embroidered works and larger abstract patchwork pieces for exhibitions, a number of which have won awards. It was inevitable that issues of war and memorials became part of the content in these works. Motifs like Anzac poppies, guns, crosses representing the dead, and military uniforms have appeared. Her concerns are wider than war, and for a number of years she has used the medium of stitchery to make a variety of political statements. Her imagery and use of stitchery have a number of parallels in international textile works of the past two decades.

Her most endearing works are the small, intimate embroideries worked in petit point on painted canvas. She maintains a looseness by hand-stitching directly, without designing on graph paper or sketching on the backing canvas. Her starting point is most likely to be words, and text becomes part of her imagery. Issues of content, colour and composition are paramount and she works with a rich palette. She was an early exponent of hand-dyed fabrics, and working with fabric dyes became an important component of her pieces in the 1980s. During that period she established a business selling dyestuffs to other practitioners. She often dyes fabrics for her patched and quilted works, and especially enjoys the rhythmical effects of Japanese shibori techniques.

In 1995 she created *Three out of Four (Marriages) Survive*, a work that was exhibited in a prestigious exhibition, *Art of the Stitch*, which was shown in London and Manchester. It was a wry view of statistics, showing a very personal concern about the issues. The work was loaded with references to romance; and equality was represented by scales and a biological clock ticking. The signature flag is there, and life events are recorded photographically.

The flag appears again in *Sheep May Safely Graze*, which also features images of sheep carcasses and dollar signs. Parkes' subversive social commentary is a genteel yet effective means of making a statement. By using stitchery she is using a time-honoured technique for women to protest about injustice.

**Three Out of Four (Marriages) Survive
Canvas work embroidery/cotton threads on painted canvas
500 x 260 mm
Collection of the artist**

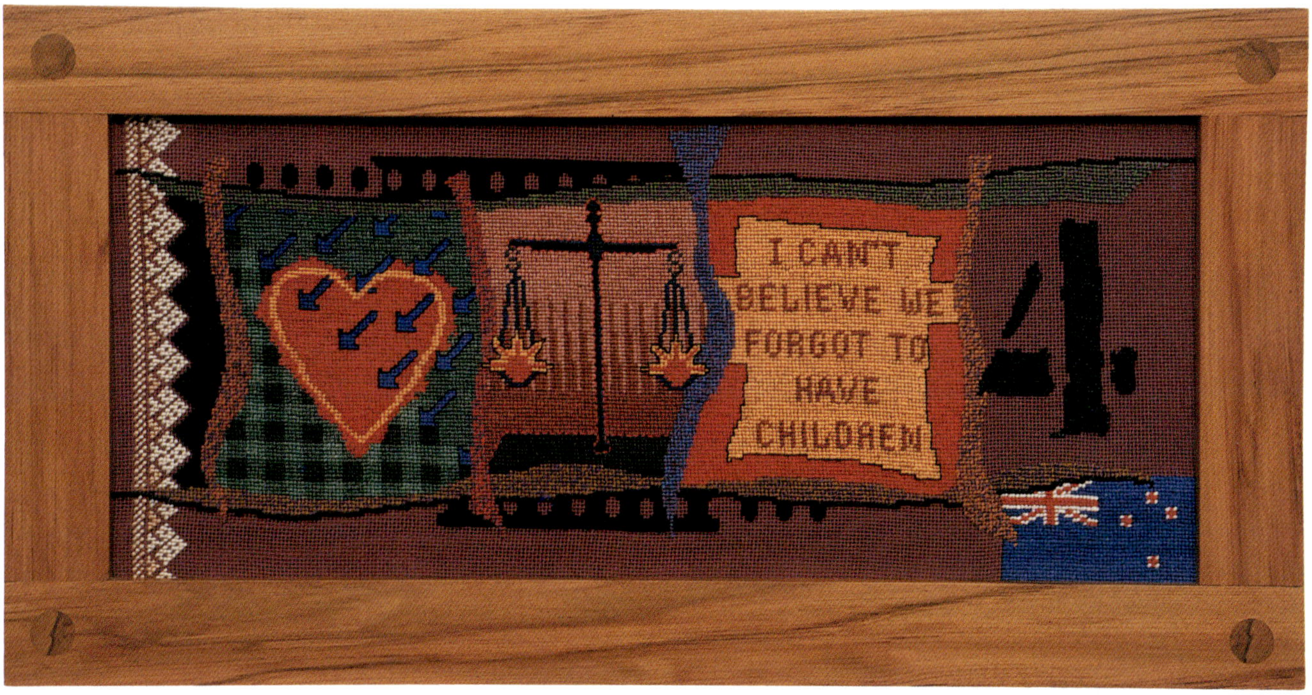
I CAN'T BELIEVE WE FORGOT TO HAVE CHILDREN
4.

TANIA PATTERSON

Born Auckland 1969.
Certificate Craft Design, Carrington Polytechnic 1987;
Dip Craft Design (Jewellery), Carrington Polytechnic 1989.
Lives in Auckland.

Moving parts give Tania Patterson's jewellery a distinctive personality. Wearing her jewellery is an activity rather than a passive display, as many of her works have a kinetic aspect which directly involves both viewer and wearer. The approach fits with her reticence in discussing the intention of her work—she prefers people to explore the opening mechanisms and discover the hidden intricacies themselves.

The hinged mechanisms are often unpredictable and always well resolved, and Patterson enjoys the challenge of creating movement. The interiors of her pieces often have an element of surprise—perhaps a tiny explosion of colour or fragmented components that spring out on opening—and the often playful contents provide a contrast to the more solid casing. In spirit these pieces sometimes bear a relationship to mass-produced novelties like walnut shells housing beetles, yet the individuality and exquisite crafting of Patterson's pieces lift them to a different realm where they are imbued with a layer of sophistication and artistry.

While a student at Carrington Polytechnic under the tutelage of Daniel Clasby, she gained confidence in experimentation and introduced humour and fine detail to her work. These remain constant characteristics, as does the marrying of organic and industrial products. While much of her work is made of silver, Patterson takes an eclectic approach to materials, and has included cherry stones, coconut shells and canna seeds as readily as gold leaf and painted wood.

Animal and plant references abound in her pieces, which are witty and sharply observed, at times fanciful. Dogs, insects, household objects and human behaviour are as much part of her pool of ideas as are plant forms. The first series of dogs, some with human hands and feet, performed on tiny stages. A subsequent series of keyhole works included more pieces about dogs and what they might do when left alone at home. These pieces also revealed tiny stages, but this time viewers were cast in the role of voyeur and spy.

Her current concerns include bracelets and necklaces which focus on wearability and relate directly to the body. The bracelets are articulated multi-component pieces, and she is interested in the fluidity which can be created with a number of joints. The concept extends the notion of moving parts, which are still important, and focuses on visual aspects of repeating images. These works celebrate materials, motifs and techniques.

Flowers that Patterson creates have never been conceived as pretty or cute, and are more likely spiky and severe. The new necklaces, in the form of single seedpods hanging from a simple wire strand, have softer lines and retain the kinetic aspect. These pods, which can be opened, suggest a beginning of life. Inviting the wearer and the viewer to engage physically implies an act of intimacy, an undercurrent to Patterson's work that makes it extraordinarily appealing.

Seedpod Pendants
Sterling silver, ebony, wood
Various from 20–40 mm
Collection of the artist

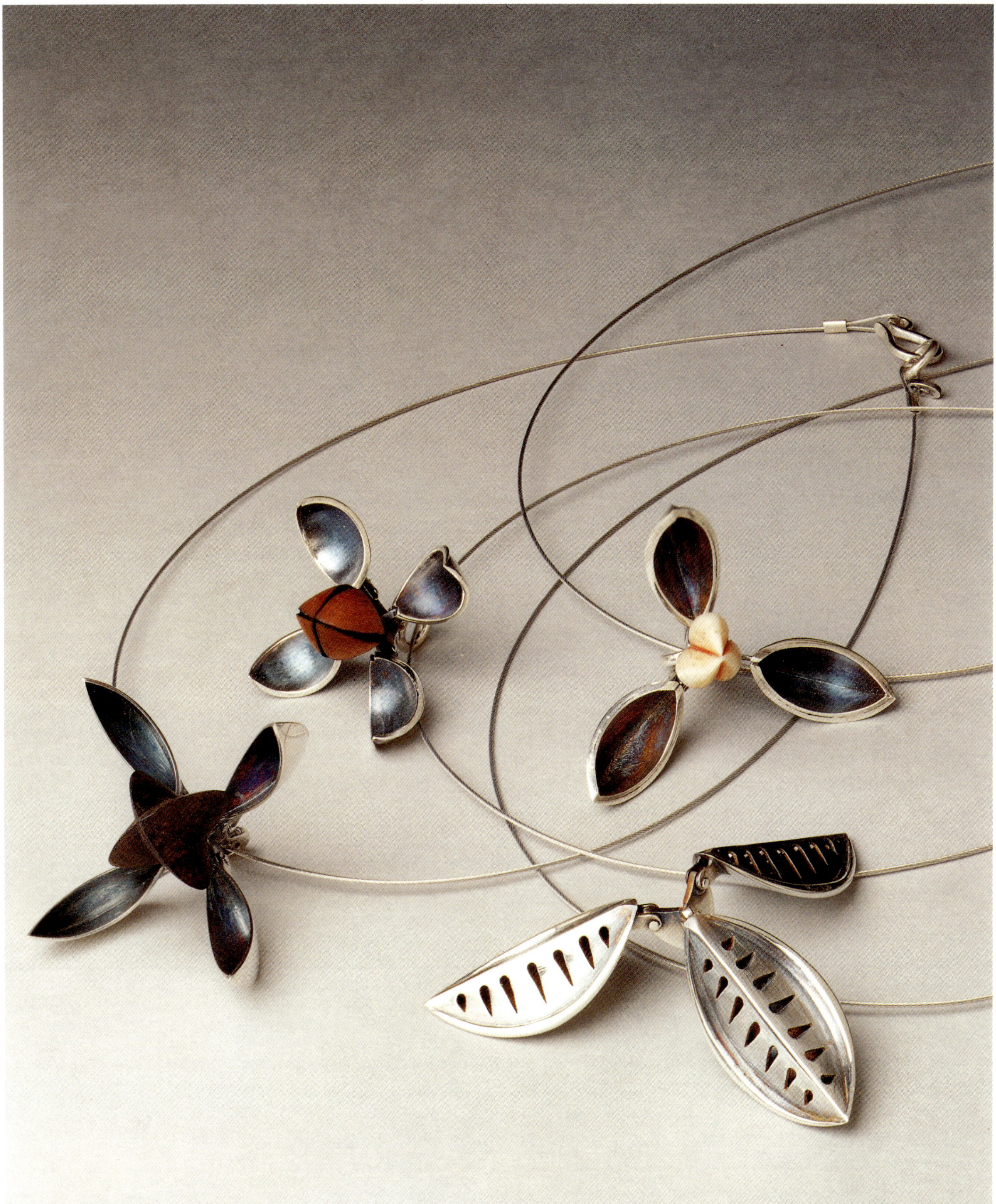

SUZY PENNINGTON

Born Wellington 1947.
Dip Industrial Design, Wellington Polytechnic School of Design 1968;
Postgraduation, Woven Textile, Leeds University 1970–71.
Lives in Wellington.

When Suzy Pennington was invited to exhibit some miniature works at *Flax 96* in Lithuania, she was offered more than just another exciting opportunity to exhibit internationally. The title of the exhibition became the trigger for a new direction in her work. Lithuania is a linen producer, hence the title for the exhibition, but Pennington recognised the chance to make a personal statement by referencing harakeke, the flax of her environment.

While working with many Polynesian people at Page 90 Artspace in Porirua, Pennington had become aware of the mana and sacredness of the mat for Polynesian people. She chose to weave a number of small mats, acknowledging that the finest mats were used to wrap the dead, that they were for sleeping on and that one never walked on them in shoes. She respectfully proceeded to build her images on them, with collage, paint, applied fibres, threads and fabrics, a process not dissimilar to the way she works on canvas. Seeking to reveal the sacred and spiritual qualities of her subject—its soul—Pennington looked to explore below the surface of her work, and to discover the intersection between the physical and spiritual world. At the time she was working on a series titled *Sacred Sites*. The connection was not lost, and the works on the mats became an integral part of the series.

The cross is a recurring theme in the *Sacred Sites* series, and its use signifies more than a religious interpretation. For Pennington there are connections to the ancient symbol for crossroads, to the tree of life and to making choices. In the potent large image on fabric, *The Shadow Lies on the Ground Like the Memory of a Past*, the cross provided a structure, fragmented and degrading, like the torn fabric of life surrounding it. This work became central to *Sacred Sites*, providing a visual and emotive focus for the cross-like layout of the exhibition.

Pennington's background in design and textiles has been critical to her work. Her early pieces were stitched 'tapestries' in the broadest sense of the word—layered, often torn fragments of fabric. The stitches and threads were integral to the visual statement which often made reference to surfaces and landscape. That sensibility has been retained in her work, and even the most painterly pieces have a textile component, the texture and tactility of fabrics and threads. The layered landscape is still important and she likens her portrayal to standing on the same piece of ground as someone before her, acknowledging the residue of human presence, the aura left behind and the effect on the landscape. The layers and threads act as a metaphor for time, and are metaphysical as well.

Pennington shares a studio with painter Helen Kedgley, and the two have exhibited together many times. She has exhibited in Lithuania, Zimbabwe, India, at the International Triennale of Tapestry in Poland on two occasions, as well as in Australia and nationally. Her work has been described as poetry in thread. She sees it as a fusion of various media, and of her Viking background, Pacific influences and the Anglo-Saxon society which has formed her.

Journey to the Inner Source
Mixed media: collage, procion dye, paint on flax
300 x 200 mm
Collection of Michael and Sandra Lee

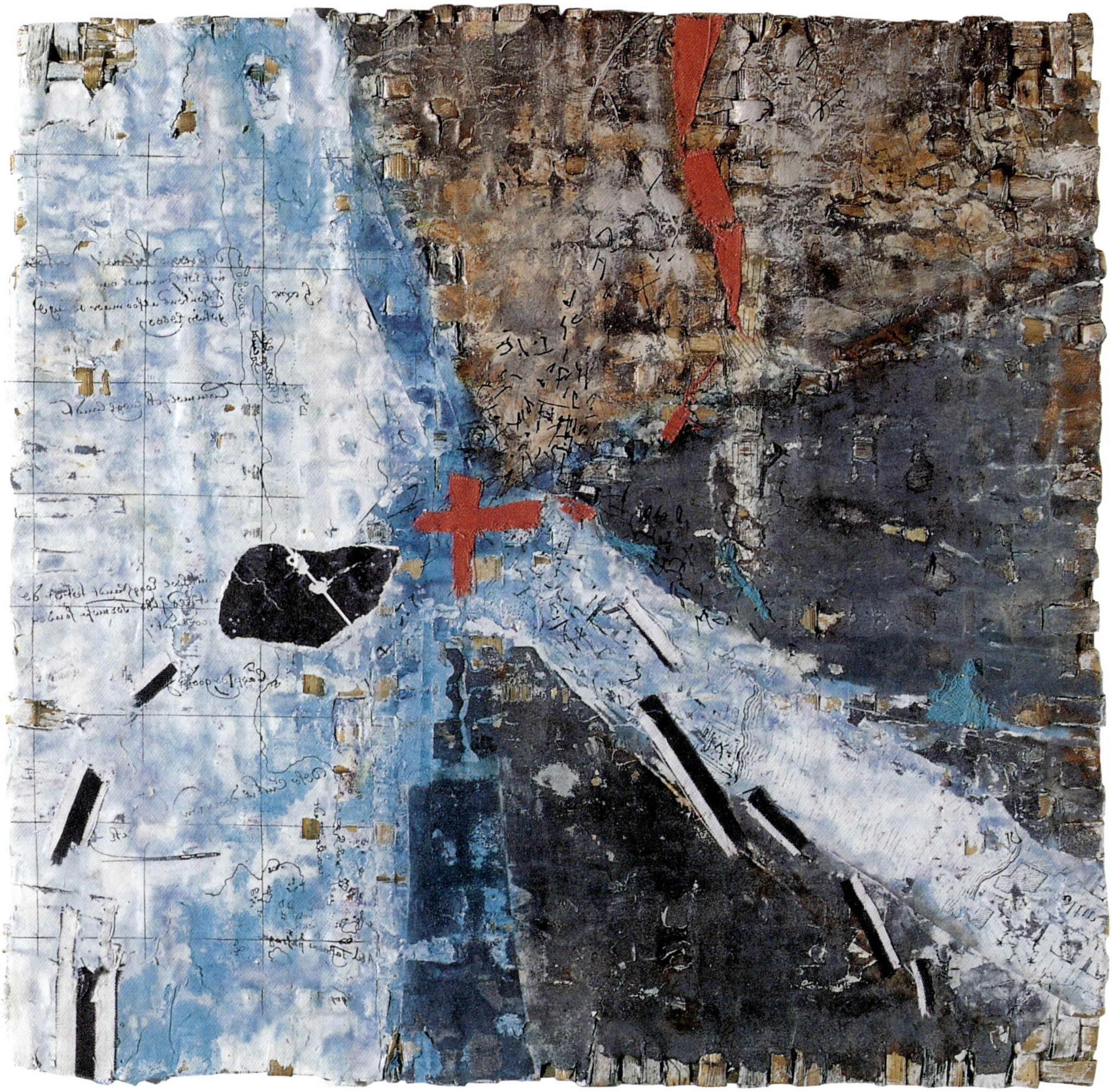

ALAN PRESTON

Born Te Awamutu 1941.
MSc (Psychology), Canterbury University 1967; jewellery classes at Camden Institute, London 1973.
Founding member of Fingers collective 1974.
Lives in Muriwai.

There were a variety of international influences on Alan Preston's early jewellery, though he first looked to contemporary English jewellery as a role model. Like other New Zealanders whose jewellery developed at that time, he was largely self-taught, looking to the exotic and the historic for inspiration.

It was after a trip to Fiji in 1979 that Preston turned his attention to the Pacific, initially incorporating vibrant colour and tropical imagery in his enamelled work, and starting to incorporate shell, coconut shell and fibre in the early 1980s. In 1982, at a workshop conducted by German jeweller Hermann Junger, Preston created paua circles with saw-tooth edges, cross-referencing details between Western and Pacific jewellery. The saw-tooth edge he perceived as an old European jewellers' technique for containing stones in a metal setting, while in Pacific culture the setting might have been made of bone or stone.

In 1983 Preston and Warwick Freeman (27) were invited to teach in Fiji. Preliminary research of the Auckland Museum collection heightened Preston's awareness of Pacific adornment. He started to make work that drew attention to the generous scale of Pacific artifacts, and these pieces bore a strong relationship to Fijian breastplates. Later work came much more from his own personal consciousness—bold graphic works made in the materials of Pacific cultures but unlike anything made before.

In his newest work Preston contrasts the positive and negative images that occur when he cuts into oyster pearl shell. Conservation of resources suggests that he use both portions of shell and there is a sense of satisfaction in using it all, a certain purity of concept. He began the series by creating large, dynamic chains out of shell loops. The interior cutouts he joined as crosses that evoked the frangipani flower, and these were strung on vau, the hibiscus bark fibre used in Fiji. For Preston the cross refers to the Celtic cross and the four-leaf clover, and he enjoys the simplicity of this graphic imagery and its multiple use in many cultures. What interests him is the way others identify his work with Pacific culture when he uses pearl shell.

A good deal of Preston's work is informed by his politics, the issues of identity and Maori sovereignty. He created a series of kiwi badges like military insignia, the bodies made of pressed silver and the pins reinforcing the vulnerable beaks. They were titled provocatively—*Kiwi Attacks the Crown, Off with her Head* and *Frightened Kiwis*, a reference to the Muldoon years in politics in the 1970s and '80s. Preston kept the kiwi image going for a number of years, with the same pressed bodies given their own identities and personalities through variations in their colour, spikes and beaks.

By seeking to express identity through his striking work Preston has attracted some controversy. He is a pioneer, a role model for younger jewellers and respected by those who seek to express New Zealand visually as a country in the Pacific.

Four Pointer Brooch and Breastplate
Black lip oyster shell, vau, silver
113 x 100 x 18 mm;
70 x 70 x 10 mm
Collection of the artist

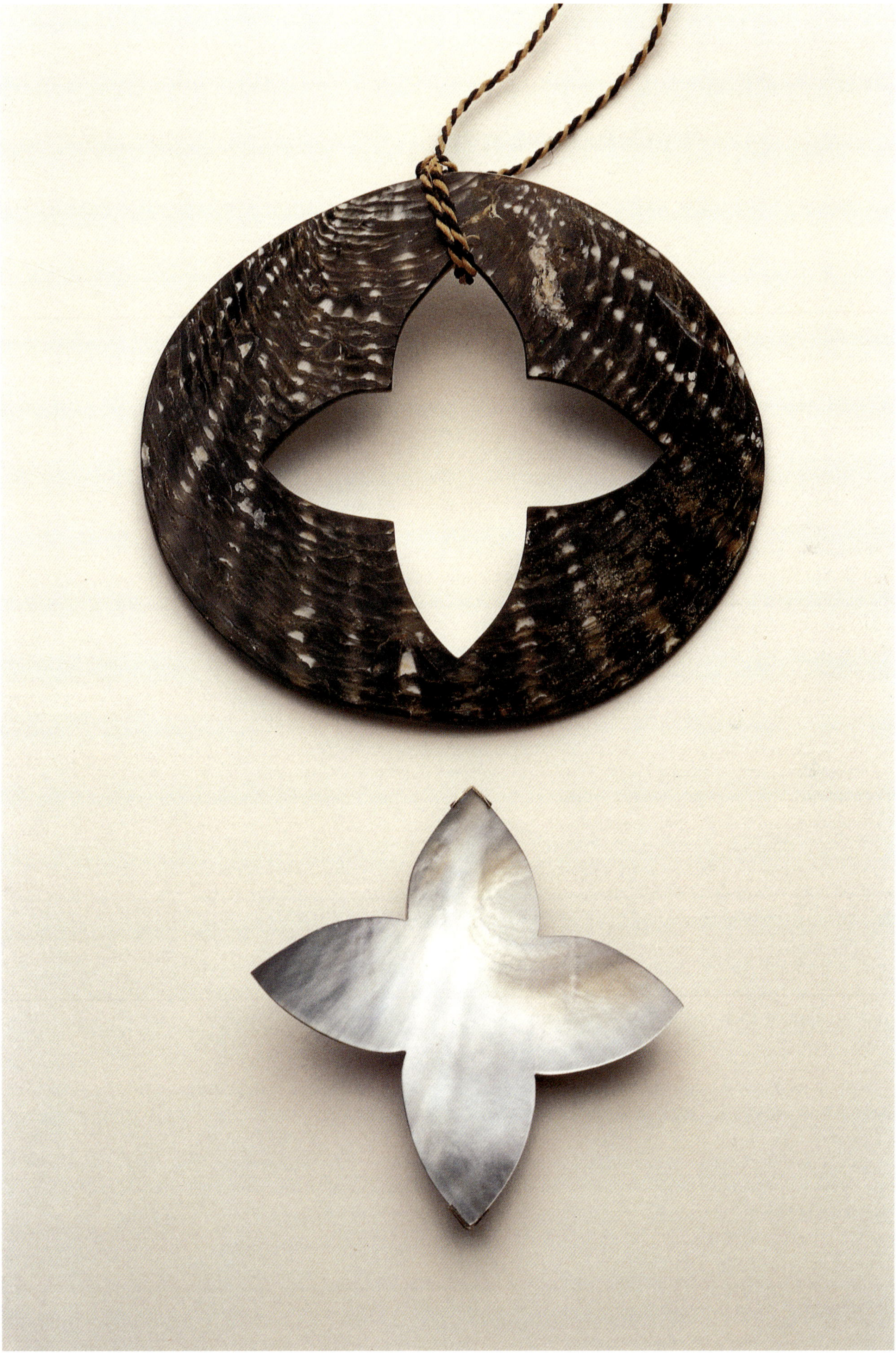

LOUISE PURVIS

Born Pahiatua 1968.
Certificate Craft Design, Hawke's Bay Polytechnic 1989;
Dip Craft Design (Maori), Waiariki Polytechnic 1990.
Lives in Auckland.

First-hand experience on a building site gave Louise Purvis the subject matter for a recent exhibition of sculpture. Like many artists she subsidises her art practice with other paid work, and stone masonry on the refurbishment of Auckland's St Matthews in the City church was such a project. The building site, perhaps an unusual context for a woman, inspired her exhibition *Site*, which could be interpreted as an exploration of measuring material, time and equivalent work between genders. One of the works, *Cup Stack*, made reference to the sacrosanct tea breaks on the job, and at the same time paid homage to Constantin Brancusi's famous *Never Ending Column*.

Purvis uses humour and wit to deliver her messages—not the strident feminist messages that abounded in the '70s and '80s, but rather wry revelations, slightly subversive understatements that provoke a smile rather than a reaction. Humour is important to her, and she enjoys twisting ideas around, animating static objects or adding a human element. The tools she makes are designed to fit her small hands—a commentary on the large, heavy tools more usually designed for male hands. Her tools sometimes acquire human features, which might replace a functional aspect. The meaning of the object shifts, and the gender connotations change with it.

She likes using parts of the human figure—hands, feet, limbs—wanting viewers to hone in on the beauty of small details. One approach is to replace an expected straight line with a leg or an arm, using them as part of the composition, a re-contextualisation, a surrealist viewpoint. By taking discrete parts of bodies and putting them into unexpected compositions, she confronts viewers, amuses them and allows them a new understanding of the objects.

Carving and casting are her basic modes of working. It is demanding work, physically and mentally, and a challenge she relishes. In *Tipple*, a recent sculpture Purvis focused solely on feet, the toes curling over the edge of the pedestal. The feet appear to be completely decontextualised in an almost classical way, yet the curling toes reveal muscles, energy and a connection to a brain. There seems no agenda other than realism and accuracy, but it is an accuracy that involves a real person. It is the same quality she brought to an earlier work in the form of a pair of stiletto-heeled shoes, and to the feet she added to her tools. These feet are beautifully carved, revealing her skill in working with stone and her love of materials which developed during her days of craft design training a decade ago.

Purvis received the Pacific Region Commonwealth Fellowship for Arts and Crafts in 1994, and worked as a sculptor in France and Scotland during that year. Now she works from a home studio, making sculptures with content that is forever evolving. Yet her fundamental premise remains constant while she follows her normal practice of looking to her immediate environment for inspiration, and poking fun at it. Whether it is a building site or the farm of her youth, Purvis brings an irreverent and surrealist point of view, suggesting that all is not what it might seem.

Tipple
Carrara marble
ca. 560 x 400 x 145 mm
Collection of the artist

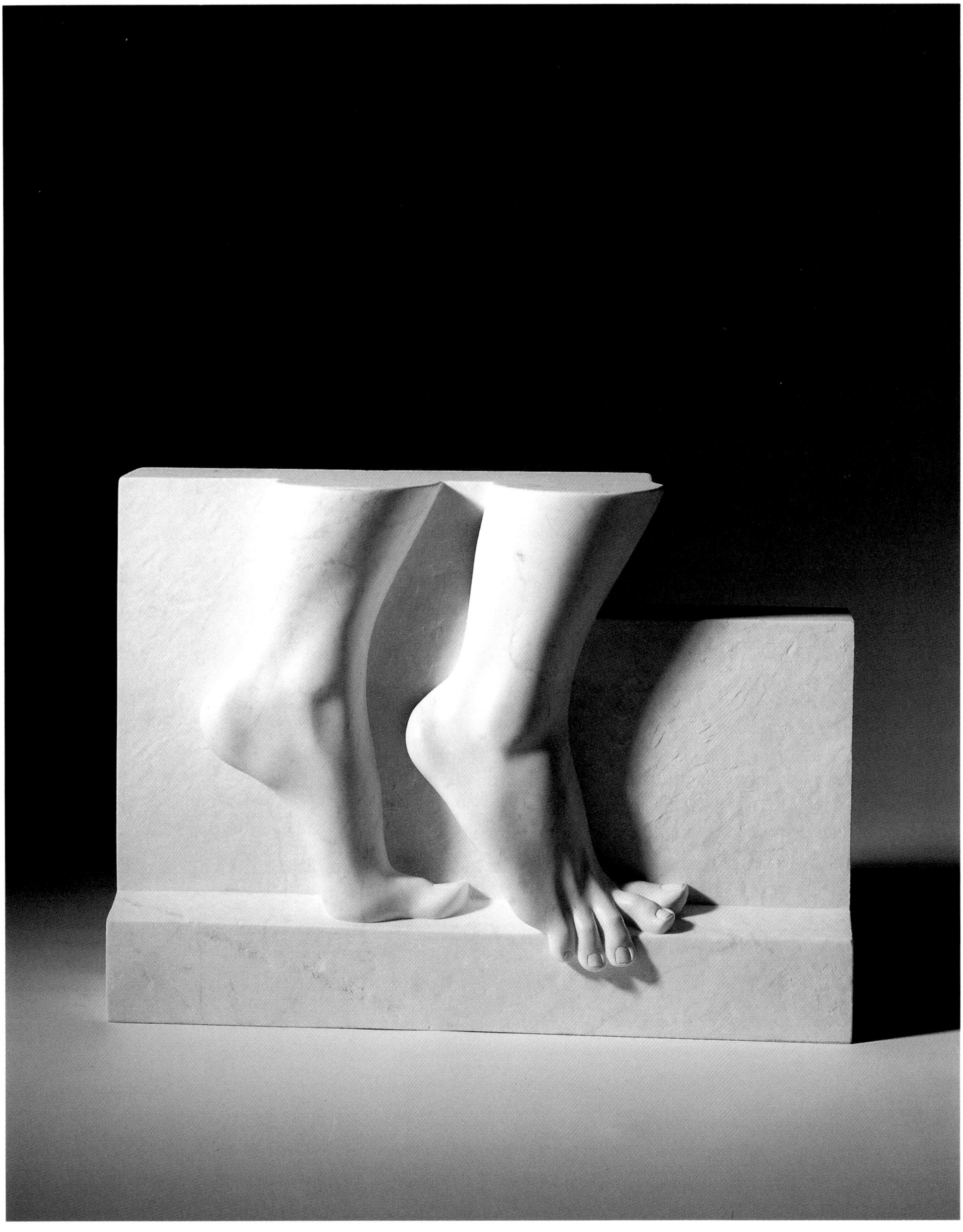

70

BAYE PEWHAIRANGI RIDDELL

Born Tokomaru Bay 1950.
Ngati Porou, Whanau a Ruataupare.
Set up first studio pottery in Christchurch 1974.
Lives in Tokomaru Bay.

Concepts of guardianship and custodianship inform Baye Riddell's ceramics. Belief that he has a responsibility to those who went before him and those coming behind is manifested in his knowledge of history and whakapapa as well as his major commitment to teaching. In 1989, on a Fulbright Scholarship, he went to the USA to study with Native American potters. It was the beginning of a number of exchanges, including opportunities for him to exhibit there. In 1996, he was asked to develop arts programmes as part of a strategy for development within his tribal area of Ngati Porou, and this work has been of major significance to him.

As a Maori potter in the 1970s Riddell pioneered a medium which had not traditionally been part of Maori culture. Working with clay was symbolic of an alternative lifestyle that attracted him while he lived in Christchurch—the concept of self-sufficiency was appealing. In 1979 he returned to Tokomaru Bay where, together with Helen Mason, he established a pottery. He subsequently worked with Harry Davis and Barry Brickell (10), later with Para Matchitt (Vol. 2, 57) and Jacob Scott. In 1987 Kaihanga Uku, an organisation for Maori ceramic artists, was formed and held its first national hui at Tokomaru Bay.

He has frequently produced glazed domestic ware, but it is with his sculptural work that he makes comment about the issues important to him. His press-moulded figurative sculptures are narratives about the marae, ancestors, challenge, welcome and the closely knit community standing together—a reminder of responsibility to those of the past, present and future.

In his work Riddell explores the spiritual concepts, analogies and symbolic vocabularies of Christianity and Maoritanga. These two streams—wai e rua—converge to produce the metaphors in his work. Faith, tradition and a sense of social responsibility anchor his concepts, which flourish within these apparent constraints. Self-imposed restraints and disciplines have confirmed for Riddell that what may seem restrictive leads quickly to discovery and innovation.

The theme becomes literal and a number of his works become doorways or gateways, representing opportunities, the unknown, rites of passage and life decisions. Some gateways stand alone: others span a vessel. Partially thrown, partially handbuilt, the vessels express a number of his ideas, often through the carved and moulded additions. He likens vessels to holes in the ground and the mystery they contain—holes that people fall into or in which they find themselves, or the unknown. He sometimes uses fibre as a visual relief and contrast. It represents offerings, family ties and connections to the land—the issue of custodianship that is fundamental to his work.

Working with terracotta clay he digs from his family land, Riddell creates unglazed forms for the many exhibitions to which he is invited. Wood-firing is a direct approach, enhancing the colour of the clay and affirming his strong connection to the land.

**Tangata Whenua
Woodfired terracotta
900–1000 mm (h)
Collection of Celia Dunlop**

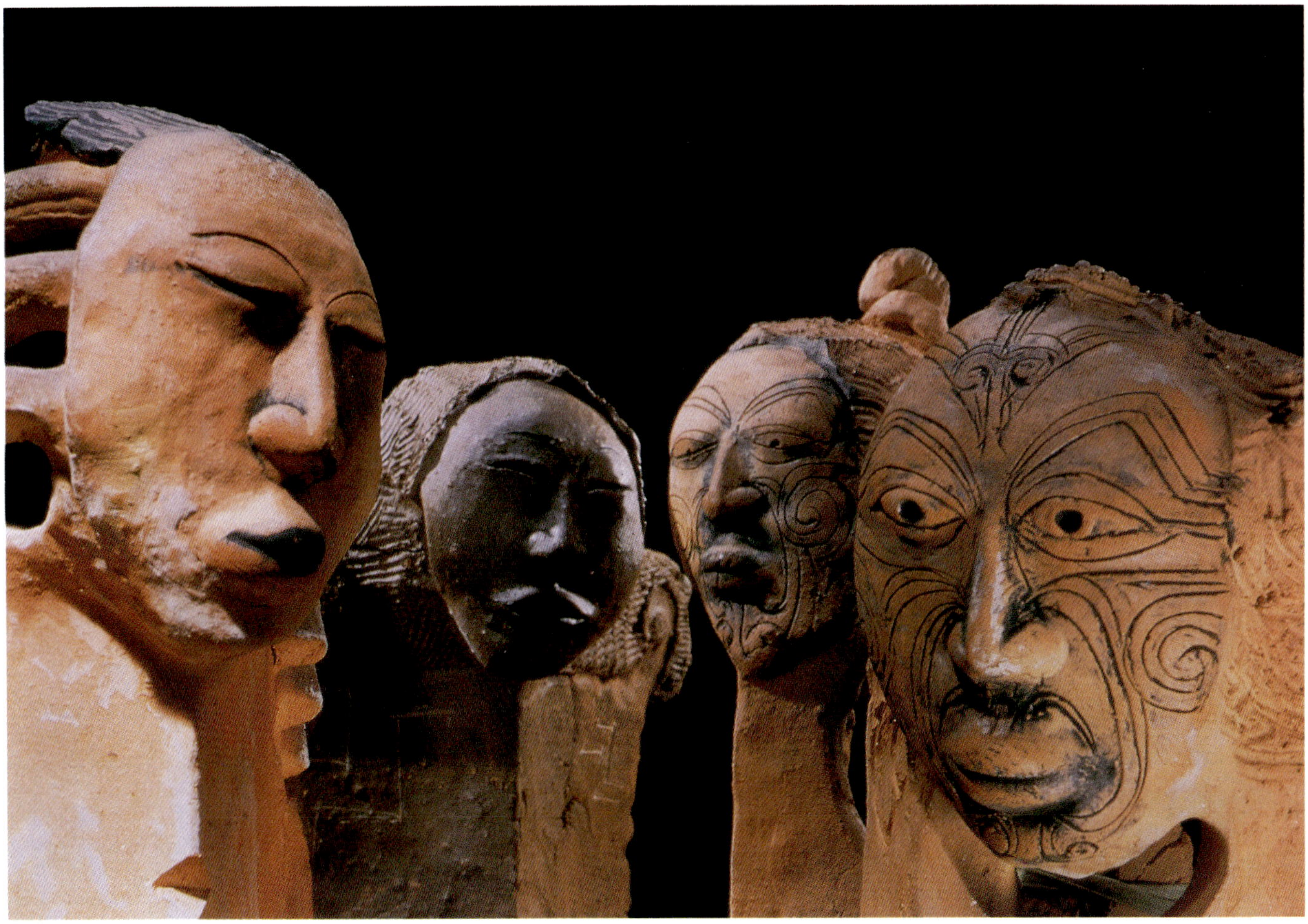

DARRYL ROBERTSON

Born Reefton 1955.
Apprenticeships 1972–79: with Harry and May Davis; Jack Laird; Christopher Vine; Sonja Ankatel, Queensland; Holga Hornum, Queensland; John Davidson, England; Brian Jasper, Queensland.
Lives in Nelson.

Seven years of apprenticeship and travel gave Darryl Robertson sound technical skills and aspirations for high standards. In 1980 he and his partner Lesley Robertson established their first pottery. His creativity and individuality, which were nurtured during those early years, flourished in 1986 when he decided he no longer wanted to be a wholesale producer of pots.

Taking this risky step was important—it freed him to produce experimental works, and to participate in numerous national and international exhibitions as well as to complete many prestigious commissions. One of his most recent was for presentation to the Emperor of Japan by Jenny Shipley, the New Zealand prime minister, in 1998. The response to his work has been encouraging and his works have been purchased for many international collections. Corporate and private commissions have, however, given him more than a living—he learns about human thought and behaviour from his interactions with clients, and this feeds back into his work.

Two strands of work developed—his wood-fired 'elemental' pots, and a series of painted clay works. He was fascinated by both processes and eventually integrated them. Essentially he created simple forms like plates—surfaces on which to paint. He won many awards in New Zealand, Australia, Egypt, Japan and France, which encouraged him to develop this work into more sculptural forms and explore further the content of his painting. In 1990, on an Anzac Fellowship, he was Artist in Residence at Monash University, Gippsland, and in 1991 he received a QEII Arts Council grant.

One of the most creatively challenging periods occurred when his father's death coincided with an invitation to participate in *Treasures of the Underworld* at World Expo, Seville, 1992. Two images emerged from a dream before the funeral: the Southern Cross and a dead whale on the edge of a breaking wave. For Robertson the cluster of stars of the Southern Cross became discs that represented members of his family; a pukeko flying away became his father; and the whale's tail on the edge of the wave seemed to pose the question: 'Are you going to crash or ride it out?' Somehow Robertson completed the massive work, just meeting his deadline—a low point in his life, but a healing period and a creative high point. Similar images appeared in later works. Robertson enjoys painting on large expanses of clay that are designed to be wall-hung. He makes stains specifically for each project but takes an uncomplicated approach to glaze technology—images are more important than technicalities.

Lizard Rock, exhibited at the Fletcher Challenge Ceramics Award, 1998, is part of a recent series based on animal life which receives little attention from humans. It is a tribute to a hardy lizard Robertson encountered in a bathroom of a multi-storey building in Singapore. He was intrigued that it had entered to drink water, then retreated, and he admired its ability to survive against all odds. The resulting work was a tall monument growing out of a rock and supported on feet, implying the possibility of mobility. Robertson recognised he was giving the subject the level of importance that a child might—it was a satisfying feeling.

Lizard Rock
Ceramic, handbuilt clay, handpainted surfaces
630 x 360 x 300 mm
Collection of the artist

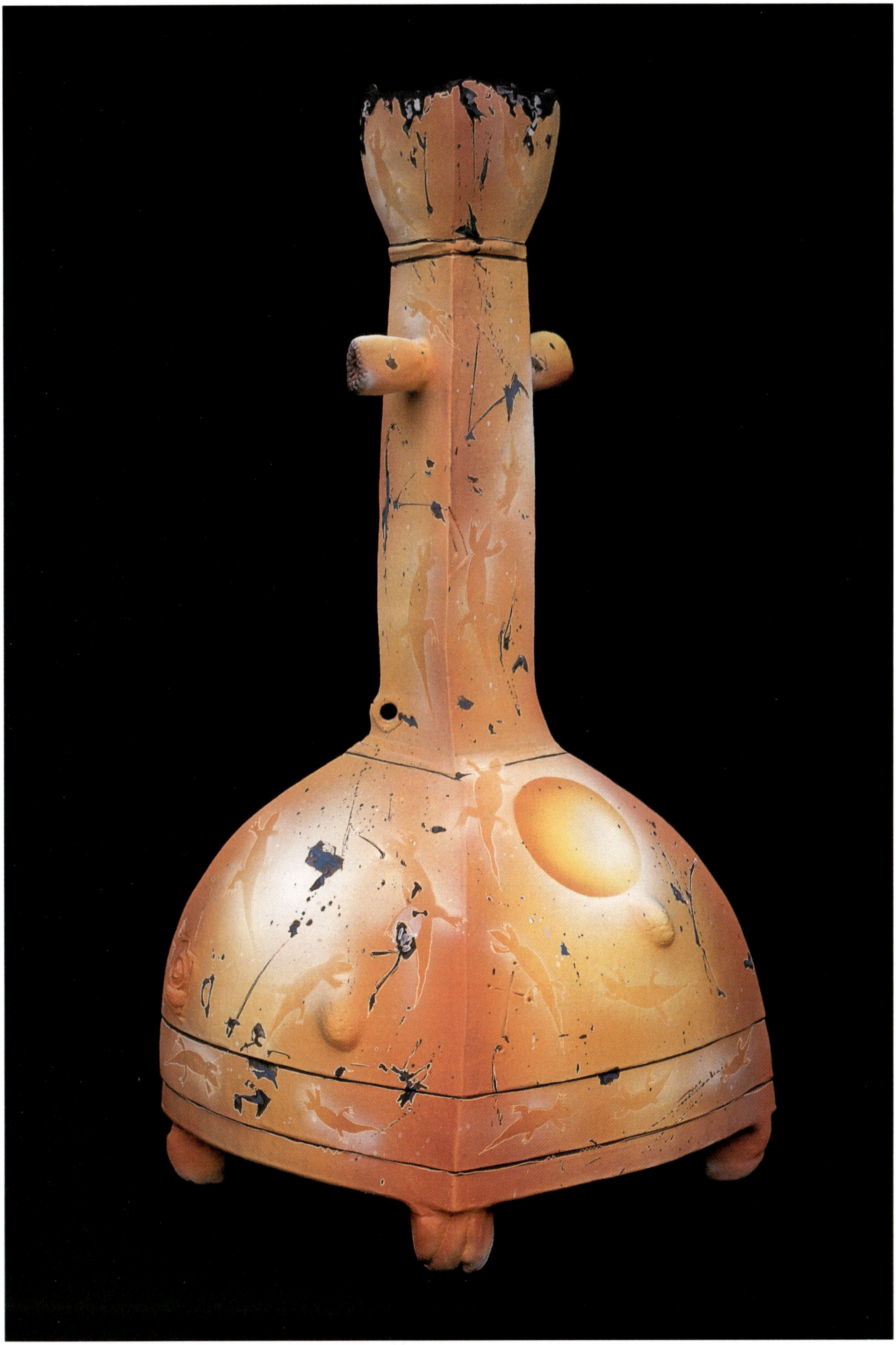

ANN ROBINSON

Born Auckland 1944.
DFA, University of Auckland 1980.
Lives in Karekare.

Since 1982 Ann Robinson has been casting glass vessels—sumptuous, simply defined, heavy, translucent pieces that celebrate the medium and delight their viewers. Her reputation is as much for her modesty and generosity with students and peers as for pioneering her casting process, which evolved from the bronze casting of her student days. But it is her outstanding design of three-dimensional forms that makes her a leader in her field.

She is respected internationally and, as well as exhibiting widely in New Zealand, Australia, Japan, USA and Europe, she has taught at the prestigious Pilchuck Glass School in USA. Robinson has had many competition successes, including winning the Philips Glass Award in 1984 and 1986, and the Winstone Biennale Award for craft in 1987. Her work was featured at the New Zealand Exhibition of Craft at Expo in Brisbane in 1988 and in *Treasures of the Underworld* at World Expo in Seville in 1992. *Casting Light*, a touring survey exhibition initiated by the Dowse Art Museum in 1998, broke new ground by being the first exhibition of craft art accepted for showing at the New Gallery in Auckland.

Nine years of glass blowing ended for Robinson in 1988. She had developed considerable expertise, and the last pieces in this genre included a series of gourd-shaped forms, decorated with loosely abstracted nikau chevrons. As with the later cast works, she looked to her environment for inspiration, and the bush setting of her home studio on the west coast of Auckland has provided this.

The forms of her cast-glass works have evolved over time, becoming progressively more graceful and assured, crisply carved, refined in detail and adventurous in scale. Robinson strikes a balance between achieving scale and solidity without her works becoming ponderous. She creates a basic wax blank that defines the generic shape of the work. The blank is embellished by relief carving or adding decorative motifs that frequently refer to leaves, petals or nikau fronds. From this she can make either one-off works or editions. Occasionally she builds her pieces from several components to reduce their weight and to exceed the more usual domestic scale. The challenge is always to push the limits of her technical knowledge.

Recently she has tended to reduce the edition size, even creating a number of one-off, innovative pieces. The days of struggling with 'glorious failures' of cracked glass have been over for some time. She has a unique working relationship with Gaffer Glass, colleagues from her glass-blowing days, who supply her with lead crystal in rich colours of her choosing. She produces effects from earthy to acidic, ice-like to jewel-bright.

Robinson has been unswerving in her quest to master and refine casting techniques, and she has a real understanding of the vagaries of the process. She is interested in sculptural form and mass. The process and considering herself to be a craftsperson have been paramount for her, and, typically self-effacing, she sees herself as only just maturing creatively. Her audiences may think otherwise, as her work has been highly sought after for several years. Her pieces have never been made as social comment; rather her aim has been 'to lift the spirit and still the mind', crafting objects of timeless beauty.

**Orchid Vessels
45% crystal glass:
lost wax casting
625 x 160 mm;
630 x 190 mm
Collection of the artist**

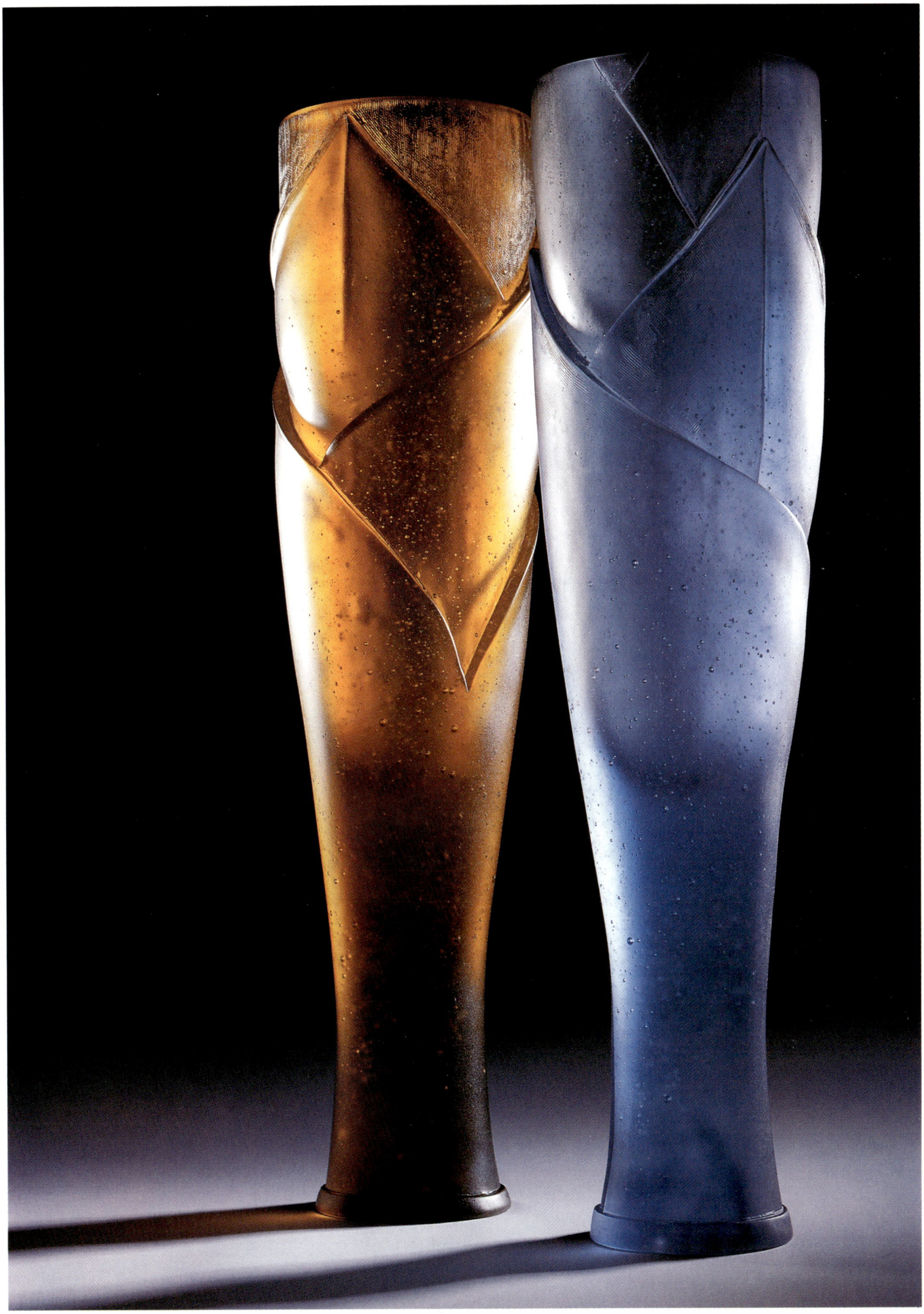

CAROLINE ROBINSON

Born Stratford 1968.
Teachers Training College, Palmerston North 1986; BA (Sociology), Massey University 1990.
Lives in Auckland.

Caroline Robinson's work has developed in a way more familiar to a previous generation. She was a student of sociology when she first started making clothes to sell at markets. This evolved into a business based in New Plymouth under the label *Cabal*. She produced hand-dyed, screen-printed, casual street wear at the 'wearable art' end of the spectrum. Within four years she had seven outlets around the country, had been involved in costume design for a number of theatrical productions, participated in her first wearable art exhibitions and received her first awards.

Robinson's study of sociology has helped her to understand issues of power in society. She had no desire to fight in a political way, but allowed her ideas to emerge more subversively through art—the time-honoured way. With her clothing label she had seen how wearing vibrant colours could shift people's perceptions of themselves. She believed that incremental changes could cumulatively translate into political change.

Robinson never stayed in one place for long after she left New Plymouth in 1993. One of the reasons she closed her clothing business was a growing environmental awareness, and her search for sustainable materials with suitable qualities continues. For four years, more than half of which she spent overseas, she involved herself in special projects like installations, costume design and set design in places as diverse as Ireland, California, Germany and Auckland. Performance and dance were part of her repertoire.

Developing skills in fabric manipulation and dyeing was a pragmatic journey, largely self-taught. She uses those skills creating costumes for the film industry, and completed an installation using fabric and laser lights at the Aotea Centre and Town Hall, Auckland, for the 1998 Youth Arts Festival. Inspiration has come from various sources including musicians. However, Robinson's boldest, most experimental work has been developed for wearable art events, and she has used these opportunities as time for personal discovery and healing.

This was especially so with *Freya*, 1997, with which she won the silk section of the New Zealand Wearable Art Awards in Nelson. She perceived *Freya* as a goddess—a queen of love, sexuality and death. Robinson's interpretation was based on the concept of the cocoon, a theme she had been developing for a couple of years. She attributed dual characteristics to the cocoon—soft, like a womb, a safe protector, and hard, like a place that confines, a prison.

Freya also defined the end of an emotional journey that coincided with Robinson settling in Auckland. She had carried a piece of silk on her travels and it was, by then, disintegrating. As an act of emotional conservation, as well as of saving material resources, she bonded the silk with additional layers of silk, cotton, nikau fibre and plant roots from the beach—a sculpted rather than stitched work. Beneath this 'jacket' was a soft silk jersey and dupion dress that had been hand-painted and screen-printed, then patchworked and handstitched together. Dyed colour was added after the garment was constructed. The costume was topped by an elongated papier mâché mask which transformed *Freya* from an outfit to a mythical character. Creating *Freya* was a personal odyssey for Robinson—a self-portrait.

**Freya
Dupion, Paj and jersey silk, paper, nikau fibre, tree roots, cane, wool
1800 mm
Collection of the artist**

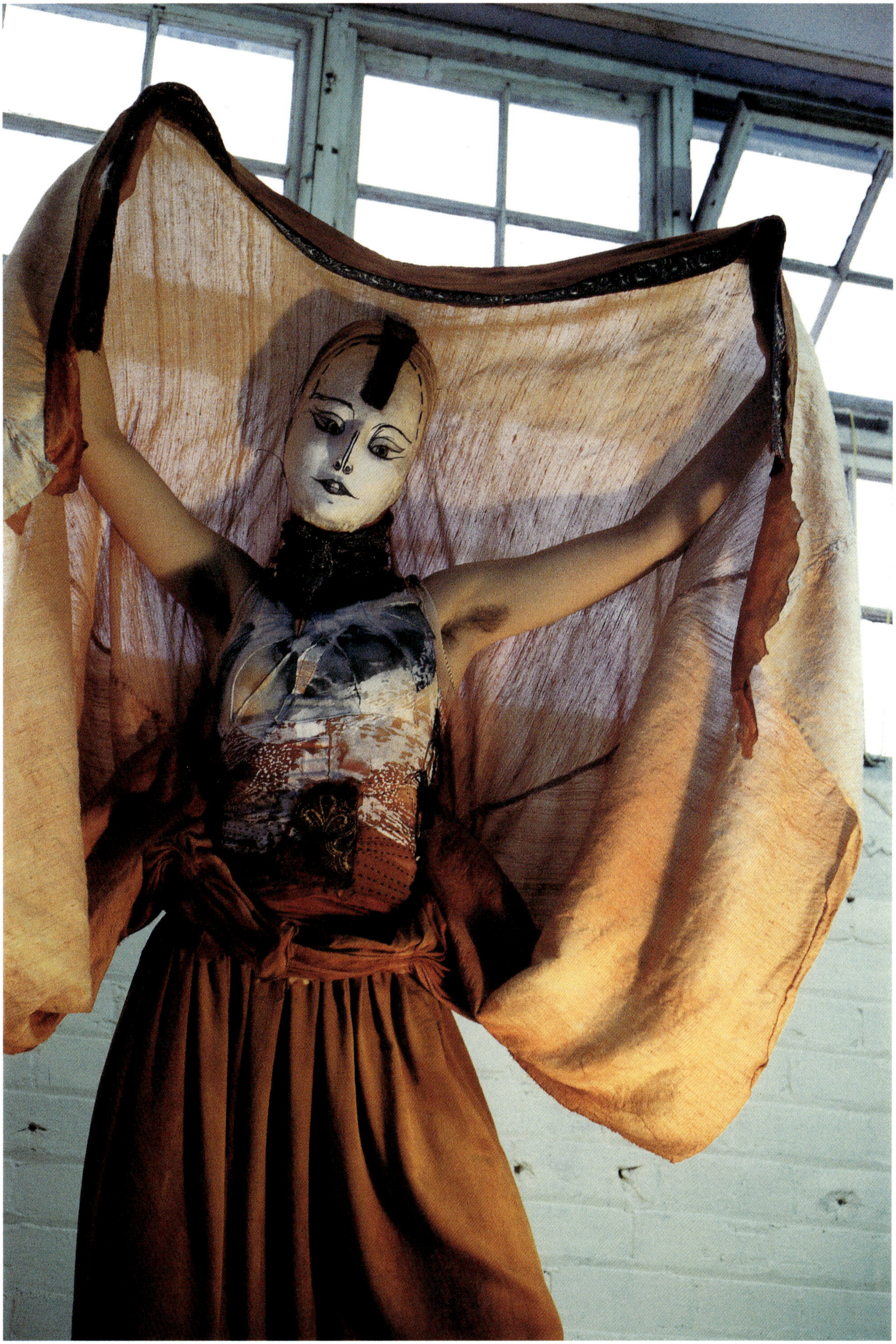

WILLA ROGERS

Born Nelson 1925.
MA, Canterbury College 1947.
Lived in USA 1955–87.
Lives in Nelson.

The baskets that Willa Rogers makes are very much about the materials she uses. She grows a wide range of these—montezuma and torrey pines for coiling, flax from which she makes paper, cabbage trees for strong fronds, as well as watsonia and yucca. She gets great pleasure from gathering local materials seasonally, storing them, then transforming what was dead and discarded into a form that is lasting and can evoke memories and emotions. The development of contemporary baskets in Australia and USA has influenced her and, like many she sees overseas, a number of her baskets are less about being used than about making reference to function and containment.

Rogers first made baskets in the mid-1980s when she lived in California. She was inspired by her teachers and the workshops she attended, and was aware of the considerable interest in contemporary baskets in the USA. In the South West Museum in Los Angeles she saw work by native Americans that excited and stimulated her. She learnt, too, of the wonderful waterproof baskets made of grasses by the Southern Californian desert Indians.

Most important for Rogers was the recognition that in many cultures people have used what was just outside their doors. Many of the same techniques appear in different parts of the world, and she realised that the materials dictated the techniques. Since retiring to Nelson in 1987, making baskets has been the most important thing in her life. Here she is surrounded by beautiful hills and bays which influence her designs. Maori kete, and the use of harakeke, became a model, and her inspiration has come from practitioners like Aromea Tahiwi and Bhana Paul.

Rogers' baskets combine weaving, braiding, coiling and twining, and she believes that the way she works three-dimensionally is a primitive instinct. Her forms, although derived from traditions that are thousands of years old, bear her personal stamp of self-expression. All parts of the nikau palm inform many of her works.

At times she integrates handmade paper into her baskets, forms that are a derivation of some Appalachian baskets she saw in Tennessee. She paints the paper with acrylic paint in colours that evoke the past as well as mirroring her environment. Strong feminist feelings about injustice and inequality emerge through these works. She wants to give credence to the voices that were never heard in the past, the women who were taught to fade into the shadowy background and the work that was anonymous, much of which has vanished. Her work is a tribute to those women, not as echoes of what they made but as contemporary individual statements that acknowledge the debt to the past.

Occasionally Rogers makes masks from handmade paper. They are moulded from real faces and some are contained in frames made like her baskets. Yet these real people also appear to be silenced and anonymous. Any strength that the masks imply is a facade—hollow and empty. Along with her baskets, these masks have been exhibited widely. Rogers teaches her craft, was the recipient of a QEII Arts Council grant in 1991, and has won a number of awards.

Paper Construction
Handmade paper (harakeke), supplejack, acrylic paint, cabbage tree
250 x 400 mm
Collection of the artist

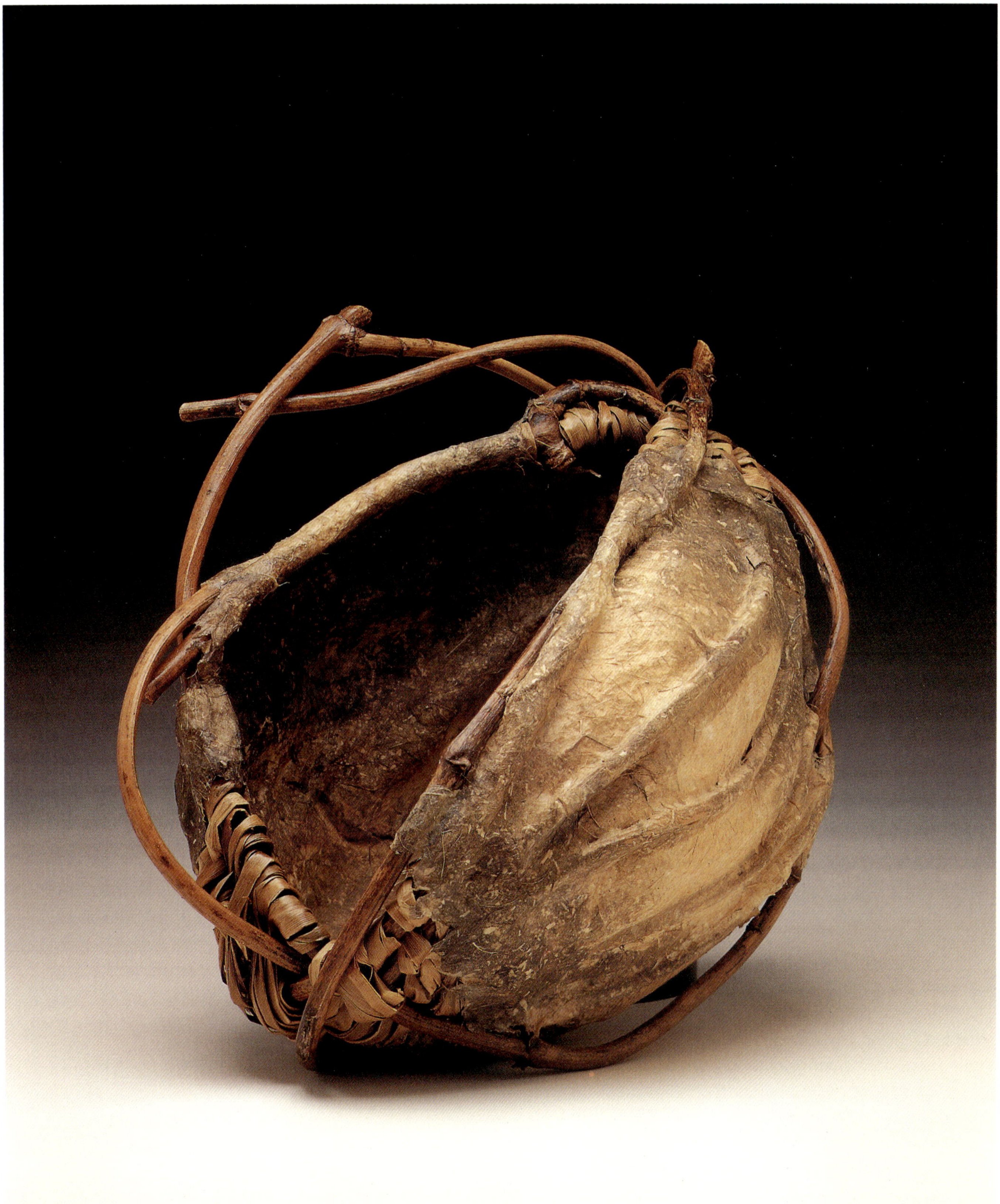

75

RICK RUDD

Born Great Yarmouth, England 1949.
Dip Art and Design, Wolverhampton College of Art, England 1972.
Arrived in New Zealand 1973.
Lives in Wanganui.

The common thread to Rick Rudd's ceramic work is the emphasis on line and form, accompanied by a functional reference and generally a restrained palette. Many have been in black, grey and white; the occasional periods when he has used lively colour have been like brief flirtations. He became known for sculptural, raku-fired vessels, and achieved a number of successes in the Fletcher Brownbuilt Pottery Awards. They were based on wavy lines and spirals in the 1970s, then the geometrical form of Mobius twists in the '80s. The Mobius twists were intriguing, convoluted, tightly defined forms that hinted at teapots, bottles and boxes. They became Rudd's signature pieces.

A QEII Arts Council grant in 1992 allowed him to experiment with glazes, and with that came one of the most dramatic shifts in his work. Raku firing gave way to experiments with lively colour and texture in 1993, and for the last time the definitive Mobius twist appeared, barely recognisable, as a richly encrusted teapot-like form. The playful bottles and boxes that followed were equally untraditional in form, but nonetheless retained the integrity of the pot, including being glazed inside, which has always been an important feature for him.

Rudd's newest works, *Bowls,* are large, monumental pieces that are about as big as he can fit in his kiln. The Stonehenge-like forms evoke his English heritage, and have evolved since a trip to England in 1995. A pair of 'pylons' is separated and linked by a sphere, a device which defines the space between them and implies secret cavities. The sphere echoes the round hand forms of the past and suggests erosion, the theme of an earlier series. *Erosion* was about single blocks—hollowed, fractured and vulnerable—and *Bowls* extended the concept. Rudd's pieces have often had a certain precariousness but his latest works, for all the risks associated with their size, have a new, solid self-confidence, and only the positioning of the spherical link creates the sense of vulnerability.

The monumental forms present a new direction, one where profiles seem hand-drawn rather than precisely tooled. The last vestige of the vessel is barely apparent. The evolution from a series of column bowls reveals new art historical and architectural references to entrances and gateways. Rudd walks a tightrope with these coiled works, aiming for substance and weight without appearing clumsy. He balances their stone-like appearance with his desire not to imitate nature directly nor to lose their essential clay-vessel quality. Formed intuitively, and occasionally preceded by maquettes, the loosely defined forms are sponged with thinly applied glaze, revealing every nuance of the form. They are conceived as indoor works, visualised in a severe setting rather than in an organic garden. These are stark, verging on the over-simplified; like Stonehenge, they engender a strange fascination.

Rudd has had periods of working figuratively, when he has created pieces featuring animals or human torsos. Many of these were challenging works that have pushed boundaries. Some retained the concept of platter or box, but a number appeared as sculptural works, with all trace of function removed. Nonetheless, Rudd's roots as a potter continue to draw him back each time to create a new generation of provocative, inventive, vessel-based forms.

Bowl
Multi-fired ceramic
1200 x 950 x 250 mm
Collection of the artist

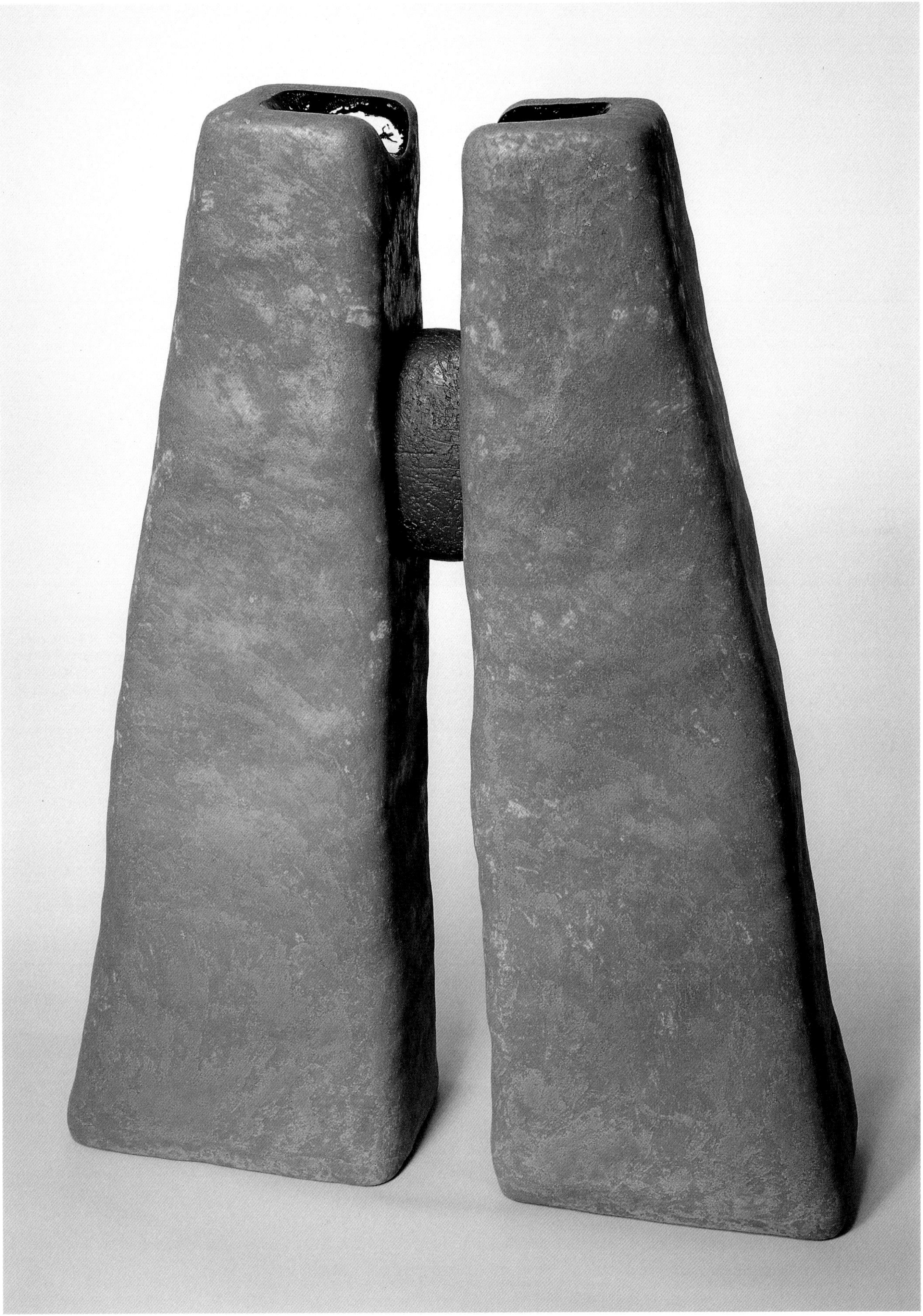

EMILY SIDDELL

Born Auckland 1971.
Carrington Polytechnic Craft and Design Course 1990–92.
Lives in Auckland.

A youthful viewpoint can occasionally be sharply focused, especially when coupled with talent and skill. Emily Siddell has been working for a relatively short time, yet her work is lively, energetic and extraordinarily well resolved. She has received considerable recognition for her glass and mixed media work.

She discovered the magic of casting glass while a student at Carrington Polytechnic, and work experience with Ann Robinson (72) was a major formative experience. But Siddell doesn't view herself solely as a glass artist, and seeks a broader visual vocabulary. That vocabulary now includes crochet, weaving and twining—simple domestic, often suburban crafts that pay homage to women of her grandmothers' era. Her European ancestry informs her range of craft skills but Siddell also looks close to home for inspiration and techniques. Her upbringing in Auckland has exposed her to the richness of the arts of the Pacific region, and in her work she treads, with a light step, the often awkward line between appropriation of a culture and paying homage to it.

Current works are in the form of small handbags—bags that are given an urban feel by her choice of industrial materials like fine wire, recycled window or bottle glass, and scraps from picture framers. She transforms these into objects of beauty. She sees the small handbags as a universal concept, and cites little feathered kete and small beaded Victorian handbags as examples she admires. Her handbags have a redefined purpose as wall-hung art works, although there is no real reason why some could not be used. That their perceived value alters in an art gallery context has not escaped Siddell's notice.

Earlier work was in the form of glass leis. Now similar glass components have been reinterpreted as embellishments for some of her bags. She favours clear transparent glass, in which the reflection and refraction of light are important aspects. Sometimes the glass echoes the fringes of Polynesian bags. Glass fragments define edges, exploding into a three-dimensional dance against the background of metallic surfaces that are sometimes so delicately crocheted that the glass dominates and the wire structure becomes almost a whisper. At other times the glass is subservient to a tight, assertive weave. The woven and twined bags make direct reference to Pacific precedents, while the crochet patterns allude to an Irish ancestor. There is no strong pull to delve into that heritage, rather a passing acknowledgement of it as one of her influences.

The results are joyous and celebratory, focusing on small details, the tiny pleasures. They celebrate the repetitive processes and reflect the pleasure of making. Siddell comes from a post-feminist generation. Her intention is not to change the world, but to enjoy the gains resulting from the activism of her parents' generation. Her work is an acknowledgement of those gains. Her use of materials and the content of her work have New Zealand and international precedents, but she brings to it freshness of image, a lively aesthetic sensibility and an empathy for the processes.

1. Kete Metal
2. Konae
3. Pacific Purse
1. Whatu aho patahi in metal twine;
2. Takitahi in braided cable with fused glass lei;
3. Irish chain lace crochet in binding wire with fused glass fringe
1. 250 x 250 x 30 mm;
2. 250 x 230 x 140 mm;
3. 300 x 290 x 60 mm
1. Collection of Dowse Art Museum;
2. Collection of Sylvia Siddell;
3. Collection of the artist

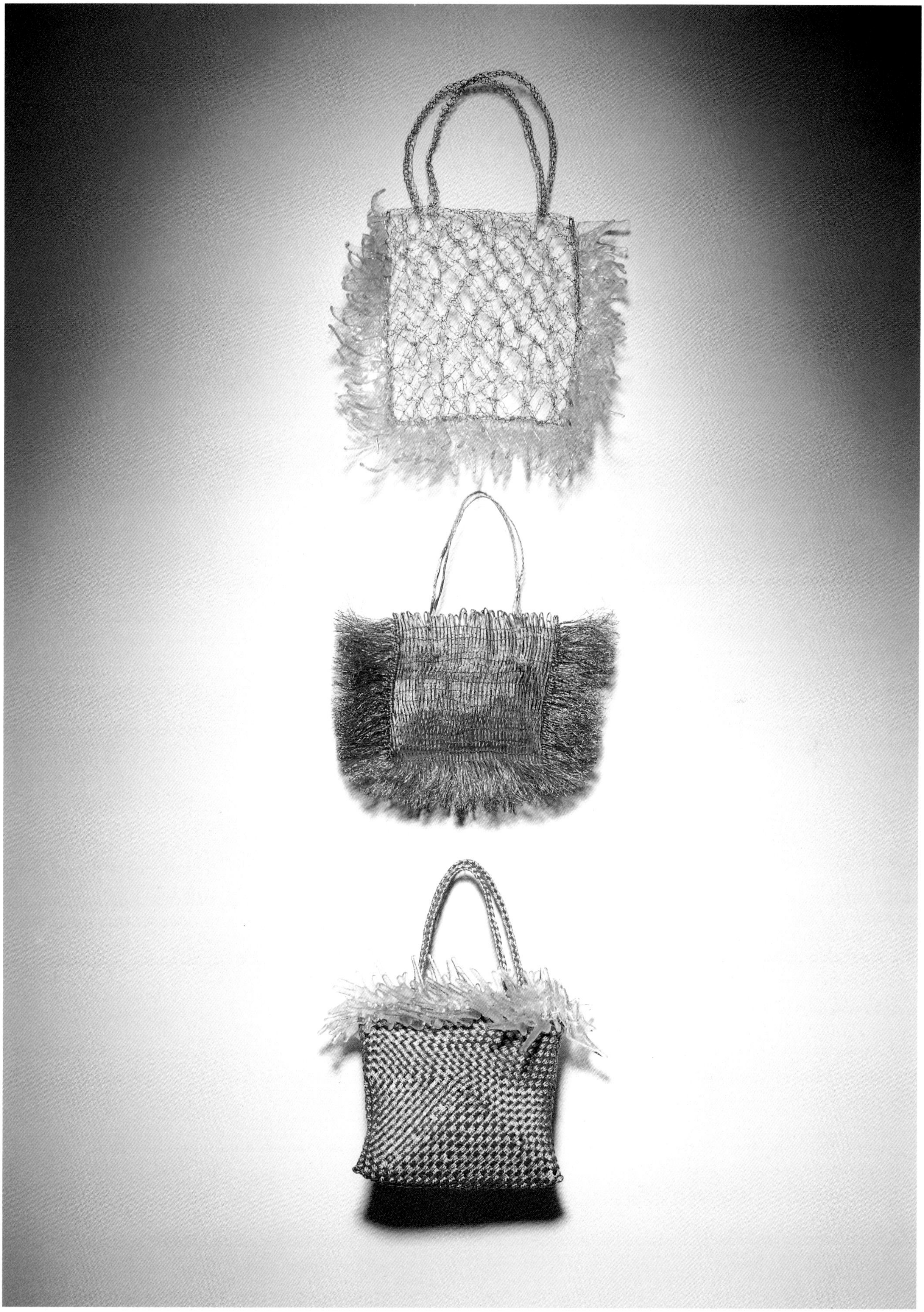

YVONNE SLOAN

Born Auckland 1941.
Began weaving while an Art and Craft Advisor, Dept of Education 1963;
studied weaving at Satergiantan, Sweden 1966.
Lives in Auckland.

When Yvonne Sloan and her husband Ian Spalding established a professional weaving partnership in 1977 there were few who hand-wove professionally, a situation that continues to this day. In 1978 they completed the commissioned curtain and hangings for the Berkeley Theatre at Mission Bay, Auckland.

Many awards and commissions have come Sloan's way, and she is represented in a number of public and private collections. In 1994 she was Artist in Residence at Waikato Polytechnic, where she thrived on the opportunity to experiment and to focus exclusively on her work in a creative environment. Her most recent accolade was an invitation to exhibit at the Crawford Art Centre in St Andrews, Scotland, in 1998.

Sloan's weaving is based on traditional twill, and she has developed a system of inlaying motifs that depends on a lively interaction of warp and weft. Her designs are based on balanced colour bands, intersecting diagonals, verticals and horizontals. The structure produces small spots of colour, which react with each other in a manner that resembles pointillism. She recalls Annie Albers' philosophy of acknowledging the importance of the structure in weaving, and recalls how confronting that was at a time when weaving in New Zealand was lumpy, bumpy and looked very handmade.

Viewing her wall-hung pieces one senses that the rhythmical process is part of her enjoyment, as is the elegant simplicity of the end product which reveals itself only on completion of the weaving. There is no clutter of added details in this work, just a ripple of vibrant, controlled colours. Sloan exploits the absorption of light on the thin strands of wool, using gradual tonal shifts rather than wildly clashing ones, and she seeks velvety mysterious effects which become apparent in subdued light.

During the Waikato Polytechnic residency she started her *Nikau Series,* which she is still developing. She experimented with imagery and colour, and introduced a theme to her work which referenced the organic yet fitted comfortably with the formal qualities of the technique. The nikau, with its crossing fronds, suited the linearity and angular nature of twill, the imagery being both an expression of the trees she loves and the medium that has engrossed her for so many years.

Sloan has introduced a new theme of large sails into her work, and she is producing pieces with a more dynamic three-dimensional quality. These sails evoke arrival in New Zealand, and she seeks to create a symbol that transcends cultural differences. The free-standing stretched triangular sails, with their frames enclosed in woven sleeves, are able to be viewed from both sides. Visibility from more than one viewpoint sets a new agenda for Sloan's weaving, and she seeks an interaction between shapes, space and movement. She aims for lightness, physically and visually, and this has led her to explore handmade paper for prototypes. Through her long-term explorations of selected themes, Sloan is creating series of superbly executed images which quietly describe a sense of place.

Nikau Series V
Weaving: wool
820 x 1720 mm
Collection of
University of Waikato

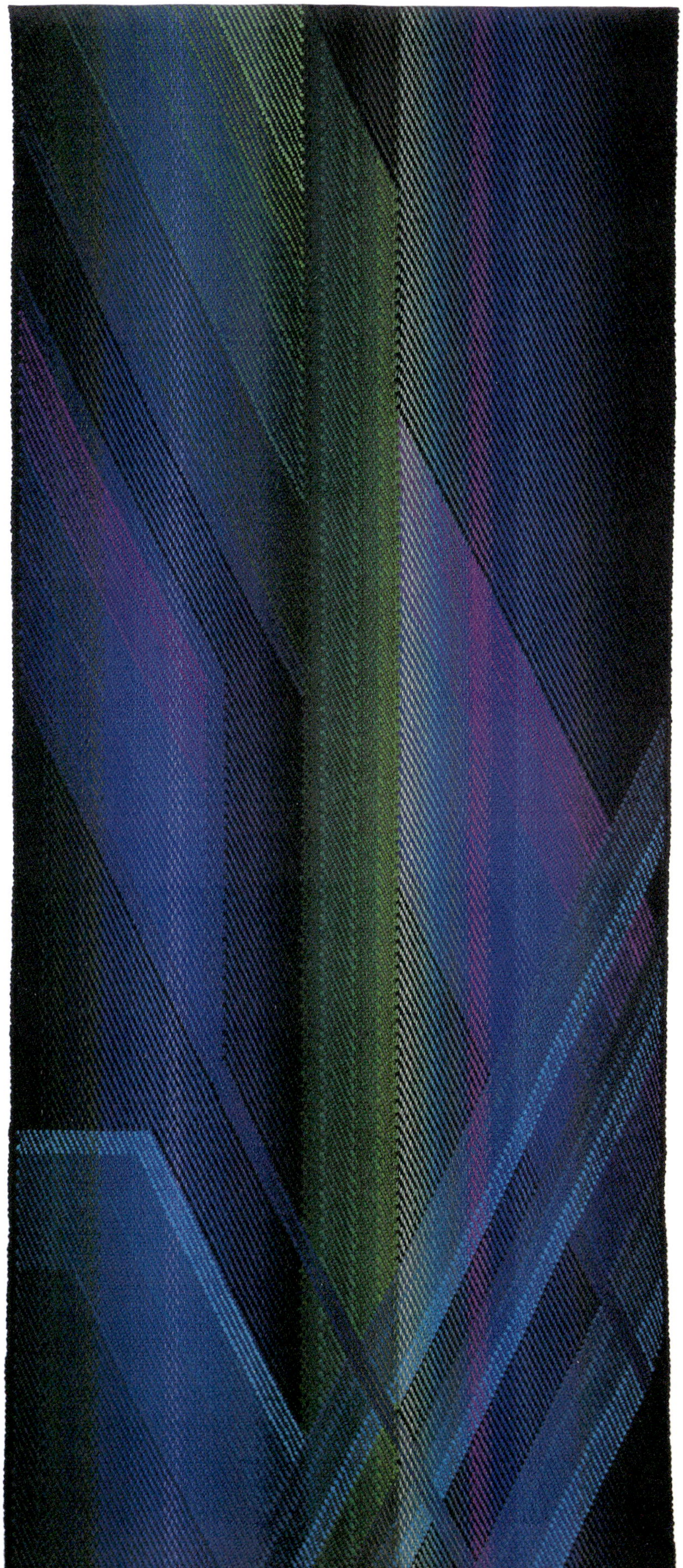

ROBYN STEWART

Born Auckland 1938.
Started working with clay at Auckland Studio Potters Centre 1975.
Lives in Mathesons Bay.

Fitting one's tools into a pencil case is not a necessary requisite for most craftspeople, but for Robyn Stewart it has been a distinct advantage when she has gone to teach clay techniques in Indonesia, Zimbabwe, India and Rarotonga. Her work with Maori communities has been a major influence on Maori ceramics, and she attributes the many teaching invitations to her simple way of working, using local combustible material and minimal equipment.

Stewart's largely self-taught process is pragmatic, a technique that developed from an affinity for pinching and coiling clay. She learnt basic handbuilding techniques from Pat Perrin, and the importance of a critical eye from Margaret Milne, at the Auckland Studio Potters Centre. However, she was inspired to experiment with burnishing and dung-firing after seeing work by the Pueblo Indian potter Maria Martinez, as well as some Neolithic Chinese pots, and she continues to use this process for her work. Burnishing cannot be rushed. It is a meditative way of working that is followed by a slow and hot dung-firing that gives variations in colour. The resultant pots have a smooth, often earth-coloured surface that invites touch, and Stewart believes that people respond well to that tactile quality and to the roundness of the pieces.

Carving into the pots has always been an important component for her. Motifs are often spirals, which she sees as universal as well as a reference to her Celtic background. Yet her work is often perceived as being inspired by Maori imagery and has achieved a certain prominence because of this. For Stewart, the pieces form a connection with the land, and the spirals depict the uncurling fern fronds she observes around her as well as Celtic spirals.

In 1997 Stewart started a new series, the *Standing Stones*, which make reference to her fascination with the large stones she saw in places like Denmark and Scotland. The burnished forms also seemed to pre-empt an experience she had while sailing near Rarotonga at the end of 1997. While on watch in the early morning she saw the exact form she had intuitively created earlier in the year appear on the horizon. Some of the pieces stand tall like guardians, as totems or markers; other large ones are placed in a reclining position, leaving viewers to make their own interpretations. These pieces generate a different response from earlier work. There is more of a desire to view from a distance than to reach forward and touch. Perhaps Stewart has unconsciously placed an ocean between the stones and the viewers.

There are other new features to this work. The pieces are still burnished and embellished with spiral motifs, but her palette has changed. There is a new greenness in her work, resulting from the application of a chrome slip, and the resultant coloration links the work to the bush environment in which she lives. Travel has inspired Stewart, but she continues to make work that speaks strongly about home.

Stelae (Standing Stones)
Black fired and burnished clay, chromium oxide
ca. 280 mm (h)
Unknown ownership

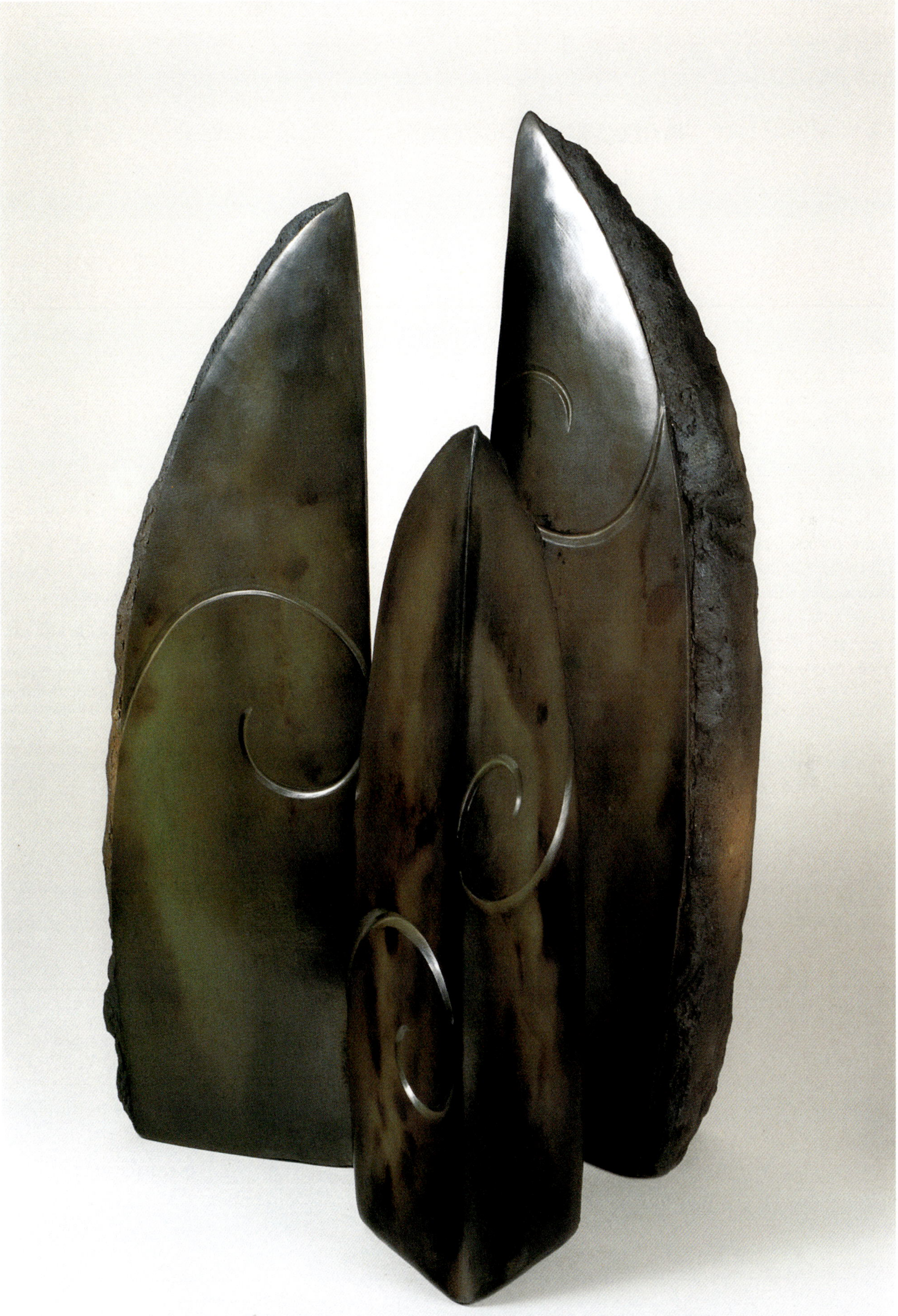

79

MARGARET STOVE

Born Palmerston North 1940.
Christchurch Teachers College 1958–59;
NZ Primary Teachers Certificate, Christchurch 1960.
Lives in Lyttelton.

Margaret Stove is known for her exquisitely fine knitted lace, and is an authority on this craft. She has written two books: *Merino—Handspinning, Dyeing and Working with Merino and Superfine Wools*, published in 1991, and *Creating Original Hand-knitted Lace*, 1995. Her impressive list of achievements includes commissions as gifts for royalty as well as innumerable private commissions; and she has exhibited and won awards both in New Zealand and overseas. Her work is held in several collections, including that of Te Papa, Wellington. She has conducted many workshops in New Zealand, Australia, UK, Canada and USA.

Stove knits primarily with handspun merino wool. She has been spinning wool since 1970 and it has become an integral part of the creative process for many of her projects. She also has a small business selling finespun merino wool as kitsets with patterns that she designs. Stove has developed a personal approach to spinning merino wool to maximise its characteristic softness, lustre and reflective quality. Her yarn is very smooth, so that pattern definition is retained in her knitted lace, and it is finer than any commercial single yarn. Knitting this merino wool on very fine needles gives her the enchanting frothy, lacy effects that are so appreciated by her international clientele.

Knitting has been part of Stove's life since she was a small child. She was taught by her grandmother who was of Danish descent and she learnt to knit in the speedy European style—a bonus for her labour-intensive work. At the age of five she learnt to knit 'V for victory' and her fascination for knitted patterns has continued to this day. She learnt to look at shapes rather than at instructions, and this proved a sound basis for her current work.

Traditional lace patterns have their origins in Northern Hemisphere motifs, and Stove builds on her knowledge of these patterns to create her own based on her environment. She looks at landscapes, seascapes, flora and shells as her starting point, and abstracts her images before transposing them into knitted motifs. The delicate tracery of creative knitted lace offers the results she seeks. She sometimes works with added colour but appreciates the liveliness of unadorned lace in space or against a contrasting background.

Stove creates christening gowns and baby shawls mainly on commission. She developed a design of ferns and rata flowers for *Christening Gown and Bonnet,* made in 1996. It epitomised her integration of tradition and personal expression—an ensemble to be cherished. The reference to her environment is the focus of her hand-dyed shawl *Sea Spray and Scallop Shells*. This was a gift for her daughter, and she worked with fewer constraints than with commissioned work. Stove applied dyes to her knitted 'canvas' of lace patterns, and the shimmer in the work resulted from merino wool and silk being spun separately, then plied together.

Other experimental works are small mounted pictures which are becoming progressively more abstracted and symbolic. Stove achieves a loose, freehand effect in an exacting medium that is usually formal and structured, and this speaks volumes about her wealth of knowledge and ability.

Rata and Fern Christening Gown and Bonnet
Handknitted, handspun 2 ply merino wool; needle size 2 mm
Shoulder to hem ca. 75 mm
Collection of Museum of New Zealand, Te Papa Tongarewa

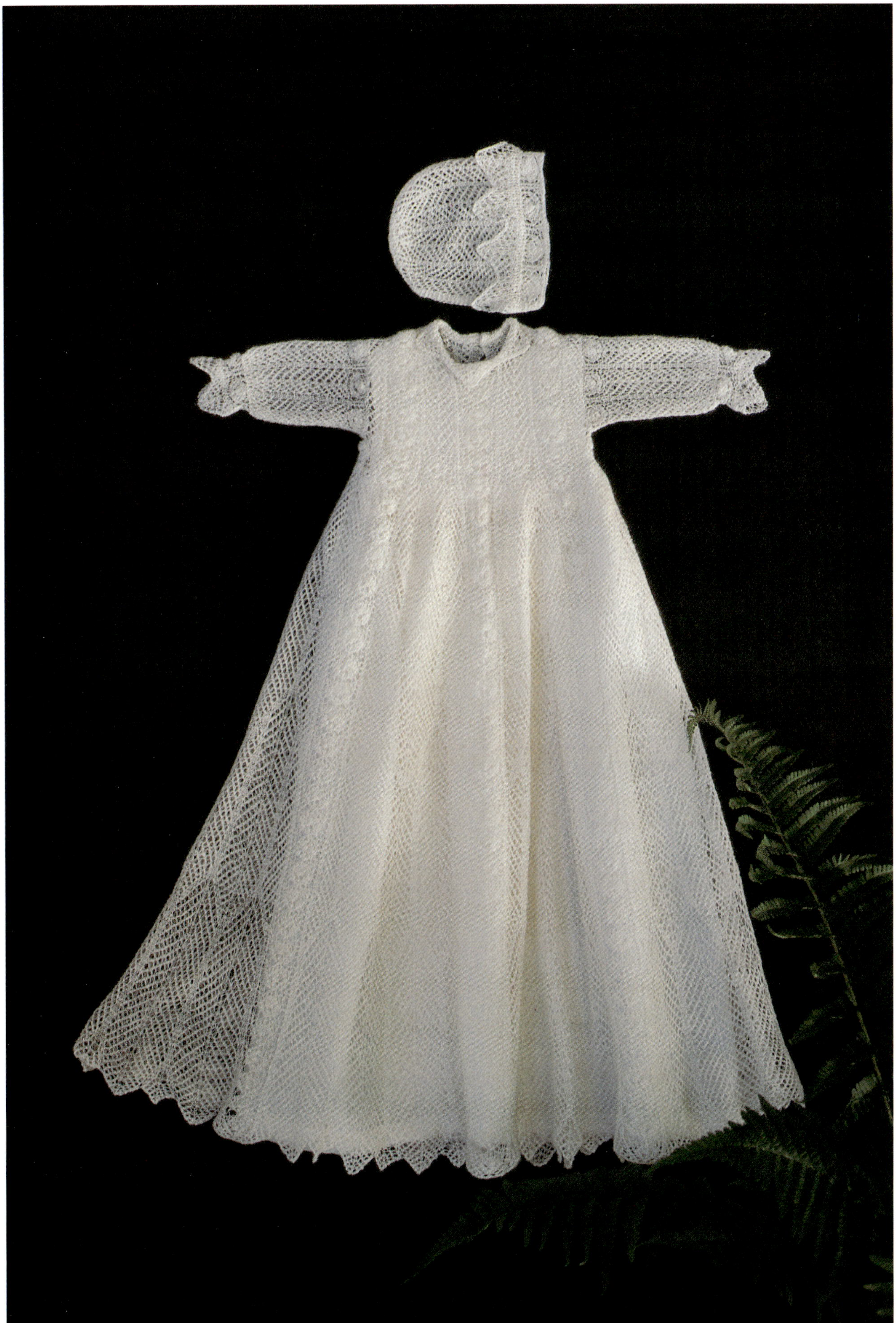

WALLACE SUTHERLAND

Born Christchurch 1946.
BSc (Geography and Geology), University of Canterbury, University of Auckland 1970;
Dip Teaching, Teachers Training College Auckland 1970;
Maori & Polynesian Art History, Twentieth Century Western Art History, University of Auckland 1993.
Lives in Auckland.

There are many dualities in Wallace Sutherland's work. He works at a small scale with jewellery, small sculptures and medallions, and at a larger scale with a number of his fabricated sculptures, thereby straddling craft art and fine art.

There are other dualities too—like three-dimensional features on flat, silhouette-like profiles, revealing his fascination for the interplay between two and three dimensions. He views this interplay as being parallel to that between intellectual concepts and the more pragmatic images we have of ourselves: the two-dimensional facades we sometimes want to maintain contrast with the three-dimensional reality. The mask, like the profile and the bust, is a form that Sutherland embraces. Each reflects his fascination with formalising imagery, like icons of art history. Again there is a duality, as the works are also about highly disorganised aspects of humanity like spontaneity and distorted emotions.

The faces he creates often present a staunch facade behind which lies human vulnerability. These faces, which have been very much part of Sutherland's imagery, often imply the self-portrait, and they acquire a certain formality when he places them on a pedestal. The exaggerated, caricatured features are strangely familiar yet also remote, often deconstructed and reconstructed in terms of individual human senses as well as facial features. The relationship between head and hands often assumes importance. Sutherland has an interest in comics, puppetry and mediaeval fairground imagery, all of which are evident in the way he seeks to capture body language, facial gesture and the complexities of human nature.

In *Hors d'Oeuvre* the facial gesture is reduced to a pair of lips—sensuous, hungry and symbolising the hunter. The work is about the predator and its prey, an eel, a traditional New Zealand food in a surreal tableau which utilises the found and the fabricated. The vitality of the eel suggests it could escape from what might be seen as a pretentious way of eating. Sutherland becomes an observer of the contradictions between his role as the fisherman and as the urban sophisticate, and uses wit as a way to reconcile them.

The processes he uses, almost invariably involving metals, mediate between the organised and the disorganised, the positive and the negative. He likes the resistance of metal, and recently has been using the ancient process of casting from carved cuttlefish. He enjoys the direct contact with antiquity and alchemy, and seeks a balance between controlled and uncontrolled effects when working with heat. He thinks through his fingers, allowing the work to emerge from a well-resolved philosophy as he fabricates and develops the surfaces of his distinctive forms.

Medallions are an important part of Sutherland's production. These have been exhibited internationally, with one included in the collection of the British Museum, and have been the subject of a number of commissions. He enjoys the historical associations with ancient coins and medals, and the way bas relief mediates between two and three dimensions. The medallions seem to summarise a number of issues that inform his work.

**Hors d'Oeuvre
Bronze and silver
cuttlefish casting
and found objects
120 x 200 x 155 mm
Collection of the
artist**

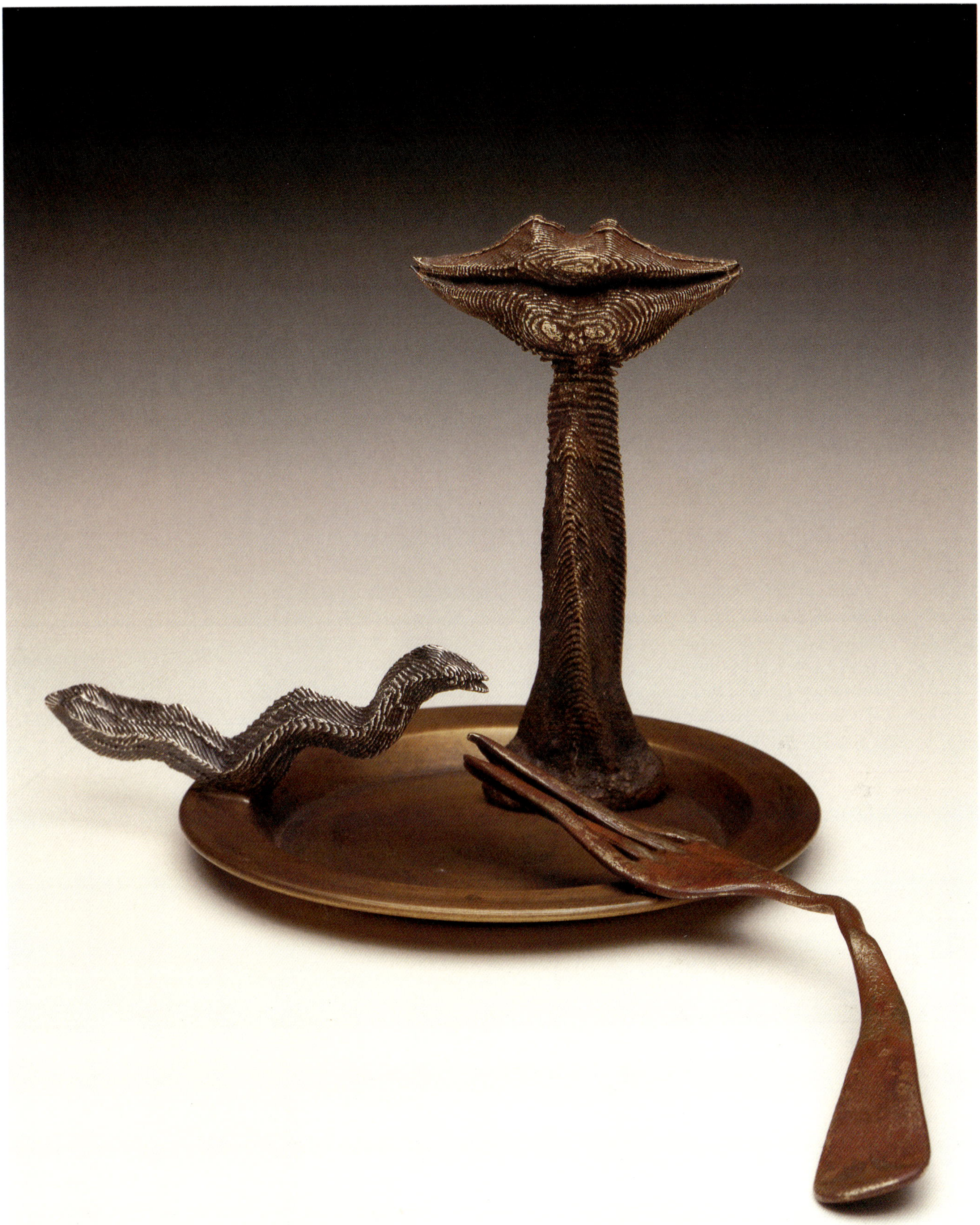

81

WI TAEPA

Born Wellington 1946.
Te Arawa, Ngati Pikiao, Te Atiawa.
Prison Staff College 1978; Food, Maori language, Wellington Polytechnic 1980; NZ Certificate Craft Design, Whitireia Polytechnic 1989; Dip Craft, Whitireia Polytechnic 1992; Maori Design, Massey University 1997.
Lives in Levin.

Wi Taepa was a display artist before he enlisted for the New Zealand Army and served in Vietnam. He later worked in security, in the penal system and the Department of Social Welfare. In 1983 he was involved in the carving projects at the Michael Fowler Centre, Wellington, and the Orongomai Marae, Upper Hutt. He followed this with a period of study in craft design at Whitireia Polytechnic and has been a tutor there since 1993.

As a student he worked with a number of media, including clay, which offered him a welcome level of freedom. It contrasted with the tight specifications usually imposed when he carved stone or wood. His imagery evolved from his Maori heritage: the designs of the past and listening to historical narratives fed his fertile mind. Whakapapa provided the content, and he honoured this by revisiting early styles of working.

Taepa enjoys reclaiming and transposing little-known processes to his clay work. One of the techniques he uses is punch marking, which is an old way of working that evolved from notching in very early Maori carving and is only occasionally seen. He looks to the way curvilinear lines were created without stone chisels, and replaces very basic tools like sticks with contemporary man-made tools. The simple stick marks are replicated with an egg slice or a ball-point pen, and patterns are rolled as if onto fabric. There are references to rolled colour and punch marks in the Lapita pottery traditions of Samoa, and Taepa is keen to explore any possible connections between Maori carving and Lapita pots.

His works are handbuilt and unglazed. Taepa likes to work very fast to capture the spontaneity of his first thoughts. He recognises that clay is not a medium which can be wholly controlled. He likes to let the colours from the earth emerge during firing as they do in nature—not just the red, white and black usually associated with Maori art, but a broad colour spectrum that includes maroons, the silvers and greys of trees as well as the colours of animals, sea and plant life.

His earliest forms in clay referred to utensils like gourds and pieces of weapons. The asymmetrical growth rings of trees like kanuka inspired their surface treatment, and the forms were made slightly off-centre to personalise them. Some of his forms come from Maori ceremony, but by expanding the scale of them the way the viewer engages with the work changes. He is able to present a different viewpoint. An example is a huge feeding funnel which would be used in order not to break the tapu that is imposed when a moko is applied. He also makes canoe forms that evoke how Maori came to New Zealand.

The beautifully detailed, doughnut-shaped work *Ipu* (vessel) was created for *Uku! Uku! Uku!* at the International Festival of the Arts, Wellington, 1998. So too were a number of sculptural pieces like boundary pegs. In the past Maori would define boundaries with groups of stones or carved pieces of wood. Taepa created minimalist, faceless works in clay that evoked these markers—like god-sticks. They are a shift from his earlier, more easily recognised figures: here the stance or shape of the head gives viewers clues, yet allows them to tell their own stories.

Ipu
Pot fired clay
ca. 450 mm
Private collection

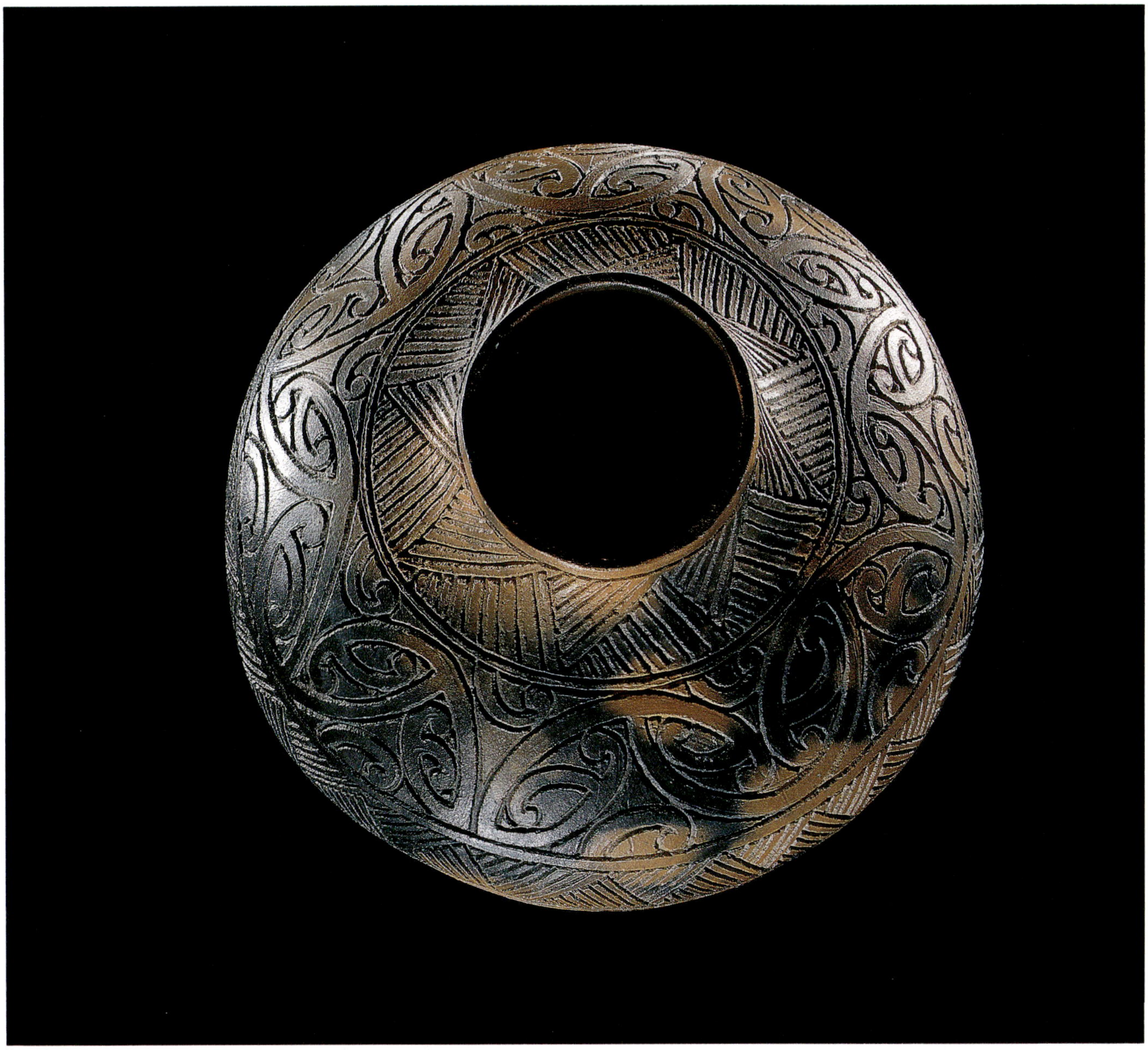

JULIET TAYLOR

Born Christchurch 1948.
Attended many workshops in New Zealand and USA.
Lives in Auckland.

Juliet Taylor makes quilts for beds. She came to quiltmaking about fifteen years ago the way many women have—as a natural extension to homemaking. The medium accommodated her interest in mathematics, an appreciation of the mosaic quality of quilts, and her passion for fabrics and stitchery. She has no inclination to make 'art quilts', although some of her works do find a place on walls; nor does she choose to add embellishments. She prefers to make large usable quilts—ones that can wrap round a person and be used daily to give comfort and warmth.

There is a quiet dignity to the pieces she creates. Their gentle rhythms, rich fabrics and simple geometry are eloquent evocations of a tradition that has its roots in Europe and the USA. Immaculate crafting seems to come naturally, with the fabric fragments locking perfectly together. Taylor aims for a soft tactility, and quilts the patched works with a contrasting rhythm of handstitching, a meditative process which she loves.

Many exponents of the medium have achieved a high standard of crafting, but what distinguishes Taylor's work is her intuitive combination of fabrics and the way she plays with colour. The formal geometry gets shuffled slightly—occasional 'rogue' colours break up the predictable symmetry like the human disruptions to a well-ordered home. The dislocations are intentional, creating eye puzzles that give life to the quilts.

These are primarily works about fabrics, some of which, like the treasured ikats, Taylor has collected overseas. They live with her for some time before she cuts into them, and she collates the support fabrics meantime. There is always a long period of play and experimentation during which she devises advantageous ways to present the most precious fabrics, and she creates contrasts of prints, stripes, woven plaids and crafted fabrics.

Occasionally the quilts contain references to the intended owners and their environments, and allude to mountain pathways, pavements or vistas from bedrooms. One work for a dying friend was created as a 'healing quilt', reflecting some of the folklore associated with quiltmaking. Human emotion becomes part of the quiltmaking process, even when there appears to be no obvious narrative.

Taylor has been involved in teaching, lecturing and judging for a number of years, and has won a number of awards. In 1990, with a QEII Arts Council grant, she toured some of the major quilt collections in the USA and attended a symposium; it was a trip that provided a great deal of inspiration. Lately she has been creating quilts for a specific person and purpose, as a commission or gift. The quilts are less analytical and mathematical than in the past, more about emotion and intuition, reflecting the maker's sensitivity to the recipients. Joyous and usable, these quilts are fundamental to our understanding of craft in its traditional sense.

**Windsong
Patchwork quilt
2100 mm square
Collection of the artist**

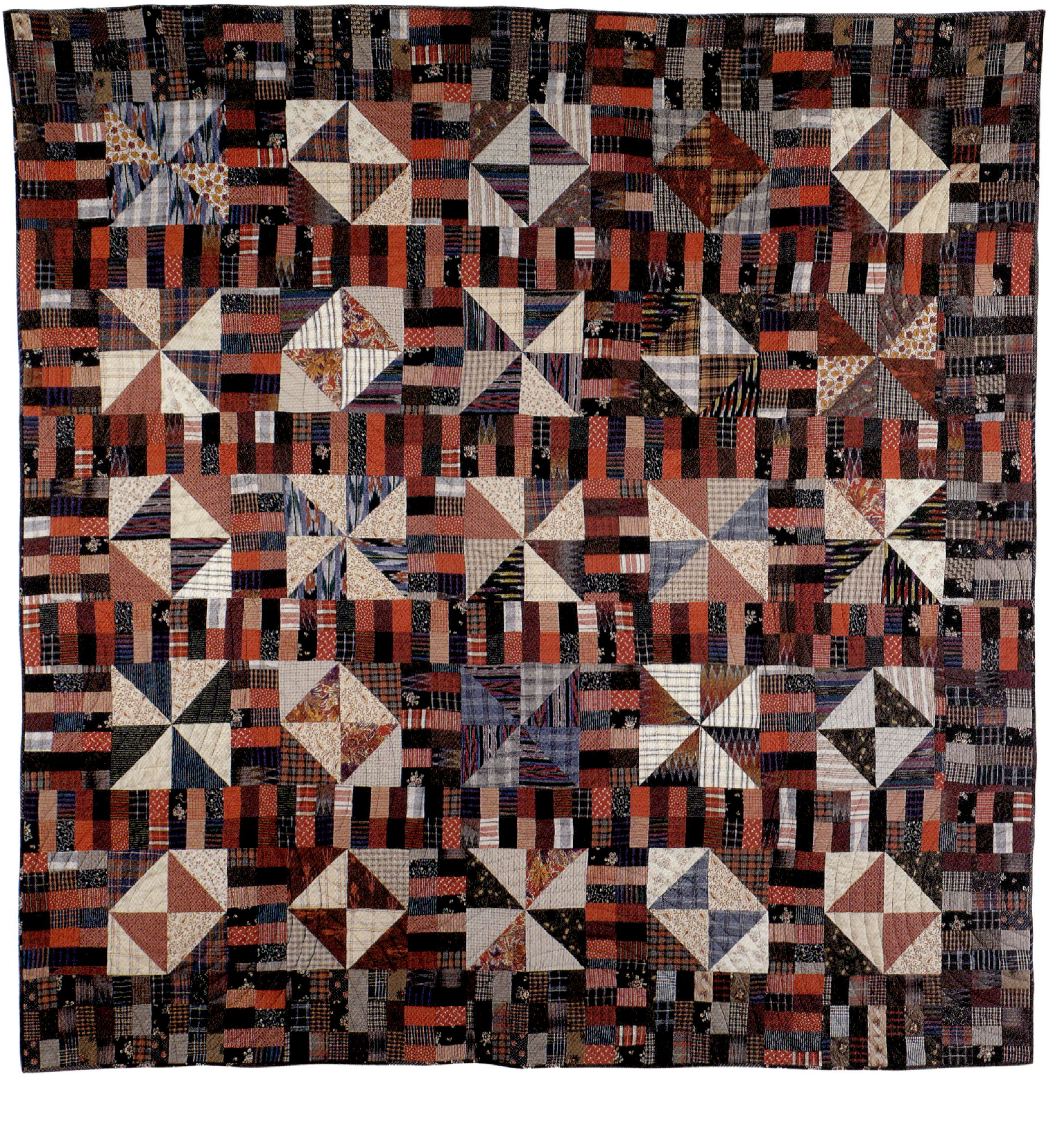

DIGGERESS RANGITUATAHI TE KANAWA

Born Te Kuiti 1920.
Ngati Maniopoto.
Received QSO Medal for Community Service 1987.
Lives in Oparure.

When Diggeress Te Kanawa first spent two days making a whariki as a child, she announced it was her first and last—she was so sore. Her mother, Dame Rangimarie Hetet, told her that if she kept going she would get broken in. That was our gain, because Diggeress Te Kanawa and her family, across all generations, have continued to keep the tradition of Maori weaving alive, producing beautiful korowai, kete and whariki.

Te Kanawa's story is a family one, about whakapapa, about skills being passed from mother to daughter, and to the community. For her, the knowledge of working with harakeke, kiekie, pingao and dyes is part of keeping the culture alive, not necessarily repeating the designs of the past but retaining the knowledge and the wairua. Weaving has been an integral part of her life—she has always made time for it, even while raising twelve children. In 1983 Aotearoa Moana Nui a Kiwa Weavers, a supportive organisation for Maori weavers, was established as a way to share ideas and to pass on weaving knowledge. Te Kanawa was invited on to the committee, and has only recently resigned.

In 1987 Te Kanawa and the late Emily Schuster went to the USA and saw a number of old cloaks in museum collections. She was struck by her forebears' wonderful eye for colour and balance, and the intuitive way they had resolved their designs, seemingly without counting threads. By contrast Te Kanawa, like her late mother, twines the muka across the warp threads from the sacred halfway line, te aho tapu, and creates rhythmical symmetrical designs. She credits her mother with being inventive, with trying new colours and exploring new ways of joining. She, too, continues to experiment.

Techniques have changed very little over time. For a korowai, 600 or more muka warp threads are supported on a simple frame, and weaving can take months or even years. The harakeke from which Te Kanawa extracts muka is grown at home and further afield, and she persists in working with muka for its fine qualities—its lustre and body. She still makes natural dyes, although suitable mud has become difficult to find. Her taniko patterns occasionally tell a story; some are inspired by nature, like matariki, the star pattern, which resembles a Fair Isle knitting pattern.

The feathers which inspire the patterns on some korowai come from diverse sources. She is intuitively a conservationist, seeking sources in which birds like weka are still plentiful. She tells the story of kaka feathers which came from her mother's collection and were originally used in mattresses. Traditionally feathers were gummed together in pairs before being locked into the weave. Te Kanawa the innovator now uses Sunlight soap to good effect.

The joy of pattern-making, of trying new ideas, sustains her. She is represented in many publications, has written *Weaving a Kakahu*, and her international recognition includes being commissioned to make royal gifts. Her list of achievements is long and her generosity in sharing her knowledge is legendary. A perfectionist and a mentor to many, she takes her place as the matriarch of weaving with aroha and humility.

**Korowai (Cloak)
Flax fibre and feathers
ca. 1000 x 1500 mm
Collection of the artist**

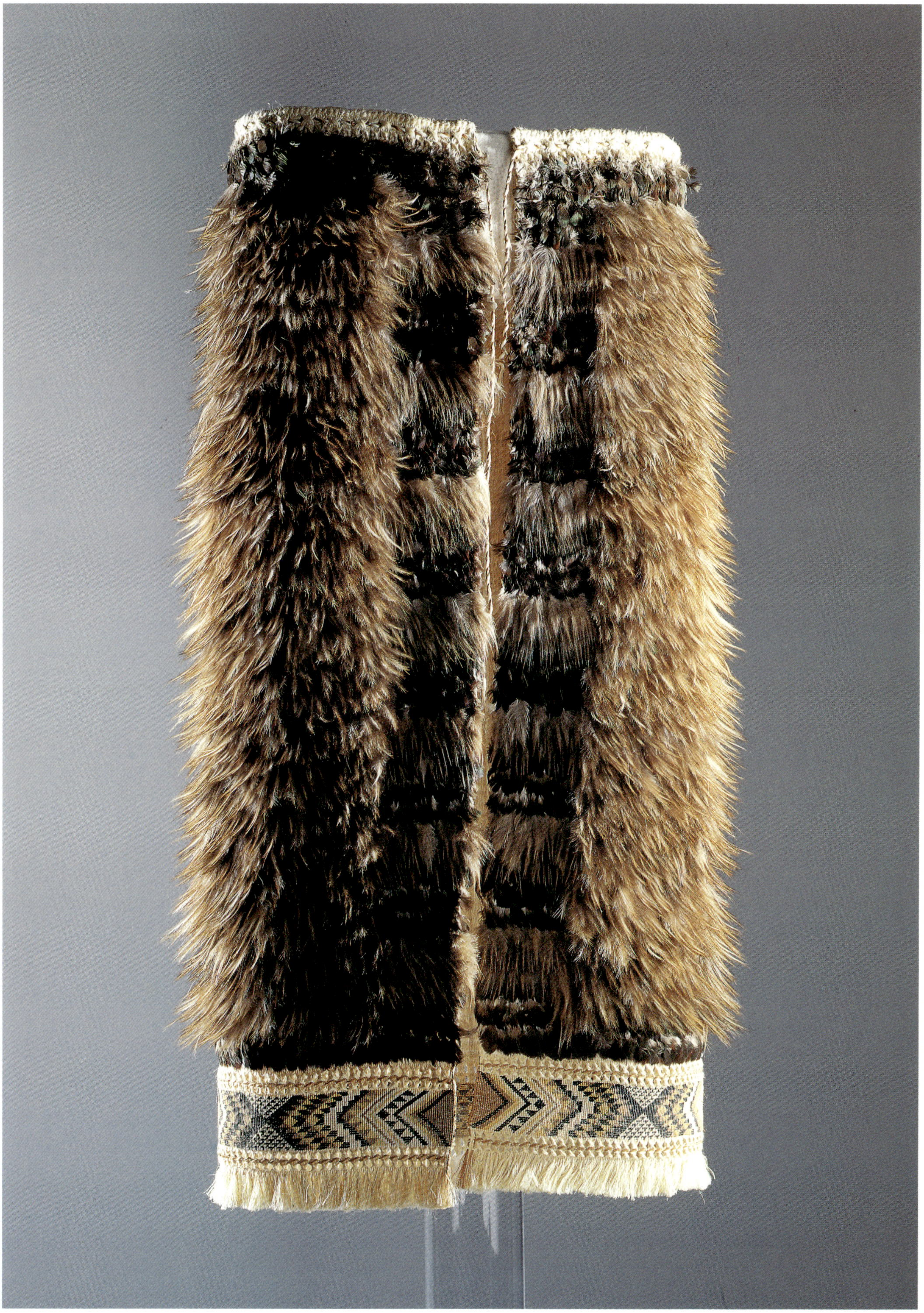

CHRISTINE THACKER

Born New Plymouth 1953.
Joined Nelson Craft Potters Association 1974;
employed at Cambridgeshire Pottery, Shelford, England 1978.
Lives on Waiheke Island.

When Christine Thacker started working with clay she brought to it the mindset of an illustrator, and painted figurative works as portraits. They were strong, generous-sized pieces, more in the realm of sculpture than pottery. Much of what Thacker has made since then has been sculptural, and can be described as shifting from interesting but 'crude' work to being skilled yet sufficiently innocent not to be mannered. It is work that has received considerable acclaim nationally as well as in Japan and Hungary, and she has been a placegetter at the Fletcher Challenge Ceramics Award on a number of occasions.

Her approach has always been to start from process. She coils her forms intuitively, not with any image or issue foremost, relying on the relationship between her hands and the material. By remaining unselfconscious about her direction, she can enjoy the challenge of resolving an awkward shape that might emerge. Years of experience have taught her to negotiate a path between the skilled and the clumsy, between the overworked and underdeveloped idea. A highly tuned critical awareness serves her work well, and she has put that skill to good use with occasional critical writing.

Organic growth has been an enduring theme in her work. The early figurative work evolved into forms that evoked the idea of growth, like stalks. Some were exaggerated shapes, one in the form of a huge hand. Painting the surface gave way to creating textures that revealed the character of the material, and she often used small, rhythmically arranged holes in the clay. The hand-pierced surface gradually gained importance, and the relationship between the heavily grogged clay body and the holes became more exaggerated.

Thacker's treatment of the surface is a contemplative process, an antidote to the physicality of preparing the clay. She works with metal oxides, engobes and slips as colourants, and often fires the pieces two or three times to achieve a deep matt finish. It is low-tech work and she enjoys the use of minimal equipment. In recent times it seems that the holes define the works: they draw the viewer in to peer through them, perhaps to observe how they have opened further or joined to a neighbouring hole.

Her recent work reveals a shift—a new feeling Thacker has for clay. Her direct references are no longer the figure or forms in nature, and she senses a need to reconnect with the work of traditional potters rather than to be a painter or decorator of clay. Her evolving self-awareness has generated new works in the form of pierced vessels, some barely dished. They are beautifully conceived, subtle forms that have mass and volume, and an intriguing contradiction of solidity and weightlessness. The pierced vessels are created beside some hand-coiled vases that evoke the 1950s and '60s, their surfaces alive with spontaneous, painterly applications of copper oxide glaze. This refocusing on the functional object in a domestic context is an apt one for Thacker, an accessible form that is easily able to touch people's lives. It is superb work that finds its way into private homes and major collections.

Dish
Clay
ca. 400 x 350 x 60 mm
Private collection

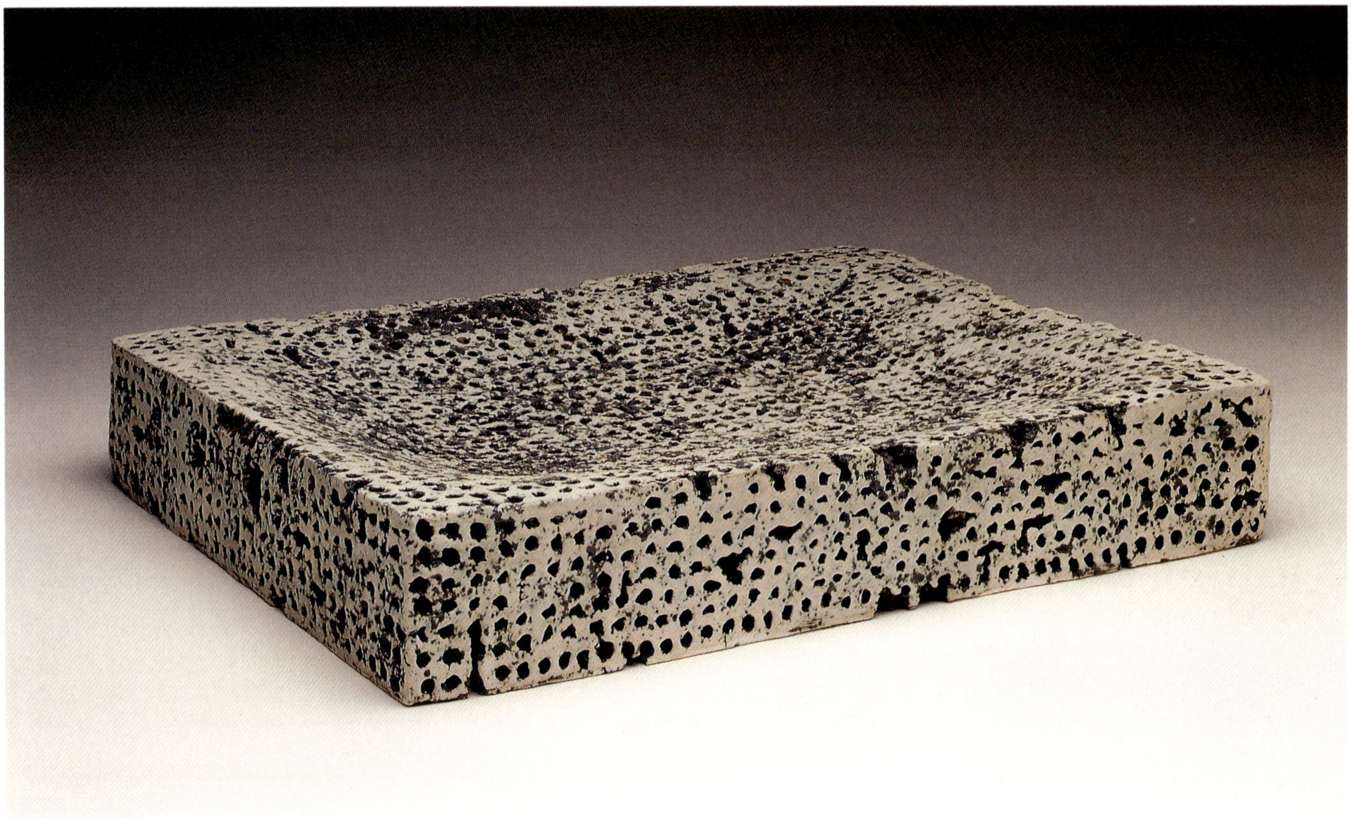

KELLY THOMPSON

Born California 1961.
Emigrated to New Zealand 1971.
BFA (Textiles), California College of Arts and Crafts, Oakland 1985;
MA, Canberra School of Art, Australian National University 1994.
Lives in Dunedin.

At the age of nine Kelly Thompson emigrated to New Zealand with her family, continuing a pattern of travel that had become an integral part of her life. Journeys have become a significant component of her handwoven narratives, which explore mapping, location and identity. Equally important is the structural integrity of the constructed, tactile cloth images.

In 1992 she created a series of multi-layered woven images for the group exhibition *Nga Kaupapa Here Aho—Fibre Interface* at Te Taumata Gallery. The work represented places that were significant to her. She had until then been exhibiting manipulated weaves in light bright colours that evoked the Pacific with non-specific land and seascape references. The shift in palette, structure and content was quite marked.

Her studies for a Masters degree in Canberra were an opportunity to challenge some of her notions about textiles. That, too, became a journey, linking past experiences with the present, juxtaposed with a theoretical study of Sumatran and Sulawesi textiles. Thompson is drawn to handwoven cloth of other cultures, to the way images are integrated with the process of manufacture, as well as to the selvedges and cut edges that express its nature. In conjunction with theory, she analysed the compositional aspects of Indonesian ikats—the way images are created, their framing devices and borders.

She adapted the ikat process, a highly specialised way of dyeing threads, to create characteristic, fuzzy-edged, illusionary images. The multi-layered narratives she revealed were about family travels—multiple perspectives reflecting a number of journeys and viewpoints. Her work was a conscious post-colonial identification of place in which she sought to make cloth speak about who she was. Because of its associated meanings about culture and identity, cloth could reflect a people, not by being bound to tradition but by bringing value back to the process of making.

Few practitioners integrate computer technology with craft as it is practised in village life, but Thompson has linked these extremes. In Canberra she first worked with a dobby loom controlled by a computer. She retained the handweaving process while programming the structure, and operated with sixteen shafts—impossible with a treadle loom. This offered her speed and fineness, and allowed her to concentrate on image and details. The process, however interesting for its computer link-up, remained, as always for Thompson, a means to draw with thread, as epitomised in her superb travelling exhibition *Passages and Postcards*, originating in 1996.

Her newest works have been created as triple weaves, intersecting layers of linen and dyed cotton that soak up the colour and shimmer in the light. They continue to explore mapping and location in a more abstract way than in the past. Small screen-like works, they hint at technology, the monitors in our lives—television, computer and medical. In this context the weave becomes pixelations, yet the focus is always on threads and their tactility.

The works are created in a context of teaching at Otago Polytechnic School of Art, and Thompson's commitment is to her students, her own work and fostering textiles as a medium for personal and cultural expression. She has been represented in exhibitions and collections in Australia and New Zealand.

Details—four components of larger work
Woven cotton linen
200 x 200 mm each
Private collection

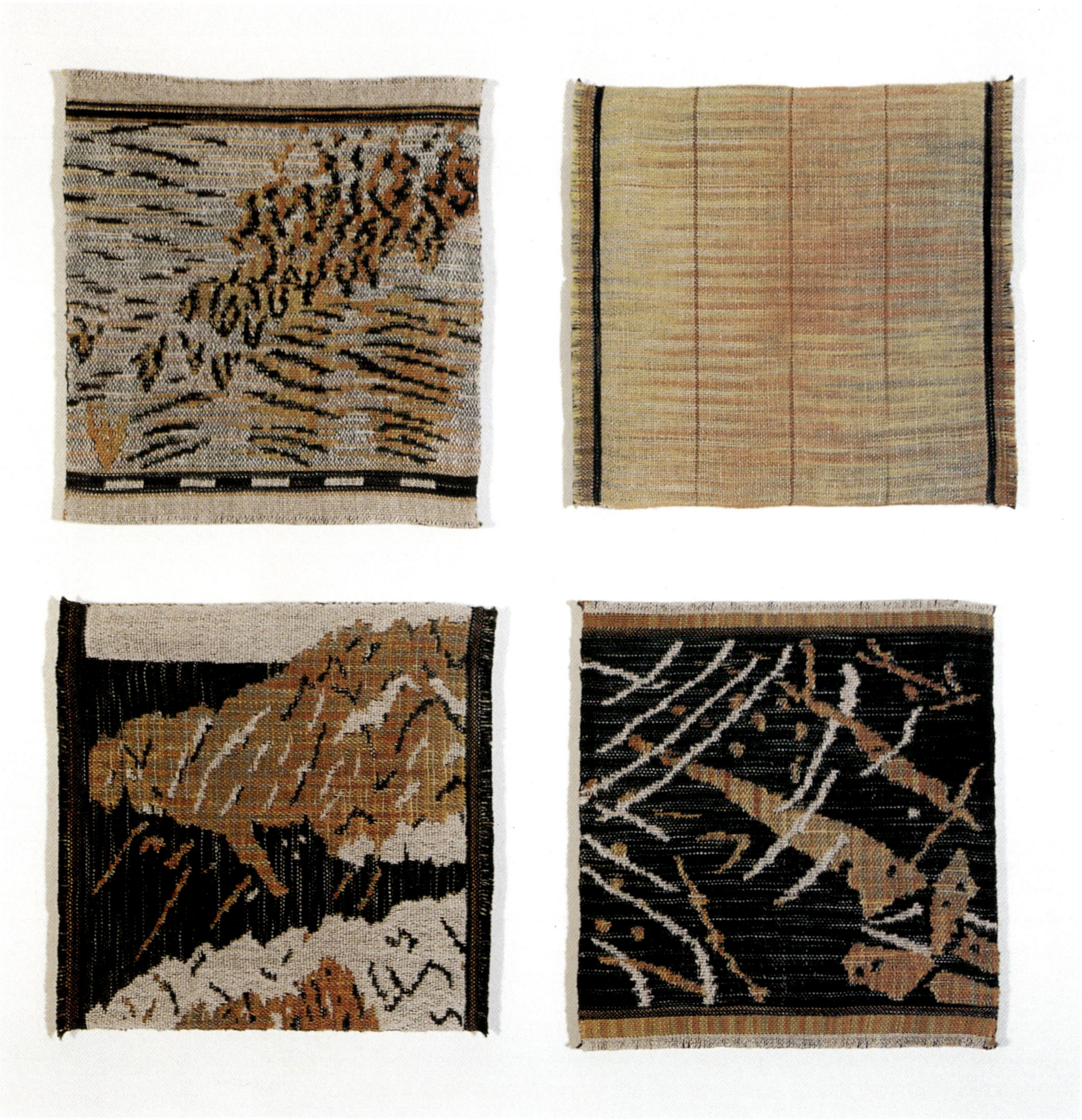

DAVID TRUBRIDGE

Born Oxford, England 1951.
BSc (Naval Architecture), University of Newcastle-upon-Tyne 1972.
Came to New Zealand 1986.
Lives in Havelock North.

David Trubridge thrives on debate about the philosophy of craft in relation to art and design, and this passion and his love of wood inform his furniture. His beautifully crafted objects have had considerable recognition within New Zealand and internationally—in England, USA, Japan, Germany and Scotland.

A four-year journey sailing to New Zealand via the Caribbean and Tahiti had a strong impact on Trubridge's furniture. At both places he made furniture to support his family, and when they arrived in New Zealand strong images of the Pacific found expression in his work. The furniture he produced was rich in sail-like forms and lashed details that evoked Polynesian vessels. He soon received recognition for this work, winning an award of merit at the first Winstones Craft Biennale in 1987; this was followed by a number of other awards over the years. Six months during 1991 as Artist in Residence at Hawke's Bay Polytechnic was a turning point in terms of process, and he acknowledges the contribution of Julia van Helden during this time.

During its evolution his work has retained a sense of the Pacific, although in recent years it is not as directly referential as in the past. Many tables now allude to the posed human figure, an idea which originated in a life-drawing class. The idea of adding an emotional element to his work appeals; it shifts the notion of the crafted furniture piece towards functional art. Finding forked and bent pieces of wood becomes the starting point for structure, as Trubridge works directly with his materials. The process is uncomplicated, the resolution of the complex intersections of angles achieved by creating small maquettes rather than drawings. The emphasis on structure is ongoing and the concept of human rather than abstract structural support is an interesting, if perhaps incidental, political statement.

Trubridge sometimes shifts the emphasis on structure to the surface of the table tops. Inspired by Gauguin's printing blocks, he saw his furniture as potential printing blocks. Marks revealed during the making process were left as a form of communication with the viewer. Trubridge inked those marks and printed the images on to paper, leaving behind ink-impregnated wood. The surface took on a patina, an implied narrative. A slight connection developed between the supporting figurative structure and the surface decoration of the table top.

What Trubridge has been seeking is a refinement of design concept, while returning to the artistic source. His use of colour epitomises his approach. In his earlier *Hornpipe Bench* he used washes of vibrant colour, with different colours applied to each of the interlocking components. The inking process of the newer works mutes the applied colour, mellows its emotive force. He wants to step sideways from the wood surface, allowing its characteristics to show but not override the work. The areas of wood left in their natural state act as contrasts: the sparkle and dynamism rather than the overriding feature. What remains dominant is a lively expression of his concerns for form, structure and detail.

**Offering II—figure
Matai, elm crotches,
artists' acrylic wash
750 x 820 mm
Collection of the
artist**

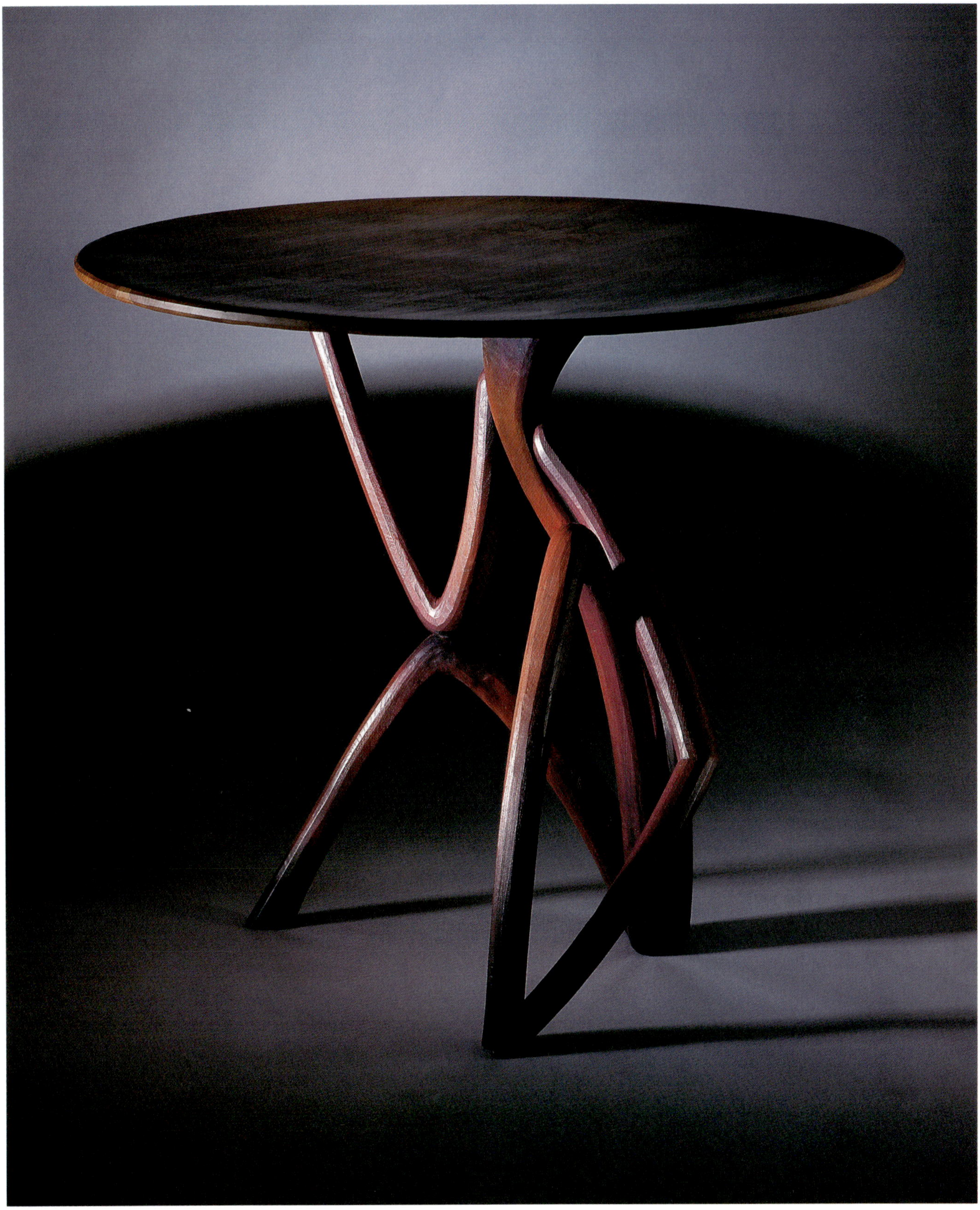

87

ANDREW VAN DER PUTTEN

Born Amsterdam, The Netherlands 1946.
Immigrated to New Zealand 1967.
Worked as a slipcaster at Crown Lynn Potteries 1967; part-time apprenticeship with Len Castle 1968–69.
Lives in Auckland.

The enchantment of the alternative craft lifestyle lasted until 1985 for Andrew Van Der Putten. During his early days as a potter, he lived and worked with potters Jeff Scholes and Helen Mason at Waiatarua while he was apprenticed to Len Castle. At the time he made functional ware in the form of stoneware and salt-glazed pots in the Hamada-Leach tradition. His pots were inspired by mediaeval English pottery, Japanese folk art and the work of pioneer potters Len Castle (14) and Barry Brickell (10). From 1975 to 1985 Van Der Putten and his partner, Jeannie Van Der Putten (88), lived in Coromandel in a thriving community of potters who made similar work in a robust, rustic style with earthy colours and little decoration. This was the era of the large wood-fired kiln that took eighteen hours or more to fire.

The decision to move to the inner suburbs of Auckland meant much more than a radical change of lifestyle. Van Der Putten found the shift from rural to urban potter was a liberating experience, and he used it as an opportunity to change direction with his work. Woodfiring gave way to firing in a gas kiln, and clay became a vehicle for decoration in the form of loosely applied, underglaze brushwork. For a decade he produced joyously coloured, expertly thrown earthenware tableware. He used housepainting brushes for speed and directness to produce gestural motifs, and his palette was lively and clean —unlike the muddier hues of the past.

The next significant change in his work occurred in 1995 when he experimented with glazes using copper carbonate and iron oxide. He wanted to pare down the decoration and reclaim some of his earlier forms, to allow the clay to come through the glaze. This was not a return to the Coromandel days of woodfiring—Van Der Putten now appreciated the efficiency of electric-fired earthenware. It was more a rejection of pots that verged on the 'competent slick'—a slightly contrived 'Pacific-ness' that had been adopted for semi-mass-produced decorated tableware.

Van Der Putten's current works have a luscious quality, and his fluid forms are eloquent expressions of his masterful throwing. Their detailing, like tiny decorative 'buttons', enlivens the surfaces yet remains subservient to the whole. The gleaming iron yellows and copper greens are like oriental glazes which he applies to terracotta clay with a layer of white slip under the glaze. The results differ from similar duller tones he has seen in Korean ceramics, and his hues express the colours of his landscape in a different way from his early earthy pots. This is the most personal expression of his work to date.

His work has always been functional but he has started to make bottles and jars that are not necessarily usable yet express their 'clayness' and functional origins. These are mature, assured, understated works—an extension of the beautifully balanced, strictly usable vessels. International exhibitions, awards, a QEII Arts Council travel grant and invitations to select a number of exhibitions have acknowledged Van Der Putten's abilities. In 1997 he was a Creative New Zealand-funded Travelling Potter, teaching his many skills throughout the South Island of New Zealand.

Jug
Clay
300 x 200 mm
Collection of the artist

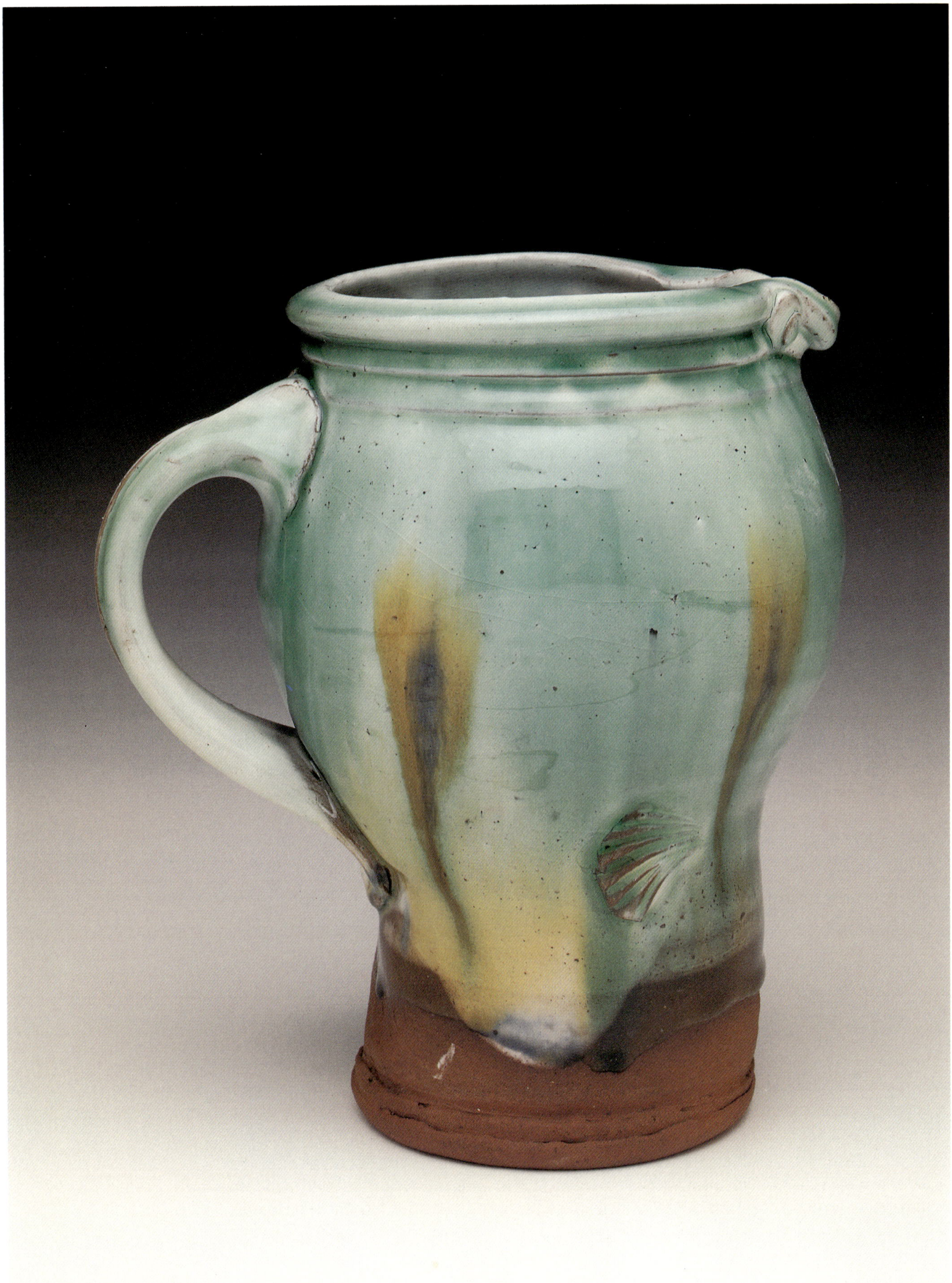

JEANNIE VAN DER PUTTEN

Born Kuala Lumpur, Malaysia 1947.
Arrived New Zealand 1950.
Elam School of Art, Auckland University 1965–66.
Lives in Auckland.

Jeannie Van Der Putten learnt to paint at Elam School of Art but in the early 1970s she turned to clay as a viable craft. Learning was by trial and error as a 'kitchen-table potter' working around small children. At a time when most potters were throwing stoneware vessels she was handbuilding. In 1971 she formed a partnership with potter Andrew Van Der Putten (87) and they moved to Helen Mason's house and workshop, where she handbuilt vases and platters. This was followed by ten years from 1975 to 1985 at Coromandel, where she developed a process of laminating porcelain and stoneware.

A move to the inner suburbs of Auckland in 1985 changed her life and her work. She started to make oxidised earthenware pieces—mainly handbuilt and occasionally cast—on which she freely brushed lively colour, with the forms as a backdrop to flamboyant expression. She looked to her immediate environment—Auckland as a Pacific city—as inspiration for her imagery.

A QEII Arts Council grant in 1991 made an electric kiln possible and the following year, on an overseas trip, the idea of painted tiles took seed. In 1993 Van Der Putten made the most significant changes to her work. For four years she was the designer for the Fletcher Challenge Ceramics Award exhibitions. Repetitive strain injury coincided with the death of her father, designer John Crichton, in whose studio she found many mosaic tiles. Partly as a tribute to him, and as a creative approach to the difficulty of working, she handbuilt and cast small clay shapes to apply to tiled murals and frames for mirrors. The imagery she had painted on her earlier work became solid, three-dimensional icons.

Georges Braques Bird in the Pacific Basin was an important series of tile paintings, protesting against French nuclear testing on Moruroa in 1996. The Pacific Basin was portrayed as a teacup amid symbolic motifs from French and Pacific cultures. *Botany Lessons* was less political—a more whimsical series in which cast clay components like cups were filled with resin and supported handbuilt organic shapes like *Palms, Mother-in-Laws Tongues* and *Bird of Paradise*.

Wall works made Van Der Putten more conscious of using clay in an architectural context, and she made some tiled furniture with her partner. She also developed work using her repertoire of sculpted clay motifs and grouped them in visual phrases, like pictograms, on walls. Flowers, fronds, birds, stars, fish, waves and crosses evoked Pacific influences, especially tapa; crowns, ladders, jugs, bowls and cups were domestic references. These images, about the size of a hand, were cut out of clay and used on lintels or fireplaces and as 'punctuations' around gateways and doors.

The assemblages of wall pieces have some of the spirit of Richard Killeen's works (Vol. 1, 42) but Van Der Putten sees them more as free-form domestic tiles—relief pieces for the wall. In 1997 the tiles were developed further in a collaboration with sculptor Virginia King (Vol. 2, 48) for a public work involving school children in Tole Street Reserve, Auckland. It was the first instance of Van Der Putten taking clay out of the domestic or gallery environment, and opened the door to new possibilities.

**Ten Oceanic Pieces
Earthenware clay
1150 x 650 mm
(wall hung)
Collection of the artist**

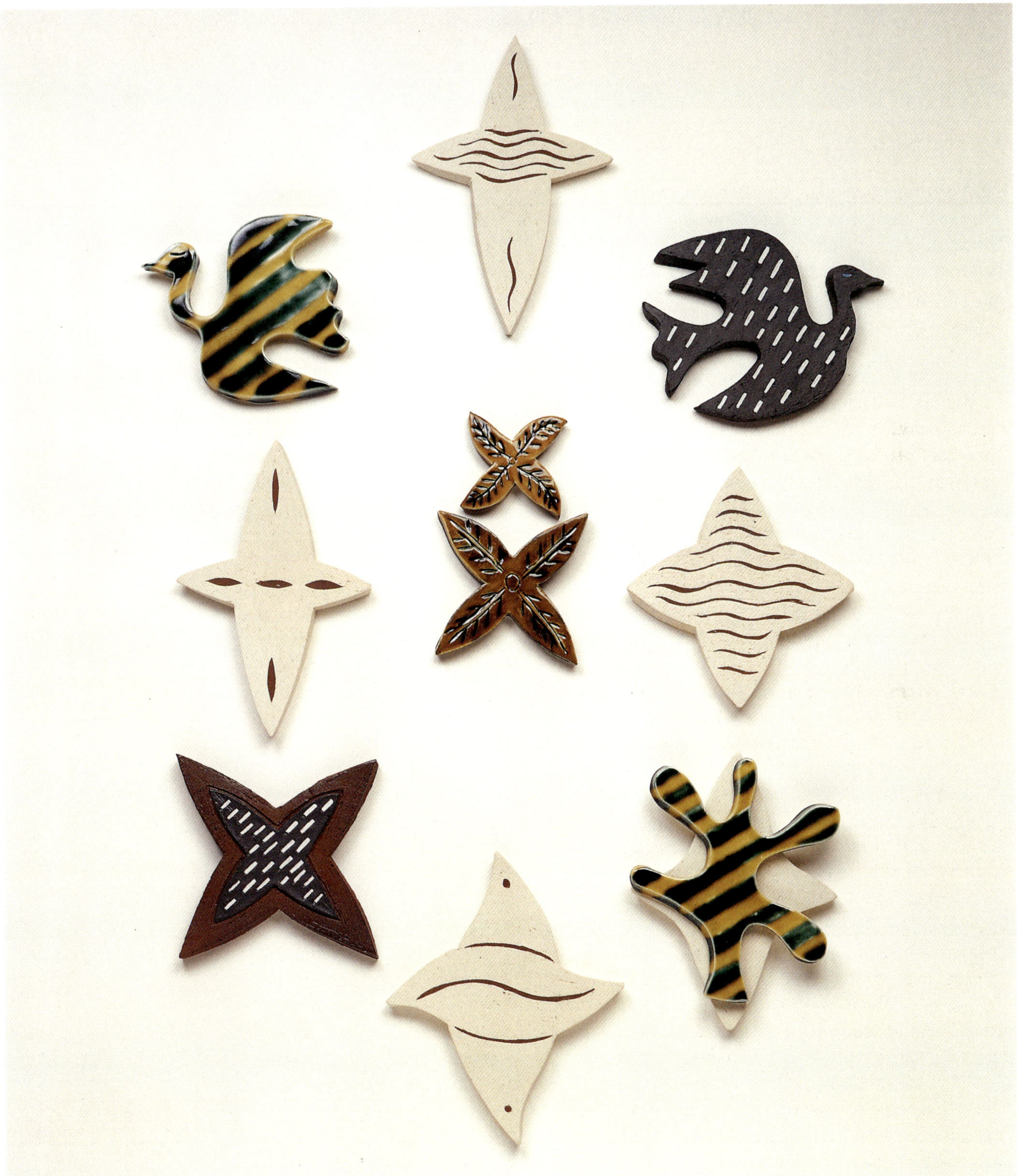

ANN VERDCOURT

Born Luton, Bedfordshire, England 1934.
Luton School of Art 1948–52;
NDD Diploma (Sculpture and Ceramics), Hornsey School of Art, London 1955.
Moved to New Zealand 1965.
Lives in Dannevirke.

When Ann Verdcourt exhibited the first of a series, *Ceremonial Elbow No. 1*, at the Fletcher Challenge Ceramics Award in 1993, it won a Judge's Commendation and a large number of smiles. The spotted elbow, like all her work, has a number of meanings, and typifies her penchant for humour and ability to play with realism. The idea for the work originated while Verdcourt was sculpting human figures and looking at body parts—in this instance an image of Nubians who had painted their skin white then applied black spots. She saw humour in the notion and created the elbow in black clay to her own recipe, applied white slip, then black ceramic stain spots, and fired it raw. There was a desire to make people look at the object in a new way and, upside down, the elbow resembled a hill. It also appeared to be pushing the viewer away, implying rejection.

As a trained painter, Verdcourt sees everything as a picture, often with art historical references. When she looks at an existing picture she imagines what is missing and visualises the figure in the round. In *Not Quite Magritte*, the whimsical figure is recognisably based on the surrealist's *Man in the Bowler Hat*. She admires Magritte's images and the way he titled his works. What really delights her audiences are her mischievous re-interpretations and the way she plays with titles. *Bridegroom with Borrowed Clothing*, with its elongated head, borrows from Modigliani and demonstrates Verdcourt's portraiture skills. They are skills she puts to good use in reference to a number of artists including Matisse.

Humour, satire and language are important in her sculptures, fitting with her love of clay and pleasure in being unpredictable with her imagery. Her direct approach to clay sees her squeezing and pinching it when appropriate, as well as handbuilding or throwing on a wheel. She prefers not to make preliminary drawings or maquettes, choosing to work directly into the actual piece to keep the image fresh rather than overworked. Learning new skills is ongoing for Verdcourt who, in recent years, has studied bronze and ceramic shell casting and working with paper clay.

When she makes vessels and objects they belong in a group, like components of a painting, rather than having a life of their own. A number of these still-lifes make reference to Giorgio Morandi's paintings and are composed of ordinary thrown pieces like bottles. Some of her works have been compared with groups of vessels by Australian Gwyn Hanssen Piggott, but unlike her, Verdcourt does not perceive herself to be a maker of jugs and bottles—they are always components of, and less important than, the sculptural 'picture'.

For *Treasures of the Underworld*, exhibited at World Expo, Seville 1992, Verdcourt created seventy pieces titled *Something about Columbus*. The work was extraordinary in scope and conception and, to accompany it, she was commissioned by the Ministry of External Affairs to create the *Abel Tasman Memorial Work*. The accolades she has received as one of the most outstanding artists working in clay are numerous. Verdcourt has won many awards, received a number of QEII Arts Council/Creative New Zealand grants and exhibited widely.

**Ceremonial Elbow
Black stonewall clay with white and black slips
ca. 390 x 330 mm
Collection of the artist**

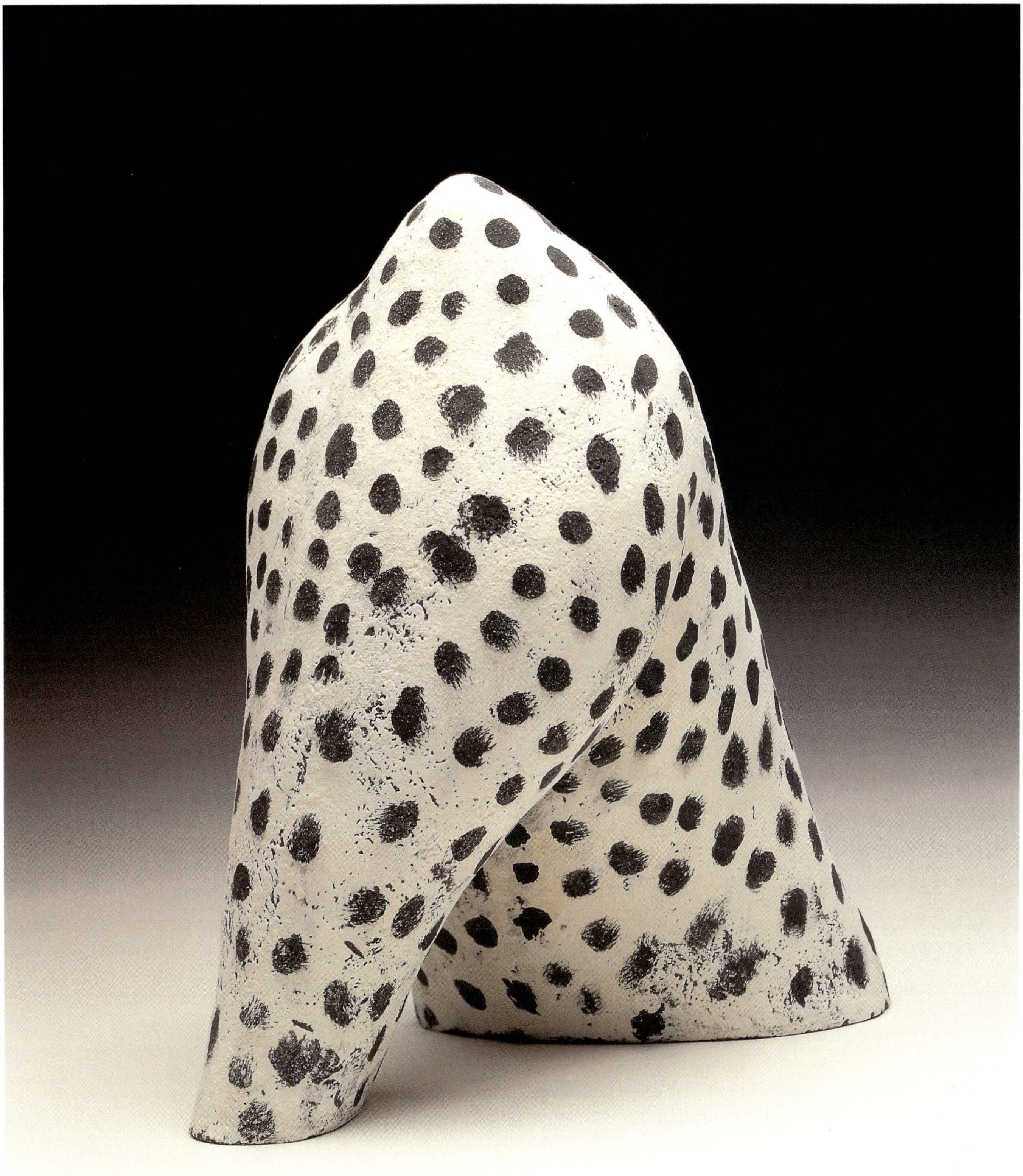

PETER VIESNIK

Born London, England 1939.
Arrived New Zealand 1974.
Self-taught; built his first glass studio facility in Albany, 1979.
Lives in Auckland.

The New Zealand studio glass movement was in its infancy and the public was just beginning its infatuation with the medium when Peter Viesnik started blowing glass in Albany. A year later he and Peter Raos established the Hot Glass Company at Devonport, in a partnership that lasted for ten years.

Being self-taught, Viesnik, like many other craftspeople at that time, benefited greatly from workshops by internationally renowned glass artists. American Richard Marquis's visits had considerable influence on locally blown glass. He introduced the Italian technique of murrini—the decorative, jewel-like 'buttons' of multi-coloured glass which became a favoured decorative device not just for Viesnik but for many of his colleagues. Inspiration and knowledge also came from others—from Italy, USA and Japan.

Viesnik has always worked intuitively, primarily making blown production ware, occasionally teaching workshops. In the tradition of craft, he has generally been process-driven, and has developed a critical eye for form through observing work in other media. He looked to ceramics for inspiration: to the Japanese potter Hamada, who had such an impact on New Zealand ceramics, and a number of New Zealand ceramists. Extensive travel also influenced his aesthetics.

After closing the Hot Glass Company, Viesnik operated from a number of studios, including eighteen months at Sunbeam Glass with Garry Nash (59) and later at the Elam School of Fine Arts facility prior to its demolition. In 1992, with the assistance of a QEII Arts Council grant, he attended a *Creative Flameworking* workshop by Paul Stankard at Pilchuck Glass School in Seattle. On his return he set up a flameworking workshop and became engrossed in the more intimate process of bead-making.

Flameworking was simple, quiet, clean and meditative in contrast to blowing glass, and Viesnik enjoyed being part of a tradition that dated back to Egyptian times. He made intricate beads, murrinis and tiny objects like fish. The diverse processes nourished each other, and soon the delicate flameworked details were integrated into his blown glass.

From 1995 to 1997 he and flat-glass artist Dermot Kelly ran GlassArts Gallery and workshop. He continued to blow glass part time, first at Northland Polytechnic, then at Burning Issues, a new hot-glass workshop in Whangarei, where he now works more frequently. He continues to live in Auckland, where he maintains a flameworking studio.

Viesnik makes a range of blown work that includes vases, stoppered bottles, paperweights and bowls. However, he is best known for his loose, flamboyant goblets which are designed to exhibit the qualities of the molten glass. Sometimes looped canes intersect the goblet or wrap around the stem or bowl. His love for colour is expressed at times in the restraint of a single colour threaded through the canes, as well as in wild blushes of variegated colour 'smudged' through the bowl. The placement of the loops often pushes the pieces into asymmetric balance and vulnerability—that is part of their appeal. Viesnik enjoys giving them individual personalities, and the most dynamic pieces are exuberant and fluid, often organic in form. One can visualise the dance of their creation.

Hand blown glass goblets
Molten glass
220–230 x 70–75 mm
Collection of the artist

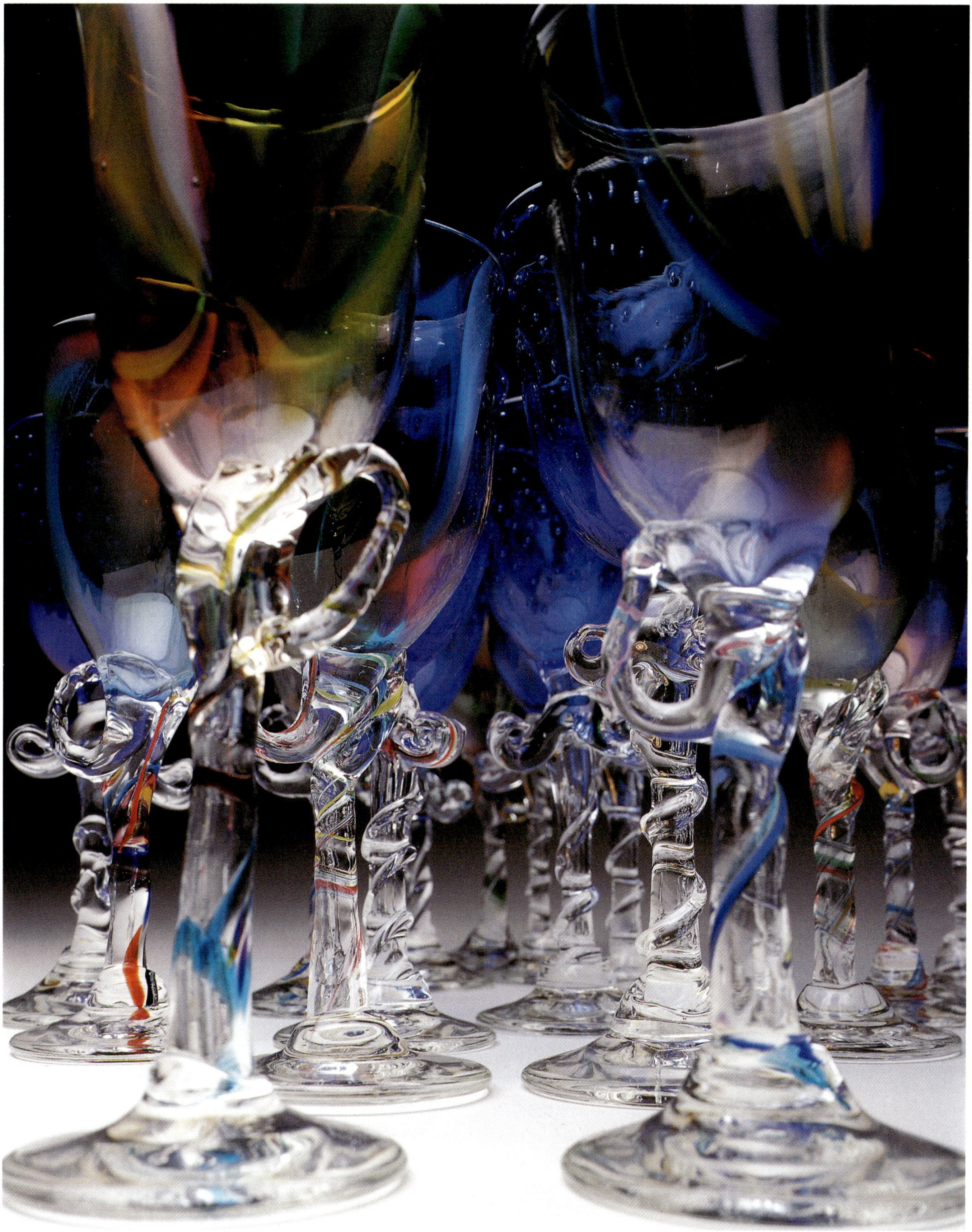

GWEN WANIGASEKERA

Born Moonlight, West Coast 1948.
Many quiltmaking workshops; part-time study of batik, shibori, paper-making 1987–89.
Lives in Hamilton.

The beauty and essence of fabrics has captivated Gwen Wanigasekera since childhood, but it is only in the past decade that she has made quilts for exhibition and commission. During that period she has created work for exhibitions in USA, France, Switzerland and within New Zealand, as well as a number of major commissions. Although largely self-taught, she has attended a number of workshops and classes, especially with Susan Flight.

Quilts at the Fisher Gallery in 1993 was her most significant exhibition, the culmination of considerable research into the beginnings of quilt-making and many months of intensive sewing. It followed a trip to the UK on a QEII Arts Council Study Grant in 1991. She worked with a large selection of silks, satins, cottons and velvets, some hand-dyed, as well as an assortment of men's ties, seeking inspiration close to home to create a sense of place. The role of the bed quilt in society was ever-present in these wall-hung works, a number of which alluded to conception, birth and death—life-changing events associated with beds. There were references, too, to quilting traditions, like log cabin patterns, and the traditional roles of textiles in society.

Wanigasekera resists making 'art quilts' favoured by a number of practitioners. Hers are quilts in the traditional sense, honouring the processes and materials of the past, and grounded in a historical and sociological context. Yet in no way is she locked into reproducing quilts of the past. Where appropriate they take the form of triptychs or multi-panelled works. She pieces together, by hand or machine, small fragments of fabric, often fine strips, in complex combinations.

Mastery of techniques is fundamental, so that her focus can be on content, composition and colour. She wants her work to transcend, yet to be about process, with nothing to detract from the quality of the fabrics and their tactility. Sophisticated use of colour and an experimental approach to colour harmony give Wanigasekera's quilts a unique and lively presence. The colours modulate and contrast, their textures adding to the dancing rhythms of her pattern-making. She aims for impact from a distance, the way many quilts are primarily viewed, with many fine details to be discovered on viewing more closely. Her approach to using colour has been influenced by the knitting and needlepoints of artist Kaffe Fassett, and she, too, seeks inspiration from diverse sources such as ancient artworks and nature.

In *Pacific Cloak*, created in 1994 for Manukau Polytechnic, there were connotations of cloaks, kites and birds. Wanigasekera was less interested in a literal interpretation than in evoking a sense of the Pacific through colour and illusion. Her palette embraced blues from the depths of the ocean and the hues of warm, sun-baked sand using many different fabrics, a number of which were hand-dyed. Triangles pointing upwards were used to create an uplifting feeling as well as to evoke Pacific imagery, and the panels were overlapped to create shadows and depth.

Currently Wanigasekera is studying landscape design, and finds that her work is inspired by the quilts that she continues to make spasmodically. The fabrics and beautiful gardens that have always been part of her life are interwoven with her enjoyment of history, culminating in beautiful quilts for daily use and for the wall.

Pacific Cloak
Patchwork: cotton,
silk and other fibres
4000 x 2200 mm
Collection of the
Manukau Polytechnic,
School of Catering
and Tourism

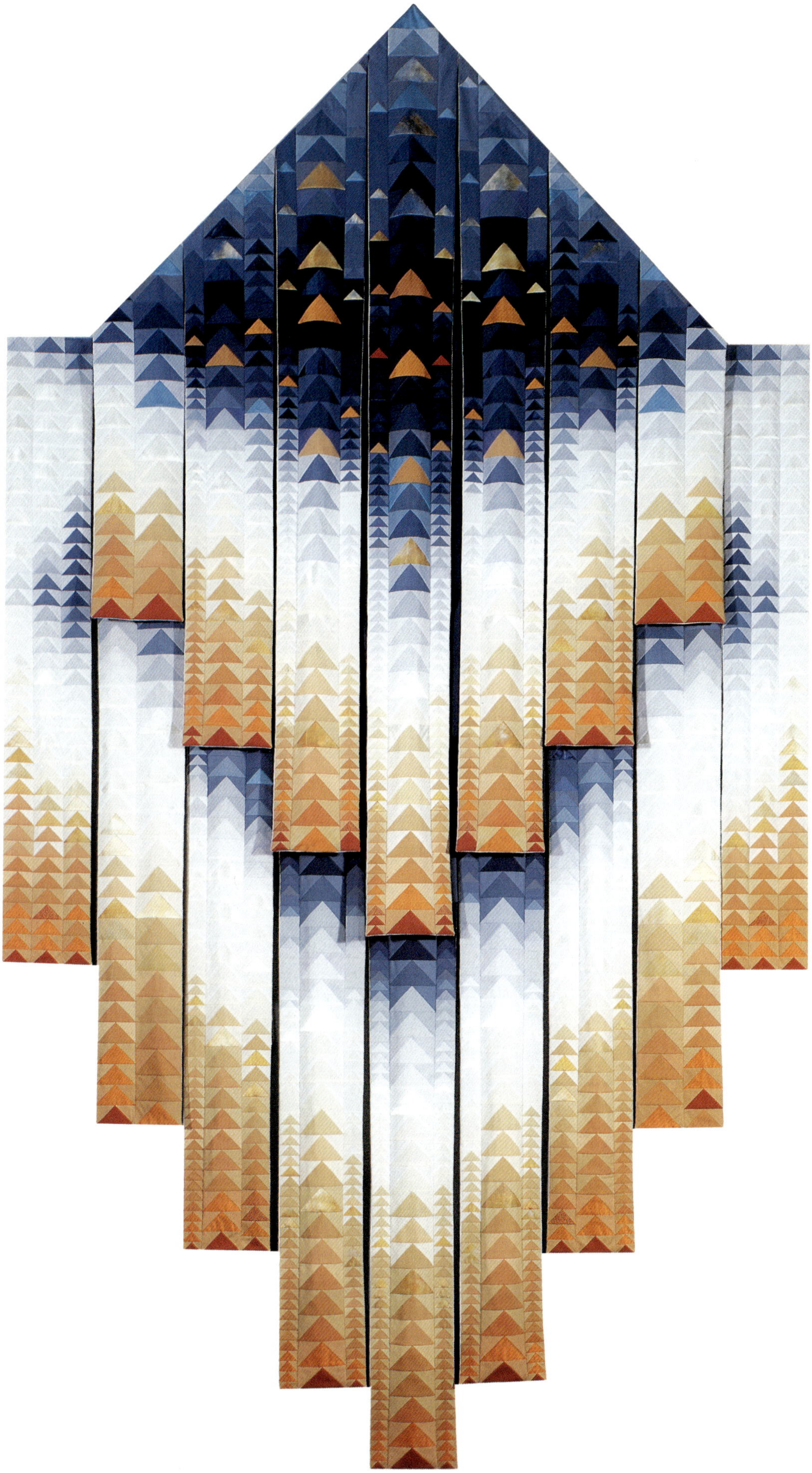

CHRIS WEAVER

Born Te Awamutu 1956.
Dip Fine and Applied Arts, Otago Polytechnic 1975;
Certificate Ceramics, Otago Polytechnic 1976.
Lives in Hokitika.

Form is of utmost importance to Chris Weaver. He makes clay tableware that is generally devoid of surface decoration—the last thing he wants is for any embellishment to hide the form. They are strong forms that reflect their functionalism, but they are never sterile, are superbly made and sensitively detailed. His work has won many national awards and is exhibited from his local co-operative in Hokitika to international exhibitions in Japan. He has consistently exhibited at the Fletcher Challenge Ceramics Award.

When Weaver started working with clay he made stoneware finished with traditional glazes in the Bernard Leach tradition. Pit firing became popular and he developed a personal style of low-temperature salt-fumed pieces on which surface decoration was a product of the flame. His interest in form was already apparent, but it was not until 1993 that his work moved to a direction that truly expressed his individuality as well as his expertise.

Using a white high-firing clay he created a number of teapots based on an old cast pressing iron. He threw the components on the wheel, then altered and assembled them. He covered the teapot with a simple black glaze which had the characteristic of breaking slightly on the edges of the clay to reveal the material underneath. The laminated handles and tiny details, all meticulously turned to fit perfectly, were of heart rimu. The resulting works had a crispness of definition and a slightly industrial appearance. Precise edges were defined by the breaking glaze. The teapot became the starting point for a range of tableware always based on a single solid colour.

Weaver has been interested in ancient Iranian ceramics for many years, and has admired the work of sculptors Henry Moore and Jean Arp. In 1995, on a Creative New Zealand travel and study grant, he visited USA, UK and Ireland. His interest in sculpture was heightened by seeing the stone sculptures of Henry Moore as well as many stone vessels. The sculptural aspect and the presence of the Moore sculptures—their mass, surfaces and solidity—were qualities he wanted in his functional ware.

Recently Weaver has started a new series using clay alone. He is emulating the white surfaces and sculptural quality of the stone works he admired. His aim is to be true to the material and to allow it to reveal its qualities. There is still an element of precision, but there is also a new looseness and a greater acknowledgement of the qualities of clay. The pieces are gentler and more curvaceous, inviting caress. His process has not changed to any great extent, but now he alters the components while they are still wet rather than waiting until they are leather-hard as in the past. There are more 'accidents' as a result, small details that communicate the process.

More than ever, through intuitive handling of clay, Weaver is expressing himself with integrity. He always works directly rather than drawing first, and the clay reveals itself as he works. He repeatedly reworks the clay, perfecting the body before adding details of spouts and handles, and the beautiful pieces reflect his love of the material and process.

Teapot
Clay
140 x 170 x 120 mm
Private collection

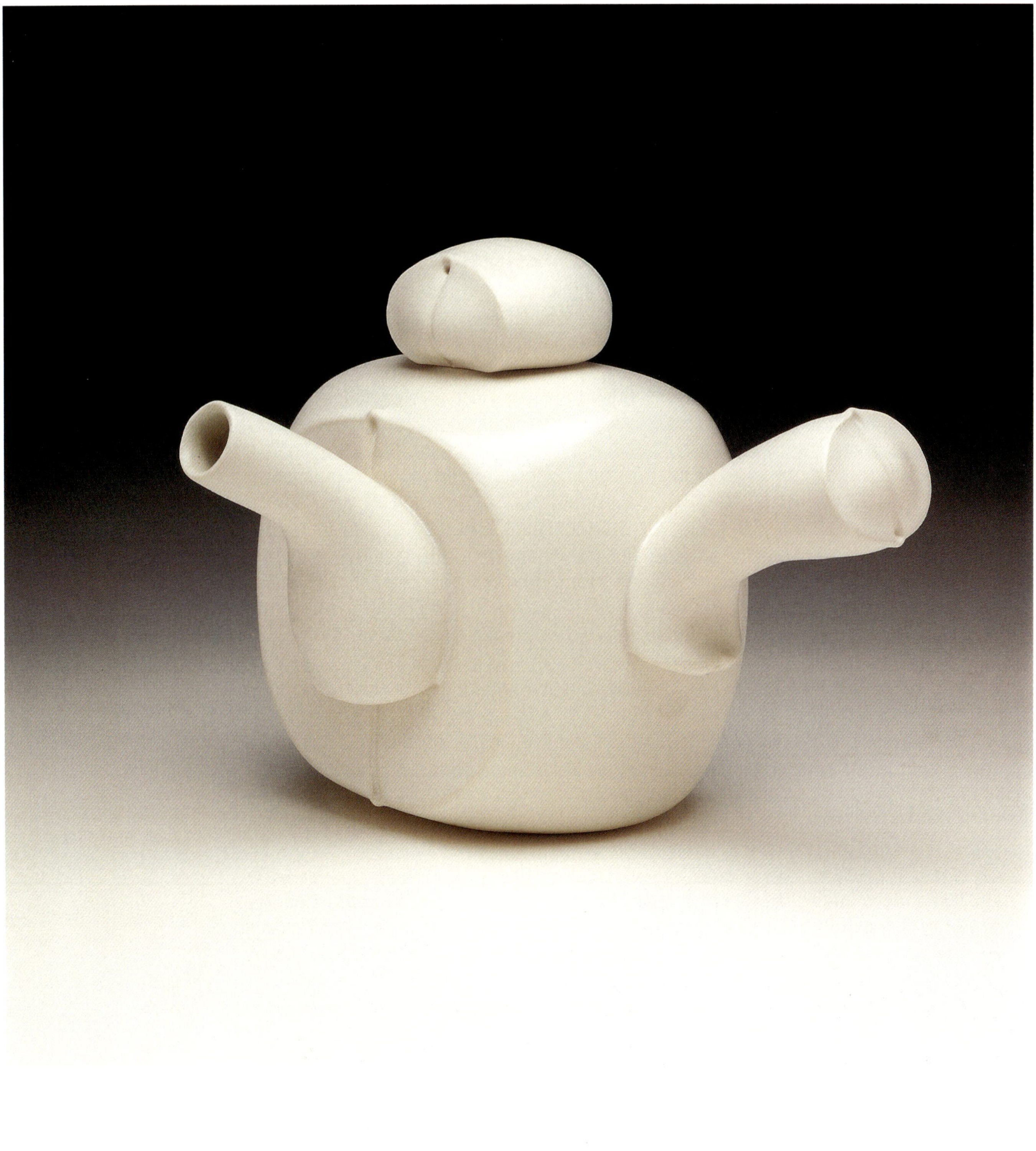

KATE WELLS

Born Foxton 1961.
Dip Textile Design, Wellington Polytechnic 1983.
Lives in Auckland.

Designing Dilana rugs has become an important part of Kate Wells' recent work. They fit well into a career that merges her interests as a designer and maker. Wells became known for producing some of the finest tapestries in the country during the 1980s. An impressive list of commissions and acquisitions in public collections testifies to her ability to produce consistently exquisite work, which is characterised not only by superb crafting but also by potent images which express humanity and vulnerability. She set a new benchmark for weaving in New Zealand in 1990 with her wonderful travelling solo exhibition *Fish out of Water*.

Tapestry is an exacting and time-consuming medium. In the past Wells set a gruelling pace, proofreading by night in order to weave during the day. She now observes that through the meditative tapestry process she was able to cushion her emotions in her early work and thus process life events. This suited her temperament and she especially enjoyed the subtlety she could achieve through manipulation of the fine strands.

Drawing has always been important for Wells, as has printmaking which she learnt from John Drawbridge (Vol. 2, 29). This opened the door to designing for other media as well as her own weaving, and since 1991 a major part of her work has been designing Dilana rugs. Here her training as a textile designer, her crafting skills, her real understanding of the medium and her empathy for the process are all put to good use. She understands the collaborative process that is required for working effectively with those who execute the rugs, and her knowledge of printmaking informs the design process.

She recognises the significant differences between tapestries and designing 'functional' works of art which can dominate an interior space. No less a vehicle for personal expression, the rug needs to have longevity as an interior design component and to fit with different design trends. Eye contact with a rug differs from the connection with a wall work, and poses a different challenge. Humour needs to have a punchline that is easy to live with. There needs to be a sense of being able to engage physically with the work and not be too precious about walking on it. Wells responds to this design brief with panache. Her love of colour is evident and she enjoys designing large-scale rugs. Her images are whimsical rather than cartoon-like. They have a narrative quality and her knowledge of the characteristics of wool are put to good use. The flat, non-reflective character of the yarns and the availability of rich, dense colour are qualities she knows how to exploit.

Wells hasn't abandoned tapestry. In her studio/showroom there are tapestries in progress—small, intimate works that have been pared down to simple ideas that reflect her life and her environment. She resists the urge, common to many working in textiles, to overload the content and effects. The tapestries are created in a context of family responsibilities, occasional teaching, designing Dilana rugs for national and international markets, and design projects for Waitakere City Council.

**Tall Sheep I
Handtufted rug/wool
2000 x 1800 mm
Collection of the artist
and Dilana Rugs**

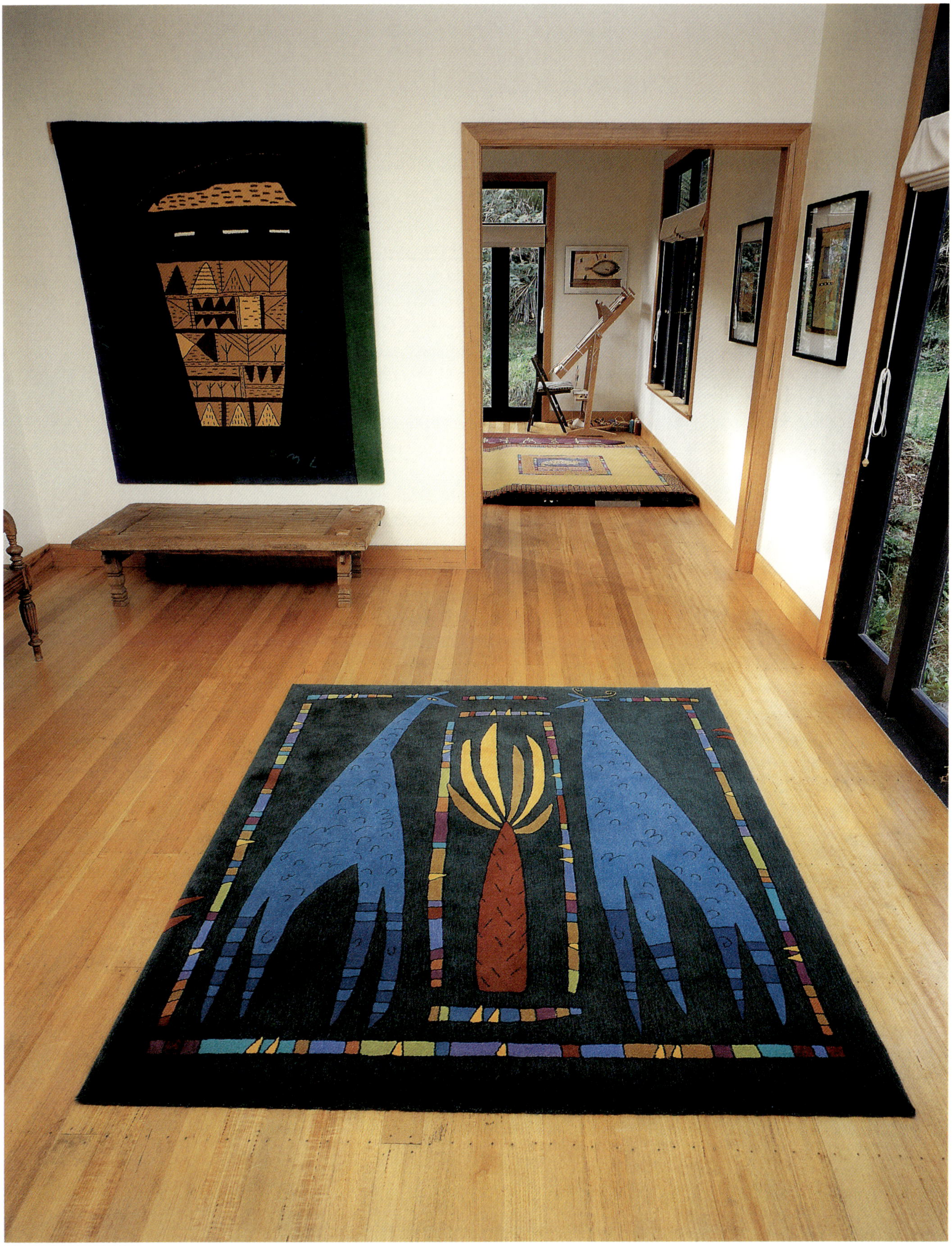

ARETA WILKINSON

Born Kaitaia 1969.
Ngai Tahu, Ngati Irakehu.
Dip Design (Jewellery), Carrington Polytechnic 1991.
Lives in Helensville.

When Areta Wilkinson wanted to use native feathers in her jewellery, she had to apply to the Department of Conservation. She gained access through her iwi and received permission, but with that came responsibility and an awareness of ownership issues. The resultant feathered brooches—one of kereru, two of kea—can never be for sale. The pieces were donated to her iwi, Te Rununga Ngai Tahu. They form part of a larger group of works owned by Auckland Museum which were assembled for exhibition in a manner that evoked weaving patterns and symbolised the mountain Aoraki.

It is significant that the latter works are owned by a museum, because a good deal of Wilkinson's recent work has explored the cataloguing and referencing of material in museums. The triangular brooches of her *05 Series* are stamped with DO NOT TOUCH on the back, and they bear catalogue numbers. The museum also provided a source of imagery, the taonga which informed this series. On a background of sterling silver, natural fibres—harakeke and the muka extracted from it, pingao and kiekie—inspired one group. Pounamu, argillite and basalt represented stone carving, and traditional carving was represented by totara and red oxide. Paua and bone are also represented.

Her *04 Series—labels* are sandblasted numbered tags, like dog tags or shopping labels, to be placed around the neck as human tags. They raise issues about jewellery as a label that signifies wealth or marital status, as well as the different connotations of identity tags. The numbered tags also emphasise a sense of series and the loss of individuality. Wilkinson realises that she is creating a false history in which numbers could just as easily reference a tax number or a birth or death date, and she links this to the arbitrary nature of cataloguing. Her interest in labelling and cataloguing grew from the relationships she observed between groups of her early works that focused on form and materials. Along with her desire to record them came the realisation that she was in fact creating a collection.

Labelling brings up issues of identity for Wilkinson, defining who she is and where she has come from—a recognition of her Pakeha upbringing and more recent exploration of her Maori culture. Maori culture informs her work, and with it comes an awareness of the privilege of her new knowledge and connections. Her respect extends to the senior practitioners from whom she has learnt her craft.

In Wilkinson's current creative exploration she is making clay tags, a reference to land settlements. The price tags are cut with biscuit cutters, and depict pounds and dollars. She also continues to work with semi-precious and found materials. Her approach has parallels in other media, yet there is a freshness and a particular cultural perspective in her work. She works at Workshop 6, an Auckland studio shared with a group of jewellers, and this provides a forum for debate, as does tutoring. That discourse, together with valuing crafting skills, is a significant feature and a sound basis for her burgeoning work.

05 Series Brooches: sterling silver, flax, pingao, kiekie, muka, pheasant feathers, basalt, argillite, totara, pounamu, paint, paua, bone. Wooven inserts made by Medina Hauraki. 62 x 42 mm each Collection of the Auckland Museum Te Papa Whakahikau

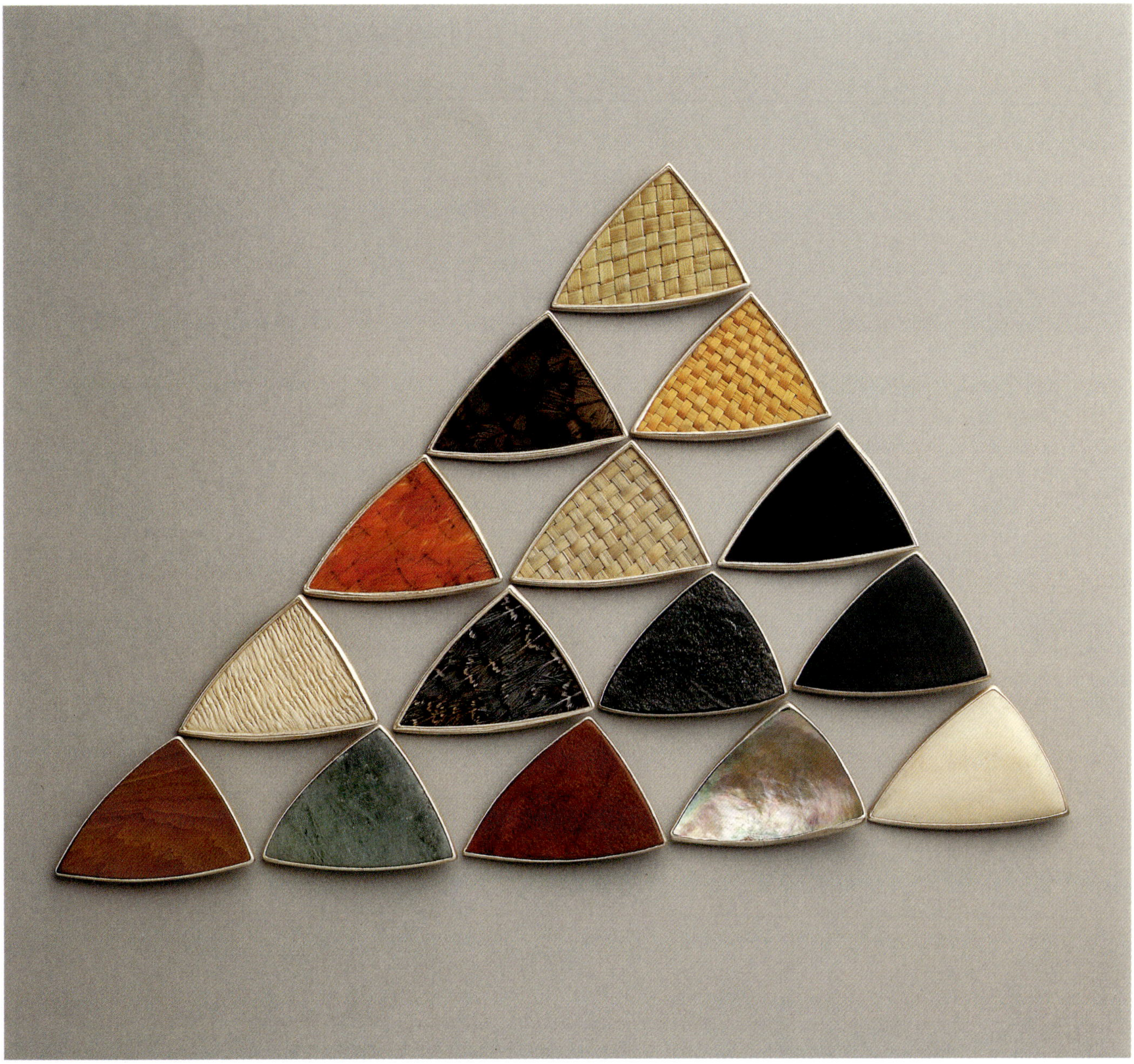

CARIN WILSON

Born Christchurch 1945.
Ngati Awa, Ngai Te Rangihouhiri.
Professional Member of Designers Institute of New Zealand;
Honorary Dip Art & Design, Whitecliffe College of Art and Design.
Lives in Auckland.

Beds for sitting on and chairs for lying on: thinking about how furniture is really used has pointed Carin Wilson into redefining the pieces of furniture he makes. He wants to accommodate a casual lifestyle, with chairs designed for reclining and reading, and beds as social places for young people. His philosophy is a developing one—Wilson likes to turn ideas around, to probe, discuss and think in three dimensions.

Wilson is a self-taught furniture maker, and his career path is an unorthodox one. He has followed his passion for designing and making since 1974. Along the way he has been president of the Guild of Woodworkers New Zealand, of the Crafts Council of New Zealand and of the Designers Institute of New Zealand, as well as a board member of the World Crafts Council. During the last five years he has assisted in introducing a number of innovative initiatives within his iwi community.

The impact of all these activities on his work has been considerable. A number of Arts Council grants since 1982 have given him time for research, and he has developed working relationships with the design industry and in education. He enjoys the interplay between functioning as the 'designer-maker' and working as a designer who relinquishes some of the making. At times he works collaboratively or as a co-ordinator.

For Wilson, exploring the boundary between functional furniture and more sculptural notions has been fruitful. One body of research began during a short Australian residency in Gippsland in 1987. It culminated in 1995 in an exhibition based on the story of Ngati Awa's Treaty of Waitangi claim presented to the Tribunal in 1995–96. His personal involvement gave him an emotional as well as intellectual rationale for the exhibition, which took him further away from functional furniture than ever before.

After the exhibition the pendulum swung back to furniture, which Wilson now sees with a much wider vision. Making sculptures clarified for him that the most successful furniture defines the space in which it lives. The sculptures were a practical way of making discoveries, like drawing in space with lines, and exploring the idea of floating in space and the way solid mass impacts on that space.

Recently Wilson was Artist in Residence at Nelson Polytechnic, and he sees this period as a milestone in his development. His daughter had provided him with a brief for a bed, along with some concept drawings, and his response was a bed that could be a prototype for further production. The design, executed in sycamore which had been milled in the centre of the South Island, is based on a single uninterrupted line. The line starts on the edge of one leg and continues through the whole piece. He compares it to composing music on one note. Striving for such conceptual simplicity led him into uncharted territory, a challenge he welcomes. It fits with his passionate enthusiasm for life, design and windsurfing—and the bit of Italian blood in his veins.

Bed
Sycamore
2800 x 850 x 2380 mm
Collection of Tulia Wilson and Greg Murrell

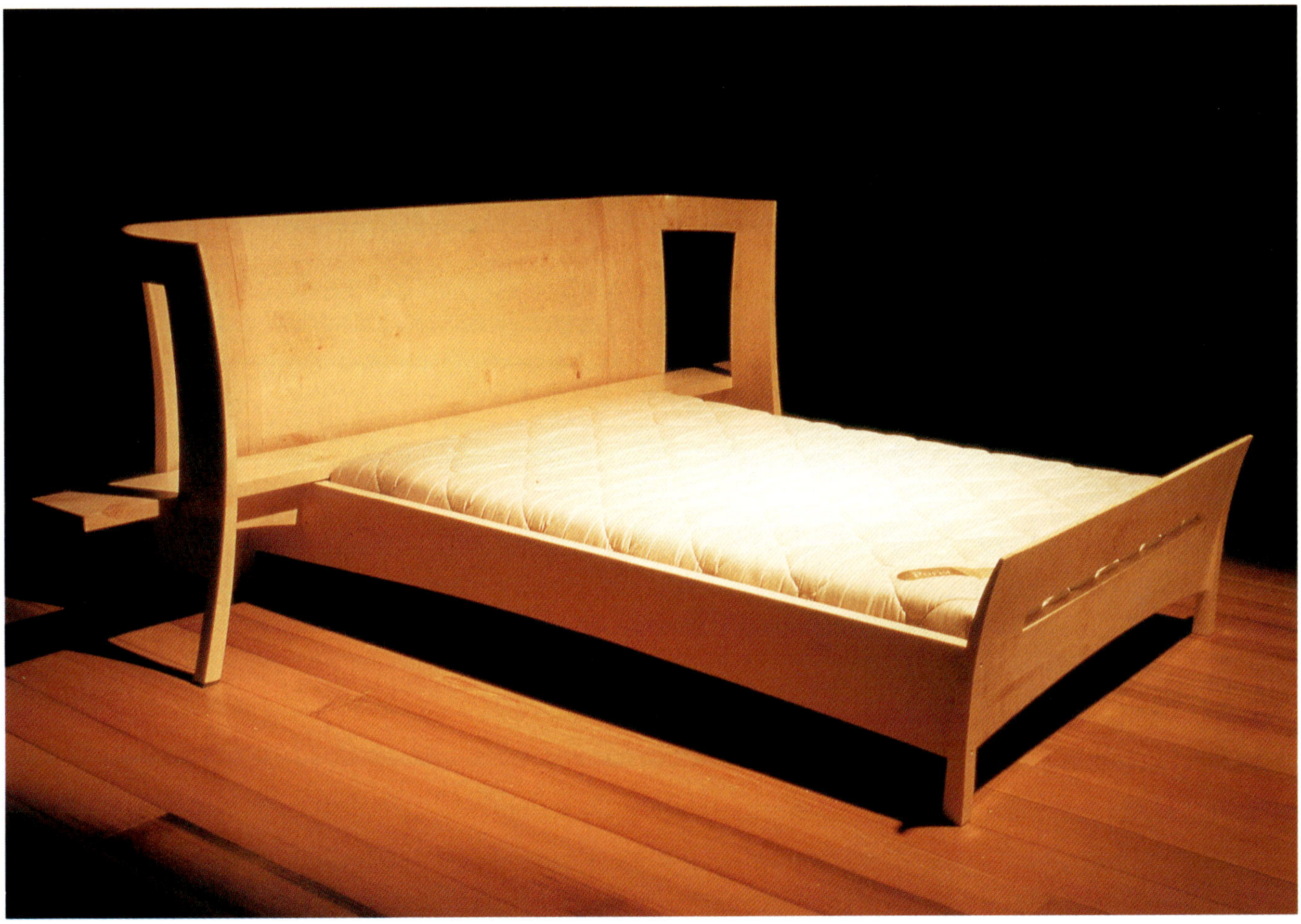

CHRISTINA HURIHIA WIRIHANA

Born Rotorua 1949.
Ngati Maniopoto, Ruakawa, Tainui, Ngati Pikiao, Te Arawa.
First and most significant weaving teacher, her mother Matekino Lawless.
Lives in Rotoiti, Rotorua.

Most of Christina Wirihana's weaving time is spent in the company of her mother Matekino Lawless, and they share a love of materials and process. A strong sense of whakapapa informs her approach to weaving and she has always looked upon Dame Rangimarie Hetet, Diggeress Te Kanawa (83) and Emily Schuster as her mentors. Wirihana has a sense of destiny; she acknowledges the tupuna for giving her the skills, and feels she was chosen to do the weaving, to discover and pass on her knowledge of traditional and contemporary fibre to her students. For some years she has taught at Waiariki Polytechnic, Rotorua, and at workshops.

Neinei is a favourite material, and she never discards any part of it. She enjoys its personality and rich colour, and especially the spoon-like butt ends which, when massed, ruffle like feathers. The neinei is found in the bush on the West Coast of the South Island and among the kauri trees in the Waipoua Forest. It grows as a small version of a cabbage tree, and Wirihana uses brittle fallen leaves which she softens to a leather-like consistency in hot water. The moisture appears to strengthen the leaves and enhance their colour. She interlaces the leaves in the same way that she would construct a whariki, and groups the ends into an undisciplined tangle. They become wall works or nests, celebrating the structure of the leaves, and are designed to adorn a space more than to be handled.

Experiments with unusual natural materials has proved fruitful for Wirihana. Lacebark has recently revealed its magic to her. She based her research on kete she had seen in museums, made from lacebark found in the Ureweras. After months of soaking the bark in fresh baths of water she was able to release the layers for weaving. Her knowledge of working with harakeke didn't prepare her for the restricted movement of the lacebark with its many claws, but her perseverance was worthwhile—the resultant *Kete Hoheria* looked as if she was weaving with light.

In her work with the more familiar harakeke, pingao and kiekie, she has developed a personal approach to detailing. Rather than cutting off the ends Wirihana leaves fringes of unwoven portions. The fringes give a visual softness and catch any breath of air, but most importantly they give the viewer an appreciation of the whole leaf, reflecting the holistic approach she applies to all of life.

There are nonetheless occasions when there are trimmings and offcuts. For a number of years Wirihana, ever the conservationist, has converted these scraps into sheets of handmade paper and given them a new life. This fits with traditional cultural practice: when you take from nature, you also give back. The process is also appropriate for teaching in Australia, which she does from time to time. She can take harakeke with her, providing she observes the Ministry of Agriculture rules, so she returns with the leaves transformed into sheets of paper.

The richness of Wirihana's works, their strong grounding in tradition and their enchanting contemporary expressions have earned her a considerable reputation. She has won a number of awards, and has exhibited widely in Australia, Germany, England, India, USA and throughout Aotearoa.

**Kohanga Neinei
Neinei—candelabra tree—*Dracophyllum latifolium/D. traversii*
200 x 300 mm
Collection of
Barry Dabb**

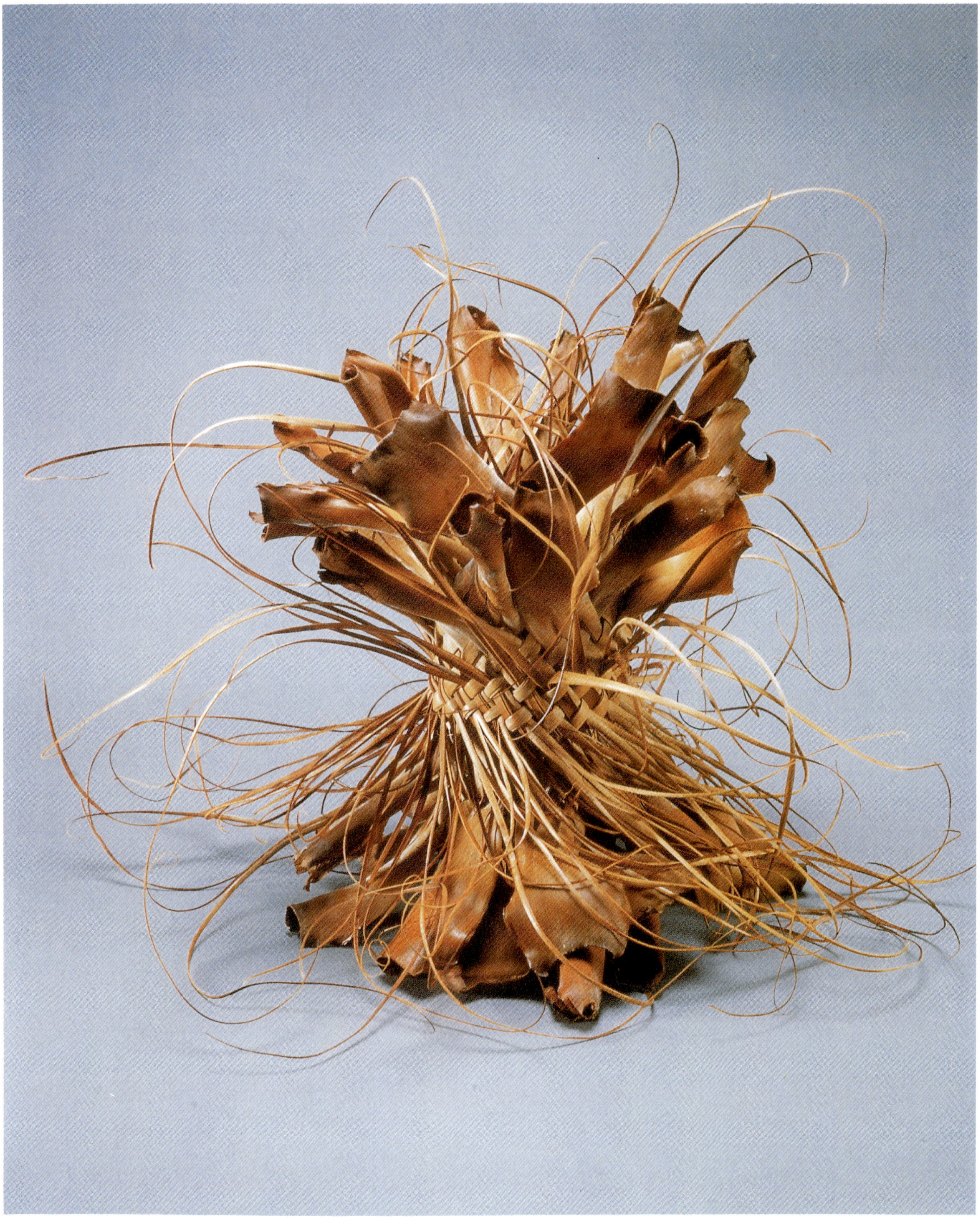

MERILYN WISEMAN

Born 1941.
Preliminary Diploma, Elam School of Art, Auckland 1959;
National Dip Design, Goldsmiths School of Art, University of London 1963;
Art Specialist Teachers Diploma, Goldsmiths College, University of London 1964.
Lives in Redvale.

When Merilyn Wiseman wants to express a visual idea she picks up a lump of clay rather than a pencil. Thinking through her fingers, she lets her vessels evolve. In a process in which pure form comes first, interpretation comes later as she starts to recognise the references like horizons, water or containment.

Graceful abstract forms seem to emerge effortlessly from her hands. In recent years each body of work has evolved naturally from the previous one. She loves working with clay, more so than painting in which she trained. It is an amorphous material with no intrinsic beauty, and Wiseman is endlessly fascinated by the extraordinary works that have been created from the material throughout history. She loves the tactility of clay, the way she deals directly with the material. She says it is a non-intellectual attraction that has stood the test of time.

The 1960s, when she started working with clay, was a vital, exciting time for craft. Wiseman had discovered the medium when in Ireland, and on her return to New Zealand she found herself involved with the beginning of the contemporary crafts movement. There was a strong Japanese influence on New Zealand ceramics at the time, and her platters and boxes with their loose gestural marks owed much to a Japanese aesthetic. Yet her impeccably crafted work had a strong personal imprint, and she received many awards and accolades, especially at the prestigious Fletcher Challenge Ceramics Award (formerly the Fletcher Brownbuilt Award). Her *Rough Diamond* series in 1989 was a major shift. These pieces made less reference to external influences and owed more to her self-knowledge and self-confidence. Her work began to evoke a sense of place, and out of this grew the *Pacific Rim* series in which she is currently engaged.

There is nothing illustrative about Wiseman's low-fired handbuilt vessels. Her visual devices are colour, textures and occasionally gestural marks, and she makes glazes to meet her needs. Surface treatment is an ongoing development. The *Pacific Rim* series, like earlier works, is based on the notion of containment. Large, generous forms stretch out gracefully like dancers with outstretched limbs, their scale seemingly determined by human arm spans. Wiseman wants them to engage with human scale in an emotional rather than literal way. Her objective to have the work appear effortless, rather than laboured or technically difficult, is realised. The newest sensuous vessels, each poised on a small foot ring, have rolled rims that appear pliable, still moist. The voluptuous edges of the vessels are strongly horizontal, and in these she sees references to rolling waves.

Wiseman has the courage of her convictions, always producing work from her need to make rather than from what the market dictates. It is a challenging existence that includes occasional teaching yet fulfils her creative urge to continue pushing boundaries.

Pacific Rim
Clay
1300 x 450 x 380 mm
Collection of
Roger Dale

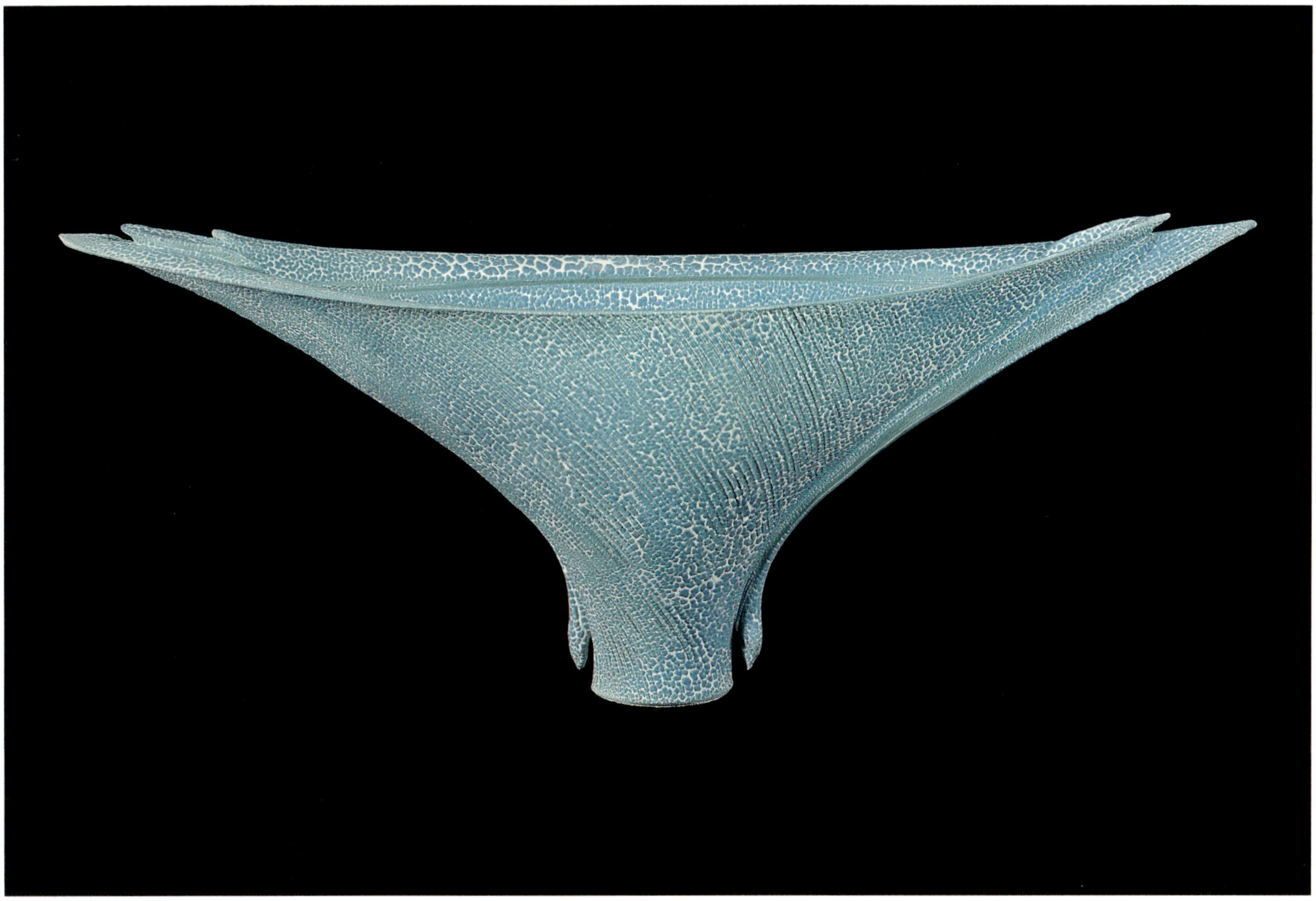

PETER WOODS

Born Eltham 1952.
Worked for Jens Hansen, Nelson 1973–74; Elam School of Fine Arts 1978.
Lives in Auckland and San Miguel de Allende, Mexico.

Contemporary silver hollow ware has few exponents in New Zealand, unlike the genre in Australia, and this makes the beautifully resolved, meticulously crafted forms of Peter Woods all the more precious. His approach eschews the avant garde and trendy, and instead celebrates the strong history and traditions of silversmithing. Wood creates elegant contemporary heirlooms that speak quietly to the viewer. Lasting design values are important, and many commissioned pieces acquire content by reflecting the interests of their owners.

The works are a response to traditional ways of working, retaining formal elements and reflecting an understanding of how objects have been assembled for centuries. Woods sees himself as part of a continuum: his works are very much of the present, not about a nostalgic past. As part of that continuum he acknowledges his responsibility to pass on skills, and he was involved in the development of the Craft Design courses that were introduced to the polytechnics in the mid 1980s. More recently he has been involved in training artisans in Mexico, where there is a strong silver tradition, and where he lives for most of the year.

When he worked for Jens Hansen (33) in the 1970s, his work was in the form of jewellery—large fabricated Scandinavian-inspired pieces, hollow bangles that were almost like vessels. At that point he made a choice to develop the works as vessels and pursue silversmithing rather than jewellery. In the early 1980s he worked full time restoring antique silver and learning much about domestic silver objects.

Since early 1996 he has been creating a dining set for the James Wallace Charitable Arts Trust, starting with a sculptural centrepiece, moving to flatware and later to serving dishes, gradually replacing antique silver with a contemporary equivalent. It follows another private commission of a dining set created in 1995 which features slender silver handle details echoed in puriri on the tea and coffee servers. The tray is embellished with small feet using the same detail. Each part of the set is beautifully balanced in itself and together they form a harmonious grouping.

The huge subject of silversmithing remains Woods' driving force. Historically this included everything from jewellery and domestic objects to architectural detail. He has participated in all of these, embracing a number of related skills including lapidary and bronze casting, and enjoying the development of skills and their relationship to materials. In 1993 he became a founding member of the New Zealand Contemporary Medallion Group.

Hands-on involvement—making the pieces, doing his own foundry work and casting—remains significant, but he has a new awareness of being able to delegate. His role is evolving as he undertakes larger, more comprehensive commissioned projects that require more designing and facilitating. He is still constantly in touch with each piece, checking methodology and the high standards he requires, and he creates the wax forms for casting. Woods' involvement ensures that the resulting works are beautiful, functional and carry his personal imprint.

**Tea and Coffee Set
Sterling silver and puriri
220 x 400 mm
J.L. Reid Collection**

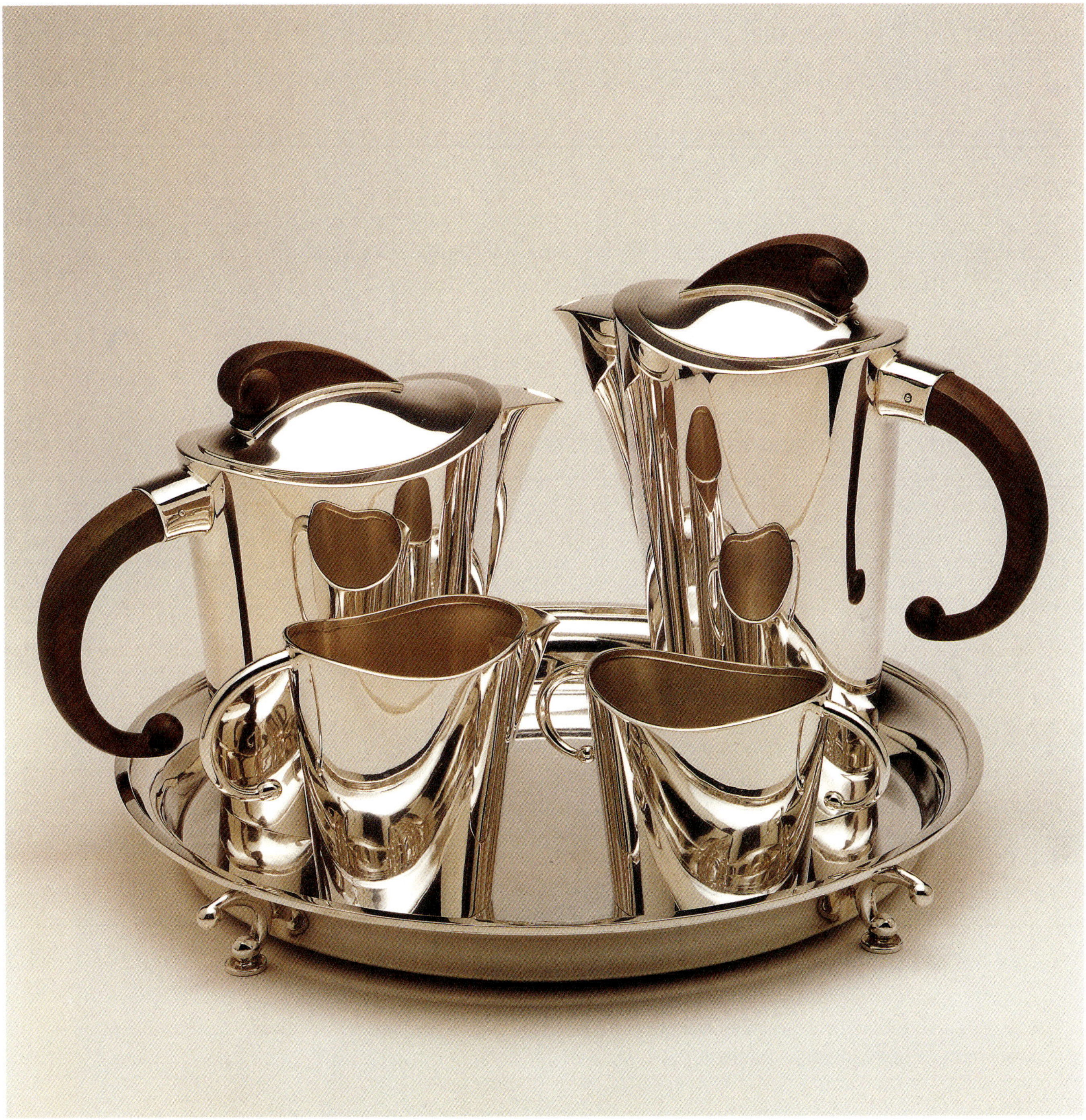

GLORIA YOUNG

Born Queensland, Australia 1941.
Resident in New Zealand since 1967.
NZ Certificate in Ceramics, Otago Polytechnic 1979.
Lives in Wellington.

Gloria Young likes to capture a reference to history in her ceramic works. She believes that pottery indicates how people have lived, and she has an appreciation of ancient Persian and Chinese ceramics. Her work is characterised by the use of majolica painting on earthenware, a Mediterranean technique popular in the fifteenth and sixteenth centuries. Young's process also includes a 'dash of Bloomsbury', an early twentieth-century English influence.

In the early 1980s Young, together with Gillian Kersey, established a gallery/workshop in Wellington, and in 1983 she went on to establish a co-operative workshop. Extensive travel in 1987 and a residency at Wanganui Regional Community College in 1989 had considerable impact on her work. In 1993, with the assistance of the QEII Arts Council, she established 'Bloomsbury for Decorative Arts', a gallery/retail shop/workshop.

There is a playful element to her domestic ware and semi-functional pieces, with trompe l'oeil used to good effect. She seeks to make pots that look like paintings of pots, and paintings that function as pots: a loose drawing on a slab of clay can become the façade of a vase thrown on the wheel. Her focus is the painted image on the front, as distinct from the vessel behind it.

A series of fruit bowls created as boat shapes formed from rolled clay slabs attracted considerable attention. The imagery was two-dimensional on one side, three-dimensional on the other, with space for real fruit. Going against what she had been taught, Young made work that appeared to have a single frontal viewing point, yet one needed to see the back to appreciate the humour and trickery. This later developed into more 'drawings' of the fruit bowl, coloured on one side, a black and white sketch on the other, with occasionally a single fruit coloured in as a light-hearted reference to colouring-in books.

Young was concerned that the fruit bowls would become stale, and this led her to seek out other vessel forms. Inspired by urns and vases of antiquity, she drew old Persian ceramics, reinterpreting the patterns, and made paintings of the three-dimensional shapes. These became the flat fronts of three-dimensional pieces. Some urns emulated marble, echoing the revival of fake paint decoration in interiors. Two different colour schemes, one on each side, played with interior decorating concepts, as did the contrast of New Zealand motifs with references to Chinese work. She wanted to go beyond the pedestal, and placed some works onto boxes or plinths which evolved into Grecian capitals. To give the tops of columns a function, she created secret trinket boxes inside. These, like a series of Japanese pillows, became works in their own right.

Her newest abstracted works are inspired by Cubism. They are distorted still lifes, composed of hollow forms and assembled like a painting. They follow her work based on fruit bowls with distorted shapes which were conceived as representational paintings, but these are less static, more abstract. She enjoys an element of movement in the new works—a certain 'wonkiness' that has always been part of her work. This looseness, and keeping interior design trends in view, has provided Young with a lively, satirical way of working.

The Fruit Bowl
Earthenware clay/
majolica glaze
320 x 350 x
360 mm (h)
Collection of the
artist

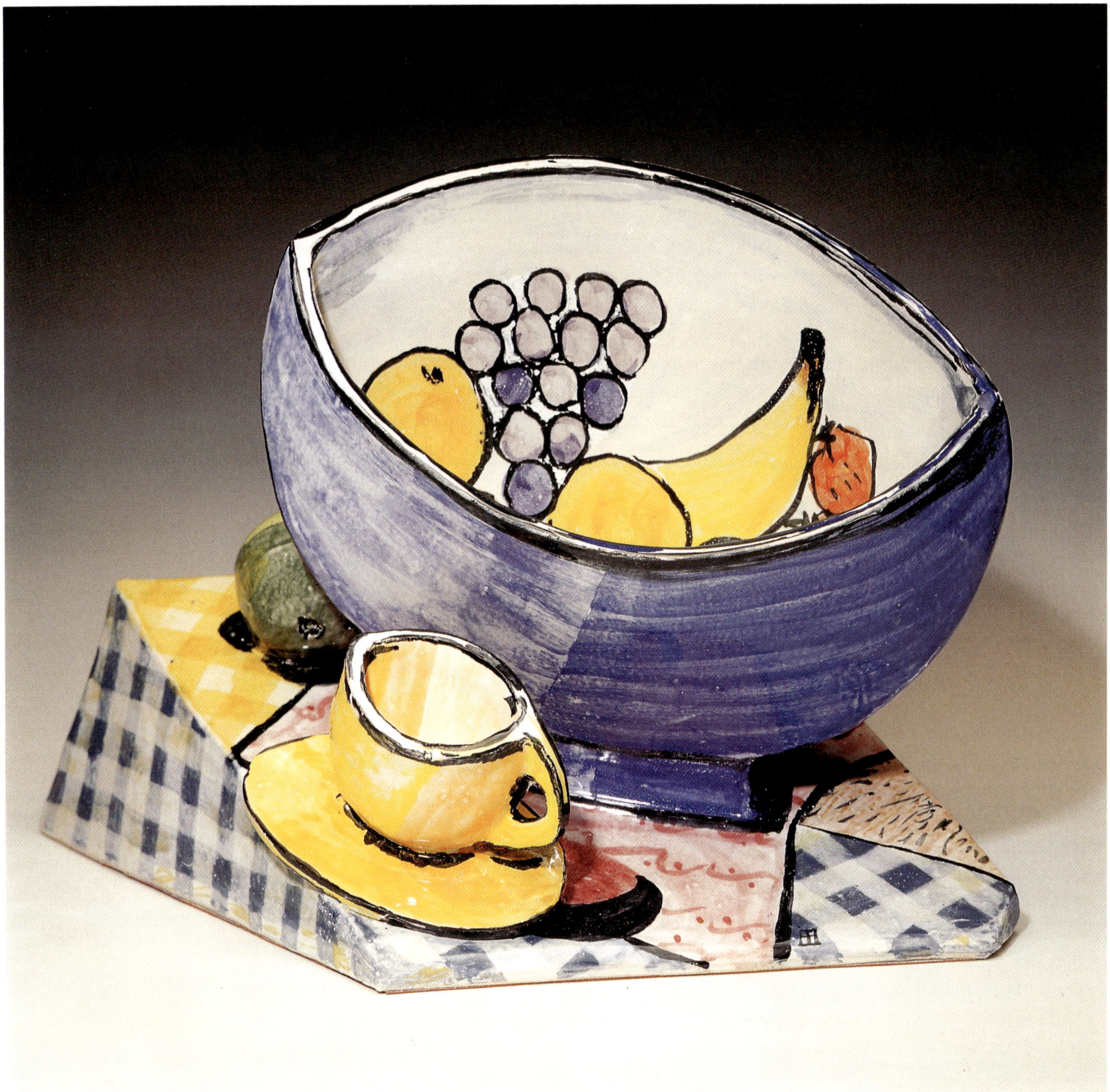

MARC ZUCKERMAN

Born Brooklyn, New York 1945.
Geological Engineering degree, Colorado School of Mines 1969;
MSc (Mining and Exploration Geology), James Cook University, Northern Queensland 1975.
Moved to New Zealand 1971.
Started designing and making furniture 1977.
Lives in Kowhitirangi, out of Hokitika.

Trends have little to do with the furniture that Marc Zuckerman makes. He has been clearly focused on minimalist functional furniture for over two decades. The aesthetic that dominates his work has its origins in the furniture he lived with in the 1950s when his parents replaced their over-stuffed furniture with Scandinavian wooden furniture.

Working with wood began when he built his home in 1976 and renovated a house for a friend. Designing and making solid timber kitchens led to making furniture and a strong interest in design. Visits to the USA always included museums and design shows, and Zuckerman gradually developed a philosophical basis for his own furniture designs. Classical designs interested him, and he wanted to create work with depth and substance more than to follow a 'rock show bandwagon' of design. In his occasional teaching at Christchurch Polytechnic from 1988 to 1996, this was a fundamental principle.

Choosing to live in the idyllic isolation of New Zealand's West Coast has meant that there has been no pressure to conform to interior design trends, so Zuckerman has made furniture that satisfies him rather than responding to external hype. He is less interested in constantly breaking new ground than in allowing progress to be in the form of small refinements. As a matter of integrity he refers to his own cultural history and does not seek to identify with Pacific culture.

Yet Zuckerman's furniture, like that of Humphrey Ikin (39), is a response to living in New Zealand. Whereas Ikin has articulated his position as a New Zealander clearly, Zuckerman has been less forthcoming. Nonetheless, his aesthetic and philosophy reflect not just his cultural roots and his aim to be true to himself. It is also a response to his environment and the quality of light, to materials and process, and he brings a lightness of touch and a functional approach to his work. This is particularly evident in the carefully detailed *Glass Settee*, 1996, made of sycamore and glass. The joints are beautifully expressed, with some of the components painted, and the use of thick glass as seat and back offers a surprisingly pleasant seating experience.

For some time he worked with rimu and matai, and more recently with sycamore, making tables, chairs, desks and coffee tables. In 1985 he became a founding member of the thriving Hokitika Craft Gallery and this continues to be a primary outlet. After the financial crash of 1987 he started making small gift and tourist items like clocks, dishes and serving implements as well as furniture. With everything he makes he applies the same well-considered design values, and the two genres of work have recently begun to overlap. Features of clocks occasionally appear in pieces of furniture, and details can be repeated at different scales.

Quality of crafting and hand-sanding as the ultimate finish remain constants in Zuckerman's work. He recalls that early designs may have been clumsy, but they were always consistently finished to the same standards he demands of himself now. Those were characteristics that helped establish his reputation and win him a number of awards.

Settee
Sycamore, painted sycamore and glass
1500 x 620 x 600 mm
Collection of the artist

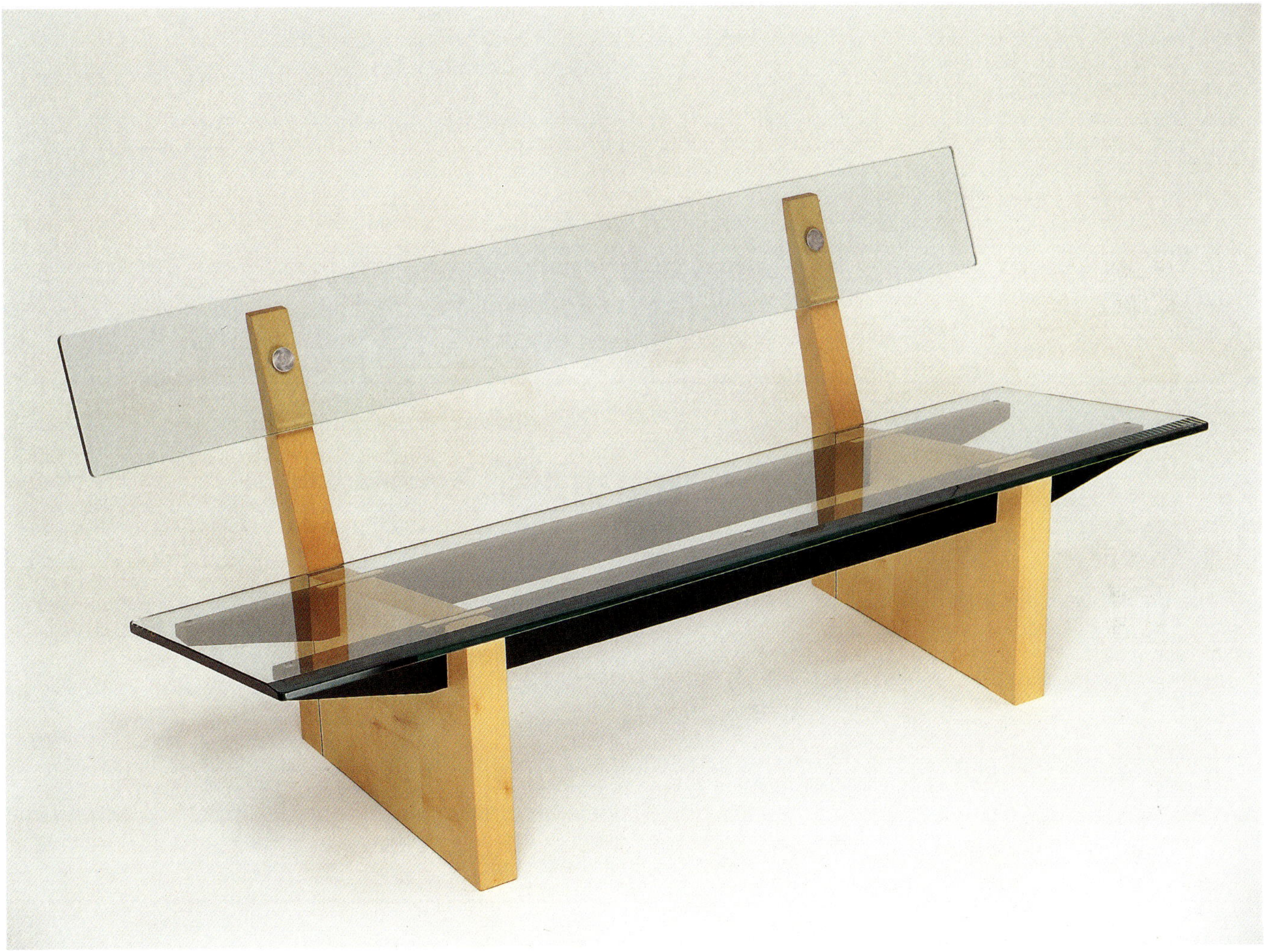

GLOSSARY OF MAORI TERMS

harakeke: *Phormium tenax*; New Zealand flax.
kai moana: food from the sea or lake.
kaitiaki: guardian.
kete: basket made of interlaced strips of flax.
kiekie: a climbing plant (*Freycinetia banksii*).
korowai: cloak ornamented with black twisted thrums.
kowhaiwhai: painted scroll ornamentation.
moko: tattooing on the face or body.
muka: prepared fibre of flax.
pingao: *Desmoschoenus spiralis*; a sedge grass which grows near the seashore; the leaves, which dry a bright golden yellow/orange colour, were much used for weaving.
piupiu: a garment consisting of a heavy fringe, about 45 cm diameter, attached to a band for the waist.
poi: a light ball with a short string attached to it, which was swung and twirled rhythmically to the accompaniment of a song, the so-called poi dance.
pounamu: greenstone, jade.
raranga: weave, plait.
taonga: property, anything highly prized, treasure.
taniko: traditional finger-woven coloured patterns for the ornamental borders of cloaks.
tukutuku: ornamental lattice-work between the upright slabs of the walls in house.
tupuna: ancestor, grandparent.
wairua: spirit, unsubstantial image, shadow.
waka huia: a container for treasures, originally for prized feathers.
whakapapa: recite in proper order genealogies, legends.
whariki: woven mat.
whatu: weaving garments and baskets, etc.
whare nui: large house.

GLOSSARY OF CRAFT TERMS

anagama kiln: an Oriental-style kiln called by a Japanese word meaning hole or cave, it consists of a single chamber, often 5 m or more in length: and placed on a slope, usually of 17 degrees, so that the chamber acts as a draught. These kilns are fired for extended periods (up to 10 days) to give full vitrification of the clay and natural-ash deposited glazes.
architectural glass: also known as flat glass. Includes stained glass, leadlighting and other techniques for colouring and joining sheet glass.
art deco: a stylised form of design and decoraton popular in the 1920s and 1930s.
art nouveau: an elaborate art style popular in the 1890s and 1900s.
bas relief: sculpture in low relief.
Bauhaus: a revolutionary German design school, 1919–33, founded by Walter Gropius. It played a central role in the emergence of the Modern Movement.
block printing: technique for hand-printing patterns onto cloth using a carved wooden or linoleum block.
Bloomsbury: an English art movement of the early 20th century.
blowpipe: a pipe used for glass-blowing, through which a stream of gas is directed at a flame to increase its heat.
cast glass: also known as warm glass, as is slumped or fused glass; glass formed in moulds.
cubism: an art style originating in the early 20th century, aiming to analyse the structure or form of objects by expressing them in geometrical shapes.
de Stijl: an architectural group in Holland in the 1920s.
deconstruction: the process of taking accepted structures of popular images, language and the signs we live by, pulling them apart, then re-presenting them.
dobby loom: a mechanical wooden loom that can accommodate many harnesses.
earthenware: One of the three main types of pottery, the others being stoneware and porcelain. It is opaque, relatively soft, and porous unless covered with glaze. The firing temperature can be as low as 800°C, as with some African pottery, or as high as 1200°C before it starts to vitrify and technically becomes stoneware.
engobe: *see* slip.
engraving: cutting marks such as letters or designs into a hard surface.
etching: engraving a picture on a metal plate by scratching the design through a layer of wax then letting acid eat into the exposed metal.
expressionism: a style of painting using simple exaggeration and distortions of line and colour to achieve emotional impact.
form language: working with a three-dimensional visual vocabulary of shape, colour, texture, etc.
glass cane: A thin rod of clear or coloured glass, often of concentric layers, used as stems on certain glassware, sometimes cut in slices for millefiore or mosaic glassware.
grogged clay: raw clay coarsened with powdered brick.
grunge: post-punk anti-establishment aesthetics.
ikat: resist technique achieved by binding and dyeing warp or weft threads (or both) prior to weaving.

kitsch: any art, literature, etc. which is considered to be pretentious or in bad taste, pandering to the lowest common denominator of popular taste.

lapidary: the art of cutting and polishing precious stones.

Lapita pottery: ancient pottery, the remains of which have been found in Samoa.

lustre glaze: a glaze or on-glaze that achieves an iridescent metallic surface.

majolica: earthenware covered with a soft tin-lead glaze, often with a lustre decoration. The ware (made by Islamic craftsmen) originally came from Spain and derived its name from the island of Majorca, which lay on the trade route to Italy.

minimalism: art which uses reduced means to force the observer to concentrate on such basic matters as shape, colour, texture or materials.

Minoan ceramics: decorated pots from prehistoric Crete.

Mobius twist: a one-sided surface formed by joining the ends of a rectangle after twisting one end through 180 degrees.

modernism: non-traditional, non-academic art movement from about 1850 to 1980.

on-glaze: a glaze applied to a previously glazed and fired clay work.

paper clay: moist clay with paper pulp added for strength.

percentage dyeing: the process of colouring fabrics and yarns using proportional amounts of dyestuffs according to pre-determined formulae.

pop art: a movement where images are taken from the everyday commercial world, including advertising slogans and comic strips.

porcelain: a white clay body which is fired to 1300°C or more, which, if thin enough, will be translucent and ring like a bell.

post-modernism: art since 1980 which regards all art before that time as available for re-use, appropriation, style-mixing or using in any chosen way.

press moulding: the process of casting clay forms by pressing clay into moulds.

Pueblo pottery: ceramics made by the Pueblo Indians of South America, characterised by unglazed burnished surfaces.

raku: a style of ceramic wares originating in Japan. Work is fired at 1000°C; biscuited pots are glazed and thrust into a small kiln for a few minutes before being pulled out red-hot.

rococo: an 18th-century style of art and architecture developed from and more exaggerated than baroque, characterised by shell motifs, scrolls and curves in general.

salt glazing: a technique developed in Germany which is achieved by tossing a quantity of common salt into the kiln during firing. The salt volatilises and forms a thin, distinctive glaze-like coating resembling an orange rind.

screen printing: a method of printing by squeezing ink through a stretched fabric screen, prepared by blocking off non-printing areas with a stencil.

sgraffito: a decoration created by scratching onto a surface, especially through a slip and/or glaze to reveal a contrasting colour beneath.

shibori: general Japanese term for tie-dye, stitch- and pleat-resist techniques.

siapo: *see* tapa.

slip, engobe: a liquid mixture of clay and water that has been filtered and mixed to a creamy consistency. When mixed with a colourant, it is sometimes referred to as an engobe.

slip casting: a technique used for making moulded ware. Liquid slip is poured into a porous mould which absorbs the liquid and leaves the clay form behind.

stoneware: a clay or mixture of clay used by potters to make permanent vessels that have the hardness of stone. Firing is usually in the 1200 to 1300°C range, and the result is impervious to acids.

surrealism: a 20th-century movement in art and literature seeking to reveal the inner world of fantasy arising from dreams and psychoanalysis by using distorted images.

tapa: (Pacific) a fabric made from beaten vegetable fibres.

treadle loom: floor loom controlled by a foot lever to raise the harnesses.

triple weave: three layers of fabric woven simultaneously.

trompe l'oeil: illusion, suggesting the surface of other materials.

twill: a woven fabric with the threads forming parallel, diagonal lines.

twining: a two-element construction in which two or more weft yarns are twisted around one another as they interlace with the warp.

West Coast American ceramics: Innovative abstract expressionist ceramics that disregarded ceramic traditions.

ABBREVIATIONS

ATI:	Auckland Technical Institute
BA:	Bachelor of Arts
BArch:	Bachelor of Architecture
BFA:	Bachelor of Fine Arts
BSc:	Bachelor of Science
DFA:	Diploma of Fine Art
MFA:	Master of Fine Arts
Vol.1	*100 New Zealand Paintings by 100 New Zealand Artists*, Warwick Brown, Godwit Publishing, Auckland, 1995
Vol. 2	*Another 100 New Zealand Artists*, Warwick Brown, Godwit Publishing, Auckland, 1996

Note: all measurements are height x width x depth

OTHER PRACTITIONERS MENTIONED IN THE TEXT

NEW ZEALAND

Clasby, Daniel. American/New Zealander sculptor/jeweller, teacher; known especially in the 1980s for intricate, humorous and quirky work.

Davis, Harry and **May**. Pioneer potters from England; built pottery on totally self-sufficient principles; also worked in South America.

Dilana Rugs. A firm based in Christchurch, headed by Hugh Bannerman, which specialises in creating rugs designed by leading New Zealand artists.

Elliott, Tom. Wood carver known best for his wall panels.

Elliott, Wailin. Potter known best for figurines.

Feu'u, Fatu. Samoan/New Zealander painter/sculptor/printmaker who works in a contemporary way, drawing mainly on imagery of Samoa.

Flight, Susan. A textile artist and respected teacher who now lives mainly in Queensland; known primarily for her painted and dyed textiles.

Graham, Fred. Maori sculptor and teacher; known for contemporary carvings based on current as well as historical issues.

Harrison, Hinemoa. Maori weaver known for weaving mainly tukutuku, raranga, whatu and taniko.

Harrison, Paki. Maori master carver of a number of whare nui.

Hetet, Dame Rangimarie. Probably the best-known Maori weaver and teacher; much loved and respected for her exquisite weaving, generous teaching and her key role in reviving Maori weaving; died 1996.

Laird, Jack. Potter and teacher, established Waimea Pottery.

Lawless, Matekino. Maori weaver for over 30 years.

Mahy, Keith. Pioneer glass-blower, teacher at Northland Polytechnic.

Mason, Helen. Pioneer potter who spent some time in Japan; established communal pottery and living facilities in the Waitakeres before moving to Coromandel; founder of New Zealand Society of Potters, first editor of *NZ Potter*, influenced a number of significant practitioners.

Maxwell, Eddie. Maori weaver who began by repairing old whariki; one of few men to weave; known for contemporary work.

Milne, Margaret. Auckland pioneer potter who spent some time in Japan and participated in pottery exchanges.

Mulqueen, Steve. South Island jeweller and sculptor.

Paul, Bhana. Maori weaver; has woven for about 15 years.

Perrin, Pat. Known for her teaching at Auckland Studio Potters and her pioneering work in domestic ware.

Raos, Peter. Pioneer glass blower known for paperweights and vessels.

Rust, Yvonne. Pioneer potter who taught ex-miners pottery on the West Coast; later went to Whangarei and established The Quarry, a centre for art and craft.

Salt, Donn. Known for his jade carving which is inspired by traditional Maori work; published *Stone, Bone and Jade*, a book about carving.

Scholes, Jeff. A respected potter; lives in Auckland.

Schoon, Theo. (1915–85, Java/New Zealand). He recorded South Island Maori rock drawings and was greatly influenced by Maori art.

Schuster, Emily. Maori weaver known for fine Maori weaving and teaching; died 1997.

Scott, Jacob. Maori artist and educator at Eastern Technical Institute, Naper.

Smisek, Mirek. Immigrated to New Zealand from Czechoslovakia; significant pioneer potter who spent time in Japan and at St Ives with Bernard Leach; received OBE in 1990.

Stitchbury, Peter. Potter who trained with Bernard Leach at St Ives and with Michael Cardew; taught at Ardmore Teachers' College; known for well-crafted domestic ware, especially his teapots.

Spalding, Ian. One of very few full-time professional weavers; came from background in teaching.

Tahiwi, Aromea. Contemporary Maori fibre artist.

Tippett, Warren. Influential potter, lived in Christchurch in the 1960s, later worked with Barry Brickell at Coromandel, moved to Sydney 1984 and broke away from Leach-Hamada traditions; pioneered technique of setting plastics and ceramics in concrete mix in large works and tiles during Carrington Polytechnic residency; died 1994.

Urlich, Colleen Waata. Teacher and one of the first Maori potters.

van Helden, Julia. Primarily a painter, but has created handbuilt porcelain works as vehicles for sgraffito surface decoration; teaches at Eastern Institute of Technology.

Vendelbosch, Carl. Potter; taught at Waimea Pottery, Nelson.

Vivieaere, Jim. Cook Islands/New Zealand artist and curator.

OVERSEAS

Albers, Annie (1899–1994, Germany/USA). Highly respected textile designer and weaver who taught at the Bauhaus and was head of the weaving workshop 1931–32; received many accolades in USA; published *On Weaving* in 1965.

Arakawa, Toyozo. Highly respected Japanese potter, a living treasure; responsible for the revitalisation of shino tea ware, a leader of the classical revival.

Arp, Jean (1887–1966 France). Dadaist, worked with philosophy of eclectic freedom to experiment; known for wooden relief constructions and sculptures evoking human anatomy, water-worn stones and fruit, influenced Henry Moore and countless other sculptors of 'modern' rounded forms.

Brancusi, Constantin (1876–1957, Romania). Known for rugged fetishistic wood sculpture and smooth, flame-like forms in marble and bronze.

Cardew, Michael (1901–83, Britain). Studied pottery with Bernard Leach; influential teacher in New Zealand.

Cavalan, Pierre (1954– , France/Australia). Known for bricolage combining assemblage and montage techniques with traditional jewellery skills.

de Chirico, Giorgio (1888–1978, Italy). Seen as the link between romantic art and surrealism. One of the strongest influences on

the surrealist painters who admired the way his work predicted surrealism.
Duchamp, Marcel (1887–1968, France). Known for invention of conceptual art, merger of life and art, the idea of the found object.
Fassett, Kaffe (1937– , USA). Has lived in England, and is known for use of colour in knitting and more recently needlepoint tapestries.
Hamada, Shoji (1892–1978, Japan). Probably the most widely known and influential potter in the western world; he helped Bernard Leach establish the pottery at St Ives before returning to Japan. Known for warmth, generosity and genius with clay.
Hepworth, Barbara (1903–75, Britain). Known for abstract sculpture: curved, hollowed-out forms strung with wires like harps; organic rather than angular shapes.
Junger, Hermann (1928– , Germany). Influential metalsmith and teacher, makes precious metal jewellery in contemporary idiom.
Klee, Paul (1879–1940, Swiss). Worked in small scale but with a huge diversity of style, ranging from child-like to abstract. Paintings were often like coloured-in line drawings. Generated many ideas taken up by others in larger paintings.
Kunzli, Otto (1948– , Switzerland). Jeweller, a pioneer of 'New Jewellery' using non-precious materials, allusions to things known in other contexts, witty/ironical presentation.
Lalique, René (1860–1945, France). Known for decorative glass, often moulded, and jewellery.
Leach, Bernard (1887–1979, Britain). One of the most influential potters in the western world; he combined Japanese aesthetics and philosophies with mediaeval English wares.
Magritte, René (1898–1967, Belgium). Late surrealist painter whose works were primarily stories as snapshots of the impossible.
Marquis, Richard (1945– , USA). Known for colourful expressionist blown glass.

Martinez, Maria (1887–1980, New Mexico). Pueblo Indian potter, known for her 'blackware', the decorated burnished pots that were characteristic of the south-west, and utilised techniques that pre-dated contact with Europeans.
Matisse, Pierre (1869–1954, France). His figurative style has been one of the most influential of the century. Confident, sweeping, simplified drawing; bold, clean colour; assured unusual composition; use of decorative elements; dynamism of figures and objects creating a rhythm.
Mies van der Rohe, Ludwig (1888–1969, Germany/America). Modernist architect known for geometric purism, the functionalist aesthetic of 20th-century design.
Modigliani, Amadeo (1884–1920, Italy/France). Primarily a painter known for graceful, reclining, female nude figures; also stone carvings in the manner of Brancusi.
Moore, Henry (1898–1987, Britain). Influenced by surrealist ideas, he made many sculptures based on the human form, but greatly abstracted into forms resembling water-worn stones.
Morandi, Giorgio (1890–1964, Italy). Showed in his still lifes that it is possible to interpret and re-interpret limited subject matter, using a limited palette, without becoming formulaic.
Picasso, Pablo (1881–1973, Spain). Co-invented cubism and went on to explore a wide range of modernist distortions of objects and the figure in his paintings and sculpture. Some figures were thick-set and adopted classic poses; others were wobbly surreal forms; still others were like angular cardboard cut-outs or stick figures.
Piggott, Gwyn Hanssen (1935– , Australia). Known for delicate, almost paper-thin, minimalist wood-fired porcelain pots.
Rietveld, Gerrit (1888– ,Holland). Modernist architect and furniture maker.
Stankard, Paul (1942– , USA). Known for intricate botanical detail in glass paperweights.

BIBLIOGRAPHY

The following books, catalogues and periodicals provided some background to this book. They offer readers further information about historic and contemporary craft art in New Zealand and internationally.

BOOKS
Beatson, Dianne and Peter, *The Arts in Aotearoa New Zealand—Themes and Issues*, Sociology Department, Massey University, Palmerston North, 1994.
—— *The Crane and the Kotuku*, Manawatu Art Gallery, Palmerston North, 1994.
Blumhardt, Doreen and Brake, Brian, *Craft New Zealand — The Art of the Craftsman*, A.H. & A.W. Reed, Wellington, 1981.
—— *New Zealand Potters, Their Works, Their Words,* A.H. & A.W. Reed, Wellington, 1976.
Brickell, Barry, *A New Zealand Potter's Dictionary: Techniques and Materials for the South Pacific*, Reed Methuen, Auckland, 1985.
Cape, Peter, *Artists and Craftsmen in New Zealand*, Collins, Auckland and London, 1969
Cochrane, Grace, *The Crafts Movement in Australia: A History*, New South Wales University Press, Sydney, 1992.
Freeman, Warwick, *Owner's Manual/Jewellery* (photos Patrick Reynolds, text Julie Ewington), Starform, Auckland, 1995.
Gardner-Gee, Robin, *A Practice called Craft in a Country called New Zealand: Readings of Craft New Zealand 1982–1993*, MA Art History Thesis, University of Auckland, 1996.
Hughes, Robert, *The Shock of the New—Art and the Century of Change*, British Broadcasting Corporation, London, 1980.
Ioannou, Noris, *Australian Studio Glass: The Movement, its Makers and their Art*, G+B Arts International, Craftsman House, Sydney, 1995.
—— (ed), *Craft in Society—An Anthology of Perspectives*, Fremantle Arts Centre Press, Western Australia, 1992.
—— *Masters of Their Craft*, Craftsman House, Sydney, 1997.
—— *The Culture Brokers: Towards a Redifinition of the Crafts*, Crafts Council of South Australia and State Publishing Unit, Adelaide, 1989.
Leach, Bernard, *A Potter's Book*, Faber, London, 1945, 1976.
Lucie-Smith, Edward, *The Story of Craft—The Craftsman's Role in Society*, Van Nostrand Reinhold Company, New York, 1981.
Manhart, Marcia & Manhart ,Tom (eds.), *The Eloquent Object—The Evolution of American Art in Craft Media Since 1945*, The Philbrook Museum of Art, Tulsa, 1987.
Mansfield, Janet, *Contemporary Ceramic Art in Australia and New Zealand*, Craftsman House, Sydney, 1995.
——*Salt-Glaze Ceramics: An International Perspective*, Craftsman House, Sydney, 1995.
Margetts, Martina (ed), *International Crafts*, Thames & Hudson, London, 1991.
Mayer, Barbara, *Contemporary American Craft Art—A Collector's Guide*, Peregrine Smith Books, Salt Lake City, 1988.

Mead, Hirini Moko, *Magnificent Te Maori, Te Maori Whakahirahira*, Heinemann, Auckland, 1986.
Nicholas, Anne, *Fabrications: Works by Forty New Zealand Fibre Artists*, Random Century, Auckland, 1990.
Parker, John and Parkinson, Cecilia, *Profiles: 24 New Zealand Potters*, Bateman, Auckland, 1988.
Pendergrast, Mick, *Feathers and Fibre—A Survey of Traditional and Contemporary Maori Craft*, Penguin, Auckland, 1984.
——*Te Aho Tapu—The Sacred Thread*, Reed Methuen, Auckland, 1987.
Rowley, Sue (ed), *Craft and Contemporary Theory*, Allen & Unwin, Sydney, 1997.
Salt, Donn, *Stone, Bone and Jade—24 New Zealand Artists*, Bateman, Auckland, 1992.
Smith, Paul J. and Lucie-Smith, Edward, *American Craft Today—Poetry of the Physical*, American Craft Museum, Weidenfeld & Nicolson, New York, 1986.
Stove, Margaret, *Creating Original Hand-Knitted Lace*, Kangaroo Press, Sydney, 1995.

CATALOGUES AND PERIODICALS
'Bone, Stone, Shell'—New Jewellery, New Zealand (ed Geri Thomas), New Zealand Ministry of Foreign Affairs, Wellington, 1988.
Craft New Zealand, 1991–1993.
Decorative Arts and Design from the Powerhouse Museum, Powerhouse Publishing (part of the Museum of Applied Arts and Sciences), Sydney, 1991.
Framed—A Studio Furniture Survey , travelling exhibition, 1997.
Making the Molecules Dance—Len Castle Ceramics—a retrospective exhibition, 1947–1994, travelling exhibition.
Mau Mahara—Our Stories in Craft, Random Century, Auckland, 1990.
New Zealand Crafts, 1982–1991.
Nga Kaupapa Here Aho—Fibre Interface, Te Taumata Gallery, 1992.
No Man's Land—Extending the Boundaries of Women and Art in Aotearoa, Dowse Art Museum, Lower Hutt, 1993.
Open Heart—Contemporary New Zealand Jewellery, travelling exhibition, 1993-94.
Past Pacific—Jewellery by Niki Hastings-McFall, Creative New Zealand, 1997.
Same but Different—The Second New Zealand Jewellery Biennial, travelling exhibition, 1996.
Taonga Maori—Treasures of the New Zealand Maori People, 1989.
Te Maori—Te Hokinga Mai—The return home, Auckland City Art Gallery, 1986.
The Human Touch—Contemporary New Zealand Craft, The Bathhouse, Rotorua, 1989.
Under Southern Skies—Contemporary Stitched Textiles from New Zealand, Barbican Centre, London, 1996.